**Desktop Publishing with
PageMaker 5.0 for the Macintosh**

D1309392

TIM MOODY
3290 BALLTOWN RD.
SCHENECTADY, N.Y. 12304

"Information through Innovation"

James Shuman

Marcia Williams

Bellevue Community College

Desktop Publishing with PageMaker 5.0 for the Macintosh

boyd & fraser publishing company

I(T)P™ An International Thomson Publishing Company

Danvers ▪ Albany ▪ Bonn ▪ Boston ▪ Cincinnati ▪ Detroit ▪ London ▪ Madrid ▪ Melbourne
Mexico City ▪ New York ▪ Paris ▪ San Francisco ▪ Singapore ▪ Tokyo ▪ Toronto ▪ Washington

Acquisitions Editor: Anne E. Hamilton
Production Editor: Patty Stephan
Production Services: Gary Palmatier, Ideas to Images
Interior Design: Kaelin Chappell
Cover Design: Cuttriss and Hambleton
Manufacturing Coordinator: Bob Warner
Marketing Coordinator: Daphne J. Meyers

bf © 1995 by boyd & fraser publishing company
    A division of International Thomson Publishing Inc.

I(T)P The ITP™ logo is a trademark under license.

This book was laid out by Robaire Ream in PageMaker 5.0. Aldus and PageMaker are registered trademarks of Adobe Systems, Inc. Macintosh and Apple are registered trademarks of Apple Computer, Inc.

Printed in the United States of America

❀ This book is printed on recycled, acid-free paper that meets Environmental Protection Agency standards.

For more information, contact boyd & fraser publishing company:

boyd & fraser publishing company
One Corporate Place • Ferncroft Village
Danvers, Massachusetts 01923, USA

International Thomson Publishing Europe
Berkshire House 168-173
High Holborn
London, WC1V7AA, England

Thomas Nelson Australia
102 Dodds Street
South Melbourne 3205
Victoria, Australia

Nelson Canada
1120 Birchmount Road
Scarborough, Ontario
Canada M1K 5G4

International Thomson Editores
Campose Eliseos 385, Piso 7
Col. Polanco
11560 Mexico D.F. Mexico

International Thomson Publishing GmbH
Konigswinterer Strasse 418
53227 Bonn, Germany

International Thomson Publishing Asia
221 Henderson Road
#05-10 Henderson Building
Singapore 0315

International Thomson Publishing Japan
Hirakawacho Kyowa Building, 3F
2-2-1 Hirakawacho
Chiyoda-ku, 102 Tokyo, Japan

1 2 3 4 5 6 7 8 9 10 PR 8 7 6 5 4

Library of Congress Cataloging-in-Publication Data

Shuman, James E.
    Desktop publishing with PageMaker 5.0 for the Macintosh / James
Shuman, Marcia Williams.
        p.   cm.
    Includes index.
    ISBN 0-534-23376-7
    1. PageMaker (Computer file) 2. Desktop publishing.
I. Williams, Marcia, 1950–   . II. Title.
Z253.532.P33S54 1995
686.2'2544536—dc20   94-44461
                                        CIP

To Barbara and Bruce for their support and
encouragement throughout this project.

CONTENTS

P R E F A C E

TO THE INSTRUCTOR

This text provides a practical, hands-on approach to developing skills in the use of the most popular desktop publishing program, Aldus PageMaker 5.0 for the Macintosh. After completing this text, students will be able to use PageMaker to develop professional-looking publications including newsletters, advertisements, stationery, flyers, business cards, and announcements. The text requires active participation as the students develop these real-world applications. The emphasis is on learning by doing. The learning process becomes exciting and motivating for students as they create a portfolio of their work.

Text Organization

This text is presented as a self-paced tutorial, designed to be used in a lab setting. A concept is presented, such as resizing a graphic. The process is explained, followed by the actual steps so students learn the "why" along with the "how." In each chapter students work through examples so that new commands are practiced as they are presented. Exercises and end-of-chapter projects are used to reinforce learning by requiring students to apply skills as they are learned. Figures duplicating the monitor display guide students through the operations involved in completing a particular exercise. This approach allows you to determine your level of involvement—from providing presentations that supplement the text material to acting as a resource person.

Chapters are organized as follows:

- Chapter objectives
- Self-paced tutorials to teach new commands and techniques

- Exercises to reinforce learning
- End-of-chapter
  Key terms
  Questions
  Projects

Features and Benefits of This Text

Explanation of underlying concepts: Students gain an understanding of desktop publishing using PageMaker.

Sequential instruction: Step-by-step instructions allow students to progress at their own pace. They learn the basic commands first and then move to more advanced features. This approach allows students to redo a section for reinforcement or review. Chapters may be completed in an open lab setting where the instructor need not be present and where students can aid one another in the learning process.

Extensive use of figures: Students can check what is displayed on the monitor with more than 400 figures provided in the text. These figures guide students through the sequential instruction.

Exercises: Once a command is learned, students are challenged to use the skill to complete a practical exercise.

Realistic examples: This text uses actual publications developed by companies using PageMaker.

Case study: The Inn at Portage Bay is used as a comprehensive case study throughout the text. This case provides a realistic example of how desktop publishing can be used in a business setting.

Numerous projects: In addition to the case study, end-of-chapter projects provide practical applications to stimulate interest and reinforce learning.

Help questions: Students are encouraged to use PageMaker's Help feature, both within the chapters and for the end-of-chapter review questions and projects.

Student-tested approach: Students familiar with word processing are able to complete this text with minimal guidance. Students like the self-paced tutorial approach and the comprehensive case study.

Data disk: The data disk (bundled with the Instructor's Manual) used with this text has more than 40 files, including publications, templates, graphics, and word processing documents. These files are used by the students to complete the tutorials, exercises, and projects. Use of the data disk simulates a business environment. In addition, students are able to work with more complex and larger publications without having to spend time entering text.

Most popular desktop publishing program: Students learn advanced features of the most widely used desktop publishing program, the same program that is used for business, government, and personal applications.

Separate chapter on design concepts: Chapter 8 emphasizes the importance of design as a part of desktop publishing. It includes many examples by professional designers.

Appendix: The appendice provides a quick-reference section that includes shortcut keys and menus.

Configuration

The exercises and projects developed in this text were written using an Apple Macintosh IIci computer, with a color monitor and an HP LaserJet 4MP printer.

TO THE STUDENT

The average business spends 8 percent of its operating costs on printing and publishing. To reduce these costs and to maintain control over the printing process, more and more companies are turning to desktop publishing.

This text provides a practical, hands-on approach to developing skills in the use of the most popular desktop publishing program, Aldus PageMaker. After completing this text you will be able to use PageMaker to develop professional-looking publications such as newsletters, advertisements, flyers, announcements, stationery, and business cards.

The text allows you to work at your own pace through step-by-step tutorials. A concept is presented, such as resizing a graphic. The process is explained, followed by the actual steps. Throughout the text, figures show appropriate screen displays to help keep you on track. Examples, exercises, and projects will reinforce your learning. A case study, The Inn at Portage Bay, provides a real-world application of how desktop publishing can be used in a business setting.

To learn the most from the use of this text, you should:

■ Proceed slowly: Accuracy is more important than speed.

■ Understand what is happening with each step before continuing to the next step.

■ After finishing a process, ask yourself: Can I do the process on my own? If the answer is no, review the steps.

■ Check your screen display with the figures in the text. *Note:* At times the text figure may not exactly match your screen display—usually because of the font (type style and size) used.

Enjoy learning PageMaker!

ACKNOWLEDGMENTS

The authors would like to thank the following individuals for their support in the development of this text. Freda Cook and Craig Danuloff of Aldus Corporation for their invaluable technical support. Francine Walls for her research efforts. Bob and Lula Cusack, Mike Larson, Larry Jablinski, Ken Shafer, Ken Trimpe, Sheila Hoffman, Dorothy Mulligan, Overlake Hospital, Kathy Spangler, and Mithun Partners for providing design materials. 3G Graphics for providing an electronic image, Conference.eps. Our spouses, Bruce and Barbara, the artistic ones, for their drawings; Bruce created Portage.tiff, Cottages.tiff, and Golf Green.tiff, and Barbara created Fort.tiff. Patti Connors and Elizabeth von Radics for careful testing and constructive feedback. Gary Palmatier for his superb efforts and font help. The reviewers who were so important to the development of this text: Betty A. Allen, Columbus State Community College; Gerald Locke, Grayson County Junior College; Peggy Magee, Robert Morris College; Gail M. Miller, Belleville Area College; Jeff Mock, Diablo Valley College; Lloyd Onyett, Santa Rosa Junior College; Cyndi Reese, Santa Rosa Junior College; Judith Scheeren, Westmoreland County Community College; Peggy Terrell, Indiana Vocational Technical College; and Robert Willette, University of Georgia.

**Desktop Publishing with
PageMaker 5.0 for the Macintosh**

Upon completion of this chapter you will be able to:

- Define the term *desktop publishing*

- Trace its development

- Specify the tools used in page description

- Compare traditional and desktop publishing methods of page design and printing

- Explain the advantages and disadvantages of using desktop publishing

- Specify the components of a desktop publishing system

- Compare software programs

CHAPTER 1

Introduction to Desktop Publishing

The term *desktop publishing* was coined in 1984 by Paul Brainerd to describe his product, PageMaker. Brainerd is founder and CEO of Aldus Corporation, which manufactures **PageMaker**, currently the country's most popular desktop publishing program. Since the term was first used, a billion-dollar industry has developed that includes computer-related equipment, software programs, training, trade associations, specialty magazines, and thousands of jobs. As has been typical in the computer field, a few major technological advances gave birth to a new industry. These advances included the development of personal computers that could produce graphics, the development of **desktop publishing programs**, and the invention of the **laser printer**. This chapter provides an introduction to desktop publishing, presents its history, and describes how companies use it.

WHAT IS DESKTOP PUBLISHING?

Desktop publishing is the process of using a personal **computer** and a software program to develop quality printed material that merges text (words, headings, titles) and graphics (pictures, illustrations, graphs). Companies typically use desktop publishing to develop documents such as newsletters, advertisements, price lists, and brochures. Prior to the development of desktop publishing, a company could either send their work to outside typesetting and printing firms or use a computer, word processing program, and printer to create their work in-house. The typesetting house produced quality type for the printing process, but the finished product was very expensive and time-consuming to create. The computer and word processing program, although cheaper and, in the right hands, faster, produced poor quality documents and until recently could not incorporate graphic images (such images were added by a graphic designer in both these processes). Desktop publishing picks up where word processing ends, allowing a company to create in-house, high-quality, modestly priced documents that utilize illustrations, borders, multicolumns, and different type styles and sizes.

DEVELOPMENT OF DESKTOP PUBLISHING

To understand how desktop publishing has developed, it is useful to look at the broader field of publishing. **Publishing** involves the creation, production, and distribution of printed material. The most common form of printed material is the page, such as is found in a newsletter, advertisement, or flyer. Some of the creative and production aspects of publishing describe how a page will look, that is, what will be placed on it and where placement will be—a process termed **page description**. What will be placed on a page falls into one of two broad categories: text (words, headings, titles) or graphics (pictures, illustrations, graphs). The selection and placement (layout) of the text and graphics are limited by the tools used to produce the page and, of course, by the skills of the persons doing the work.

TOOLS USED IN PAGE DESCRIPTION

The tools used in page description can be classified as manual, mechanical, and electronic. The pen, printing press, and computer are examples of tools fitting these classifications. Some questions that could be asked in evaluating these tools are:

■ Does the tool enhance creativity? That is, does the tool allow you to use different type styles, such as script or block, and type sizes? Can you easily change the size of the graphics and rearrange the layout (design) of the page?

■ How effectively does the tool merge text and graphics? Can the text be developed and then the graphics easily incorporated into the page?

■ Who controls the process? That is, can a company use this tool to create and produce the printed material in-house?

■ What will be the quality of the printed material?

■ What will the process cost?

■ How long will the process take?

The oldest and least complex tool used for page description is the pen. In the hands of a skilled craftsperson, this tool can be used to create text in various styles and sizes, as well as illustrations. Using a pen permits an almost endless number of ways to arrange (lay out) the text and graphics on the page. This manual process enhances the creative process, increases quality, and leaves control of the finished product with one person, but it can be very slow, and even minor changes might require rewriting the entire page.

The development of the printing press (printing from movable type) by Johannes Gutenberg in the mid-1400s was revolutionary. As a page description tool, it dramatically reduced the amount of time necessary to produce printed material. This mechanical process also made possible the mass distribution of books and contributed to a higher literacy rate and the spread of knowledge. However, the craftsperson lost creative flexibility and most control of the page description process. The style and size of type was limited as was the type of graphics. Control over the process was reduced because production was done in the print shop instead of at the craftsperson's desk.

With the twentieth-century development of **phototypesetting** equipment, a computer was used to generate text and send it electronically to a typesetting machine. However, until recently these computers have been dedicated machines, whose programs were linked directly with the type-setting equipment and not used for other purposes. Specialists are needed to operate these computers and insert text codes to control the typesetter's operations. Also, the input was limited to text. No graphics could be developed or incorporated into the page design using the computer.

From the time the printing press was developed until recently, the publishing process had become more and more specialized. Each new technological advance, such as phototypesetting, required specialists. The publishing process, once done at the desk with pen and paper, now required writers, editors, illustrators, graphic designers, and typesetters. With the development of the personal computer, page description software, and the laser printer, control over many aspects of the publishing process returned to one person. What follows is a simplified view of the steps involved in producing a printed page and a comparison of the traditional method and the desktop publishing method of doing so. Figure 1.1 illustrates this comparison.

TRADITIONAL METHOD OF PAGE DESIGN AND PRINTING

1. **Creating the concept.** This process generates ideas to be included in the page. For example, a company working on a direct-mail advertising campaign would hold a brainstorming session to generate a theme and other ideas for the campaign. This step also involves determining the advertising objective. Every publication contains a message communicated not only by what is said, but also by how it is said. For example, an advertising objective might be to have the reader make a phone call. To accomplish it, the reader's attention could be drawn to a phone number typeset in bold type.

Figure 1.1
Comparison of the
traditional and desktop
publishing methods of
producing a printed
page

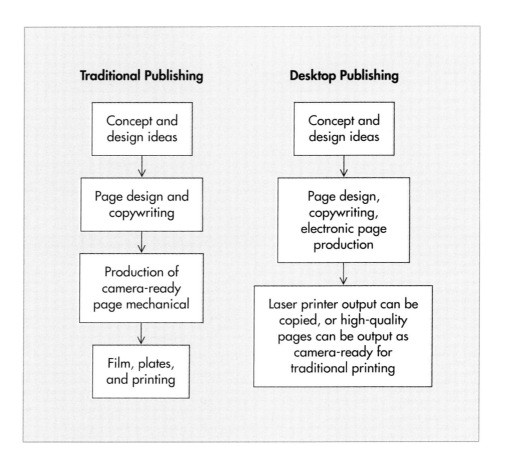

2. **Creating a preliminary page design.** A rough layout of the elements of the advertisement (headline, copy, illustrations, logo, and so on) would be developed. A copywriter would write the text and an artist would sketch out the illustrations. An editor and those involved in the advertising campaign, such as marketing personnel, would review this preliminary work. Rewrites and redesigns would follow this review.

3. **Preparing the page for printing.** Depending on time, cost, quality, and quantity considerations, the advertisement could be prepared for printing in several ways. If the ad were to be high quality, color, and include photographs, a manual pasteup process would be needed to prepare the page for printing. A computer could be used to lay out the text, leaving blank areas where photos would be placed (pasted). After the pasteup, the camera-ready page would be photographed and printing plates made.

4. **Printing.** Assuming good quality is desired, a printing process called offset lithography would be used. This process uses film to expose a photo-sensitive emulsion on a metal plate, which is then placed around the rollers of a printing press. The image area of the plate, created by the exposure to light, is coated with a material that accepts ink. The plate is inked and paper is fed through the rollers, creating the printed page.

DESKTOP PUBLISHING METHOD OF PAGE DESIGN AND PRINTING

1. The concept development step does not change in the desktop publishing environment.

2. & 3. Creating a preliminary page design and preparing the page for printing can be combined. One person could incorporate into the page design both text, written by a copywriter using a word processing program, and an artist's illustrations. Alternately, one person could write the text, draw the illustrations electronically, and scan in photographs to be used in the page design. Editing text and rearranging the ad elements could be done quickly. Additionally, the finished page design can be viewed before printing. This feature is called **WYSIWYG** (What You See Is What You Get) and is not available in traditional methods of page design.

4. Printing could be accomplished with the use of a desktop laser printer and a copier. Or a quick-print shop could produce a printing plate from the laser printer output. If a higher-quality ad is desired, the desktop publishing page design could be sent electronically to a high-end laser printer producing type of greater visual clarity and definition. If photographs or color are desired, the page design could be used as part of the pasteup for a camera-ready page to be made into a plate for an offset printer.

ADVANTAGES OF USING DESKTOP PUBLISHING

The primary advantage of desktop publishing is greater control over the publishing process. Desktop publishing provides the opportunity for a company, depending on its needs and resources, to do some or all of its publishing in-house. This method allows the company to determine its own time lines. If a project has a high priority, it is not delayed by being sent outside the company. Projects previously spread over several weeks can now be done in a few days. Furthermore, fewer specialists are needed, and time taken in rewriting and redesigning is reduced.

DISADVANTAGES OF USING DESKTOP PUBLISHING

As desktop publishing systems become more and more common, the potential for misuse increases. Placing such a powerful tool in the hands of a novice can result in poor quality documents. It is very easy for a person lacking design skills to get carried away in using too many type styles and sizes and produce something resembling a ransom note instead of an effective communication. In addition, companies are concerned with image. Some want to be thought of as conservative, others as caring, or innovative. Advertisements, catalogs, annual reports, and so on can reinforce or contradict the desired image. For example, a company trying to portray itself as tough and assertive might not want to use a script type in its publications. Yet, if the marketing, public relations, product development, and accounting departments can all create their own publications, the possibility of contradiction increases.

THE DESKTOP PUBLISHING SYSTEM

Once a company determines that the advantages of using a desktop publishing system outweigh the disadvantages, it must decide on a system—including the computer, printer, software, and options. Figure 1.2 shows a typical system with an Apple Macintosh computer and a laser printer (right). A **scanner**, used to transfer photographs, drawings, and other printed material into the computer, is on the left. Also required is the software package for a desktop publishing program. Depending on the power of the computer, the quality of the printer, the sophistication of the program, and the need for options, desktop publishing systems generally cost between $3,000 and $10,000.

Figure 1.2
Typical Macintosh desktop publishing system

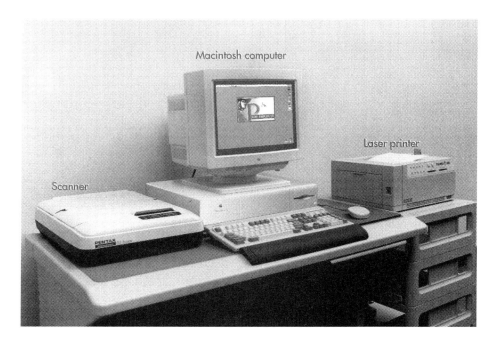

The Computer

In choosing a computer consider the programs to be used, which in turn determine the necessary processing speed and amount of memory required. Desktop publishing works with graphics, and these take longer for a computer to manipulate than text. Graphics also require a great deal of computer memory. A minimum configuration would be a Macintosh II series computer with 4 megabytes of memory. The Macintosh II series provides the minimum necessary processing speed.

Computers with faster processing speeds, such as the Macintosh Quadra, and more memory (8 megabytes) are more desirable for desktop publishing.

The Printer

Although desktop publishing programs will work with dot-matrix printers, laser printers provide higher-quality output. A measurement of printer quality is dots-per-inch (dpi): the more dots, the higher the quality. Figure 1.3 shows the same heading printed on two laser printers, one with 300 dpi and the other with 1,200 dpi. Notice the difference in quality between the two headings.

Figure 1.3
Comparison of output from laser printer and high-resolution imagesetter

The computer and printer can be used for different applications, such as word processing and database management. What turns this **hardware** (computer and printer) into a desktop publishing system is a set of instructions called a **software** program.

The Program

A variety of desktop publishing programs are available, ranging in price from $100 to $1,000 or more. The least expensive programs lack the advanced features—especially the ease in merging text and graphics—of the more expensive programs. The cheaper programs with fewer options are best suited for in-house publications, such as newsletters and announcements. The following features are common in more powerful desktop publishing programs.

- Insert graphics into the page and have text flow around the graphics automatically

- Rotate text and graphics

- View the page as it will be printed (WYSIWYG)

- Develop book-length documents that include a table of contents and an index

- Adjust spacing between characters and lines of text

- Enlarge or reduce graphic images

- Develop publications that use color

- Link files created using other programs and automatically update a publication using these files

Recently, the more sophisticated word processing programs have added features comparable to those of the low-end desktop publishing programs.

Deciding which program to buy is based primarily on anticipated needs and on budget and hardware considerations. If a company plans to produce only newsletters, announcements, posters, and other simple in-house-only documents, a sophisticated word processing program might be adequate. If a company plans to produce brochures, product specification sheets, annual reports, book-length documents, and other materials that will be seen outside the organization, or if color is to be used, a high-end desktop publishing program would be more appropriate.

In deciding which program to purchase, a company should ask these questions: How much are we currently spending on publishing? How much of our publishing could we realistically do ourselves? Do we have the expertise to publish in-house or will we need to hire new personnel and/or train existing employees? What are the start-up expenses, such as those for hardware, software, and training? What are the time considerations? And, ultimately, what is the net savings of doing part or all of our publishing in-house?

The Options

Although desktop publishing can be accomplished with a computer, a program, and a laser printer, numerous options, both in hardware and software, can enhance the basic desktop publishing system. Among these options are scanners allowing you to transfer in graphics, drawing programs for freehand illustration, clip-art files containing ready-made illustrations, and additional software fonts that will give you more design flexibility. A useful option for a computer system is a CD-ROM drive to read compact discs capable of holding more than 650 megabytes of items, such as illustrations and photographs.

Finally, the decision a company makes about whether to go desktop is concerned not with replacing current publishing activities, but with how best to supplement them. The following four examples show how desktop publishing is being used in some businesses.

ROI is a one-person accounting service. Sandra Gilbert, the owner, uses a personal computer, a laser printer, and a sophisticated word processing program—Microsoft Word for Windows—to create simple documents. She publishes a quarterly newsletter (see Figure 1.4) to inform her clients of changes in tax codes and pending tax legislation. She also develops promotional flyers to send to prospective clients. These documents include both text and graphics. She uses borders, shading, and various type sizes to enhance the documents. Because of the relative simplicity of the documents, she does not need to supplement Word for Windows with any other software packages, such as drawing programs.

Figure 1.4
ROI newsletter

R O I

N E W S L E T T E R

First Quarter

Capital Gains Tax

Representative Griffey of Washington State has proposed a reduction in the Capital Gains tax. Her proposal would set the maximum tax rate at 15%, down from the current maximum of 28%. Her intent is to stimulate investment in hopes that this will give a boost to our stagnate economy. She faces some stiff opposition from Democrats who see this as a tax break for the rich.

Quarterly Tax Payments

For those of you who make quarterly tax payments, your next installment is due at the end of March.

New Employee (Intern)

I am happy to announce that Ann Grey will be joining ROI as an intern. She is a senior at City University and will complete her degree (BS Accounting) in June. Her arrival is very timely because of the tax return season that is quickly approaching.

Property Tax Assessment

All property in King County was re-assessed beginning on January 1. You will receive a valuation notice by June 1. As you know property values have been sky rocketing the past 18 months. However, the price of residential property has increased at a higher rate than commercial property. Therefore, homeowners will find that their taxes will increase while commercial investors may actually see a tax decrease. You may appeal your reevaluation up to 30 days after receiving the notice. The most important evidence to support an appeal are comparable's -- prices of properties that are comparable to yours and have sold recently. If you would like help with your appeal, call me.

Vacation

I am planning a two-week trip to Hawaii to visit my brother and the office will be closed from May 15 - 30.

Sandra Gilbert, Editor

World Trade Network is an international marketing firm employing 12 people. The company specializes in athletic equipment and sells more than 80 products worldwide, primarily through trade shows. The company uses a personal computer, a laser printer, a scanner, and a desktop publishing program—PageMaker—to create several kinds of documents, including product specification sheets, price lists, promotional brochures, and sales reports. The scanner is used to capture an electronic image, called a graphic, of a product from a photograph. The graphic is used with text to create the product specification sheets. The company uses a drawing program for freehand artwork and a clip-art program (which provides predesigned artwork) to enhance its promotional brochures and sales reports. Also, the company produces a product catalog and annual report with the help of an electronic publishing service. This service provides high-resolution printing, color printing, and binding using equipment too expensive for World Trade Network to purchase. Figure 1.5

Figure 1.5
World Trade Network product specification template

WORLD TRADE NETWORK
100 East 35th Street
San Francisco, CA 95222
(415) 555-4387
Fax (415) 555-4823

"The Key to International Markets"

PRODUCT SPECIFICATION SHEET

Product Name:

Product Description:

List Price: U.S.$

Quantity Discounts:

Terms:

Shipping Weight:

shows a **template** (a predesigned document) containing a standard page layout. When World Trade Network acquires a new product, the template is used to create a product specification sheet. Blank areas of the template allow for a graphic of the product and data (such as the description and price, which varies from product to product) to be inserted.

Cusack's Alaska Lodge is a family-owned lodge catering to hunters and fishermen. The lodge is located on Iliamna Lake in southern Alaska between Lake Clark National Park and Katmai National Monument. The lodge is accessible only by floatplane. The company works with a graphic designer to develop various publications. Figure 1.6 shows several

Figure 1.6
Various publications of Cusack's Alaska Lodge

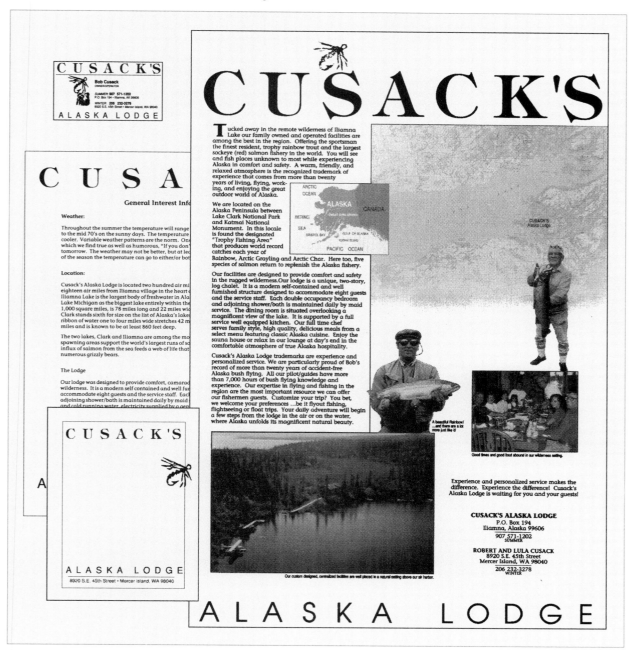

of the publications, including a general information sheet on company stationery, a business card, and a brochure. These publications were developed using PageMaker on a personal computer. Text was created with a word processing program, and a scanner was used to incorporate photographs. The brochure, which includes color maps and photographs, was printed using an offset printer. This is a good example of how a company can tie together a variety of publications. Notice, for instance, how the company name, CUSACK'S, and the logo, a fly-type hook, are used repeatedly.

SEAFIRST BANK is a large regional bank with more than 6,000 employees. The company creates several publications including brochures, bulletins, and forms. The Administrative Services department oversees three publishing areas—Forms Management, Graphic Services, and Publications—that provide publishing services to the entire company. For example, a specialist in the Forms Management area might work with the Marketing department to create a credit card application. The specialist would provide expertise in layout and design and ensure quality and continuity with other corporate publications. In addition to the basic desktop publishing system—computer, laser printer, PageMaker program—the company uses a high-resolution (high-quality) printer called an **imagesetter**. In essence, SEAFIRST has its own in-house publishing service. Figure 1.7 shows an application form created by SEAFIRST personnel using a desktop publishing system and printed on a high-resolution printer.

Figure 1.7
SEAFIRST application form

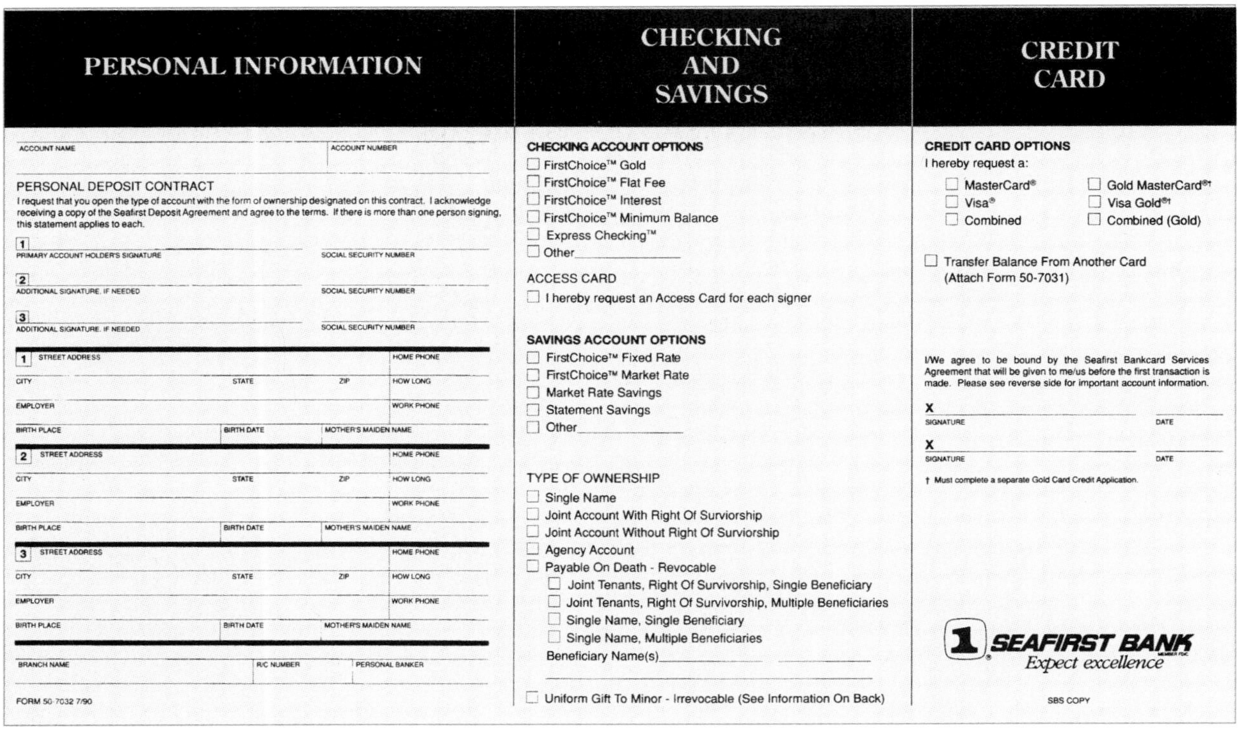

PERSONAL INFORMATION

ACCOUNT NAME | ACCOUNT NUMBER

PERSONAL DEPOSIT CONTRACT
I request that you open the type of account with the form of ownership designated on this contract. I acknowledge receiving a copy of the Seafirst Deposit Agreement and agree to the terms. If there is more than one person signing, this statement applies to each.

1 PRIMARY ACCOUNT HOLDER'S SIGNATURE | SOCIAL SECURITY NUMBER
2 ADDITIONAL SIGNATURE, IF NEEDED | SOCIAL SECURITY NUMBER
3 ADDITIONAL SIGNATURE, IF NEEDED | SOCIAL SECURITY NUMBER

1 STREET ADDRESS | HOME PHONE
CITY | STATE | ZIP | HOW LONG
EMPLOYER | WORK PHONE
BIRTH PLACE | BIRTH DATE | MOTHER'S MAIDEN NAME

2 STREET ADDRESS | HOME PHONE
CITY | STATE | ZIP | HOW LONG
EMPLOYER | WORK PHONE
BIRTH PLACE | BIRTH DATE | MOTHER'S MAIDEN NAME

3 STREET ADDRESS | HOME PHONE
CITY | STATE | ZIP | HOW LONG
EMPLOYER | WORK PHONE
BIRTH PLACE | BIRTH DATE | MOTHER'S MAIDEN NAME

BRANCH NAME | R/C NUMBER | PERSONAL BANKER

FORM 50-7032 7/90

CHECKING AND SAVINGS

CHECKING ACCOUNT OPTIONS
☐ FirstChoice™ Gold
☐ FirstChoice™ Flat Fee
☐ FirstChoice™ Interest
☐ FirstChoice™ Minimum Balance
☐ Express Checking™
☐ Other______________

ACCESS CARD
☐ I hereby request an Access Card for each signer

SAVINGS ACCOUNT OPTIONS
☐ FirstChoice™ Fixed Rate
☐ FirstChoice™ Market Rate
☐ Market Rate Savings
☐ Statement Savings
☐ Other______________

TYPE OF OWNERSHIP
☐ Single Name
☐ Joint Account With Right Of Surviorship
☐ Joint Account Without Right Of Surviorship
☐ Agency Account
☐ Payable On Death - Revocable
☐ Joint Tenants, Right Of Survivorship, Single Beneficiary
☐ Joint Tenants, Right Of Survivorship, Multiple Beneficiaries
☐ Single Name, Single Beneficiary
☐ Single Name, Multiple Beneficiaries
Beneficiary Name(s)______________

☐ Uniform Gift To Minor - Irrevocable (See Information On Back)

CREDIT CARD

CREDIT CARD OPTIONS
I hereby request a:
☐ MasterCard® ☐ Gold MasterCard®†
☐ Visa® ☐ Visa Gold®†
☐ Combined ☐ Combined (Gold)

☐ Transfer Balance From Another Card (Attach Form 50-7031)

I/We agree to be bound by the Seafirst Bankcard Services Agreement that will be given to me/us before the first transaction is made. Please see reverse side for important account information.

X______________ SIGNATURE ______ DATE
X______________ SIGNATURE ______ DATE

† Must complete a separate Gold Card Credit Application.

SEAFIRST BANK
Expect excellence

SBS COPY

The manner in which these four companies use desktop publishing ranges from the very simple to the very sophisticated. The common thread in each application is the use of a personal computer, laser printer, and software program that allows the merging of text and graphics to create a serviceable, attractive publication.

THE PAGEMAKER PROGRAM

As mentioned at the beginning of this chapter, PageMaker is currently the country's most popular desktop publishing program. It offers extremely sophisticated features, yet is relatively easy to learn. If you have worked with a personal computer and a word processing program, you have valuable skills transferable to the desktop publishing environment. The ability to use the keyboard and disk drives, as well as to save and retrieve work, will speed up the process of learning PageMaker. When you begin the program, you may notice one significant difference between the use of your word processing program and PageMaker. With some word processing programs, you use the keyboard to enter and edit text, execute commands (such as Save or Print), and move around the screen using cursor keys. With a desktop publishing program, you use a pointing device, called a **mouse**, to move around the screen and to execute commands. This process speeds up the use of the program and relieves you of the burden of memorizing keystroke combinations. (Many of the more sophisticated word processing programs, including all of those that are Windows-based, also allow you to use a mouse.)

In Chapter 2 you will begin learning the PageMaker program. The steps to start up the program can vary, and you should check with your instructor or lab assistant before beginning Chapter 2. The data disk accompanying this text has several files you will use in the following chapters. These files include publications developed using PageMaker, documents developed using a word processing program, graphs developed using a spreadsheet program, and graphics developed using a drawing program. With the exception of Chapter 8, Design Concepts, which can be completed at any point, each chapter builds upon the previous ones, so it is important that you work carefully through the chapters in the order they're presented.

SUMMARY

This chapter has introduced desktop publishing. You have learned how it can be used as a tool in page description and how it compares with traditional methods of page design and printing. You know the components of a desktop publishing system and some of its advantages and disadvantages. Keep in mind that desktop publishing will not allow you to eliminate those printing situations requiring typeset- or photographic-quality documents, but it can be used to enhance them.

KEY TERMS

PageMaker

desktop publishing programs

laser printer

desktop publishing

computer

publishing

page description

phototypesetting

WYSIWYG

scanner

hardware

software

template

imagesetter

mouse

QUESTIONS

1. Define *desktop publishing*.

2. Explain the phrase "Desktop publishing begins where word processing ends."

3. Briefly trace how desktop publishing developed.

4. What is meant by the phrase "Desktop publishing is a tool used in page description"?

5. Compare the traditional versus desktop publishing methods of page design and printing.

6. Explain the advantages and disadvantages of using desktop publishing.

7. List and explain the functions of the components of a desktop publishing system.

8. List four features common in more powerful desktop publishing programs.

1. Visit a company or organization and obtain a publication its staff has developed using desktop publishing. Then determine:

   - the basic hardware and software program being used
   - other equipment and programs used in the publishing process
   - steps involved in creating the publication
   - the people involved and the skills each must have to do the job adequately
   - the time needed
   - what, if any, outside services being used

2. Through library research, write a review of a magazine or newspaper article that deals with desktop publishing. Include:

   - the name and date of the publication, the name and page length of the article, and the author, if specified
   - a one-page summary of the article specifying two or three main points

3. Describe the desktop publishing features of the word processing program you use.

To complete this chapter you must:

- Be able to start up the PageMaker program
- Have the data disk accompanying this text

Upon completion of this chapter you will be able to:

- Use the mouse pointer, pull-down menus, and shortcut keys
- Use a dialog box
- Describe the components of the PageMaker screen
- Open a publication
- Describe the components of the Toolbox
- Print a publication
- Use the Help menu

The PageMaker Environment

This chapter presents an overview of how PageMaker works. The chapter walks you through the PageMaker environment and teaches you how to use the menu system. A **menu** is a list of options or commands. For example, the File menu has a Save command and a Print command. You will learn how to select a menu and execute a command in the practice session later in the chapter.

The chapter also introduces you to The Inn at Portage Bay, a luxury resort hotel located near the ocean in Washington State. As you will learn, the Inn is known for its quality service and dramatic views of the ocean, distant islands, and the Olympic Mountains. The Inn at Portage Bay needs many documents that can be produced using a desktop publishing system: a newsletter, employee benefit booklet, brochure, menu, advertisement, price list, and stationery, to name a few. Some of these you will create by following specific directions within the chapters, and others are part of projects at the end of the chapters.

USING THE MOUSE POINTER

Before starting the PageMaker program, you need to learn to use the mouse pointer. The **mouse** is a small device connected to your computer that works with PageMaker to select different commands. As you move the mouse around your desk, an arrow moves on the screen. If you run out of space to move the mouse, simply lift the mouse off the desk surface and reposition it in a location that allows you to continue.

You can do all PageMaker tasks by a combination of typing at the keyboard (for text and numbers) and using four mouse techniques: **click, double-click, press,** and **drag**. Each technique requires a different action and has a specific function as indicated below.

Technique	Action	Function
Click	Press and release mouse button.	Selects an option or changes a setting.
Double-click	Quickly click and release mouse button twice.	Highlights an item or shortcuts a process. For example, when opening a file, you can double-click on the file name displayed onscreen.
Press	Press and hold mouse button. Release when done.	Displays pull-down menus and selects commands.
Drag	Press and hold mouse button while moving mouse in any direction.	Moves objects, such as a drawing, around the screen, selects a screen area, or draws graphics.

You will use all four mouse techniques to execute PageMaker instructions.

In the following sections you will start the PageMaker program and learn about the PageMaker environment. Throughout the chapter you will be directed to carry out specific actions, such as pointing and clicking the mouse. All actions are numbered and displayed in color. Carefully work through this practice, pausing to study each figure presented. Make sure you understand what is happening as you proceed through the exercise. If you are unsure of what is happening, return to the last point you understood, or return here and start again.

1. Start the PageMaker program according to the procedure for your computer. (A copyright statement will appear briefly onscreen.)

2. After the copyright statement disappears from the screen, find the mouse pointer (an arrow pointing up and slightly left) onscreen.

3. Take a moment to move the pointer around the screen. (Do not click the mouse button.)

When you first start the PageMaker program, one or more windows may appear onscreen (see Figure 2.1). These windows are not part of the PageMaker program. They can be left on the desktop or removed by clicking on the Close box for each window (Figure 2.1). If you remove the windows, you will need to choose Aldus PageMaker 5.0 from the Finder icon in the upper-right corner of the screen (Figure 2.1).

Figure 2.1
Two open windows
that may appear when
starting PageMaker

Finder icon

Close box

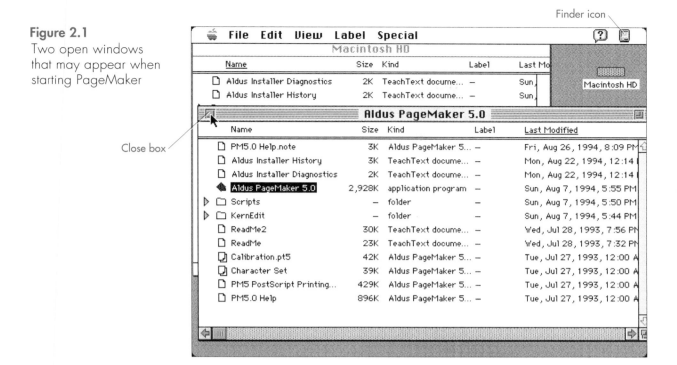

UNDERSTANDING PULL-DOWN MENUS

Figure 2.2 shows the PageMaker menu bar. When you point to a word in the menu bar and press the mouse button, PageMaker displays a pull-down menu. A **pull-down menu** is a list of related **commands** that can be selected. PageMaker has seven pull-down menus in the menu bar: File,

Figure 2.2
The PageMaker
menu bar

Menu bar

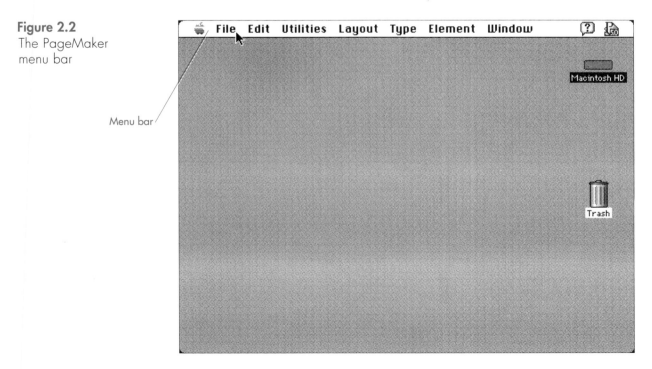

Edit, Utilities, Layout, Type, Element, and Window. For this practice you will work with each pull-down menu, starting with File.

First, you need to understand some features common to all the pull-down menus. Using the mouse, select the File menu as follows:

1. Point to File in the menu bar.

2. Press and hold the mouse button.

Several features are notable in the File menu. Options, such as Open, Preferences, Page setup, and Quit, are in black; others—Save, Place, and Print—are in gray. Black options are active and can be selected. Gray options are inactive; selecting them will have no effect. PageMaker "knows" which options are appropriate at any time in your session. For example, since you are just starting a session and have opened no document, there is nothing so far to print, so the Print option is in gray.

Many options, such as Open and Page setup, have an **ellipsis**, three periods, after them. Selecting such an option will give you a screen, called a **dialog box**, with additional choices to make before the option will be executed. For example, selecting the Page setup option displays a dialog box that allows you to change the page size, margins, and resolution of printer you are using. Options without an ellipsis, such as Close and Save, will execute when you select them and usually require no additional choices.

3. Release the mouse button.

Selecting a Menu Option

To select an option with the mouse you must first display the appropriate pull-down menu by pointing to the menu and pressing and holding the mouse button. Then point to the desired option and release the mouse button. If you make a mistake and choose the wrong option, you can usually choose Cancel from a dialog box or press the (ESC) key.

Using Shortcut Keys

Some options can be selected directly from the PageMaker window without first displaying the pull-down menu. Menu options with an entry to the far right, such as:

New...   ⌘ N

can be selected by holding down the Command key (represented by ⌘) and pressing (N). These are called **shortcut keys**.

Throughout this book the directions will use the first method of option selection, that is, selecting pull-down menus and commands with the mouse. After Chapter 3 you will be familiar with the pull-down menus, and the shortcut keys will be listed.

Using Pull-Down Menus

In this section of the practice, you will familiarize yourself with the options in the menu bar by pointing and pressing the mouse to display the various menus. Each part of the practice has a short explanation of the options available in that pull-down menu. Then you are directed to select different options. Don't be concerned now with the details of each option—it will be explained when used in an application. This practice is intended only to show you how to use pull-down menus and what is contained in each.

FILE MENU

Figure 2.3 shows the File menu, which allows you to open, save, close, and print publications; place text and graphics, developed using another program, in a publication; and quit PageMaker.

Figure 2.3
File menu

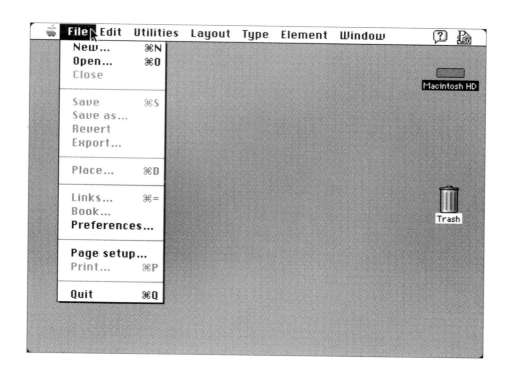

Starting a New Publication

To start a new publication, you must tell PageMaker about the publication. How many pages does it have? What is the page size? How wide are the margins? These and other settings can be specified, using the Page setup dialog box, before or after you bring text and graphics into a page.

For this practice you will select the New option from the File menu to start a new publication, and use the Page setup dialog box to change the top margin setting. In Chapter 3 you will take this process one step

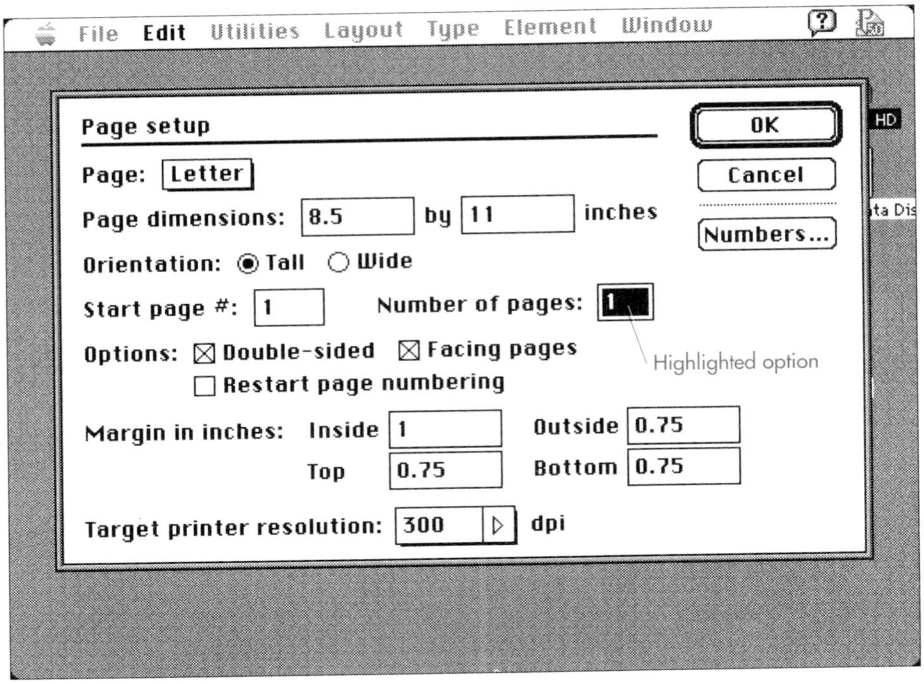

Figure 2.4
Page setup dialog box

further by entering text into the publication window. *Note:* The New option in the File menu is used to start a new publication, and the Open option is used to open a previously saved publication. Now select the New option from the File menu.

1. Point to File in the menu bar.

2. Hold down the mouse button to display the File pull-down menu.

3. Point to New...

4. Release the mouse button.

The Page setup dialog box appears, as shown in Figure 2.4.

WORKING WITH DIALOG BOXES

A dialog box allows you to issue instructions to the program or specify characteristics about a publication. For example, when you are just beginning a publication, you use the Page setup dialog box to specify margin settings and number of pages in the publication. Or if you want to retrieve a previously saved publication, you use the Open publication dialog box to specify the file name and which disk drive holds the file. Each dialog box has a name, such as Page setup, Preferences, or Open publication. Also, most dialog boxes have two buttons, OK and Cancel. You click on the OK button after you've made changes in the dialog box and are ready to continue. You click on the Cancel button if you displayed the dialog box accidentally. Clicking on the Cancel button returns you to the publication page or another dialog box.

Study the Page setup dialog box in Figure 2.4. Several settings, called default settings, are specified. For example, the default Page size is Letter with dimensions of 8.5 × 11 inches; and the Margin in inches settings are Inside (left), 1; Outside (right), 0.75; Top, 0.75; and Bottom, 0.75. These, as well as other settings in this dialog box, can be changed in two ways. First, if the setting is simply a choice among options, such as Tall versus Wide, the mouse can be used. If a setting requires you to enter text or numbers, such as changing a margin setting, you must first select the option and then make the entry from the keyboard.

Notice that the 1 in the Number of pages option is highlighted, which means this option is selected. Typing another number replaces the 1. Three methods can be used to highlight an option.

Method 1— [TAB]

By pressing the Tab key you can highlight the various options.

1. Press [TAB] four times.

The highlight moves through five options to the bottom margin setting. To change this setting, you would type another number.

**Method 2—
Double-Click**

Another method for highlighting an option is to point to the option and double-click the mouse button.

2. Point to the 8.5 page dimension.

3. Double-click the mouse button.

The 8.5 is highlighted and can be edited.

**Method 3—
Point and Drag**

You use the mouse to highlight an option by pointing the arrow at the setting and dragging the pointer to the right.

4. Point to the left of the 0 in the top margin setting (Figure 2.5).

5. Hold down the mouse button and drag the pointer to the right.

6. Release the mouse button.

The setting 0.75 is highlighted and now you can enter a new number.

7. Type 2.

The 0.75 changes to 2. Now you will leave the dialog box and display the page setup with these new settings.

8. Click on OK.

Figure 2.5
Positioning the pointer

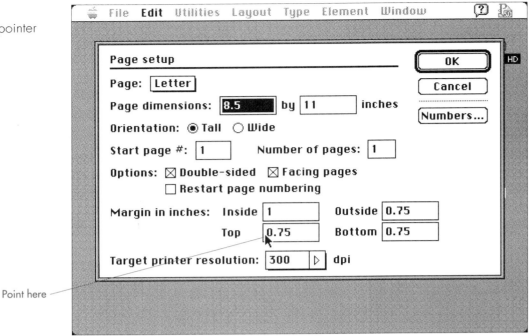

Point here

THE PUBLICATION WINDOW

Figure 2.6 shows the **publication window** with the page setup in the middle. The window components are listed in the following table.

Component	Function
Page setup	Displays the publication's layout, including page size, orientation, and margins.
Title bar	Displays the current publication's title. Because this is a new publication, the word *Untitled-1* appears. PageMaker allows you to have more than one open publication at a time. If you were to start another new publication it would be given the default name Untitled-2.
Menu bar	Displays the menu.
Toolbox	Displays the tool **icons** (symbols PageMaker uses to suggest functions) used in entering and editing text and in drawing and manipulating graphics.
Rulers	Measurement scales used to align text and graphics within the page.
Scroll bars	Used to scroll the window and the page.
Pasteboard	Area, outside the page, holding text and graphics for later use in the page.

Figure 2.6
Publication window
with the page setup

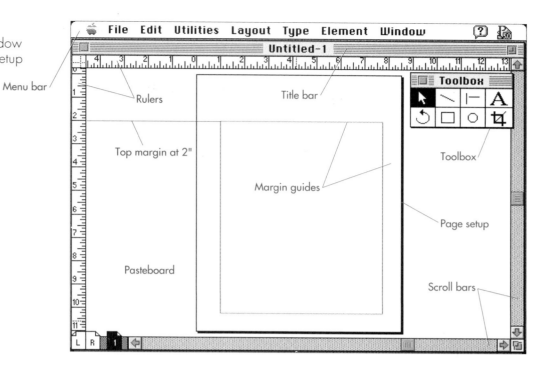

You use the Pasteboard as a desktop in that you can move items onto and off of it, as well as within it. For example, you can place text and graphics in the empty spaces on either side of the page setup, and then, when needed, bring them inside the page.

The page you are working with is bound by a solid line with standard dimensions of 8½" wide × 11" high. The dotted lines within the page are **margin guides** indicating margin settings. Notice that the top margin is at the 2" mark, the number you specified earlier in the Page setup dialog box. At this point you can add text or graphics to the page or change its design.

CREATING GUIDES

In addition to margin guides, PageMaker allows you to display ruler and column guides. **Ruler guides** help you align text and graphics as they are brought into the page. **Column guides** are used when you specify that the page will have more than one column, such as in a newsletter. All guide-lines are nonprinting. The following list shows how to create the three types of guides.

Type	How Created	Menu
Margin	Page setup dialog box using the New or Page setup command	File
Column	Column guides command	Layout
Ruler	Drag from ruler	None

Figure 2.7
Page setup with
ruler guides

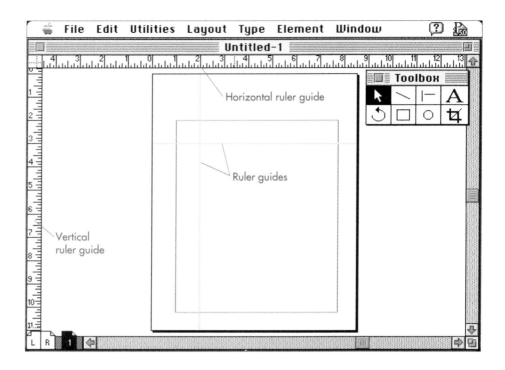

Ruler Guides

Figure 2.7 shows a page setup with ruler guides. You can display vertical and horizontal ruler guides. To display a vertical ruler guide, point to anywhere on the left ruler, press and hold down the mouse button, and then drag the line to the desired location in the page. *Note:* Point on the ruler, but do not point on the ruler's left edge.

Complete the following to duplicate Figure 2.7.

1. Point to the left ruler.

The pointer changes to a larger single arrow.

2. Press and hold the mouse button.

Figure 2.8 shows that the pointer has changed to a double arrow.

3. Drag the line to the 2" mark on the top ruler.

4. Release the button.

5. Point to the top ruler.

6. Drag the line down to the 3" mark on the left ruler.

7. Release the button.

To clear a ruler guide, simply drag it back to the ruler. Clear the ruler guides as follows:

1. Point to the horizontal ruler guide on the page.

2. Press and hold the mouse button.

When the pointer arrow changes to a double arrow:

3. Drag the line to the top ruler.

Figure 2.8
Pointer changed to
a double arrow

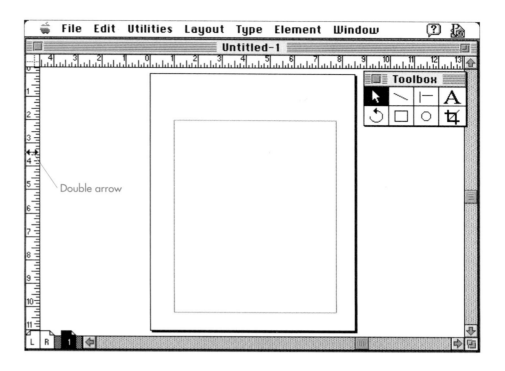

4. **Release the button.**

5. **On your own, drag the vertical ruler guide back to the left ruler.**

Column Guides

Figure 2.9 shows a page setup with column guides for a two-column layout. Use the Column guides command from the Layout menu to display the dialog box that lets you specify the number of columns.

Figure 2.9
Column guides for a
two-column layout

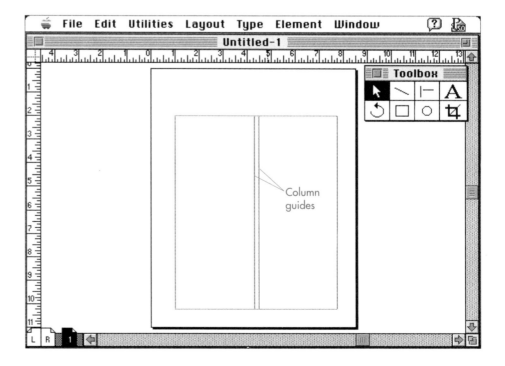

1. Point to Layout in the menu bar and press the mouse button.

2. Point to Column guides... and release the mouse button.

The Column guides dialog box appears with the Number of columns default set at 1. Notice that the number is highlighted.

3. Type 2.

4. Click on OK.

The publication window now appears with the page setup divided into two columns.

EDIT MENU

Figure 2.10 shows the Edit menu, which allows you to undo your last action and make changes to a publication, such as copying paragraphs and graphics or deleting (Clear) text. You can also use the Edit menu to insert charts or drawings into a publication and to select Story Editor—a PageMaker word processor. Many of the Edit options are inactive (gray) because as yet there is no text or graphics in the publication. To illustrate the use of the Edit menu, you will use the Undo command to remove the column guides.

1. Display the Edit menu.

2. Choose Undo guide move.

The column guides are removed from the publication page. The Undo command is useful when you change your mind about an action you have just taken. It can be used to reverse only the most recent action, however, and is not available for all actions.

UTILITIES MENU

Figure 2.11 shows the Utilities menu, which allows you to search for words in a publication, check for spelling errors, and create an index and table of contents. Also, the Utilities menu includes the Aldus Additions. These commands allow you to automate various tasks such as numbering all of the lines of text.

Figure 2.10
Edit menu

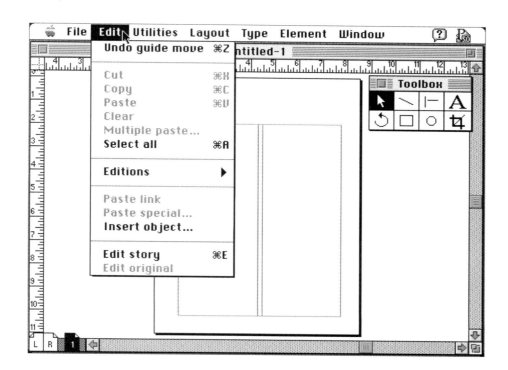

Figure 2.11
Utilities menu

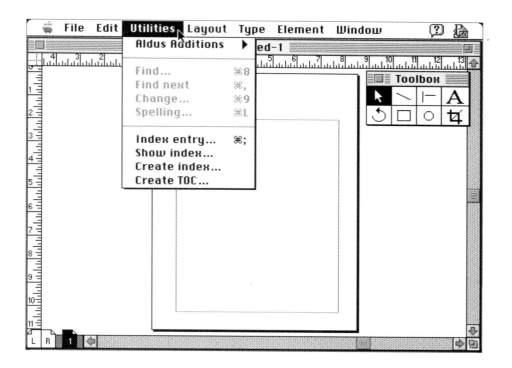

Figure 2.12 shows the Layout menu, which lists commands used to lay out the publication and to view it at various levels of magnification. You have already used the Layout menu to display the column guides for a two-column page setup. You can also use it to insert and remove pages as well as go to a particular page in a multipage document. In addition, you can change the PageMaker environment. For example, the Guides and rulers command lets you remove the ruler from the screen. Some of the commands in this menu can be made active or inactive. Commands are active when they have a check mark next to them and are inactive when not checked. To change the status of the command, simply click on it. To illustrate this, you will select the Guides and rulers option and then turn off the rulers.

1. **Display the Layout menu.**

2. **Point to Guides and rulers.**

Several options appear, some with check marks, indicating that they are active.

3. **Point to Rulers.**

4. **Release the mouse button to remove the check mark.**

The rulers are now removed from view. Now use the mouse pointer to reactivate them.

5. **Display the Layout menu.**

6. **Point to Guides and rulers.**

Figure 2.12
Layout menu

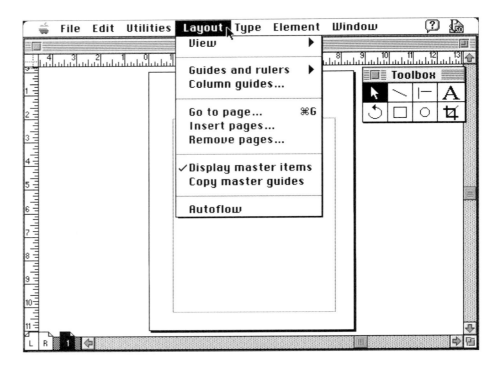

7. Point to Rulers.

Notice that the check mark is gone from Rulers.

8. Release the mouse button to display the check mark and activate the rulers.

The rulers are redisplayed.

OPENING A SAVED PUBLICATION

Before studying the rest of the menus, you will open a publication saved on your data disk as file Promo 1. As Figure 2.13 shows, this

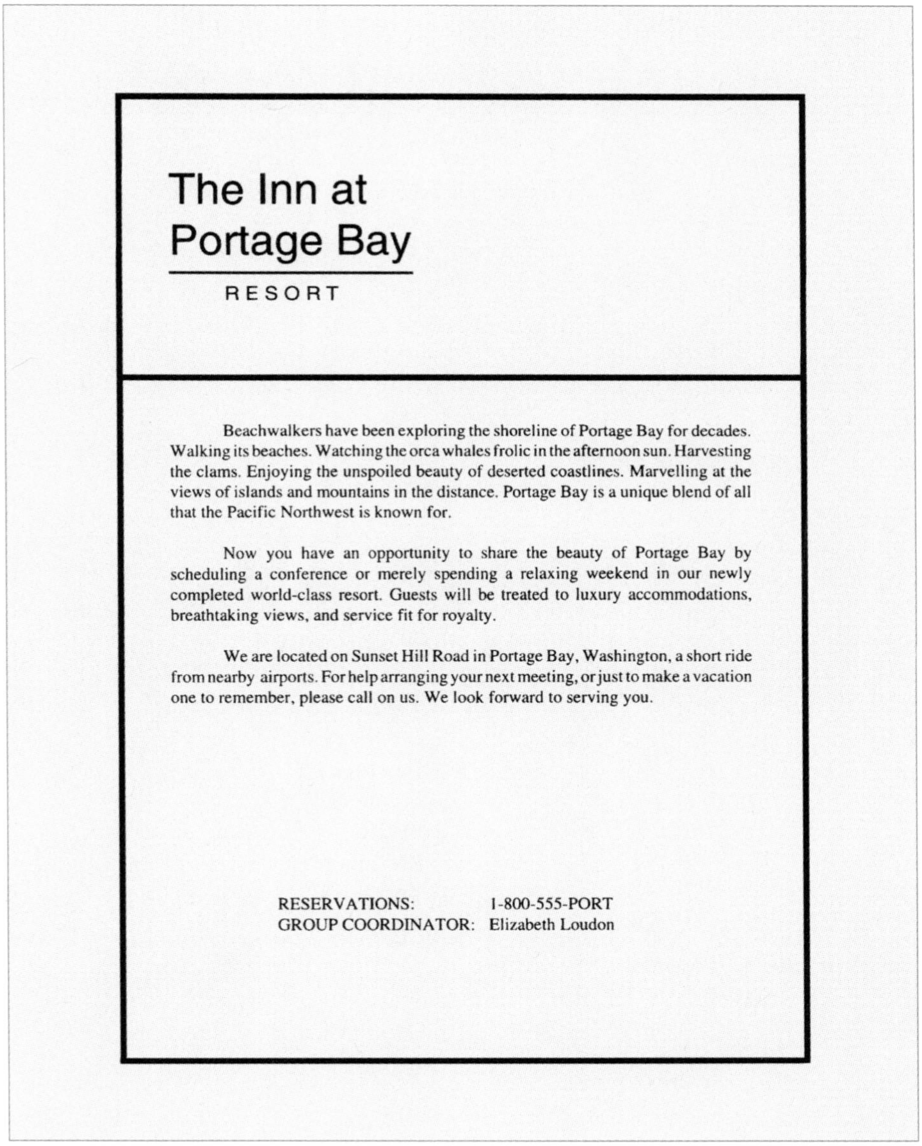

Figure 2.13
Promo 1, a promotional piece for The Inn at Portage Bay

> # The Inn at Portage Bay
> RESORT
>
> Beachwalkers have been exploring the shoreline of Portage Bay for decades. Walking its beaches. Watching the orca whales frolic in the afternoon sun. Harvesting the clams. Enjoying the unspoiled beauty of deserted coastlines. Marvelling at the views of islands and mountains in the distance. Portage Bay is a unique blend of all that the Pacific Northwest is known for.
>
> Now you have an opportunity to share the beauty of Portage Bay by scheduling a conference or merely spending a relaxing weekend in our newly completed world-class resort. Guests will be treated to luxury accommodations, breathtaking views, and service fit for royalty.
>
> We are located on Sunset Hill Road in Portage Bay, Washington, a short ride from nearby airports. For help arranging your next meeting, or just to make a vacation one to remember, please call on us. We look forward to serving you.
>
> RESERVATIONS: 1-800-555-PORT
> GROUP COORDINATOR: Elizabeth Loudon

publication is a promotion for The Inn at Portage Bay. You will use the Open command from the File menu to open it. Before starting another publication, close the current one with the Close command from the File menu.

1. Choose Close from the File menu.

A warning screen appears, asking if you want to save the publication before closing. If you choose Yes, a dialog box will appear, allowing you to enter a file name. If you choose No, the publication will be discarded. If you choose Cancel, you will return to the publication window.

2. Click on No.

The page setup disappears from the screen and the PageMaker screen replaces the publication window. Now retrieve the Promo 1 publication as follows:

3. Insert the data disk into the disk drive.

4. Choose Open... from the File menu.

The Open publication dialog box appears so you can select the name of your publication.

5. Click on Desktop.

6. Double-click on the PageMaker Data Disk option.

7. Click on the down arrow in the scroll bar to display Promo 1 (Figure 2.14).

Figure 2.14
Open publication
dialog box

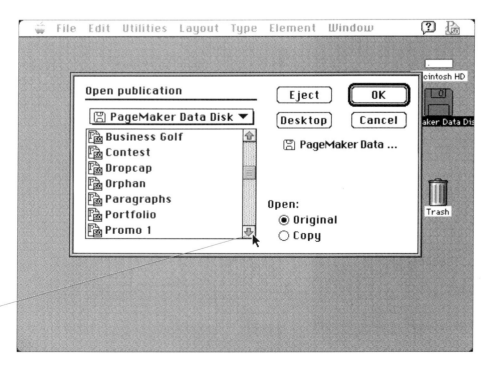

Click here

Figure 2.15
Promo 1 displayed
in Greeked text

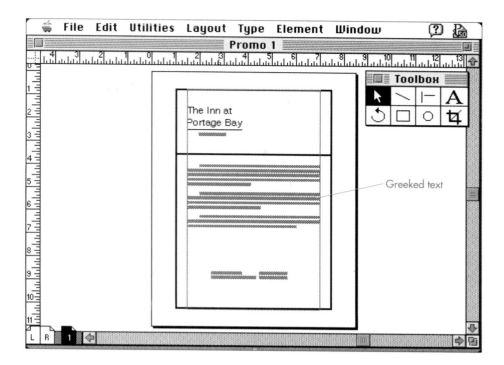

8. **Click on Promo 1 to highlight it.**

9. **Click on OK.**

The Promo 1 file is retrieved from the data disk.

Figure 2.15 shows the publication layout as it will appear onscreen. All of the text, except for the top heading lines, is simulated and illegible because the screen is too small to display the entire publication in a type size large enough to read. Despite its limitations, the full-page screen view lets you see the exact position of the publication's paragraphs and heading lines. (The heading lines are legible because they are in larger type sizes.) **Greeked text** is the term used to describe simulated text. Compare the screen view of the publication with Figure 2.13, which shows the printed publication. As you make changes in a publication, PageMaker may need to redraw the publication onscreen. Using Greeked text speeds up the redrawing process as well as allows you to see the design of an entire page. The following section shows you how to change the screen view of the publication so all the text is legible.

CHANGING THE PAGE VIEW

The Layout menu View command is used for specifying how much of your publication you see onscreen.

1. **Display the Layout pull-down menu.**

2. **Point to View.**

The eight options control the size of the publication view, as described in the following table.

Command	Displays Page...
Fit in window	as it will fit in the publication window (this is the default setting).
Show Pasteboard	with the complete Pasteboard, including all text and graphics stored there.
25% size	at 25% size it will be when printed.
50% size	at 50% size it will be when printed.
75% size	at 75% size it will be when printed.
Actual size	at size it will be when printed.
200% size	at twice the actual size.
400% size	at four times the actual size.

Now look at the publication page with five of these different views. Examine each view before moving to the next one.

3. Choose Actual size.

This view is similar to what you would see onscreen if you were using a word processing program.

4. Choose View from the Layout menu.

5. Choose 75% size.

More of the page can be seen with this view than with the Actual size view; however, the type is smaller.

6. Choose View from the Layout menu.

7. Choose 50% size.

You see even more of the page at 50% size. However, the type is displayed as Greeked text.

8. On your own, choose 200% size.

Only a small part of the page is displayed because the text is enlarged to twice the actual size.

9. On your own, choose the Fit in window option.

Using Greeked text the entire page is displayed onscreen.

PageMaker provides shortcut keys for the different views.

10. Choose View from the Layout menu.

Notice how the Command key can be used with other keys to change the view. The most useful shortcut keys are ⌘-W for Fit in window and ⌘-1 for Actual size.

11. Press ⌘-1 to display the actual size.

12. Press ⌘-W to display the Fit in window size.

Before continuing, select the Actual size option using the menu.

13. Choose View from the Layout menu.

14. Choose Actual size.

MOVING THE PUBLICATION PAGE AND THE PUBLICATION WINDOW

Using the Scroll Bars

When you use any page view, except for Fit in window and 25% size, only part of the page is displayed. However, you can use the scroll bars on the bottom and right sides of the screen to view any part of the publication. The scroll bars move the publication window up, down, left, and right while the page stays fixed in place. There are four ways to scroll the window: (1) click on an arrow at either end of the scroll bars, (2) click in the gray area of the scroll bars, (3) drag a box in the scroll bars, and (4) point to an arrow and hold down the mouse button.

Use the click method to scroll the window up.

1. Point to the down arrow in the lower-right corner of the screen (see Figure 2.16).

2. Click the mouse button five times.

Figure 2.16
Using the scroll bars to scroll the publication window

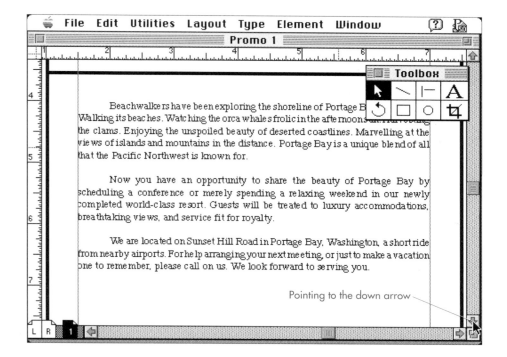

Notice that the window moves down to display the ending lines. Before continuing, change the page view to Fit in window.

1. **Choose View from the Layout menu.**

2. **Choose Fit in window.**

Using the Grabber Hand

The **grabber hand** is an icon in the shape of a hand. It allows you to "grab" your publication and move it to another place on the Pasteboard. When your view is larger than Fit in window, the grabber hand lets you bring another portion of your document into view. To use the grabber hand:

1. **Position the pointer on the page as shown in Figure 2.17.**

2. **Hold down the (OPTION) key and press the mouse button. (Note that the arrow icon changes to a hand icon.)**

3. **Release (OPTION) but keep the mouse button pressed.**

4. **Drag the mouse to the left.**

The grabber hand pulls that area of the page as you drag the mouse.

5. **Release the mouse button.**

After releasing the mouse button, the icon changes back to an arrow. Before continuing, change the page view back to Actual size.

6. **On your own, change the page view to Actual size.**

7. **Use the scroll bar to scroll the window so that all heading lines at the top of the page are displayed.**

Figure 2.17
Positioning the pointer

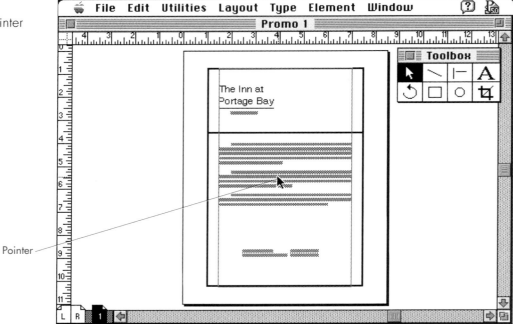

Pointer

The Toolbox appears in the upper-right corner of the screen when you open a publication. It contains eight tools for working with text and graphics in your publication. With them, you select, resize, move, and rotate text and graphics; type and edit text; and create drawings.

To select a tool in the Toolbox, point to the tool and click the mouse button, then move the mouse pointer back to the page. As you move the pointer to the page, the pointer changes to the icon representing the selected tool (see Figure 2.18). You can also move the Toolbox by clicking on the Toolbox title bar and dragging it to another location on the page, which is helpful when the Toolbox covers a portion of the publication page you want to work with.

To illustrate the use of the Toolbox tools, you will use the text tool to select the word *Inn*. Then you will use the Type menu to select the Italic option so the word *Inn* is displayed in italic.

1. Point to the text tool (A) in the Toolbox.

2. Click the mouse button.

3. Move the pointer to the page.

Notice that the icon changes to an I-beam.

4. Place the I-beam on the space before the word *Inn* (Figure 2.19).

5. Hold down the mouse button and slowly drag the I-beam to highlight the word *Inn*.

6. Release the mouse button.

Figure 2.18
Toolbox icons

Tool	Icon	Function
Pointer		Selecting text blocks and graphics
Line	+	Drawing diagonal lines
Constrained-line	+	Drawing perpendicular lines
A Text	I	Selecting, entering, and editing text
Rotating	+	Rotating text and graphics
Rectangle	+	Drawing rectangles
Ellipse tool	+	Drawing ovals and circles
Cropping		Trimming graphics

Figure 2.19
Positioning the I-beam

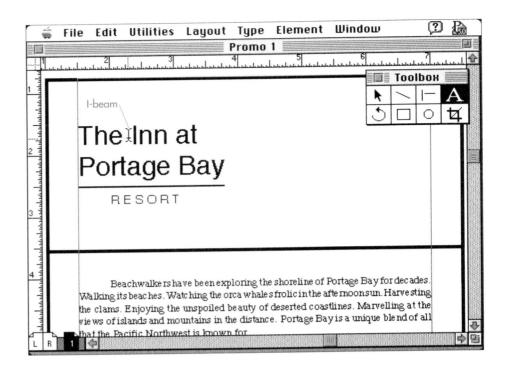

TYPE MENU

Figure 2.20 shows the Type menu, which contains commands that let you specify how text will appear in a publication. The first group of commands allows you to select the font (typeface) and size and to specify the spacing between characters. You can also specify the type style, such as bold or italic. The second group of commands allows you to format paragraphs by specifying indentation, hyphenation, justification, and type specifications. The last three commands allow you to align text (left, right, center, and justified) and to define and apply styles. A style is a set of specifications that determines how a body of text will appear. For example, you could define a headline in your publication as having a large type size, bold, underlined, and centered. You might then define a subhead to have a smaller type size, in normal type, and aligned with the left edge of the text.

Now use the Type menu to change the word *Inn* to italic.

1. Display the Type pull-down menu.

2. Point to Type style.

3. Choose Italic.

The word *Inn* is now in italic and it is still highlighted, allowing you to perform another function, such as underlining. To remove the highlight:

4. Move the I-beam to a blank area of the page.

5. Click the mouse button.

To change from the text tool (I-beam icon) to the pointer (arrow icon):

6. Click on the pointer tool in the Toolbox.

Figure 2.20
Type menu

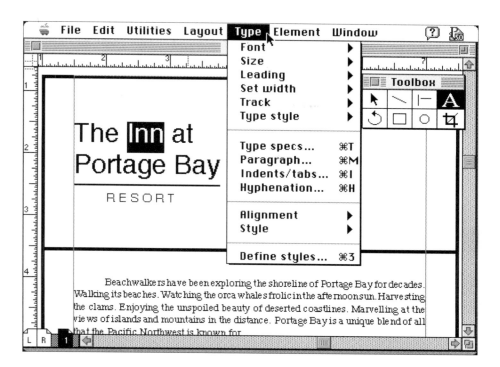

ELEMENT MENU

Figures 2.21 and 2.22 show the Element menu with the Line and Fill menus. The Line menu lists the widths and patterns available for PageMaker-drawn lines and graphics. The Fill menu lists eight shades and eight patterns for filling in shapes drawn in your publication. You will use the Line and Fill menus in Chapter 3. Take a moment to view the Line and Fill menus.

Figure 2.21
Element and Line menus

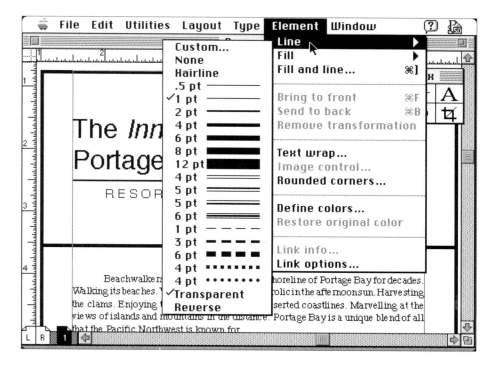

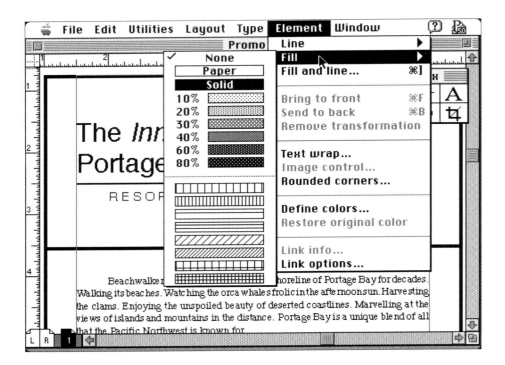

Figure 2.22
Element and Fill menus

1. **Display the Element pull-down menu.**

2. **Point to Line.**

3. **Point to Fill.**

Another feature of the Element menu allows you to work with text and graphics that overlap. For example, you could draw two boxes and have them overlap to create a three-dimensional effect. The Bring to front and Send to back options allow you to change the position of these overlapped boxes.

In addition, the Element menu allows you to specify how text will wrap around a graphic (such as flowing text around all sides of the graphic or flowing text through the graphic). You can also control the appearance of graphics (such as the lightness and contrast) and round the corners of rectangles drawn in PageMaker. The Element menu also allows you to work with colors in the publication and to specify how text and graphics developed using another program will be updated.

4. **Release the mouse button to close the Element menu.**

WINDOW MENU

Figure 2.23 shows the Window menu, which allows you to display (Tile, Cascade) all of the open publications. You can also turn on and off the display of the Toolbox and the palettes. The **palettes** are used as shortcuts

Figure 2.23
Window menu

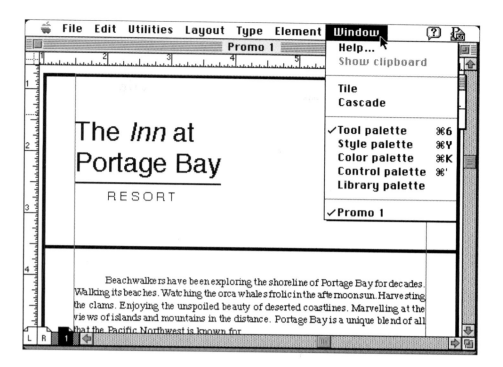

when carrying out many PageMaker functions. For instance, the Control palette can be used to change the type style and type size of text. The bottom of the Window menu shows the file name of the open publication(s). Practice working with this menu by using the Control palette to underline the word *Inn*. Start by selecting *Inn*.

1. Click on the text tool (A) in the Toolbox.

2. Point to before the word *Inn*.

3. Drag the I-beam over the word *Inn* to select it.

4. Display the Window pull-down menu.

5. Choose Control palette.

The Control palette appears, showing information about the selected text *(Inn)*. (*Note:* There are several features of this palette that you will be learning later.) Notice that the *I* is highlighted on the Control palette, indicating that the selected text is formatted in italic type. Now underline the word by clicking on the underline button on the Control palette.

6. Click on the underline button (see Figure 2.24).

Inn is underlined. Now remove the Control palette from the screen.

7. Choose Control palette from the Window menu.

8. Click on a blank area of the screen to deselect the word *Inn*.

Figure 2.24
Control palette

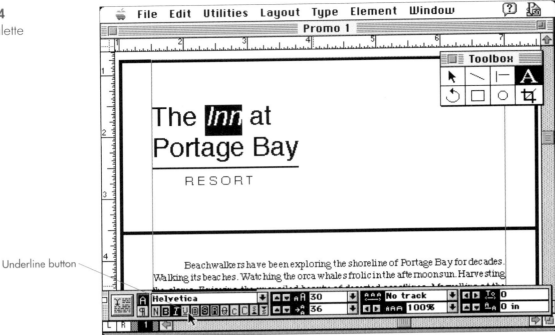

Underline button

HELP MENU

PageMaker provides a comprehensive Help function that is accessed from the Window menu.

1. Choose Help... from the Window menu.

Figure 2.25 shows the Help window. This window contains buttons, such as TOPICS and SEARCH, that can be used to display the information you need. Figure 2.25 shows seven help topics. You choose a topic by clicking on it. You will use the step-by-step instructions to display information about starting a new publication.

2. Click on STEP-BY-STEP INSTRUCTIONS.

3. Click on Publication Setup.

4. Click on Opening, naming and saving publications.

5. Click on Creating a new publication.

A window appears with information about creating a new publication.

6. Read the information in the window.

This is the same procedure you used earlier in this chapter. You can use the PREVIOUS button to display the previous screen, or you can use the TOPICS button to return to the list of topics.

7. Click on the TOPICS button.

Now use the COMMANDS topic to display information about opening a publication.

Figure 2.25
Help window

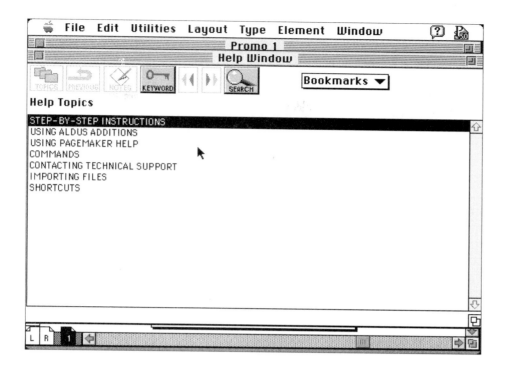

8. Click on COMMANDS.

9. Click on File menu.

10. Click on Open.

A screen appears with information about the Open command. Next use the KEYWORD button to search for how to change margin settings.

11. Click on the KEYWORD button.

An alphabetical list of words appears. You can use the scroll bar to scroll the list. Also, you can type a letter to jump to the part of the list that starts with that letter.

12. Type *m*.

The list scrolls to display the word MACROS. Now use the scroll bar to display the word MARGINS.

13. Point to the down arrow on the scroll bar.

14. Click the mouse button until MARGINS appears.

15. Click on MARGINS.

Two choices appear on the right side of the window.

16. Click on PAGE SETUP... (FILE MENU).

Information on the Page setup command, which is used to change margin settings, appears. *Note:* You would need to scroll this window to display the section on margins. When you are done with the Help

Figure 2.26
The Close box used to close the Help window

Close box

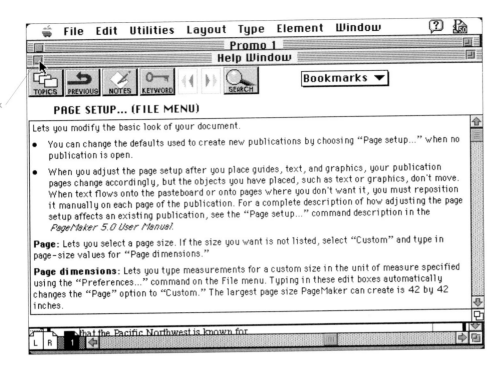

function, you can use the Close box in the upper-left corner of the window to close the window.

17. **Point to the Close box of the Help window (see Figure 2.26).**

18. **Click the mouse button.**

The Help window is closed and you return to the PageMaker publication.

The Help function is most useful after you have learned the basics of the PageMaker program. It is best used to help you through a process already learned but partially forgotten, rather than to teach you a new process.

ENDING A PAGEMAKER SESSION

Before quitting PageMaker, you must decide if you want to print and/ or save the current publication. Then you're free to close the publication and quit the program. For this practice you will print, but not save, the publication.

Printing a Publication

To print a publication, use the Print command from the File menu. Make sure your computer is connected to a printer, the printer is ready, and the paper is aligned.

1. Choose Print... from the File menu.

The Print document dialog box appears with print options, such as the number of copies to print. Normally you will not need to make changes to these settings. The name of the printer is displayed near the top of the dialog box. Make sure the printer you are using is displayed. You may need to check with your lab assistant or instructor to determine which printer you'll be using.

2. Click on Print.

At this point a window may appear, telling you the publication was not composed for your printer. This means you are not using the same printer as was used to create the document. If so, you can still print the publication by clicking on OK, but the printed document may look different than the document onscreen.

In a few moments the publication is printed.

Closing a Publication and Quitting PageMaker

Earlier you retrieved the Promo 1 file using the Open command. Now that you're done with the publication, you can use the Close command from the File menu to close this file.

1. Choose Close from the File menu.

A window appears, asking if you want to save before closing. Remember, you made a change in the document when you italicized the word *Inn*. If you specify yes, the original Promo 1 file will be overwritten. You do not want to save the changes, so specify no.

2. Click on No.

The publication window is cleared and the PageMaker screen appears. Now use the Quit command from the File menu to exit PageMaker.

3. Choose Quit from the File menu.

SUMMARY

You have now been introduced to the PageMaker environment. You have learned how to use the mouse to select pull-down menus and execute commands. You know how to use dialog boxes and the Toolbox, as well as how to open, close, and print publications. In Chapter 3 you will create your first PageMaker document.

KEY TERMS

menu

mouse

click

double-click

press

drag

pull-down menu

commands

ellipsis

dialog box

shortcut keys

publication window

page setup

title bar

menu bar

Toolbox

icons

rulers

scroll bars

Pasteboard

margin guides

ruler guides

column guides

Greeked text

grabber hand

palettes

QUESTIONS

1. Describe the four techniques for using the mouse.

2. What is a pull-down menu?

3. List and briefly describe each of the pull-down menus.

4. What are commands and how are they chosen?

5. What is the purpose of a dialog box? Give an example.

6. Briefly describe the components of the publication window.

7. How is the Pasteboard used?

8. What is the difference between margin, ruler, and column guides?

9. Describe the process for opening a file.

10. How is the grabber hand used?

11. Briefly describe the components of the Toolbox.

12. Describe the process for printing a publication.

13. Turn to the Quick Reference section of this book (Appendix B) and describe the type of information you find and how it can be used.

14. Using the Index at the end of this book, list the page numbers for the following terms:

Greeked text _____

publication window _____

ruler guides _____

1. The following exercise lets you practice many of the commands and techniques you learned in Chapter 2. On your data disk is a file called Annual Picnic. Open this one-page publication and complete the following procedures.

   ■ Use the Layout menu to change the page view to 75% size. What is the last line of text displayed onscreen?

   ■ Use the scroll bars to display the last sentence of the document in the middle of the screen.

   ■ Use the scroll bars to display the document heading.

   ■ Change the page view to Actual size.

   ■ Use the text tool to highlight the top heading line.

   ■ Use the Control palette to underline the selected text.

   ■ Deselect the highlighted text.

   ■ Remove the Control palette from the screen.

   ■ Remove the Toolbox from the screen.

   ■ Print the document.

   ■ Close, but do not save, the publication.

2. Throughout this book you will be creating publications for The Inn at Portage Bay. You may want to collect your work in a portfolio. In this project you will create a cover for your portfolio. On your disk is a file called Portfolio. This is a portfolio cover that you will customize by adding your name, the course name, and the date. Figure 2.27 shows the Portfolio publication. In the upper-left corner of the page there are place holders for your name, the course name, and the date. To replace one of these, you drag the text tool to highlight it. Then you type the desired text. Complete the following steps to create your customized portfolio cover.

   ■ Open the Portfolio publication.

   ■ Change the page view to Actual size.

   ■ Display the three lines of text at the top of the page.

   ■ Select the text tool from the Toolbox.

   ■ Drag the I-beam pointer across *(your name)* to highlight it.

   ■ Type your name.

   ■ On your own, enter the course name and date.

   ■ Print the publication.

   ■ Save the publication using the file name My Portfolio. *Note:* To save the publication, choose Save as from the File menu. Then make sure the data disk is inserted and displayed in the Save publication as dialog box. Type *My Portfolio* and click on OK.

Figure 2.27
Portfolio publication

3. On your data disk is a file called Stationery. This is a template for stationery that you can customize by inserting your name and address. The process is the same as for Project 2. Complete the following to customize the stationery template.

■ Open the Stationery publication.

■ Change the page view to Actual size.

■ Display the top of the page.

■ Select the text tool from the Toolbox.

■ Drag the I-beam pointer across *(Name)* to highlight it.

- Type your name.
- On your own, enter the address lines.
- Print the publication.
- Save the publication using the file name My Stationery. *Note:* See Project 2 for instructions on saving.

4. Use the Help function to display the keyword OPEN. Then display the OPEN topics and go to the OPEN... (FILE MENU) topic.

- What limits the number of publications you can have open at one time?
- What is the difference between the Open and New commands in the File menu?

Upon completion of this chapter you will be able to:

- Use PageMaker Help

- Set defaults for PageMaker

- Create a multicolumn publication

- Use horizontal and vertical ruler guides

- Select different line types from the Line option of the Element menu

- Create text for a publication

- Use three different methods to change the page view

- Create a simple graphic

- Copy and paste a graphic

- Save and print a publication

CHAPTER 3

Creating a Single-Page Publication

In this chapter you will create your first complete publication—a magazine advertisement for The Inn at Portage Bay. You will set PageMaker defaults and tell PageMaker about the new publication. Then you will create the publication, save it, and finally print it. In the process, you will learn about typing text, drawing lines and boxes, and copying a box. By the chapter's end you will have been introduced to many more PageMaker features and will have a completed publication.

The Inn at Portage Bay needs an advertisement to use in the Yellow Pages and in travel magazines. A media consultant has developed a design based on the decision that the piece should be simple and readable, with the headline *The Inn at Portage Bay* prominently featured. Further, the consultant and Inn management wish to include a list of the resort's amenities. To draw a reader's eye and to enhance readability, the ad will contain substantial **white space** (space intentionally left empty, white). The consultant's layout is shown in Figure 3.1. You will create the ad, using the steps listed in this chapter. Before you begin, however, you will explore PageMaker's Help utility.

USING HELP

Most software products include a comprehensive Help utility with information available to you so you don't have to look up a question in the documentation. Learning how to use this feature helps you to solve your own problems and rely less on outside support. You were first introduced to Help in Chapter 2. It is such an important resource that it merits further exploration before you create your first publication.

Figure 3.1
Finished design

In this section you will find Type specs in PageMaker Help. Figures 3.2 through 3.6 will guide you.

1. Press and drag on Window, selecting Help... (see Figure 3.2).

2. Click on SEARCH (see Figure 3.3).

3. Click an insertion point in the Search for box.

4. Type *type specs* (see Figure 3.4).

5. Click on the x in the Case Sensitive box to remove it.

6. Click on Start Search (see Figure 3.4).

The result of the search is a list of topics. To find type specs:

7. Click on the down-arrow scroll bar at the right of the screen.

8. Click on TYPE SPECS... (TYPE MENU) (see Figure 3.5).

The type specs information appears (Figure 3.6). Click on the scroll bar and read the information.

Figure 3.2
Help menu Search
option

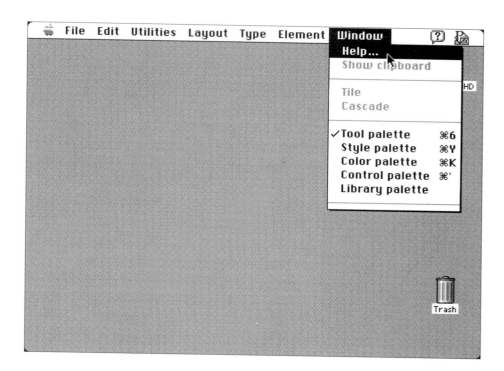

Figure 3.3
Starting a search

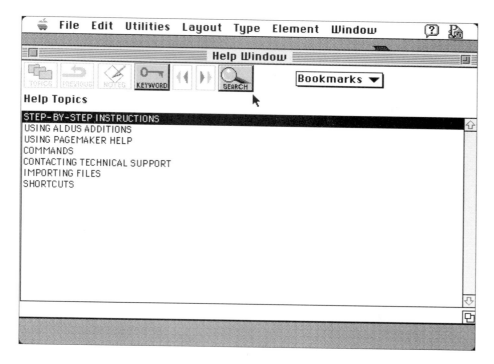

To close Help:

9. Click on the Close box.

Use Help whenever you want an explanation of some feature. It should be the first step you take before asking what something means.

Figure 3.4
Type specs Help window

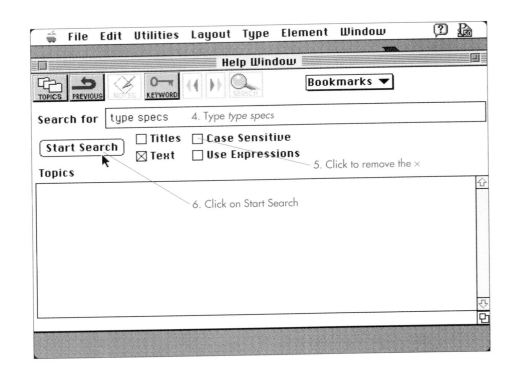

Figure 3.5
Selecting a topic

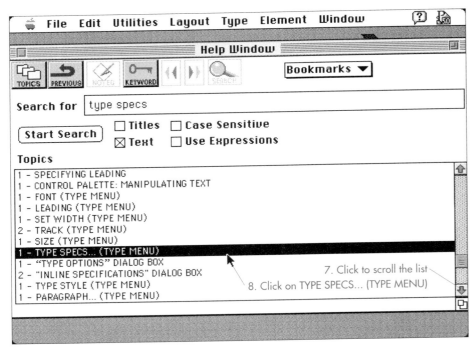

SETTING PAGEMAKER DEFAULTS

Before even opening your publication, you must set some **defaults** for it. The kinds of defaults you can set include paragraph indentation, type size, line width, and whether or not graphics, such as circles and boxes, are filled.

Figure 3.6
Type specs help
information

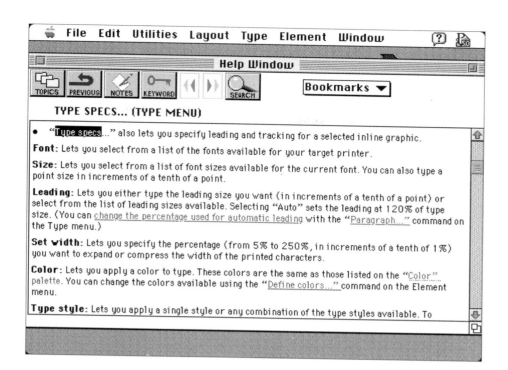

Setting defaults prior to opening a publication makes sense for two reasons. First, you need select the settings only once. For example, suppose most of the text will be set in Helvetica 12, but the last default set was Times 36 bold. You open a publication, set the type specifications at Helvetica 12, and type some text. You change to the line tool in the Toolbox and draw a line. Now you want to resume typing in Helvetica 12. You click on the text tool and continue typing. But this text will be in Times 36 bold, the earlier default, because PageMaker is designed to return to the type setting selected when the publication was first opened. Setting defaults *before* opening a publication makes the process of creating the publication easier.

A second reason to set defaults is that the process itself requires that you plan *prior* to starting a publication. Just as a graphic designer is going to set up the workspace by making sure all the needed tools are available before starting, you should set or verify default settings before opening a new publication. Planning produces better-looking documents, which in turn communicate more effectively, the ultimate goal of desktop publishing.

Predicting how your computer is set up is impossible. The PageMaker program does not have standard defaults, but a PageMaker publication and a particular computer do. The defaults on a particular machine are set by you or whoever used PageMaker last. Thus, when setting defaults you either set them or verify they're set with choices you can utilize.

About the Four Defaults

For the Inn's advertisement, you will set or verify four defaults: type specifications, align left, lock guides, and snap to guides.

First you want to tell PageMaker the kind of type you will be using for most of the publication. Type commands selected before the publication is opened are in effect for the entire publication and can be thought of as defaults. Type commands selected after the publication is opened are in effect until you move from the text tool in the Toolbox to another tool in the Toolbox.

Second, for this publication all text will be set left justified. **Left justified** means text is flush to the left margin while the right margin is uneven, or ragged. To specify left justification, select the Alignment command from the Type menu and click on Align left. Other options are Align center, Align right, **Justify**, and **Force justify**. Justify directs PageMaker to use proportional spacing between words and characters so that text completely and evenly fills a line: both left and right margins are flush. With Justify, a short line, such as the last line of a paragraph, will have normal spacing. Force justify makes a headline or the last line of a paragraph fill the alotted space. Figure 3.7 shows text left justified, centered, right justified, justified, and force justified.

Third, you will make sure the Lock guides option is *not* selected, because when it is, you are unable to move a ruler guide after you position it. Because you are just getting started with PageMaker, you may not

Figure 3.7
Left, centered, right, and justified text

Left-justified text	Centered text	Right-justified text
Waterfront location	Waterfront location	Waterfront location
224 deluxe guest rooms	224 deluxe guest rooms	224 deluxe guest rooms
Fireplaces, suites	Fireplaces, suites	Fireplaces, suites
Meeting rooms	Meeting rooms	Meeting rooms
Indoor tennis, squash, racquetball, pool, jacuzzi	Indoor tennis, squash, racquetball, pool, jacuzzi	Indoor tennis, squash, racquetball, pool, jacuzzi
Championship golf course	Championship golf course	Championship golf course
Award-winning restaurant	Award-winning restaurant	Award-winning restaurant

Left-justified text	Justified text	Force-justified text
Waterfront location; 224 deluxe guest rooms; Fireplaces, suites; Meeting rooms; Indoor tennis, squash, racquetball, pool, jacuzzi; Championship golf course; Award-winning restaurant	Waterfront location; 224 deluxe guest rooms; Fireplaces, suites; Meeting rooms; Indoor tennis, squash, racquetball, pool, jacuzzi; Championship golf course; Award-winning restaurant	Waterfront location; 224 deluxe guest rooms; Fireplaces, suites; Meeting rooms; Indoor tennis, squash, racquetball, pool, jacuzzi; Championship golf course; Award-winning restaurant

position a ruler guide correctly the first time you pull it onto your publication, so you want to have the flexibility to change its position.

Fourth, you will verify that the Snap to guides option is selected. When Snap to guides is selected, lines or graphics drawn near a ruler guide will be snapped to the guide like a magnet. In this way, your ruler guide will line up different graphic elements. This default will be important as you position the seven square bullets in a column for the Inn's magazine ad.

You may find that some of the options you are checking are already set the way the directions tell you to set them. In other cases, you will have to make a change.

Selecting the Default Type Specifications

The Type specs command in the Type menu gives you the Type specifications dialog box, which allows you to select your publication's type specifications. Type specs include font name and size, type style, position, and text case. Figure 3.8 shows the Type specifications dialog box.

A **font** is the entire group of letters and other characters of a shape, or design, in a particular size, for example, Helvetica 14. **Font name** is the name associated with a family of fonts in all sizes. Examples include Chicago, Courier, Geneva, New York, and Palatino. **Font size** is measured in points. One **point** equals about $\frac{1}{72}$ inch. Thus, a 72-point letter E is about 1 inch tall. Figure 3.9 shows six fonts in two font families.

In addition to font name and size, the Type specifications dialog box lets you make other choices about how the text will appear on the page.

Figure 3.8
Type specifications dialog box

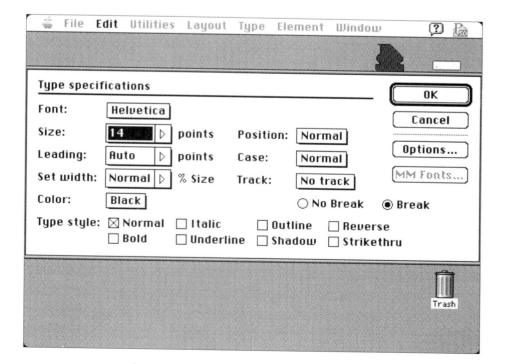

Figure 3.9
Six fonts in two
font families

Helvetica 12 Normal

Helvetica 24 Bold Italic

Helvetica 36 Bold

Times 12 Italic

Times 18 Bold

Times 48 Normal

The choices are Leading, Set width, Color, Position, Case, Track, and Type style, and a choice between Break and No break.

Type style includes the following options: Normal, Bold, Italic, Underline, Outline, Shadow, Reverse, and Strikethru. Generally, you will use Normal, Bold, and Italic. **Reverse**, white letters on a black background, does not work on every printer.

Position refers to where on a baseline the text appears. The choices are Normal, Superscript, and Subscript. **Superscript** is above the normal baseline, like an exponent. **Subscript** is below the line. In this book you will always use Normal. You may wish to experiment on your own with Superscript and Subscript.

Case refers to whether what you type is to be printed in uppercase, a mix of uppercase and lowercase, or in a version called Small caps. The choices are Normal, All caps, and Small caps. When Normal is selected, hold down (SHIFT) for capital letters. Most of what you will do will be Normal, but from time to time you will want to use All caps. An alternative to All caps is to press (CAPS LOCK) on the keyboard. Small caps is useful in certain design situations; it prints capital letters, but their height is that of the lowercase characters.

Leading (pronounced "ledding") refers to the amount of space between lines of text and is measured in points. Chapter 4 has a more complete discussion of leading, text processing, and the options available in the Type specifications dialog box.

The Break/No break option allows you to control line breaks for selected text. You may specify words that must appear on the same line regardless of where the end of the line falls.

Fonts and Points

In this section you will learn more about fonts and points. In the document you're creating you will be using two type sizes: 30 point for the headline *(The Inn at Portage Bay)* and 14 point for the rest of the text. The font used in this project is Helvetica, chosen for its clean, simple lines. If Helvetica is not available to you, use Geneva or similar font. Thus, you will be using two fonts: Helvetica 30 and Helvetica 14.

The fonts available to you are the ones listed when you choose Font from the Type pull-down menu. PageMaker 5.0 does not have its own fonts, but Apple provides fonts. Other companies such as Bitstream and Adobe make font software that works with PageMaker. Fonts are available from 4 to 650 point. You may select a size from a list of point sizes or select Other and type a number between 4 and 650. Now it's time to set defaults. To set the default at Helvetica 14:

1. **Start PageMaker.**

2. **Select Type specs... from the Type menu.**

Look at the selected font. If it is not Helvetica:

3. **Press the mouse button.**

4. **Select Helvetica.**

Look at Size. If it is not 14:

5. **Press the arrow to the right of Size, selecting 14.**

Compare your screen to Figure 3.10. When they match,

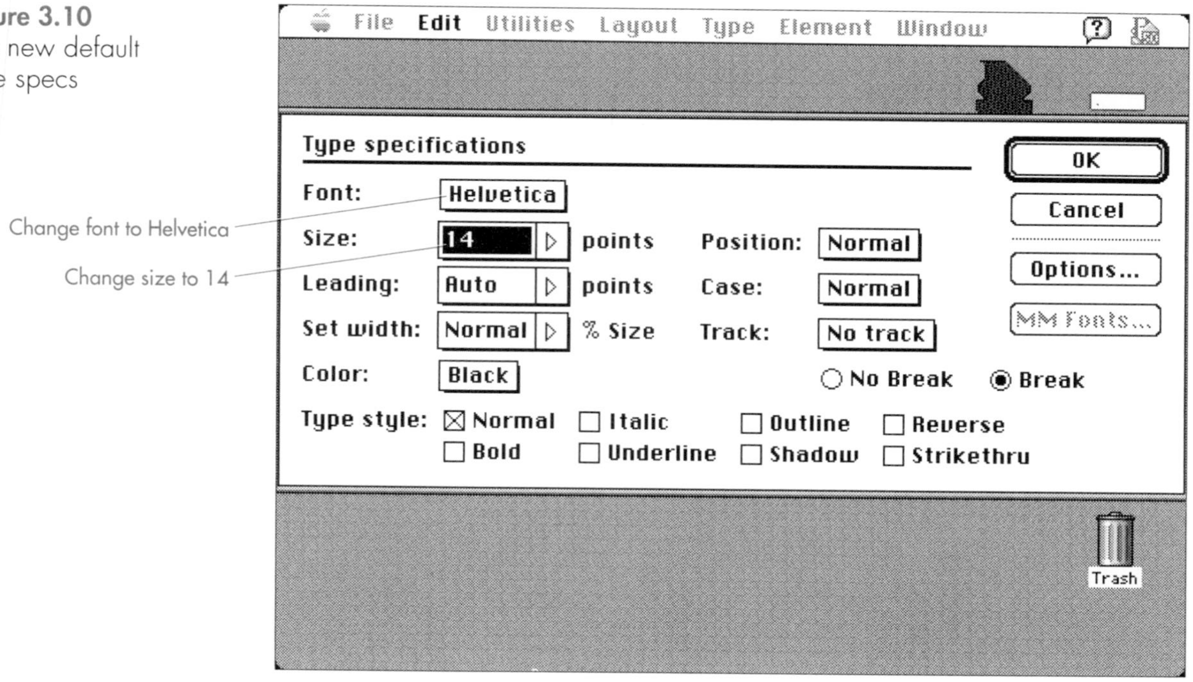

Figure 3.10
The new default
type specs

Change font to Helvetica

Change size to 14

6. Click on OK.

Even though you won't be typing text right away, the publication you open will be set at Helvetica 14 as the default type specification because you made this change before opening a publication.

To verify your selection of Helvetica 14 and see an alternate method for selecting font name and size, do the following:

1. Press and drag to see Font in the Type menu.

2. Press and drag to see Size in the Type menu.

Your default specs are indicated by a check mark.

Verifying the Align left Command

Look again at the advertisement you are creating in Figure 3.1. It has two columns, and text in each column is lined up on the left margin. Thus, you want to specify Align left as a default before opening the publication. To verify the Align left command:

1. Select Alignment from the Type menu (see Figure 3.11).

2. If Align left is not checked, select it.

Verifying Lock guides Is Off

If the Lock guides option is checked (on) when you create a ruler guide and place it, you cannot later move that ruler guide. When the Lock guides option is not checked (off), you can move guides. While you are creating ruler guides, you will want Lock guides to be off. When you have all ruler guides where you want them, you will change this setting to on.

Figure 3.11
Verifying the Align left default

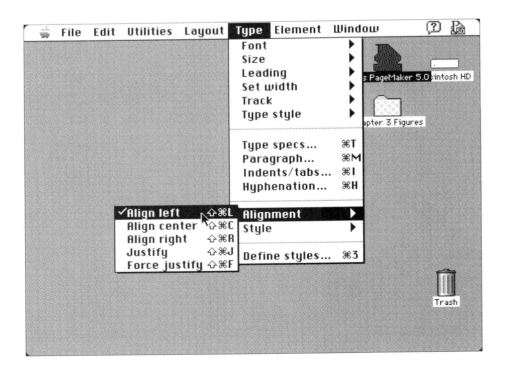

Figure 3.12
Verifying that Lock
guides is off

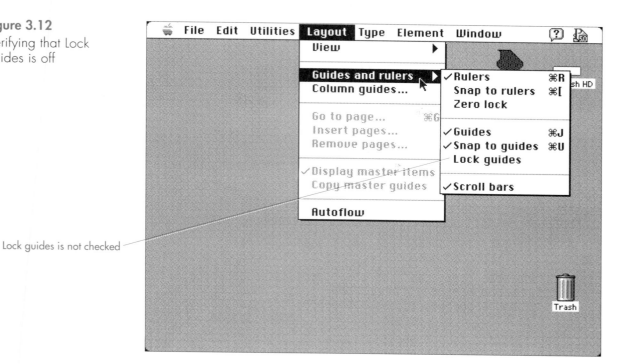

Lock guides is not checked

You need to check several settings. First, Guides must be turned on (checked). When Guides is on, you will see margin and column guides on your publication. Second, Lock guides should be off (no check).

1. Select Guides and rulers from the Layout menu (see Figure 3.12).

2. Look at Lock guides. If it is checked, click on it to turn it off.

Verifying Snap to guides Is On

Typically, you will draw vertical and horizontal nonprinting guidelines to help you place different elements on the page. Once the guidelines are drawn, you will want graphic elements such as lines, circles, and squares to line up with them. When Snap to guides is checked in the Guides and rulers option of the Layout menu, graphics will align on the guidelines. For example, if you wanted to draw two lines that start and end at the two guidelines, with the Snap to guides option selected you can be assured that both lines will do just that. If you draw the lines without Snap to guides selected, you'll have no guarantee the lines will align exactly. The critical eye will see the minor difference between the length of the two lines and how they are positioned.

To select Snap to guides:

1. Select Guides and rulers from the Layout menu (if necessary).

2. Look at Snap to guides. If it is not checked, release the mouse button on it to activate it.

3. Verify that the Guides and rulers list matches Figure 3.12. Make any changes needed to make your screen match.

**Creating a
New Publication**

Prior to putting text and graphics on a page, you must first bring a piece of paper onto your desktop and draw some guides on it. To do this electronically, you will open a new publication in PageMaker. To draw some guides on the "paper," you will use the rulers and column guides.

Files must be opened before they can be created, changed, or printed, and they must be closed when you are done with them. There are two ways to open a publication: New, which creates a new publication, and Open, which opens an existing publication. Because you are creating a new publication, for this project you will use New.

To create a new publication:

1. Select New... from the File menu.

The Page setup dialog box appears (see Figure 3.13). (It can also be accessed by selecting the Page setup command from the File menu.)

The Page setup dialog box allows you to tell PageMaker about the publication you will create and the paper you will put on the Pasteboard. How many pages will there be? What are the page dimensions? How wide will the page margins be?

2. With the Page setup dialog box onscreen, duplicate Figure 3.13 by choosing or verifying the following options. Recall that you may use either TAB or the mouse to move from option to option.

Page dimensions: 8×8.5 inches

Orientation: Tall

Start page #: 1

Number of pages: 1

Margin in inches: 0.75 for all margins

Because this publication is one page, click on Double-sided so the × in the box will disappear. Double-sided documents have odd and even pages with margins that are mirror images of each other, so when you print page 1 and page 2 back-to-back, the text on the two sides of the page will occupy the same part of the paper.

3. Compare your screen to Figure 3.13. If it matches, click on OK.

Now the "piece of paper" is on the desk. In PageMaker terms, you have an empty publication on the Pasteboard. The next step is to draw guidelines on the paper.

Creating Columns

This page will have two columns, as shown in Figure 3.14.

Figure 3.13
Page setup dialog box

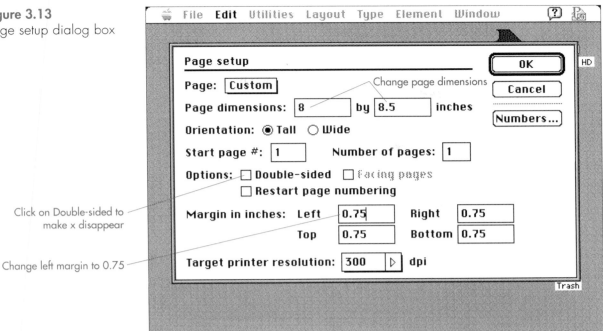

Click on Double-sided to
make x disappear

Change left margin to 0.75

Figure 3.14
Column guides

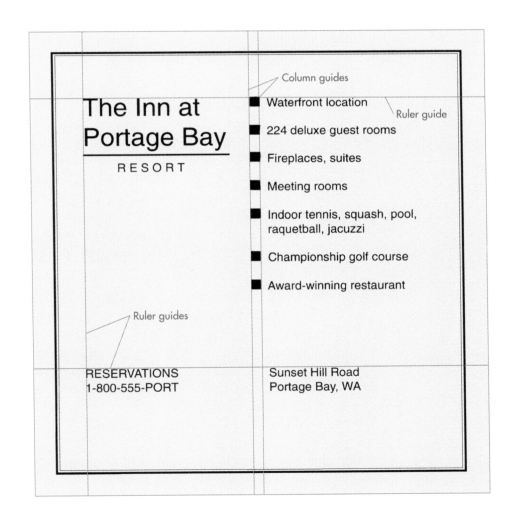

Figure 3.15
Column guides
dialog box

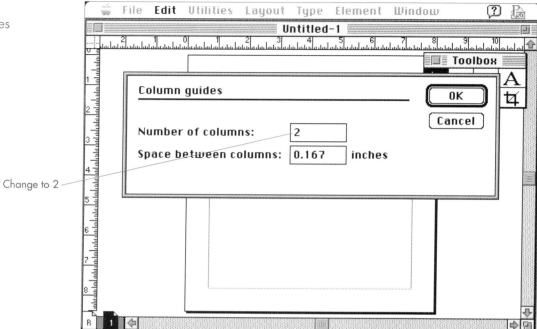

To create the columns:

1. Select Column guides... from the Layout menu.

Figure 3.15 shows the Column guides dialog box with the correct settings.

2. Enter the following change:

Number of columns: 2

3. Click on OK.

PageMaker has drawn lines on the publication indicating left and right margins for the two columns. These lines will not appear when you print the publication. The **gutter space**, or space between the columns, is 0.167 inch. Compare the column guides on your screen to the rulers on the top of the page. Verify that the distance between the two columns is about 0.167 inch, or about ⅙".

Specifying columns allows you to start text for the second column, in this case headed by *Waterfront location*, without having to use (TAB) or press the spacebar to position the cursor midline. In other words, when you are typing text in the second column and press (ENTER), the cursor will be positioned on the next line at the beginning of the second column. And remember that left justified means all text in the second column lines up on the left margin of that column.

Creating Ruler Guides

Ruler guides allow you to draw both vertical and horizontal lines to help position text and graphics on the page. Recall from Chapter 2 that to create ruler guides, you drag the lines from the vertical and horizontal

Figure 3.16
Column and ruler
guides

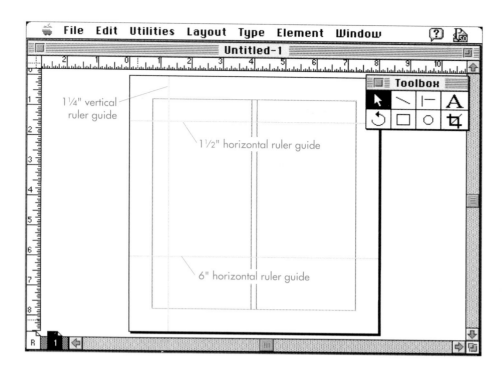

rulers. For this project you will need two horizontal ruler guides, 1½"
and 6", and one vertical ruler guide, 1¼". Figure 3.16 shows the
publication with both column and ruler guides.

If you recall from Chapter 2 how to create the ruler guides, create them
and proceed to the next section.

If you need some prompting, follow these steps:

1. **Point to the top (horizontal) ruler.**

2. **Press and drag the double-arrow pointer down until the line intersects
   1½" on the left (vertical) ruler. Release the mouse button.**

3. **Repeat steps 1 and 2 to create a second horizontal ruler guide at 6".**

4. **Point to the left (vertical) ruler.**

5. **Press and drag the double-arrow pointer to the right until the line
   intersects 1¼" on the top (horizontal) ruler.**

The ruler guides on your screen should now look like those in Figure 3.16.
If you need to move a line, point to it, press the mouse button, and drag
to reposition it.

Troubleshooting Tip: If the ruler guide does not move, select the Layout
menu, then Guides and rulers. If a check mark appears to the left of Lock
guides, select Lock guides to remove the check. Remember that when
Lock guides is selected, a ruler or column guide once positioned can't
be moved. This feature prevents you from accidentally changing
the guides. Deselecting the Lock guides option allows you to move
ruler guides.

Now that the column guides match those in Figure 3.16, lock them to prevent inadvertently moving any of them.

1. Select Guides and rulers from the Layout menu.

2. Click on Lock guides.

CREATING THE PUBLICATION

Now that you have set the PageMaker defaults, created a new publication, and set it up, you are ready to actually create the advertisement for The Inn at Portage Bay. Make sure the page 1 icon in the lower-left corner is highlighted (see Figure 3.17). If it is not, click on it. A complete discussion of page icons is in Chapter 6.

Creating a Border Around the Publication

First, create a double-line border around the publication by (1) selecting the line's pattern for the borderline, (2) selecting the amount of shading for the inside of the rectangle, and (3) drawing the rectangle.

To select the line's pattern:

1. Select Line from the Element menu.

2. Choose the double line indicated in Figure 3.17.

After you select the double line, the Line menu will disappear. To verify your selection, select the Line menu again and make sure a check mark is next to the correct pattern.

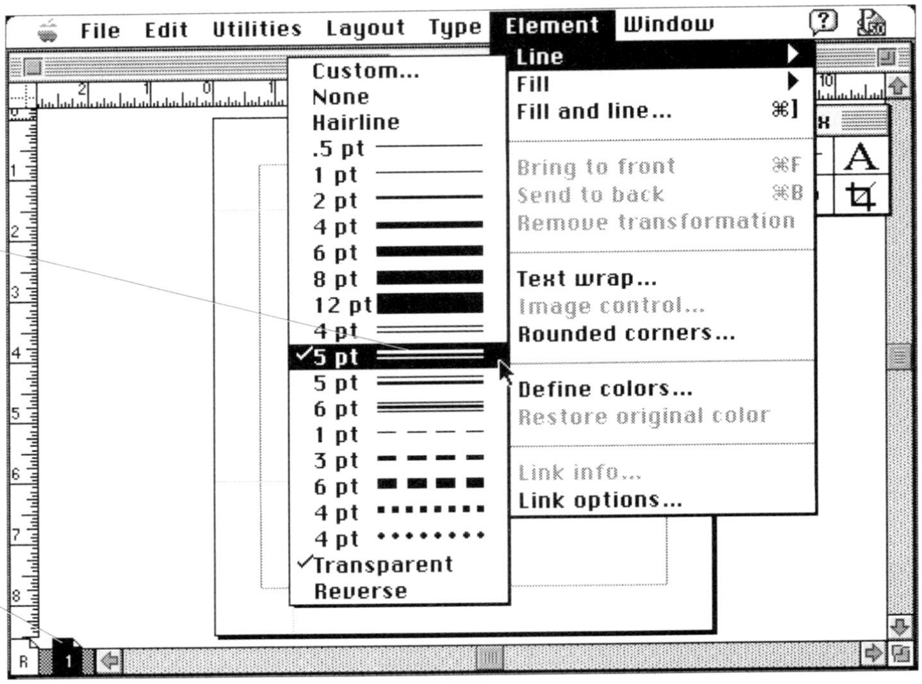

Figure 3.17
Element Line menu

Click on this line pattern for the border

Make sure the page 1 icon is highlighted

You will be drawing a double-line border, so it may seem unusual to worry about shades when you are only drawing lines. However, from PageMaker's perspective, you will be drawing the exterior of a rectangle, and a rectangle is a graphic. Graphics shading varies from no shading to partial gray shading to solid black fill. For this rectangle, you want no shading.

To select the amount of shading:

1. Select Fill from the Element menu.

2. Click on None (see Figure 3.18).

If None is checked, your choice is already made for you, so simply release the mouse button.

To give you practice drawing a rectangle, you will draw, resize, delete, and then redraw a new rectangle.

To draw the rectangle:

1. Select the rectangle tool in the Toolbox. The rectangle tool should now be highlighted, and the mouse pointer, when moved out of the Toolbox, changes from an arrow to a crossbar.

2. Position the crossbar at the top-left corner of the margin guide (see Figure 3.19).

3. Press and drag the mouse to the lower-right corner of the margin guides.

4. Release the mouse button.

The box should now be visible as a border around your publication.

Figure 3.18
Element Fill menu

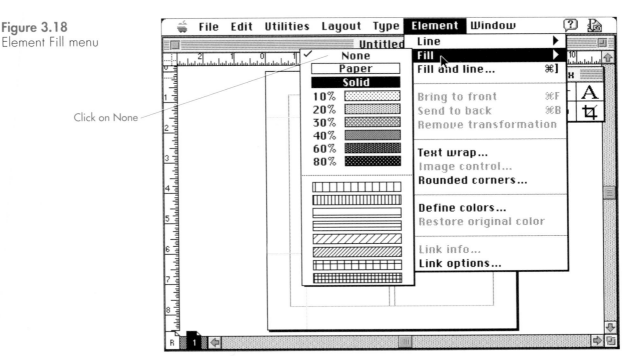

Click on None

Figure 3.19

Drawing a rectangle

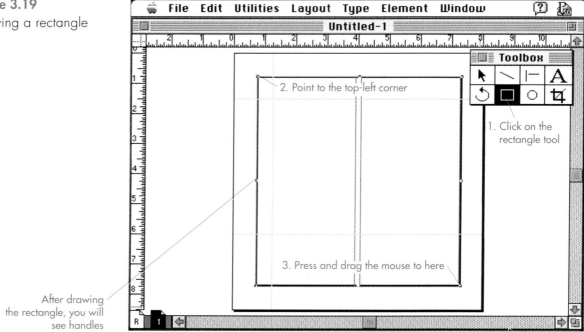

After drawing
the rectangle, you will
see handles

Notice that the box has handles at several places on each side. A **handle** is a small rectangle on a graphic. Pointing to a handle with the pointer tool allows you to resize a graphic. Pointing to a place other than the handle with the pointer tool allows you to move the graphic.

The handles on the rectangle mean that the rectangle is selected. **Selected items** may be moved, resized, or deleted. Handles at the midpoint of a line allow you to change the length or width of a box. Corner handles dragged diagonally allow you to resize length and width simultaneously. Experiment now with moving, resizing, and deleting the rectangle.

To move the box:

1. Click on the pointer tool in the Toolbox.

2. Select the box by pointing to any location on a line. Click.

3. Point to anywhere on the line but a handle.

4. Press the mouse button.

5. Drag to a new location.

6. When the box is where you want it, release the mouse button.

To resize the box:

1. Point to one of the handles.

2. Press the mouse button.

3. Drag the handle to make the box smaller. (Moving the handle inward reduces the box; moving it outward enlarges the box.)

4. When the box is the size you want, release the mouse button.

Repeat steps 1 through 4 to enlarge the box.

To delete the border:

1. Make sure the double-line border is selected (has handles).

2. Press (DELETE).

You can undo your last action in PageMaker with the Undo option from the Edit menu. To undo the delete you just did:

1. Select Undo delete from the Edit menu.

The Undo feature works for many, though not all, PageMaker actions. Look at it again. You can undo your last action, restoring the deleted box.

1. Select Redo delete from the Edit menu.

The Undo feature is context-sensitive, that is, the choices (Undo delete and Redo delete) change, depending on what is appropriate with respect to your last action.

Re-create the border by repeating the steps starting with "To select the line's pattern" on page 68. To summarize, with an abbreviated set of directions for creating the border:

1. Select a line pattern.

2. Select a fill.

3. Draw the border.

If you need to stop now, look ahead at the section titled "Saving the Publication" that starts on page 80. Using those directions and Figure 3.28, save your publication.

Selecting Large Type

Recall that before you created this new publication, you set the default type specs to Helvetica 14. Now you will set the type specs to Helvetica 30 in preparation for typing the heading, the only text in this publication not in Helvetica 14. You will also verify that left alignment is still selected.

1. Select the text tool from the Toolbox.

2. Select Alignment from the Type menu.

3. Verify that Align left is checked. If Align left is not checked, click on it and select the Type menu again.

4. Select Size from the Type menu.

5. Select 30. (See Figure 3.20.)

Figure 3.20
Type Size menu

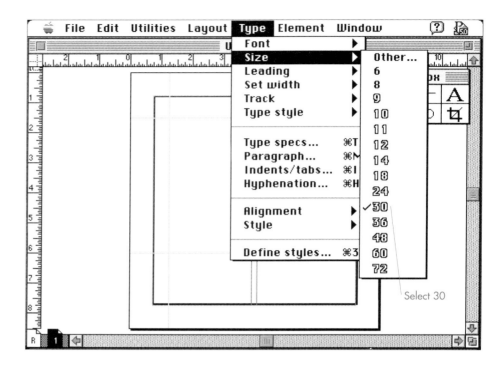

Entering the Heading

1. Position the I-beam as shown in Figure 3.21 and click the mouse button anywhere on the line.

This inserts a vertical bar, called an **insertion point**, which tells PageMaker where to place text. The insertion point will automatically "jump" to the nearest left-hand margin.

2. Press (TAB) once to move the cursor to the right.

3. Type *The Inn at.*

4. Press (RETURN) once.

5. Press (TAB) once to move the cursor to the right.

6. Type *Portage Bay.*

Drawing the Horizontal Line

Below the resort name is a horizontal line. To draw it you must select the constrained-line tool and the correct line width from the Line menu (Figure 3.17) and then draw the line.

1. Select the constrained-line tool from the Toolbox, |—.

2. Select Line from the Element menu.

3. Choose 2 pt.

Draw a line below the words *Portage Bay* (see Figure 3.22):

4. Point at the left ruler guide.

5. Press and drag the mouse to the end of the word *Bay.*

Figure 3.21
Entering the heading

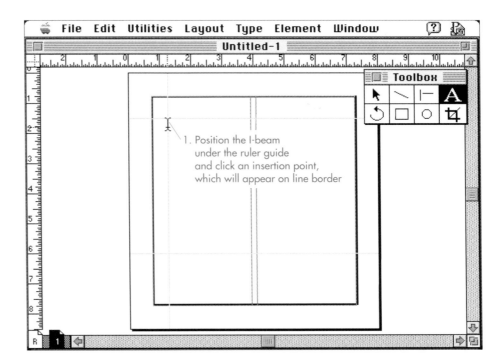

Figure 3.22
Drawing the line

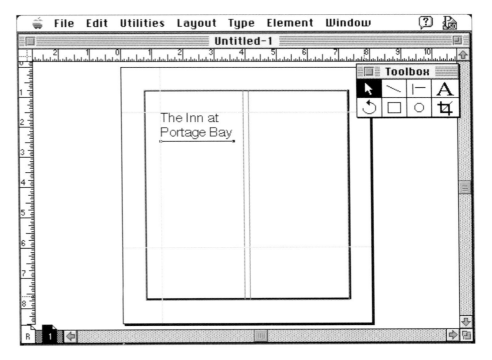

6. Release the mouse button.

Make sure the line does not touch the descenders of *g* and *y*. This would be a "crash," something a graphic designer would avoid.

Notice that the line has handles on it, meaning it is still selected. If the line is in the correct place, click the mouse button anywhere off the line to deselect it. If you wish to delete the line while it is selected, press (DELETE) and redraw the line. To move the line, select the pointer tool in the Toolbox, point anywhere on the line but the handles, and move it to the correct location.

You cannot change the location or length of the line while the constrained-line tool is selected. If you need to move the line or change its length, you must first select the pointer tool.

Typing the 14-Point Text

Now you are ready to type the rest of the text. First, you will change the page view to enlarge the area of the publication in which you will work. Second, you will select the text tool, verify the type specifications, and type the word *RESORT* in the first column. Third, you will type the list of features in the second column. Finally, you will type the lower part of the publication.

Changing the Page View

Recall from Chapter 2 that PageMaker allows you to adjust the page view to see the complete publication or to focus on a part of the page. When the publication is set to Fit in window, meaning the complete publication can be viewed on the screen, the details on the page can't be seen. When you enlarge the page so details can be seen, you lose the ability to see the complete page layout. Because you can't have both detail and layout at the same time, you must switch between different page views as the tasks demand.

For typing the smaller 14-point type, you will want to change the page view from the current Fit in window to allow you to see more detail. Several options are available to you in the Layout menu for altering page view, and you may choose whichever best suits your needs at any time during the creation of a publication. For now, the next steps will lead you through using the 75% size option. Three methods for changing the page view exist, and you should try all three. Then, as you see the need to change the page view, choose the method best for you.

Method 1—From the Pull-Down Menu

1. Select View from the Layout menu.

2. Choose 75% size.

3. Click on the scroll bars to adjust the view to see the horizontal line you have just drawn and some space beneath it (see Figure 3.23).

Method 2—From the Keyboard

To use method 2, change the page view back to Fit in window. (Select View from the Layout menu, then choose Fit in window.)

1. Press ⌘ and ⑦ at the same time.

Figure 3.23
Page view at 75% size

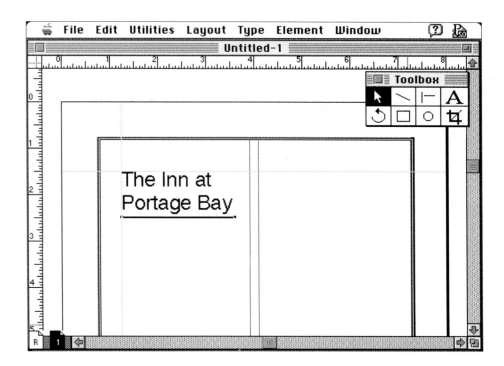

2. Click on the scroll bars to adjust the view to see the horizontal line you have just drawn and some space beneath it.

Method 3 — Toggle Between Two Sizes

Toggle means to alternate between two settings. There are two toggle options:

100%/Fit in window   ⌘ + (OPTION) + click

200%/100%   ⌘ + (OPTION) - (SHIFT) + click

To toggle between 100% and Fit in window, hold down ⌘ and (OPTION) while clicking the mouse button. The pointer can be anywhere on the Pasteboard. Try toggling between the different settings.

Adjust your page view to see the horizontal line below *Portage Bay*. Refer to Figure 3.23.

Verifying Helvetica 14

In this section you will verify that the default type specifications you selected before you opened the publication are active.

1. Select the text tool in the Toolbox.

2. Select Size from the Type menu.

3. Verify the selected font: Helvetica 14. Change the size if it is different.

Typing *RESORT*

Refer to Figure 3.24 as you complete the following steps.

Figure 3.24
Typing *RESORT*

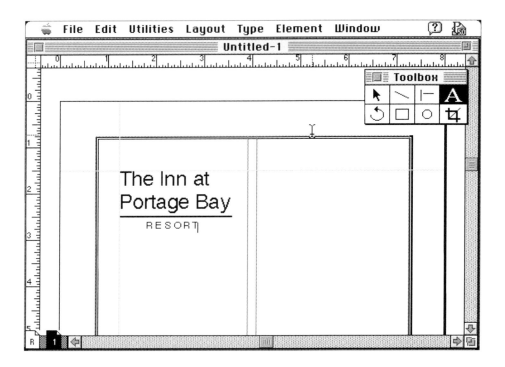

1. Point below the horizontal line and click an insertion point.

2. Select Alignment from the Type menu and click on Align center.

3. Press (CAPS LOCK) to set all caps.

4. Type *R E S O R T* (press the spacebar once after each letter).

Moving Between Columns

To move from one column to the other, simply position the I-beam in the other column and click the mouse button.

1. Click on the scroll bars to adjust the view to display the top of column 2.

2. Position the I-beam in the second column next to the words *The Inn at.*

3. Click to insert the I-beam.

4. Change to Align left by selecting Alignment from the Type menu and clicking on Align left.

Typing the List of Features

1. Press (CAPS LOCK) to turn off uppercase mode.

2. Using Figure 3.25 as a guide, type the list of features, double-spacing between lines. Press the spacebar twice to include two spaces before each feature. If you make a typing error, use (DELETE) to erase it, and then retype the text.

Figure 3.25
List of features

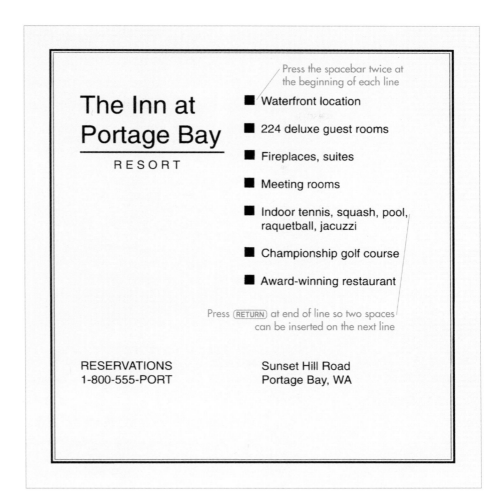

The Inn at Portage Bay

RESORT

Press the spacebar twice at the beginning of each line

■ Waterfront location

■ 224 deluxe guest rooms

■ Fireplaces, suites

■ Meeting rooms

■ Indoor tennis, squash, pool, raquetball, jacuzzi

■ Championship golf course

■ Award-winning restaurant

Press (RETURN) at end of line so two spaces can be inserted on the next line

RESERVATIONS
1-800-555-PORT

Sunset Hill Road
Portage Bay, WA

Typing the Phone Number and Address

To type the word *RESERVATIONS* and the telephone number in the first column:

1. Move the page view to see the first column under the 6" horizontal ruler guide.

2. Position the I-beam and click an insertion point.

3. Press (TAB) once.

4. Press (CAPS LOCK) to activate uppercase mode.

5. Type *RESERVATIONS*.

6. Press (RETURN).

7. Press (TAB) once.

8. Type *1-800-555-PORT*.

To type the address in the second column:

1. Adjust the page view to see the second column under the 6" horizontal ruler guide (if necessary).

2. Position the I-beam on the same line as the text *RESERVATIONS* and click an insertion point.

3. Press (CAPS LOCK) to change back to lowercase mode.

4. Press the spacebar twice so that the address will line up with the list of features.

5. Type *Sunset Hill Road.*

6. Press (RETURN).

7. Press the spacebar twice.

8. Type *Portage Bay, WA.*

Compare your publication with Figure 3.25. Make sure every word is spelled correctly and is positioned in the right place. If you need to make changes, do so before proceeding to the next section.

Adding a Square Bullet

The next step is to create a small solid-black square, or bullet, to the left of *Waterfront location* to highlight the feature. Then you will copy it once and paste it six times.

1. Adjust the page view to show the list of features (see Figure 3.26). *Hint:* Use 200% size (select View from the Layout menu, then click on 200% size).

2. You want to make sure each square bullet lines up properly with the text. To do this, set up horizontal ruler guides that touch the baseline of each line of text. (See Figure 3.26.)

Figure 3.26
200% size with horizontal ruler guides and one bullet drawn

Pull down horizontal ruler guides from the ruler

3. Select Fill from the Element menu.

4. Select Solid.

5. Select the rectangle tool in the Toolbox. The pointer changes to a crossbar.

6. Position the crossbar between the two column guides and next to the words *Waterfront location*. Make sure the crossbar is positioned at the lower-right corner of where the square will go. Refer to Figure 3.26.

7. Hold down (SHIFT) while you do the next step. This will assure you of a square; otherwise, you will draw a rectangle.

8. Press and drag the crossbar diagonally to the upper-left corner of where the square will go. The square will be slightly taller than the cap height of the text.

9. Release the mouse button.

You will see the square bullet with handles on it. If the square is not in the correct position or is not the correct size, erase it using (DELETE). Repeat the steps above to create a new square. When the square is in the correct position, move on to the next section, leaving the square selected.

Copying the Square Bullet

This publication needs seven square bullets to highlight the various amenities of the resort. You could draw seven bullets, but each could end up being a different size. A better technique is to draw one bullet, as you have already done, copy it once, and paste it six times to guarantee that the bullets will all be exactly the same.

To proceed, the square must be selected—that is, have handles around it.

1. Verify that the pointer tool is selected. If it is not, select it by pointing to the arrow in the Toolbox and clicking.

2. Verify that the square bullet is selected. If it is not, select it by pointing to it and clicking.

3. Select Copy from the Edit menu.

This copies the selected item, in this case a bullet, to a holding area called the **Clipboard**.

4. Select Paste from the Edit menu.

This pastes the last item (text or graphics) copied to the Clipboard onto the PageMaker publication.

Notice that the handles are now on the pasted square bullet.

5. Move the new bullet to the correct location by (1) pointing to the center of the bullet, being careful not to point to a handle, and (2) pressing the mouse button and dragging the bullet to the correct location—beside *224 deluxe guest rooms* and below the first bullet (see Figure 3.27).

Figure 3.27
The copied bullet
"snaps to" the three
ruler guides

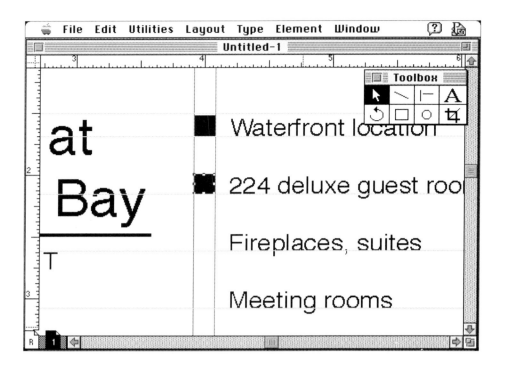

The ruler guides, along with the activated Snap to guides setting, help anchor the pasted graphic.

Repeat steps 4 and 5 to paste a bullet next to the remaining features on the list.

SAVING THE PUBLICATION

These steps will lead you through saving your publication on your own diskette. To proceed, you will need a formatted diskette. It is suggested that you save all the publications you create on a disk separate from the data disk that came with this book.

1. Insert the formatted diskette into the drive.

2. Select Save as... from the File menu.

3. Double-click on the name of your disk.

The Save publication as dialog box appears, as shown in Figure 3.28.

4. In the file name box type *Magazine ad.*

5. Click on OK.

After you return to the PageMaker screen, notice that the title bar now includes your publication's name.

From the File menu, there are four ways to save your publication: Close, Save, Save as, and Quit. If your publication is unnamed because it is a new publication, each of these selections will give you the Save publication

Figure 3.28
Save publication as
dialog box

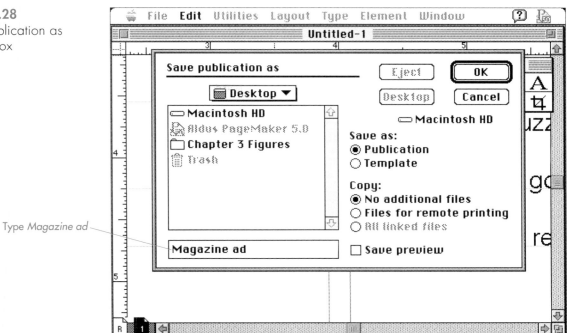

Type *Magazine ad*

as dialog box. The following table summarizes the functions of these four commands.

Command	Function
Close	Prompts you to save if unsaved changes have been made; closes the publication; returns to the PageMaker desktop.
Save	Saves the publication with the same name it already has; for unnamed publications, you will be given the Save publication as dialog box; returns to the publication.
Save as...	Saves the publication; allows you to save with a different name, save to a different location, or make a copy of the publication; returns to the publication.
Quit	Prompts you if you have not saved changes; for unsaved changes you want to save, you will be given the Save publication as dialog box; closes the publication and quits PageMaker.

PRINTING YOUR PUBLICATION

1. Make sure your computer is connected to a printer, the printer is ready, and the paper is aligned.

2. Select Print... from the File menu.

The Print document dialog box appears. Follow any special instructions for your installation.

3. Click on Print.

Leave PageMaker by selecting the File menu and choosing Quit.

SUMMARY

Congratulations! You have created a complete publication from start to finish. In the process you have used several of PageMaker's features: drawing a border, using different fonts, copying, and pasting. You planned the publication, drew guidelines, and saved and printed the publication. In the next chapter you will learn more about working with text.

KEY TERMS

white space	font size	case
defaults	point	leading
left justified	type style	gutter space
justify	reverse	handle
force justify	position	selected item
font	superscript	insertion point
font name	subscript	Clipboard

QUESTIONS

1. Use the Help feature to answer the following questions.

   (a) Explain power pasting. What are the keystrokes for power pasting?

   (b) There are two choices for saving a file, quickly and _____.

   (c) When you copy text or graphics, where does it get stored?

   (d) What is the maximum number of ruler guides you may have in any one publication?

2. Explain the purpose of white space.

3. Why is it a good idea to set defaults before opening a publication?

4. What are the results of selecting a font before and after a publication is opened?

5. Explain the differences between the on and off settings for Lock guides.

6. Why would you want to have the Snap to guides option selected?

7. How do the commands New and Open differ?

8. What two commands give you the Page setup dialog box?

9. What is the purpose of column guides?

10. Can column guides be reset? If yes, how?

11. What is the purpose of ruler guides?

12. How can you tell when a graphic is selected?

13. How can you alter a selected graphic?

14. Explain the two ways to erase a graphic.

15. Describe the three methods for changing the page view. Which method do you prefer? Why?

16. Name the four ways to save a publication. Compare and contrast them.

17. Use Appendix B of this book to name the menu in which you find each of the following:

    (a) Type specs

    (b) Multiple paste

    (c) Guides and rulers

    (d) Page setup

    (e) Find

18. Use the index of this book to find the page numbers for references to:

    (a) Save as command _____

    (b) Defaults _____

    (c) Copying several times _____

PROJECTS

1. Create a new publication and draw a square-corner rectangle border for a page using a 1-point line and 10% shading. Delete the figure using (DELETE).

2. Create a new publication and draw a square-corner rectangle border using a 6-point line and 40% shading. Delete the figure using (DELETE).

3. Using the specifications in Figure 3.29, create a business reply card.

4. The Inn wants a set of stickers to use on items such as the packet of information left in each room. Using the specifications in Figure 3.30, create the generic sticker to be used on various items at the Inn.

5. Using the specifications in Figure 3.31, create a business card for the Inn. Use the name on the card or your own name.

Figure 3.29
Project 3.3—Business
reply card (4¼" × 5⅝")

(4⅛" × 5")

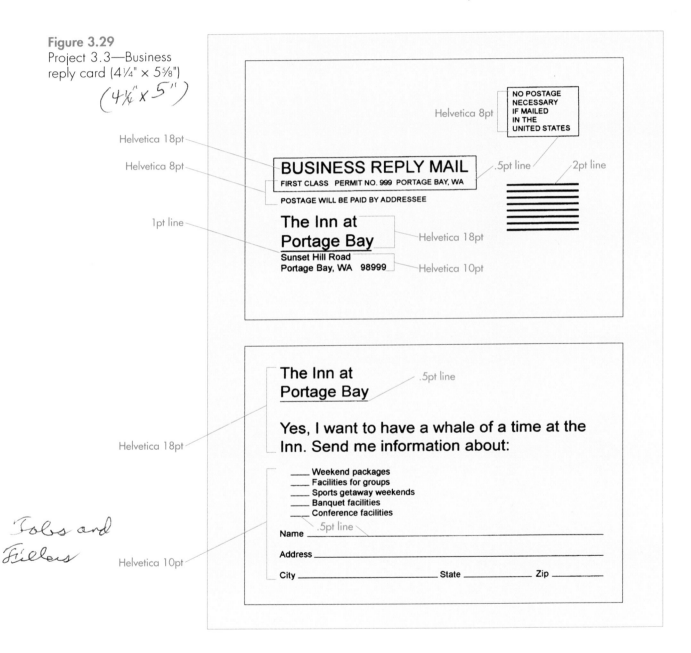

Jobs and Fillers

Figure 3.30
Project 3.4—Generic sticker (3" × 5")

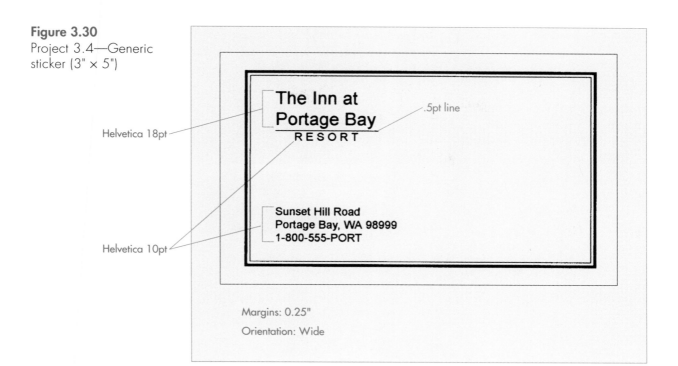

Helvetica 18pt

.5pt line

The Inn at Portage Bay
R E S O R T

Sunset Hill Road
Portage Bay, WA 98999
1-800-555-PORT

Helvetica 10pt

Margins: 0.25"

Orientation: Wide

Figure 3.31
Project 3.5—Business card (2" × 3½")

Helvetica 14pt

1pt line

Helvetica 9pt

The Inn at Portage Bay
R E S O R T

Elizabeth Loudon
Group Coordinator

Sunset Hill Road
Portage Bay, WA 98999

1-800-555-PORT
FAX (206) 555-PORT

Margins: 0.25"

Use two columns; second column is right justified

6. The Inn needs some stationery and envelopes made. Using the specifications in Figure 3.32, create a letterhead and envelope for the Inn.

Figure 3.32
Project 3.6—Letterhead (8½" × 11") and envelope (9½" × 4⅛")

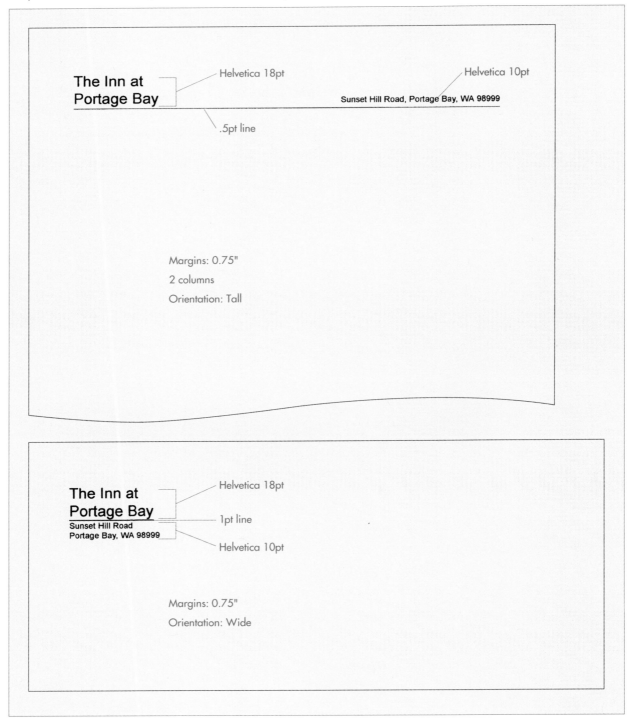

Figure 3.33
Project 3.7—Pad of
paper (4½" × 5½")

Figure 3.33 Project 3.7—Pad of paper (4½" × 5½")

1pt line

Margins: 0.25"

The Inn at
Portage Bay
R E S O R T

Helvetica 18pt

Helvetica 10pt

Helvetica 10pt

For reservations, call toll-free 800-555-PORT

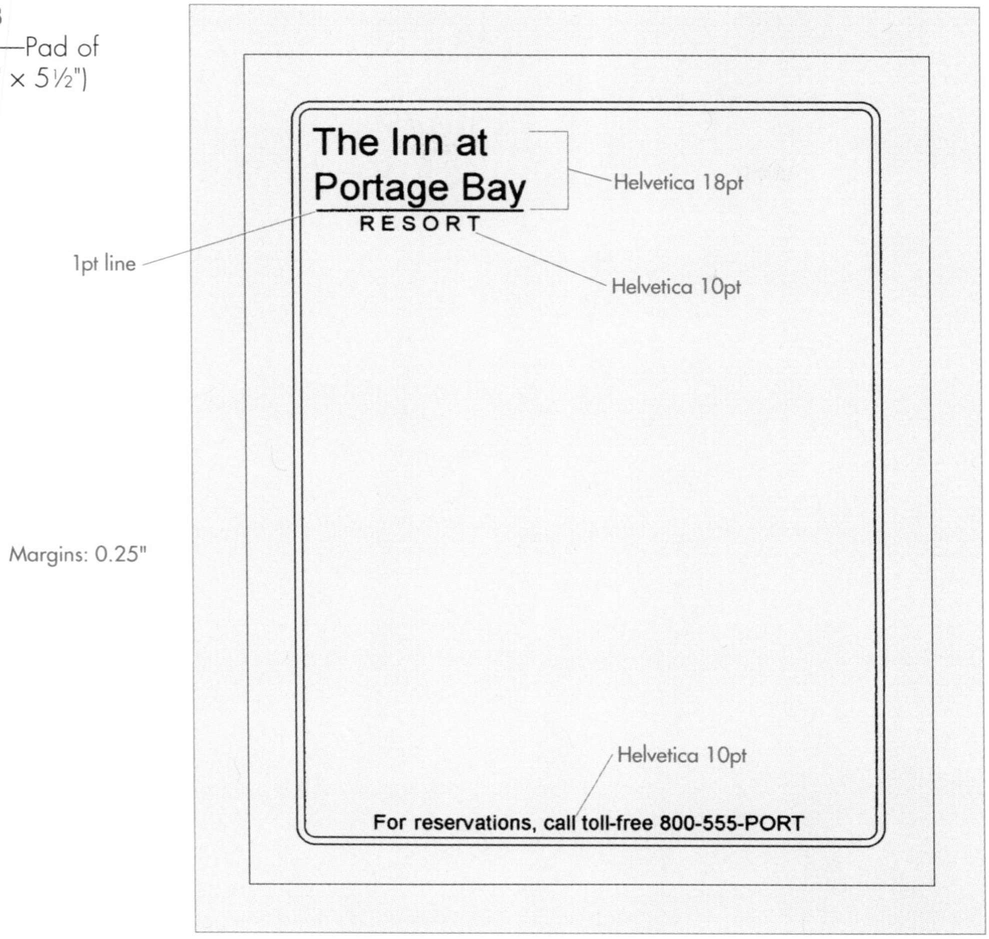

7. The Inn leaves a pad of paper on the desk in each room. Using the specifications in Figure 3.33, create the master copy that can be duplicated.

8. Create the Ambassador of Service Nomination Card shown in Figure 3.34.

9. Create the Room Service Breakfast Order form shown in Figure 3.35.

10. Create your own business card.

11. Create your own letterhead and envelope.

Figure 3.34
Project 3.8—Employee
service award
nomination (3½" × 8½")

Times 14pt

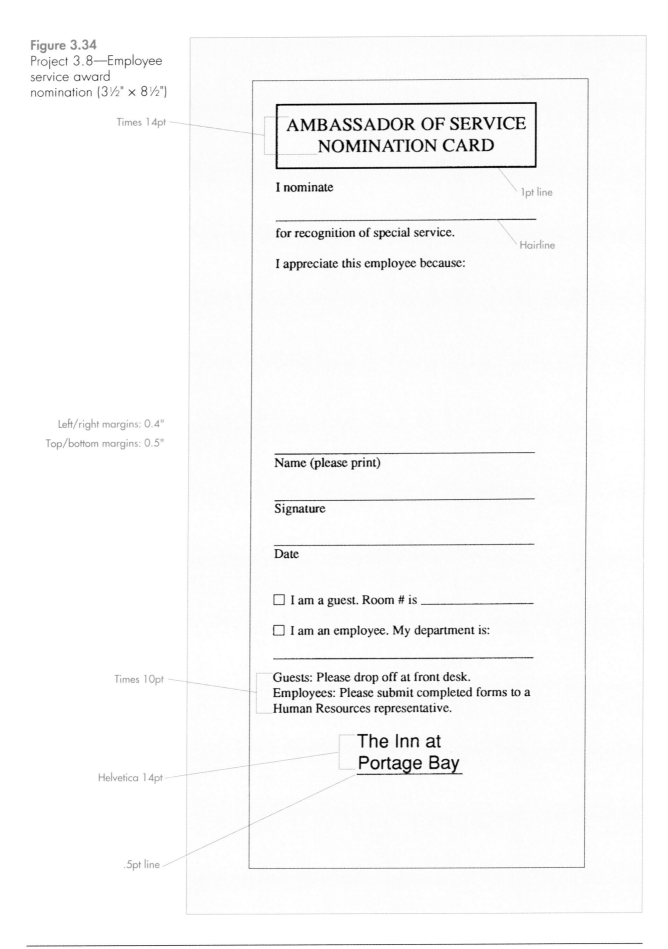

**AMBASSADOR OF SERVICE
NOMINATION CARD**

I nominate

1pt line

for recognition of special service.

Hairline

I appreciate this employee because:

Left/right margins: 0.4"
Top/bottom margins: 0.5"

Name (please print)

Signature

Date

☐ I am a guest. Room # is _____

☐ I am an employee. My department is:

Times 10pt

Guests: Please drop off at front desk.
Employees: Please submit completed forms to a
Human Resources representative.

The Inn at
Portage Bay

Helvetica 14pt

.5pt line

Figure 3.35
Project 3.9—Room
service breakfast order
form (5" × 11")

Type in text first

All type is Helvetica

Margins: 0.75"

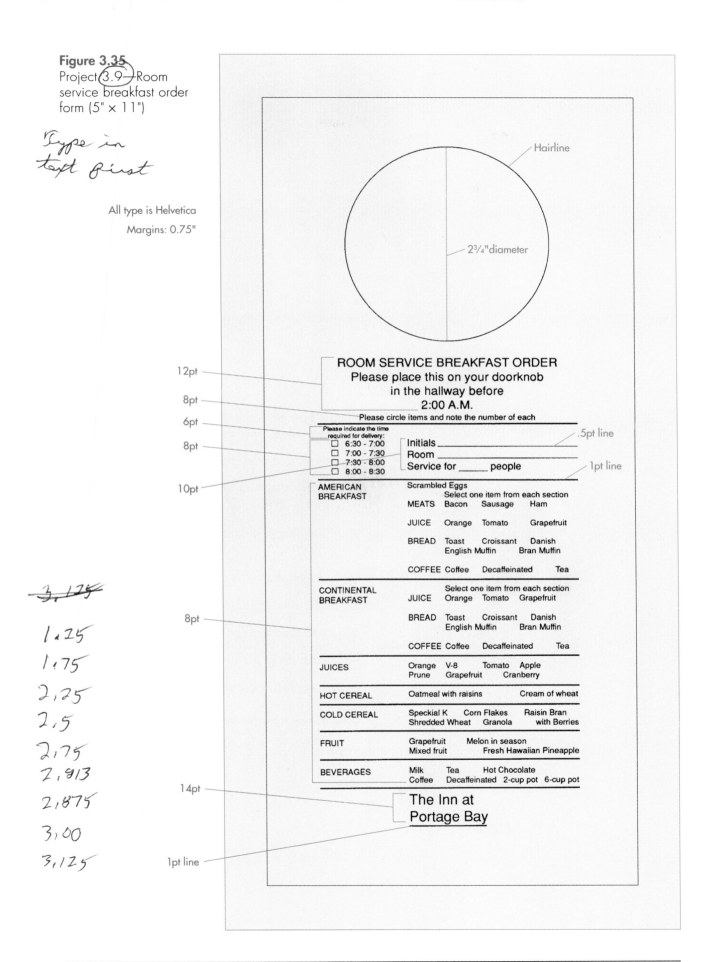

Hairline

2¾"diameter

12pt

8pt

6pt

8pt

10pt

.5pt line

1pt line

8pt

14pt

1pt line

3.125

1.25

1.75

2.25

2.5

2.75

2.913

2.875

3.00

3.125

ROOM SERVICE BREAKFAST ORDER
Please place this on your doorknob
in the hallway before
2:00 A.M.

Please circle items and note the number of each

Please indicate the time
required for delivery:
☐ 6:30 - 7:00
☐ 7:00 - 7:30
☐ 7:30 - 8:00
☐ 8:00 - 8:30

Initials _____
Room _____
Service for _____ people

AMERICAN BREAKFAST	Scrambled Eggs		
	Select one item from each section		
MEATS	Bacon	Sausage	Ham
JUICE	Orange	Tomato	Grapefruit
BREAD	Toast	Croissant	Danish
	English Muffin		Bran Muffin
COFFEE	Coffee	Decaffeinated	Tea

CONTINENTAL BREAKFAST	Select one item from each section		
JUICE	Orange	Tomato	Grapefruit
BREAD	Toast	Croissant	Danish
	English Muffin		Bran Muffin
COFFEE	Coffee	Decaffeinated	Tea

JUICES	Orange	V-8	Tomato	Apple
	Prune	Grapefruit	Cranberry	

HOT CEREAL	Oatmeal with raisins	Cream of wheat

COLD CEREAL	Speckial K	Corn Flakes	Raisin Bran
	Shredded Wheat	Granola	with Berries

FRUIT	Grapefruit	Melon in season
	Mixed fruit	Fresh Hawaiian Pineapple

BEVERAGES	Milk	Tea	Hot Chocolate
	Coffee	Decaffeinated	2-cup pot 6-cup pot

The Inn at
Portage Bay

Upon completion of this chapter you will be able to:

- Import text into a publication

- Use the text tool and the pointer tool to select a portion of text

- Move, copy, and delete text

- Change the appearance of text and paragraphs

- Work with text blocks

- Use the Control palette

- Create drop caps

- Rotate, flip, and slant text

Working with Text

In previous chapters you have learned how to develop a PageMaker publication. You know how to set up a grid for a new publication and how to type in text. You also know how to save and print a publication. Although the skills you have learned allow you to develop many different kinds of documents, so far you are limited in editing text and controlling a publication's appearance. For example, even after placing text, you may want to move or delete a large portion of it, or you may want to change the text's appearance by right-justifying each paragraph.

ADDING TEXT TO A PUBLICATION

PageMaker provides three ways to add text to a publication. Assuming you have set up the publication page with the desired margins and column and ruler guides, you can enter text onto a page by (1) typing text using the text tool, (2) importing text from a word processing program, or (3) pasting text from the Clipboard.

You have already learned the first process. Typing text directly onto the publication page involves selecting the text tool, positioning the I-beam at the desired location, clicking the mouse button to set the insertion point, and typing the text. Because PageMaker is not a word processing program, you should use this method only to type small amounts of text, such as titles and headings, and to edit text by inserting and deleting words and correcting spelling errors. *Note:* PageMaker has a Story Editor with word processing capabilities, which is covered in Chapter 9.

PageMaker provides a holding area for text called the **Clipboard**. To copy or move a portion of text from the page, you use the pointer or text tool to select the desired text and then choose the Cut or Copy command from the Edit menu to place the text on the Clipboard. Once you determine where in the publication the text is to be copied or moved to, you choose the Paste command from the Edit menu.

Text on the Clipboard is not immediately visible. If you want to view it, you can choose the Show clipboard command from the Window menu. A window appears showing the Clipboard's contents. You can also paste the text from the Clipboard to the Pasteboard. The Pasteboard is similar to a desktop and allows you to hold text and graphics for use later in your document. You can also edit and resize text placed on the Pasteboard.

IMPORTING TEXT

Importing text from a word processing program involves chosing the Place option from the File menu and selecting the desired file. Then you position the text icon on the page or Pasteboard and click the mouse button. Whenever you import text, you must be concerned with the compatibility between PageMaker and your word processing program. Several word processing programs create files requiring no changes when correctly imported into PageMaker. Other programs create files incompatible with PageMaker or files that must be converted to a PageMaker-compatible format before being imported into a publication.

The following exercise will allow you to practice importing and editing text. On the data disk is a document created using Word for Windows, a word processing program, and saved with the file name Business Center.

Figure 4.1 shows this document, which is an announcement to the employees of The Inn at Portage Bay about the new business center. Start the PageMaker program and then import this document onto a new page.

1. Load the PageMaker program.

2. Select New... from the File menu (⌘-N).

Check the Page setup dialog box and verify that the settings are:

      Page size: Letter
      Margins: Inside 1"
                  Others 0.75"

3. Click on OK.

Check the blank page. There should be no column guides. If there are multiple columns, choose Column guides from the Layout menu and change the number of columns to 1.

Figure 4.1
Business Center
document

Business Center

THE INN AT PORTAGE BAY is proud to announce the opening of our new Business Center. This facility will be available to our guests starting on Monday the 15th. The services that will be provided are explained below.

To acquaint you with the center, there will be orientations on Wednesday the 10th at 9:00am and 3:00pm.

The Business Center will provide a full range of secretarial services, including taking minutes of meetings; preparing and copying documents, overhead transparencies, and slides; and desktop publishing. We are linked to CompuServe, Internet, and Prodigy.

The center has state-of-the-art equipment, including a fax machine, personal computers (IBM-compatible and Macintosh) equipped with CD-ROM drives and modems, color laser printers, and scanners. The most popular applications are available.

Location: Room 144
Hours: M-F 7:00am to 5:00pm
Phone ext.: 2311

Before placing this document, you need to select Helvetica as the font and 12 as the font size.

4. Choose Font from the Type menu.

5. Choose Helvetica.

6. Choose Size from the Type menu.

7. Choose 12.

8. Make sure the data disk is in the drive.

9. Select Place… from the File menu (⌘-D).

The Place document dialog box appears, allowing you to select the desired file. You may first have to select the disk to display the desired files.

10. If necessary, select the data disk so that Business Center appears (see Figure 4.2).

11. Double-click on Business Center.

At this point a message may appear, indicating that the Business Center document was not created with Aldus PageMaker 5.0, as shown in Figure 4.3. This message will appear if you do not have installed on your computer the application program that was used to create the document. You should be able to use any of the options as an alternate program.

12. If the message appears, click on Open.

The text icon appears; this icon represents the text to be placed.

13. Position this "loaded" icon as shown in Figure 4.4.

14. Click the mouse button.

Figure 4.2
Business Center file name displayed in the Place document dialog box

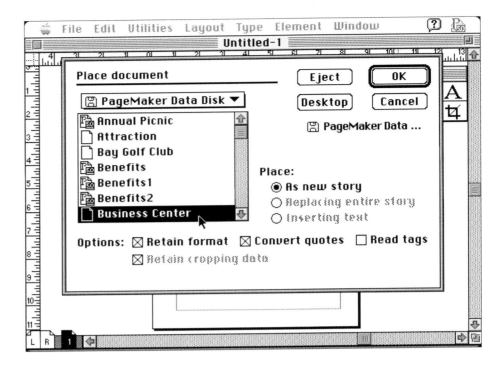

Figure 4.3
A message that may appear when placing a document

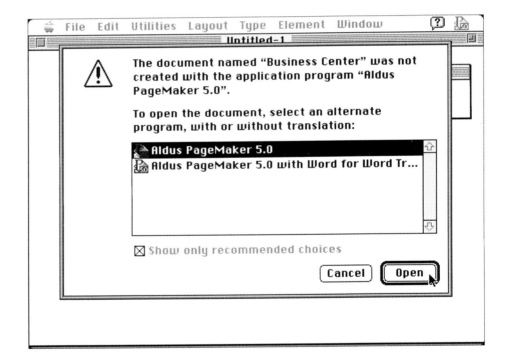

The document is placed on the page. Now use the Layout menu to change the page view to 75% size.

15. Choose View from the Layout menu.

16. Choose 75% size (⌘-7).

Figure 4.4
Positioning the text icon

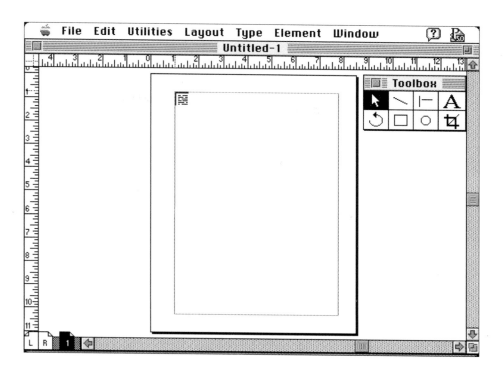

Figure 4.5
Viewing the document

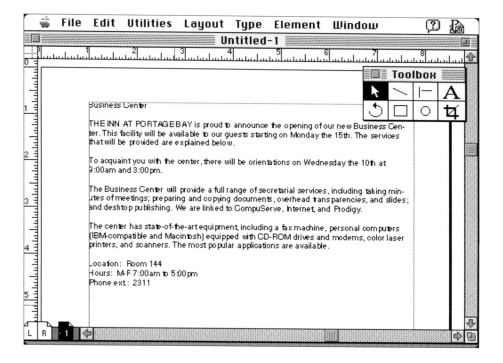

17. Use the scroll bars to duplicate the view shown in Figure 4.5.

Your document may not look exactly like the one displayed, because the type size displayed varies with the kind of monitor used.

PageMaker provides several ways to select a portion of text. The following involve using the **text tool** (I-beam icon). The **pointer tool** can also be used to select blocks of text and will be demonstrated later in this chapter. Text selected with the text tool is highlighted onscreen. You can deselect text by moving the text tool to a blank area and clicking the mouse button.

One method of selecting text is to place the I-beam at the beginning of the text to select, hold down the mouse button, and drag the I-beam to highlight the desired text. Figure 4.6 shows this process. Complete the following to select (highlight) the words *Business Center*.

1. Click on the text tool.

2. Position the I-beam to the left of the word *Business*.

3. Hold down the mouse button and slowly drag the mouse across the words *Business Center*.

4. Release the mouse button.

At this point the highlighted text could be moved, copied, replaced, or deleted. To remove the highlight (deselect the text), simply click on a blank area of the screen.

5. Position the I-beam in a blank area.

6. Click the mouse button.

This drag method can be used to select any portion of continuous text. Complete the following to select the first paragraph.

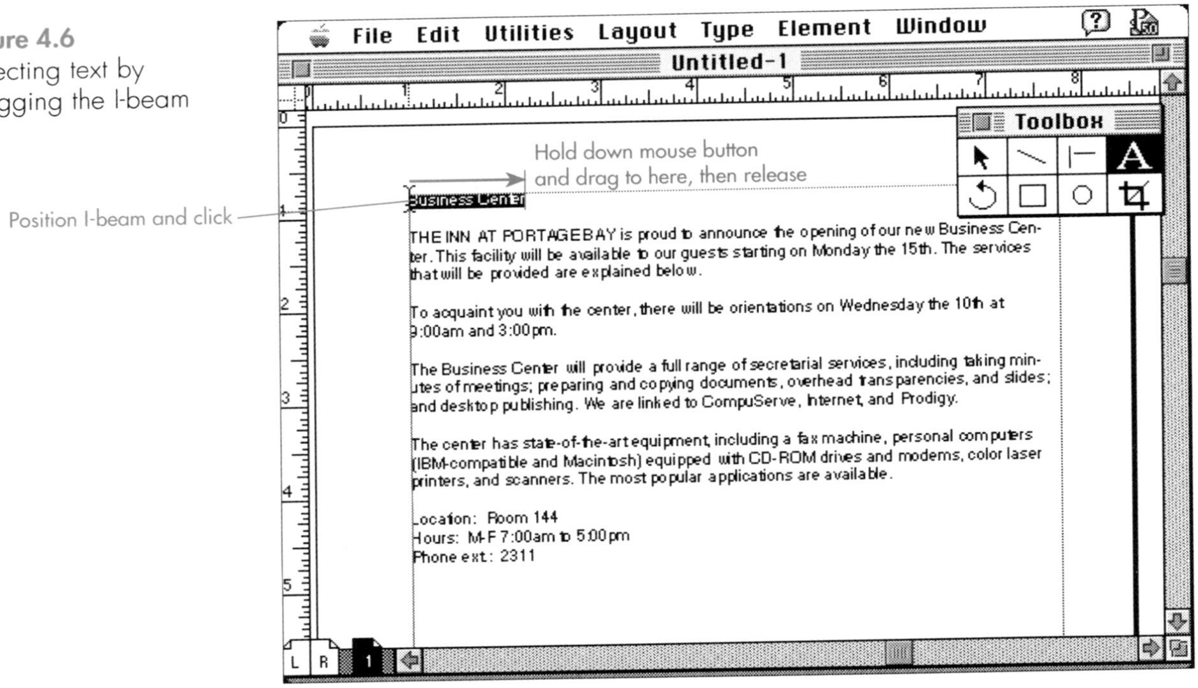

Figure 4.6
Selecting text by dragging the I-beam

Position I-beam and click

7. Position the I-beam to the left of the word *THE* in the first paragraph.

8. Hold down the mouse button and drag the mouse to highlight the entire paragraph.

9. Release the mouse button.

10. Click on a blank area to remove the highlight.

Another method for selecting text is to use the text tool to point to a word or paragraph and the mouse button to select it. The process is to position the I-beam on the word, then double-click to select the word or triple-click to select the paragraph.

11. Position the I-beam on the word *BAY*.

12. Double-click the mouse button.

The word *BAY* is highlighted.

13. Click on a blank area to remove the highlight.

To select the entire paragraph:

14. Position the I-beam on the word *BAY*.

15. Triple-click the mouse button.

The entire paragraph is highlighted.

16. Remove the highlight.

Yet another method for selecting text is to position the I-beam at the beginning of the desired text, click an insertion point, move the I-beam to the end of the desired text, hold down (SHIFT), and click the mouse button. Figure 4.7 illustrates this process.

Figure 4.7
Selecting text by clicking an insertion point, moving the I-beam, and clicking the mouse

Position I-beam and click ——

Then reposition I-beam, hold down (SHIFT), and click

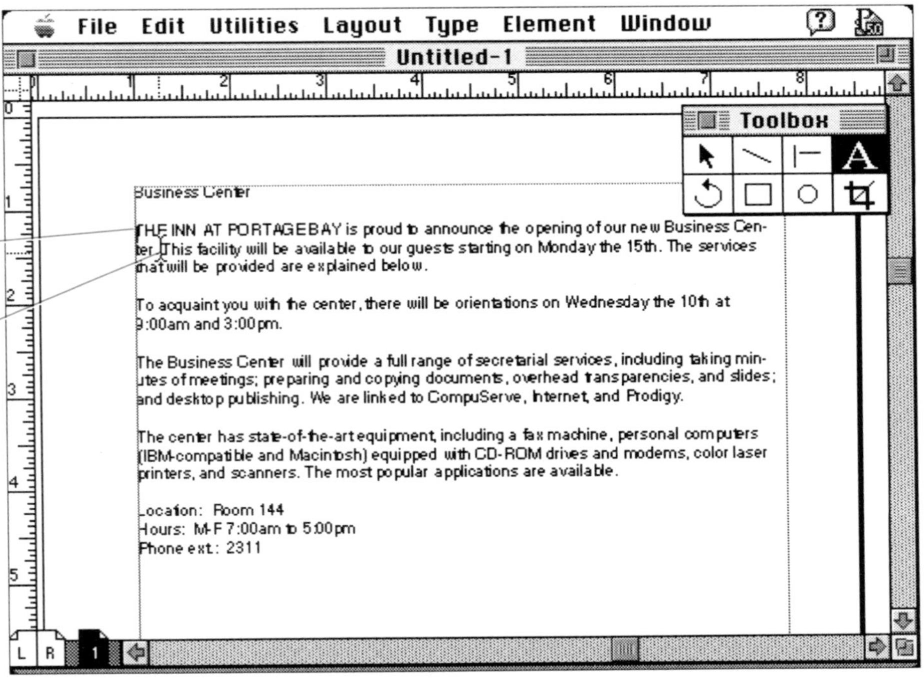

17. Position the I-beam to the left of the word *THE* in the first paragraph.

18. Click the mouse button to set an insertion point.

19. Move the I-beam to the end of the sentence.

20. Hold down (SHIFT) and click the mouse button.

The first sentence is highlighted.

21. Remove the highlight.

The previous methods of selecting text use the text tool and allow you to select a part or all of the text. You can also use the Select all option from the Edit menu to highlight the entire document. To use this option you must first click on any text with the text tool.

22. Click on any text in the page.

23. Choose the Select all option from the Edit menu (⌘-A).

Notice that all the text is highlighted.

24. Remove the highlight.

MOVING, COPYING, AND DELETING TEXT

Moving Text

Now that you know how to select text, you can practice using PageMaker's editing functions, which allow you to **cut** and **paste** text. Start by moving the second paragraph of the Business Center file to the end of the document.

1. Highlight the second paragraph including the blank line above it (see Figure 4.8).

2. Select Cut from the Edit menu (⌘-X).

The second paragraph is now removed to the Clipboard, and the text below it moves up. Now paste the paragraph from the Clipboard onto the page.

3. Position the I-beam at the bottom of the document (see Figure 4.9).

4. Click an insertion point.

5. Select Paste from the Edit menu (⌘-V).

The second paragraph is pasted onto the page at the insertion point.

Copying Text

The **copy** process allows you to place the selected text in two or more locations in the page. Practice this function by copying the title *Business Center* to the bottom of the page, as shown in Figure 4.10.

Figure 4.8
Selecting text to
be moved

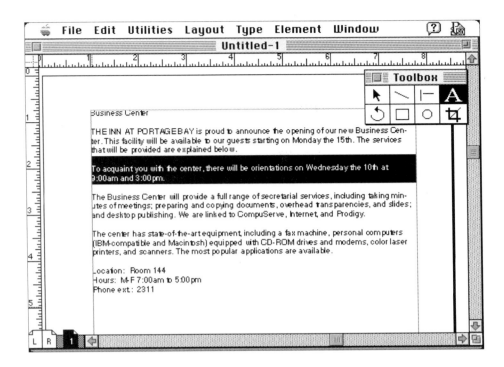

Figure 4.9
Positioning the I-beam

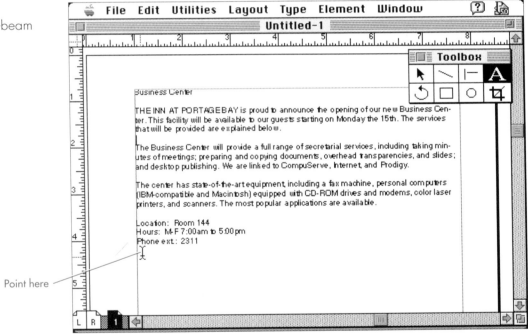

Point here

1. Use the I-beam to highlight *Business Center*. (Highlight only the words *Business Center*, the text to be copied, not the blank space following the words.)

2. Select Copy from the Edit menu (⌘-C).

A copy of the highlighted text is placed on the Clipboard.

Figure 4.10
Copying the title
Business Center

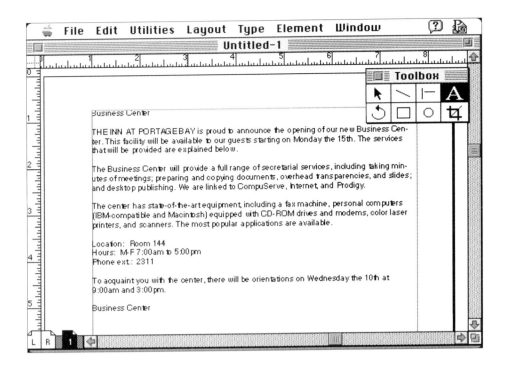

3. Position the I-beam at the bottom of the document.

4. Click an insertion point. (The vertical bar will move to the left margin.)

5. Choose Paste from the Edit menu (⌘-V).

The text is copied and the highlight is removed. However, the text remains on the Clipboard. Notice that the vertical line is at the end of the words *Business Center*. If you continue to select Paste, the text will be copied wherever the insertion point is located. Complete the following to copy the text three more times.

6. Select Paste from the Edit menu (⌘-V).

7. Select Paste again.

8. Select Paste again.

Deleting Text

The Clear option from the Edit menu allows you to **clear**, or delete, selected text. You will practice this function by deleting the words *Business Center* from the bottom of the page.

1. Use the I-beam to highlight the words *Business Center* at the bottom of the page.

2. Select Clear from the Edit menu.

The text is removed from the page. If you change your mind about deleting text, you can replace it with the Undo option in the Edit menu. Practice using this option as follows:

3. Display the Edit menu.

Notice the first option is Undo clear.

4. Choose the Undo clear option (⌘-Z).

The text is returned to the page and is still highlighted. The Undo clear command changes to Redo clear. The Redo command can be used to once again clear the selected text. The Undo and Redo options can be used with the Cut, Copy, Paste, and Clear commands. Now remove the text permanently.

5. Select Redo clear from the Edit menu (⌘-Z).

This completes the section on editing text.

WORKING WITH LINE AND CHARACTER SPACING

In any document, you are concerned with how the text appears. That is, the type style and size in which it's set, the spacing between characters, words, and paragraphs, and so on. Earlier, you learned how to use the Type specifications dialog box to change fonts and type size, and the Type menu to change type styles (bold, italic, et cetera). In this section you will change the spacing between lines and between characters.

Changing Line Spacing

Figure 4.11 shows the Type menu and the Leading submenu. **Leading** (pronounced "ledding") is the measurement of the vertical spacing between the base of one line and the base of the following line. Leading is measured in points, and the default setting is 120% of the largest type

Figure 4.11
Type Leading menu

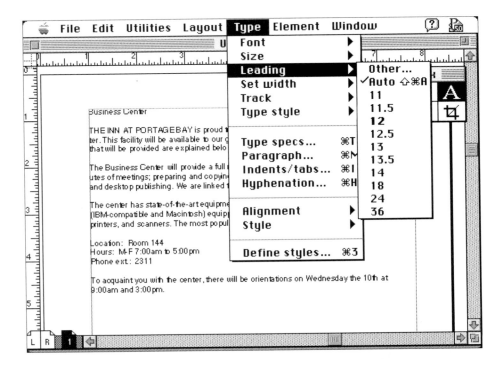

Figure 4.12

12-point type with
different leading values

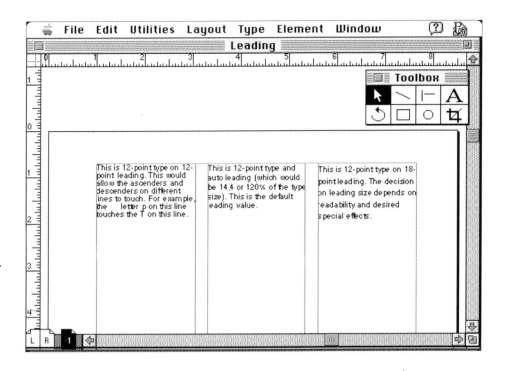

size on a line. (Remember, you can override any default setting.) For example, if the type size is 10 point, the default leading will be 12 points. Figure 4.12 shows examples of 12-point type with three different leading values. The first example, 12-point type with 12-point leading, allows the ascenders and descenders of individual letters on different lines to touch. Notice how the descender of the *p* touches the ascender of the *T*. Obviously then, if the leading is the same as the type size, characters may touch. The second example shows 12-point type with 14.4-point leading, which is the default spacing, 120%. The third example shows 12-point type with 18-point leading. The decision on how much leading to use is based on readability as well as on special design effects you may want to create. Generally, a larger type size requires less leading. Also, if you are using all uppercase characters, which will have no descenders, you may want to specify a leading smaller than the type size.

To illustrate leading you will change the spacing between the three lines (Location, Hours, Phone ext.) near the end of the document we've been working on.

1. Use the I-beam to highlight the three lines.

2. Display the Leading option from the Type menu.

A box appears with several sizes. The check mark next to Auto indicates that leading is being set automatically.

3. Choose 18.

The three lines change to 18-point leading. Now clear the highlight.

4. Click on a blank area.

Before continuing, change the page size to Actual, and scroll the page to display the top of the document.

5. Choose View from the Layout menu and select Actual size (⌘-1).

6. If necessary, scroll the page to view the top of the document.

Changing Spacing Between Characters

PageMaker allows you to change the spacing between characters. Each font has built-in spacing for pairs of characters. But certain pairs, like *WA* and *Yo,* may appear too far apart with this spacing. The process of adjusting spacing between pairs of characters is called **kerning**. PageMaker has an automatic pair-kerning function. If you want to adjust the spacing between characters manually, you can use the text tool to position an insertion point between characters. Then hold down the Command key and press the left arrow to reduce spacing. Or hold down the Command key and press the right arrow to add space. Complete the following steps to reduce the spacing between the *A* and *Y* in *BAY.*

1. Position the I-beam between the *A* and *Y*.

2. Click an insertion point.

3. Hold down the Command key, ⌘.

4. Press ⬅ two times.

5. Click in a blank area.

The spacing between the *A* and *Y* is reduced, and the insertion point is removed.

WORKING WITH PARAGRAPHS

Aligning Paragraphs

PageMaker provides several ways for you to change the appearance of paragraphs. You can align and indent them and change the spacing between them. You can also control the hyphenation used to fit lines within margins. These functions are carried out using the options within the Type menu.

PageMaker provides five ways to align paragraphs:

- **Left:** aligns the paragraph on the left margin or column guide.

- **Right:** aligns the paragraph on the right margin or column guide.

- **Center:** aligns the paragraph between the margins or column guides.

- **Justify:** spaces the words on each line (except the last line) of the paragraph so that each line is as long as the column is wide.

- **Force justify:** justifies all lines of the paragraph including the last line.

Currently, the document we're using is left aligned—the alignment in the word processing program used to create it. To change the alignment, select the desired text and use the Alignment options in the Type menu. Complete the following steps to change the alignment of selected paragraphs. Start by right-aligning the first paragraph.

1. Use the Layout menu to change the view to 75% (⌘-7).

2. If necessary, scroll the page to display the entire first paragraph.

3. Use the I-beam to highlight the first paragraph.

4. Choose Alignment from the Type menu.

Figure 4.13 shows the Type menu and the five Alignment options. The check mark next to the Align left option indicates that the highlighted paragraph is left aligned.

5. Choose Justify from the Alignment option of the Type menu (⌘-SHIFT-J).

6. Click on a blank area to remove the highlight.

Notice that the text is flush to the right margin. PageMaker inserts additional spaces between words and letters to justify text. To illustrate center alignment, center the Location, Hours, and Phone ext. lines.

7. If necessary, scroll the page to display the three lines.

8. Highlight the three lines.

9. Choose Align center from the Alignment option of the Type menu (⌘-SHIFT-C).

10. Click on a blank area to remove the highlight.

Figure 4.13
Five options of the
Type Alignment menu

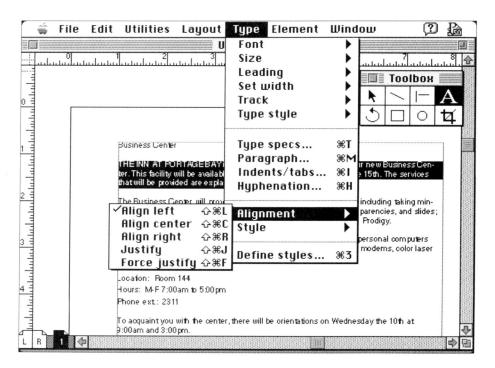

Figure 4.14
Business Center
document with different
paragraph indents

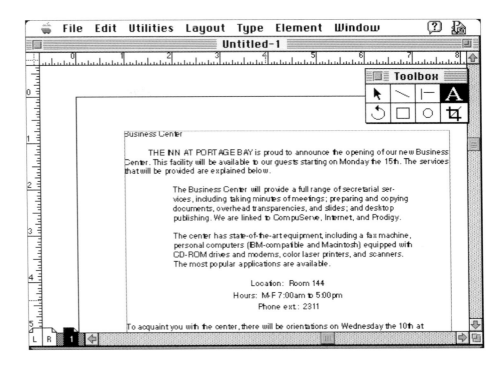

Indenting Paragraphs

In this section you will learn how to set paragraph **indents** and **tabs**. Figure 4.14 shows the Business Center document with different paragraph indents. The first paragraph has a first-line indent. The second and third paragraphs are indented from the left and right margins. Complete the following steps to duplicate this figure.

1. **Drag the mouse pointer to highlight the first paragraph.**

2. **Select Indents/tabs... from the Type menu (⌘-I).**

Figure 4.15 shows the Indents/tabs dialog box, which is used to set paragraph indents and tabs for moving the vertical insertion bar across the page. The ruler part of the dialog box shows the location of the indent and tab settings and indicates their type.

Tabs are set every half inch along the ruler and are signified by a small triangular icon pointing down, toward the ruler. You will change the tab settings later in this section. For now, you will set the indent for the first line of the highlighted paragraph.

At the left of the ruler line are two triangles used to set paragraph indents. The top triangle is used to set the indent for the paragraph's first line. The bottom triangle is used to set the indent for the entire paragraph. (In effect, this triangle sets a new left margin for the paragraph.) You will set a first-line indent for the first paragraph. Then you will set a paragraph indent for the second and third paragraphs. To set these indents, you drag the triangle to the desired location on the ruler. Figure 4.16 shows the top triangle moved to the .5" mark.

Figure 4.15
Indents/tabs
dialog box

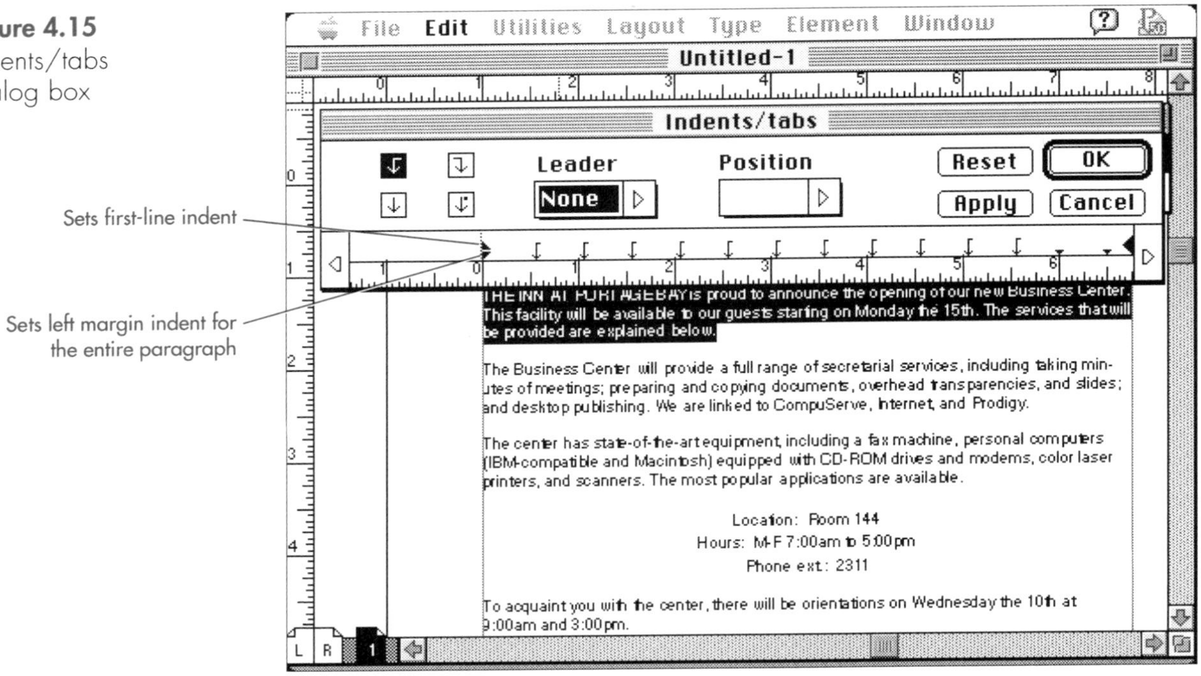

Sets first-line indent ——

Sets left margin indent for
the entire paragraph

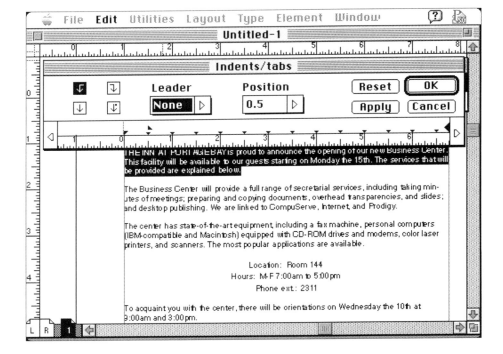

Figure 4.16
Top triangle moved
to the .5" mark

3. Point to the top triangle.

4. Hold down the mouse button.

5. Drag the triangle to the .5" mark on the ruler.

As you drag the triangle, its location is displayed under the word *Position*.

6. Release the mouse button.

7. Click on OK.

Figure 4.17
Both triangles moved
to the same position
on the ruler

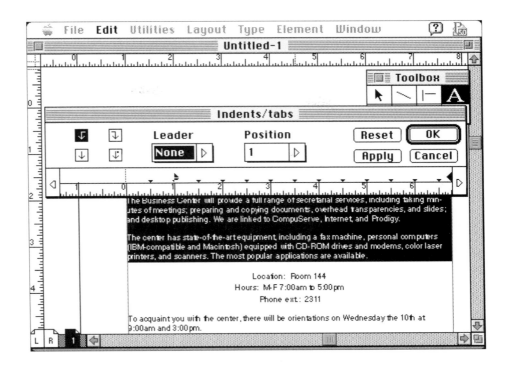

The page is displayed with the first line of the highlighted paragraph indented a half inch.

8. Click on a blank area to remove the highlight.

Now you will indent the second and third paragraphs.

9. Highlight the second and third paragraphs.

10. Select Indents/tabs... from the Type menu (⌘-I).

Because the first line will not be indented, you will move both the triangles to the same position on the ruler, as shown in Figure 4.17.

11. Point to the bottom triangle.

12. Hold down the mouse button and drag the icons to the 1" mark. (Both triangles will move together.)

13. Release the mouse button.

14. Click on the Apply button to view the changes.

The next step is to change the right indent, similar to a right margin, for the selected paragraph. Figure 4.17 shows the right indent located at the 6.75" mark. This location is the same as the right margin, indicated by a vertical dotted line. You will move the right triangle to the 6" mark to set a right indent. The process is shown in Figure 4.18.

15. Point to the right-indent triangle (see Figure 4.18).

16. Hold down the mouse button and drag the triangle to the 6" mark.

The indicator under the word *Position* will specify 0.75, which is the distance from the triangle to the right margin.

Figure 4.18
Setting a right indent

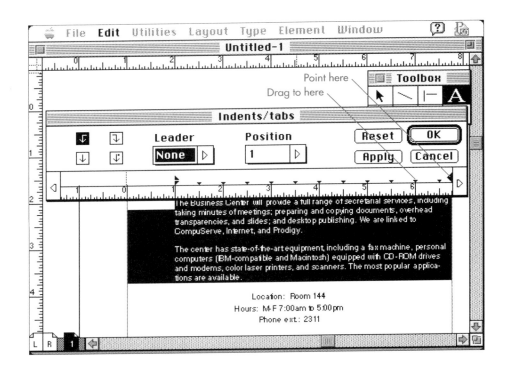

17. **Release the mouse button.**

18. **Click on the Apply button.**

Take a moment to review your actions. The dialog box shows that you have set a left indent at the 1" mark and a right indent at the 6" mark for the highlighted paragraphs.

19. **Click on OK.**

20. **Click on a blank area to remove the highlight.**

The page is displayed with the paragraphs indented.

So far, while working with paragraph indents, you have used the text tool to drag the I-beam to select the desired paragraph(s). There are two other ways of specifying a paragraph for indentation. First, if you want to work with only one paragraph that is already in the publication, position the I-beam anywhere on the paragraph and click an insertion point. Then any indent setting will apply to just that paragraph.

Second, if you want to indent a paragraph that has not yet been typed, you use the pointer tool instead of the text tool. If you use the pointer tool to set an indent, the default paragraph setting is changed so that any new paragraph entered at the end of the publication will be formatted according to the new indent setting.

Working with Tabs

Earlier you learned that PageMaker sets tabs at half-inch increments. When you press the Tab key, the vertical insertion line moves across the page to the next tab setting. To add tabs, you must specify the location of the tab on the ruler and the tab type. PageMaker provides

Figure 4.19
Left, center, and
decimal tabs

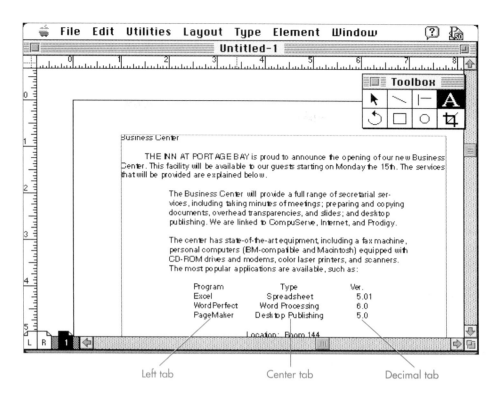

Left tab   Center tab   Decimal tab

four types of tabs: left, right, center, and decimal. If you specify a left tab, the tab is to the left of the text you type. If you specify a right tab, the tab is to the right of the text you type. Specifying a center tab centers the text at the tab. Specifying a decimal tab aligns the numbers that you type on their decimal point. This is useful for lining up a column of numbers that have different lengths. When you add tabs, all default tabs to the left are erased. Figure 4.19 shows left, center, and decimal tabs used when adding four lines of text to the Business Center document. The tab positions on the ruler (in inches) are: left, 1.5; center, 3.5; and decimal, 5. Figure 4.20 shows the Indents/tabs dialog box with these settings. Each tab has a different icon: ↓ for left, ↓ for center, and ↓ for decimal. Before setting these tabs, add the words *such as:* to the end of the third paragraph.

1. Position the I-beam to the right of the period after the word *available*.

2. Click an insertion point.

3. Press (DELETE) once to erase the period.

4. Type *, such as:*

5. Press (RETURN) twice.

Now use the Indents/tabs dialog box to set the tabs.

6. Select Indents/tabs... from the Type menu (⌘-I).

On the left side of the dialog box are the four tab-type icons. To select a tab type, you click on the appropriate icon, which is then highlighted. The first tab setting you add is to be left aligned. The left-tab icon is highlighted, so you do not have to change this setting. But you do have to

---

Figure 4.20
Indents/tabs dialog
box with tab settings

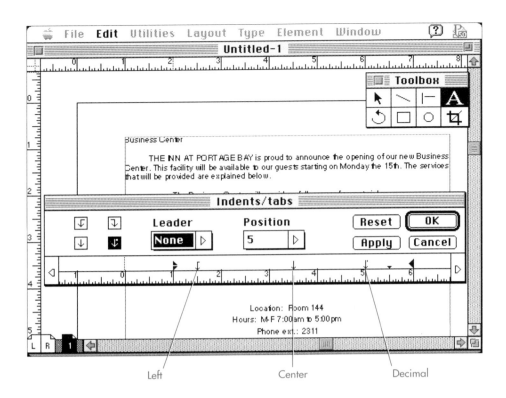

Left   Center   Decimal

specify the tab location. To set a tab, point to the desired location on the ruler and click the mouse button. To move a tab, point to the icon and drag the tab to the left or right. To reset all tabs to their original position, click on Reset. To remove a tab setting, point to the icon and drag it down through the ruler.

7. Point to the 1.5" mark on the ruler.

8. Click the mouse button.

The left-tab icon appears above the ruler. Also, all default tab settings (small triangles) to the left of the added tab are erased.

Before adding the next tab, click on a blank area in the dialog box to remove the highlight from the current tab.

9. Click on a blank area in the dialog box.

To set the next tab, first indicate that it will be center aligned.

10. Click on the center-tab icon, ↓.

11. Click on the 3.5" mark.

12. Click on a blank area in the dialog box to remove the highlight.

The last tab will be decimal aligned.

13. Click on the decimal-tab icon, ↓.

14. Click on the 5" mark.

Check to make sure your settings are the same as those shown in Figure 4.20.

15. **Click on OK.**

The page is displayed onscreen. Now enter the new lines for the document.

16. **Press** (TAB).

17. **Type** *Program.*

18. **Press** (TAB).

19. **Type** *Type.*

20. **Press** (TAB).

21. **Type** *Ver..*

22. **Press** (RETURN).

23. **Press** (TAB).

24. **Type** *Excel.*

25. **Continue to complete the new lines as shown in Figure 4.19.**

Setting Leaders

PageMaker provides a function, Set leader, that allows you to specify a string of characters to be automatically placed in front of a tab setting. Figure 4.21 shows the publication with the Location, Hours, and Phone ext. lines left aligned. Notice that there is a series of dots, a **leader**, that follows each of these headings and extends to the next tab setting. To create these lines, you will use the Indents/tabs dialog box to specify a leader type (in this case, a series of dots) and then set the desired tab. Begin by clearing these lines in the publication.

Figure 4.21
Example of a leader

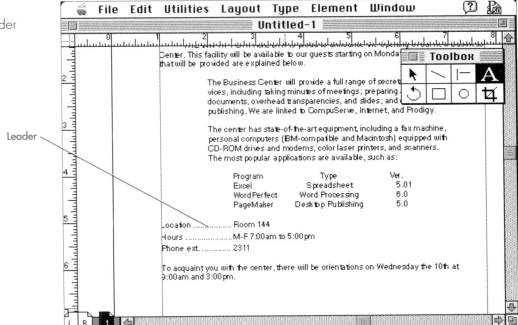

1. Highlight the three lines.

2. Select Clear from the Edit menu.

3. Select Indents/tabs... from the Type menu (⌘-I).

4. Click on Reset to clear all tabs except the default tabs.

5. Point to the triangle at the right of the word None.

6. Hold down the mouse button.

A list of options appears with a check mark next to the word None. This indicates that no leader has been selected. The option below None is a series of dots. The next two options are a broken line and a solid underscore line. The last option is Custom, which allows you to specify a character to be used as a leader.

7. Choose the dots.

The word None is replaced by dots. Now set a left-align tab at the 1.5" mark.

8. Point and click on the 1.5" mark.

9. Click on OK.

10. If necessary, choose Align left from the Alignment option of the Type menu to move the insertion point to the left margin.

11. Type *Location*.

12. Press (TAB).

The dots fill the line to the tab setting.

13. Type *Room 144*.

14. Press (RETURN).

15. Complete the other two lines on your own.

This completes the section on indents and tabs. Before continuing, close the document.

16. Choose Close from the File menu.

A message appears, asking if you want to save before closing.

17. Click on No (indicating that you do not want to save the document).

If your study time is up, use the Quit option from the File menu to exit PageMaker. If not, continue with the rest of the chapter.

Working with Paragraph Spacing and Hyphenation

Earlier you learned how to change the spacing between lines and between characters. In this section you will learn how PageMaker spaces words and letters within paragraphs and how this affects **hyphenation**. Controlling the spacing within paragraphs is especially important when you are working with justified text in narrow columns, such as might occur in a newsletter. To justify text, PageMaker must end each line at the right margin. Because few lines will have the exact number of characters to end at the right margin, PageMaker must adjust the spacing between characters and words and/or hyphenate a word at the end of the line. The amount of spacing is determined by ranges specified in the Spacing attributes dialog box, which is accessed by selecting the Type menu Paragraph option and then pressing the Spacing button.

Figure 4.22 shows the Spacing attributes dialog box with the default spacing values. The letter- and word spacing values are percentages of the overall font spacing as determined by the font designer. Thus, a spacing value of 50% would be one-half of the predetermined font spacing. The default values allow PageMaker to use word spacing of between half (50%) and twice (200%) the font spacing when justifying a line.

An important consideration in letter- and word spacing is the relationship between spacing and hyphenation. To justify text, PageMaker first adjusts the spacing between words and letters within the specified ranges. Then, if necessary, PageMaker hyphenates words. Thus, the larger the spacing range, the less hyphenation is needed. However, the larger the spacing range, the larger the gaps between words and letters. In most cases you would leave the spacing at the default values. To change the appearance of the paragraphs, you could turn off and on the hyphenation, and change paragraph alignment from justified to unjustified, as demonstrated by the following exercise.

Figure 4.22
Spacing attributes dialog box with the default spacing values

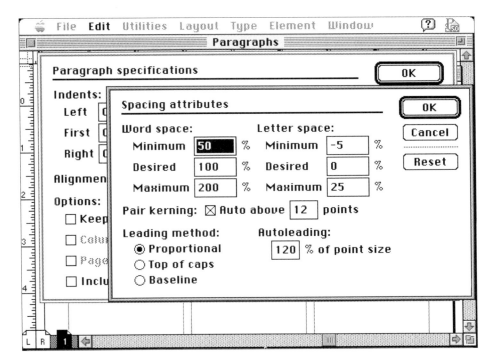

Figure 4.23

Three paragraphs with the same text and spacing values but different alignments and hyphenation

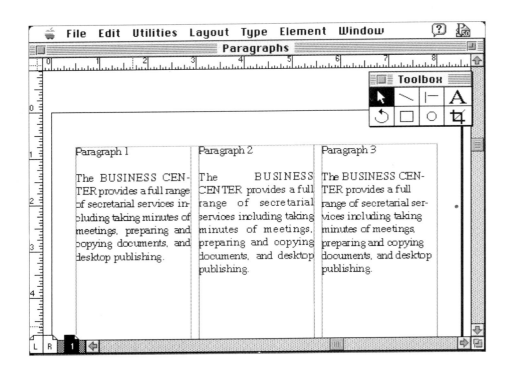

Figure 4.23 shows three paragraphs with the same text and spacing values but with different alignments and hyphenation. Paragraph 1 is justified, and the hyphenation is turned on. Paragraph 2 is justified, and the hyphenation is turned off. Paragraph 3 is not justified, and the hyphenation is turned on. You can change these settings in the Hyphenation dialog box from the Type menu. To practice using the Hyphenation dialog box, you will retrieve the file Paragraphs, which has three identical paragraphs. You will then change them to duplicate Figure 4.23. Start by opening Paragraphs. Make sure the data disk is in the drive.

1. **Choose Open… from the File menu (⌘-O).**

2. **Select the Paragraphs file from the data disk.**

3. **If needed, choose 75% size from the View option in the Layout menu (⌘-7).**

4. **If needed, scroll the page to view all three paragraphs.**

The paragraphs are identical. They are justified, and the hyphenation is turned on. Change Paragraph 2 by turning off the hyphenation. *Note:* When working with these paragraphs, do not highlight the headings.

5. **Using the text tool, highlight Paragraph 2.**

6. **Select Hyphenation… from the Type menu (⌘-H).**

The Hyphenation dialog box is displayed. This dialog box contains several options that: allow you to turn hyphenation on and off; select the type of hyphenation, such as Manual only, which permits PageMaker to hyphenate only words you specify; limit the number of consecutive lines in a paragraph that end in a hyphen; and specify the amount of space at the end of a line in which hyphenation should be allowed. You can also use this dialog box to specify where you want a particular word to be hyphenated and to specify a word that you never want hyphenated.

Continue by turning off hyphenation for the selected paragraph.

7. Click on the Off radio button.

8. Click on OK.

9. Click on a blank area to remove the highlight.

After turning off the hyphenation, PageMaker must insert additional spacing to justify the paragraph, which may create "rivers" of white space in the paragraph. Now change the alignment of Paragraph 3.

10. Highlight Paragraph 3.

11. Select Alignment from the Type menu choose Align left (⌘-SHIFT-L).

12. Click on a blank area to remove the highlight.

Paragraph 3 now displays a ragged right edge.

All three paragraphs have a different appearance due to variations in hyphenation and justification. Another appearance can be created by using track kerning. Earlier you learned about kerning, spacing between two characters. **Track kerning** allows you to adjust the space between letters and words in selected text, such as a line or paragraph. This function is useful in providing special effects, such as darkening or lightening a part of the text. If you tighten the space between letters and words, the text block will appear darker. If you loosen the space between letters and words, the text will appear lighter. Another use of track kerning is to change the spacing of lines of very small or very large text, such as captions and headlines. To illustrate this function, you will use the Track option to change the letter- and word spacing for Paragraphs 2 and 3 of the original Paragraphs publication. Begin by closing this publication and opening Paragraphs again.

1. Choose Close from the File menu.

2. Click on No (do not save).

3. Open Paragraphs.

4. Use the text tool to highlight Paragraph 2.

5. Select the Track option from the Type menu.

Figure 4.24 shows the list of options of the Track command with the No track option checked. This indicates that there is no track kerning for the selected text. Change the track kerning to Very tight.

6. Choose Very tight.

7. Use the text tool to select Paragraph 3.

8. Change the Track setting to Very loose.

9. Click on a blank area to remove the highlight.

Figure 4.24
Track command options

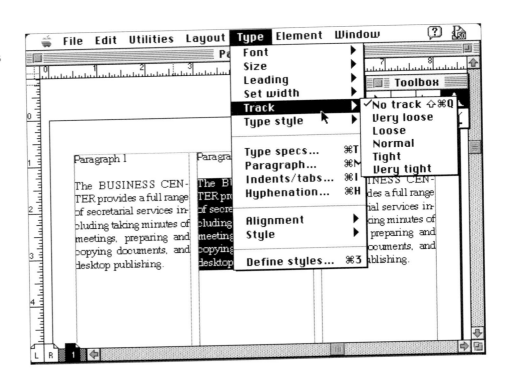

Paragraph 2 appears darker because it has less space between the letters and words, and Paragraph 3 appears the lightest because it has more space between the letters and words. Alignment, hyphenation, and spacing are adjustments that you can control to manipulate the appearance of text.

Working with the Paragraph Specifications Dialog Box

Thus far you have worked with several PageMaker functions (including indents, tabs, alignment, letterspacing, and hyphenation) that allow you to change the appearance of paragraphs. Several of these functions, and others, can be executed using the Paragraph specifications dialog box shown in Figure 4.25. Notice that paragraph indents and alignment can be specified with this dialog box. In addition, you can control spaces between paragraphs, as well as column breaks, page breaks, widows, and orphans. All of these are explained in this section.

Controlling Paragraph Spacing

The Paragraph space option allows you to specify (in inches) the amount of additional space before or after selected paragraphs. Practice this option by increasing the spacing above Paragraph 1 by .25 inch.

1. Highlight Paragraph 1 (do not highlight the heading).

2. Choose Paragraph... from the Type menu ((⌘)-M).

3. Highlight the 0 in the Before box.

4. Type .25.

Figure 4.25
Paragraph
specifications
dialog box

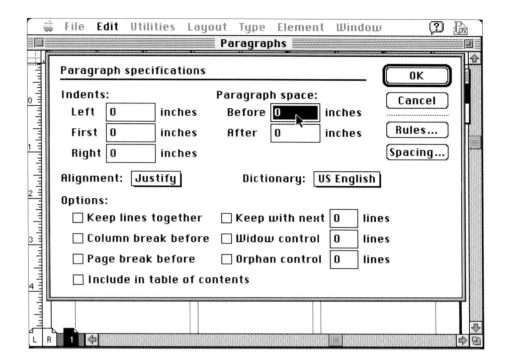

5. Click on OK.

6. Click on a blank area to remove the highlight.

Notice that the increased spacing has caused the paragraph to move down.

This completes the section on hyphenation and paragraph spacing. Before continuing, use the File menu to close the document.

7. Choose Close from the File menu.

8. Click on No (indicating that you do not want to save the document).

Controlling Page and Column Breaks, and Widows and Orphans

The Paragraph specifications dialog box has several options that control the flow of text from column to column and page to page. When working with these options, you must determine which paragraph will be affected by the option. You can use the text tool to highlight the paragraph and the Paragraph specifications dialog box to choose the option. Each option is explained in this section. Refer to Figure 4.25 as you read the following.

■ **Keep lines together**   This option allows you to specify that a paragraph will not be split at a column or page break. This is useful if you want to keep a table or list together.

■ **Column break before and Page break before**   When working with a multipage or multicolumn publication, you need to be concerned with page and column breaks. If you want a paragraph to begin a new page or column, you merely select the paragraph and choose the desired option from the dialog box.

- **Keep with next *x* lines**   This option is used to make sure that the last line of a paragraph will be placed with a certain number of lines (1, 2, or 3) of the next paragraph. This is useful in keeping headings connected to their accompanying text.

- **Widow control *x* lines**   A widow occurs when the beginning lines of a paragraph are isolated at the bottom of a column or page. Use this option to specify the maximum number of lines (1, 2, or 3) that make up a widow. Figure 4.26 shows an example of a widow without the control set.

- **Orphan control *x* lines**   An orphan occurs when the last line of a paragraph is isolated at the top of a column or page. Use this option to specify the maximum number of lines that make up an orphan.

Now take a moment to practice using two of these options: Keep lines together and Orphan control. Begin by opening a publication called Orphan.

1. **Select Open... from the File menu.**

2. **Select Orphan from the data disk.**

Figure 4.27 shows this publication. Notice that the top of the second column begins with a single line. This is an orphan—the last line of the paragraph that ends the first column. Use the Paragraph specifications dialog box to set the Orphan control to 3. Start by highlighting the paragraph.

Figure 4.26
Example of widow without the control set

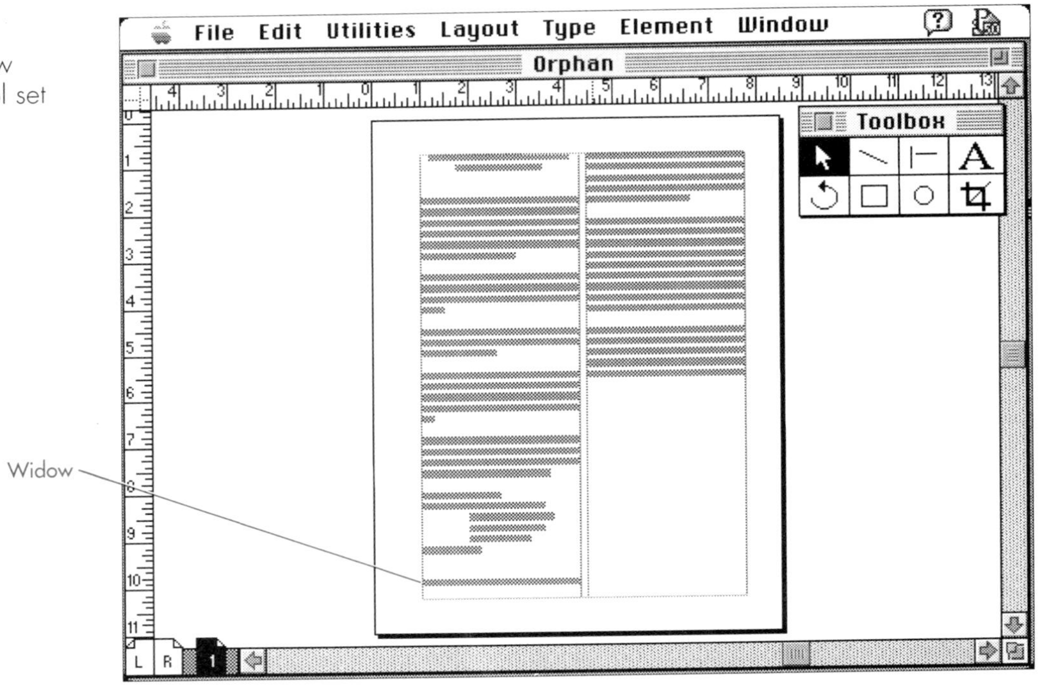

Figure 4.27
The Orphan publication

Orphan

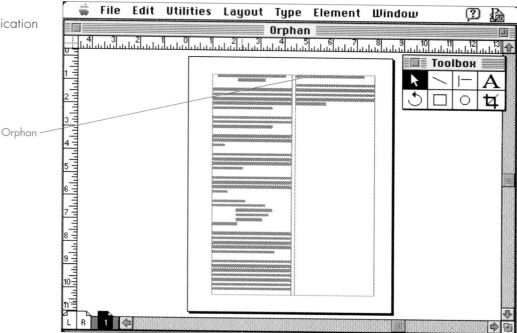

3. Select the text tool.

4. Triple-click on the last paragraph in column 1.

5. Choose Paragraph... from the Type menu (⌘-M).

6. Click on Orphan control.

7. Type 3.

8. Click on OK.

Three more lines moved from the bottom of the first column to the top of the second column. Now use the Keep lines together option. With the paragraph still highlighted:

9. Choose Paragraph... from the Type menu (⌘-M).

10. Click on Orphan control to turn it off.

11. Click on Keep lines together.

12. Click on OK.

Now the entire paragraph moves to the second column. This completes the section on controlling page and column breaks, and widows and orphans. Before continuing, use the File menu to close the publication.

13. Choose Close from the File menu.

14. Click on No (indicating that you do not want to save the publication).

Earlier you learned how to use the text tool to select a portion of text that could then be edited—moved, copied, deleted, and so forth. In this section you will learn how to use the pointer tool to select a **text block**. A text block is a rectangular area on the page that contains text. A publication page can have one or several text blocks. A text block is created when text is placed, pasted, or typed on a page. If a publication has more than one text block, the text blocks are often threaded, or linked together, so that a change in one affects the others. For example, reducing the size of one text block may increase the size of the following text block. Threaded text blocks are combined to form a story. A **story** is text that PageMaker recognizes as a unit, such as a document created using a word processing program. Publications can have more than one story.

An advantage of working with a text block is that you can change its shape and easily move it. This allows you to rearrange the text on a page to provide space for a graphic or to enhance the document's appearance. To work with a text block, you must first select it. To do this, use the pointer tool to point inside the text block boundaries; then click the mouse button.

Figure 4.28 shows a text block that has been selected. After selecting a text block, the top and bottom boundary lines, called **windowshades**, are displayed. The windowshades are used to edit a text block. The windowshades have handles, called loops, which are either empty or contain a + or ▼ symbol. An empty loop at the top of a text block indicates the beginning of a story. An empty loop at the bottom of the text block indicates the end of a story. The + symbol in a loop indicates

Figure 4.28
Selected text block

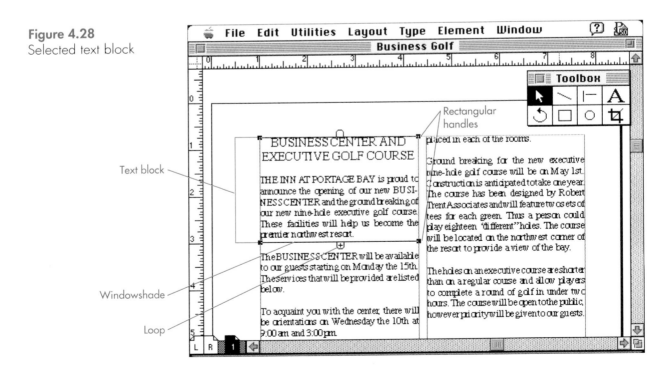

that the text block is threaded to the previous or following text block. When there is text that does not appear, the ▼ symbol is displayed in a loop. To display the text, either drag the loop lower or click on the loop to display a loaded text icon; then place the text.

At each corner of the text block is a small rectangular handle. You can use the pointer tool to select it, and then drag the handle to change the shape (such as the width) of the text block. You also can use the pointer tool to select the text block and drag it to another location on the page.

To practice using text blocks, you will open a PageMaker document named Business Golf. This is a two-column document containing announcements of the business center and a new golf course. Figure 4.29 shows a printout of this document, and Figure 4.30 shows the Fit in window view of this document. Using text blocks, you will revise the document to duplicate Figure 4.31, a printout. Figure 4.32 shows the Fit in window view of the revised document. Revising the document involves:

■ changing the size of text blocks so the amount of text in each column is approximately the same

Figure 4.29
Printout of Business
Golf publication

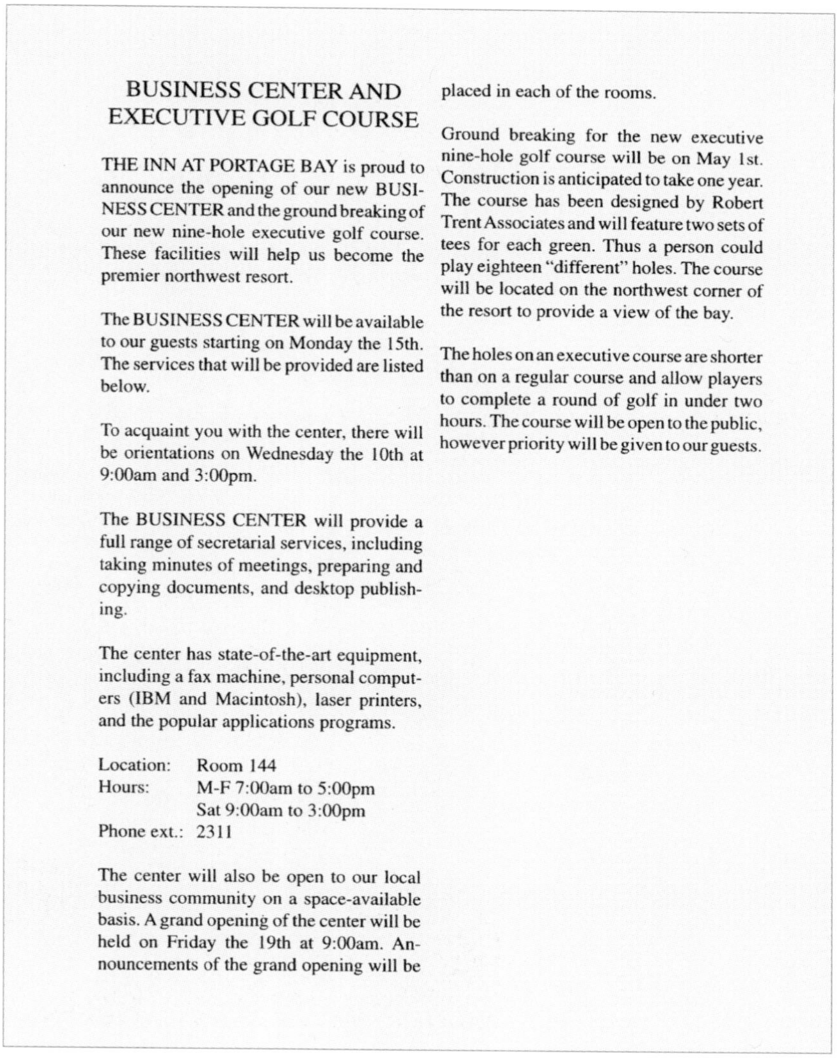

BUSINESS CENTER AND EXECUTIVE GOLF COURSE

THE INN AT PORTAGE BAY is proud to announce the opening of our new BUSINESS CENTER and the ground breaking of our new nine-hole executive golf course. These facilities will help us become the premier northwest resort.

The BUSINESS CENTER will be available to our guests starting on Monday the 15th. The services that will be provided are listed below.

To acquaint you with the center, there will be orientations on Wednesday the 10th at 9:00am and 3:00pm.

The BUSINESS CENTER will provide a full range of secretarial services, including taking minutes of meetings, preparing and copying documents, and desktop publishing.

The center has state-of-the-art equipment, including a fax machine, personal computers (IBM and Macintosh), laser printers, and the popular applications programs.

Location: Room 144
Hours: M-F 7:00am to 5:00pm
             Sat 9:00am to 3:00pm
Phone ext.: 2311

The center will also be open to our local business community on a space-available basis. A grand opening of the center will be held on Friday the 19th at 9:00am. Announcements of the grand opening will be placed in each of the rooms.

Ground breaking for the new executive nine-hole golf course will be on May 1st. Construction is anticipated to take one year. The course has been designed by Robert Trent Associates and will feature two sets of tees for each green. Thus a person could play eighteen "different" holes. The course will be located on the northwest corner of the resort to provide a view of the bay.

The holes on an executive course are shorter than on a regular course and allow players to complete a round of golf in under two hours. The course will be open to the public, however priority will be given to our guests.

Figure 4.30
Fit in window view
of Business Golf

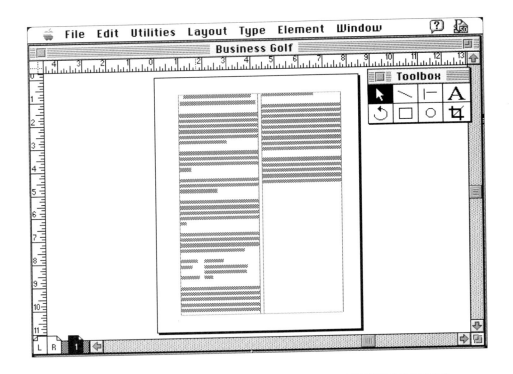

Figure 4.31
Revised publication
using text blocks

BUSINESS CENTER AND EXECUTIVE GOLF COURSE

THE INN AT PORTAGE BAY is proud to announce the opening of our new BUSINESS CENTER and the ground breaking of our new nine-hole executive golf course. These facilities will help us become the premier northwest resort.

The BUSINESS CENTER will be available to our guests starting on Monday the 15th. The services that will be provided are listed below.

To acquaint you with the center, there will be orientations on Wednesday the 10th at 9:00am and 3:00pm.

The BUSINESS CENTER will provide a full range of secretarial services, including taking minutes of meetings, preparing and copying documents, and desktop publishing.

The center has state-of-the-art equipment, including a fax machine, personal computers (IBM and Macintosh), laser printers, and the popular applications programs.

Location: Room 144
Hours: M-F 7:00am to 5:00pm
             Sat 9:00am to 3:00pm
Phone ext.: 2311

The center will also be open to our local business community on a space-available basis. A grand opening of the center will be held on Friday the 19th at 9:00am. Announcements of the grand opening will be placed in each of the rooms.

Ground breaking for the new executive nine-hole golf course will be on May 1st. Construction is anticipated to take one year. The course has been designed by Robert Trent Associates and will feature two sets of tees for each green. Thus a person could play eighteen "different" holes. The course will be located on the northwest corner of the resort to provide a view of the bay.

The holes on an executive course are shorter than on a regular course and allow players to complete a round of golf in under two hours. The course will be open to the public, however priority will be given to our guests.

Figure 4.32
Fit in window view of
the revised document

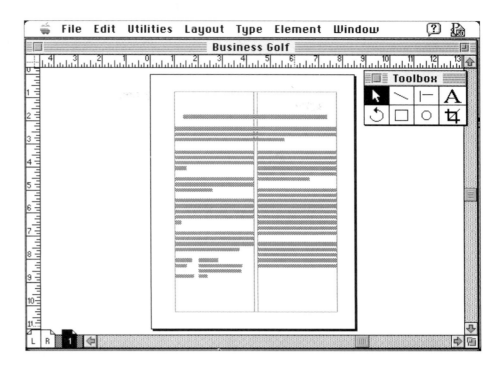

- dividing a large text block into two smaller ones to allow you to work with each text block separately

- moving text blocks

- changing the shape of a text block so it flows across both columns

Start by opening Business Golf.

1. **Choose Open... from the File menu (⌘-O).**

2. **Choose the Business Golf file.**

Displaying Text Blocks

When you first open a document, it may not be clear how many text blocks are in it. A text block can be as short as a single line or as long as the page. Because this page is divided into two columns, there are at least two text blocks. To view a single text block, you would click on the text. To view all the text blocks on a page, you can use the Select all option from the Edit menu.

1. **Choose Select all from the Edit menu (⌘-A).**

Figure 4.33 shows the windowshades and loops, indicating that there are two text blocks. The top loop in the left column is empty, signifying the story's beginning. The empty loop in the right column signifies the story's end. The loops with a + signify there are threaded text blocks before and after the windowshade. These two text blocks are threaded, which means that a change in one can affect the other. To remove the windowshades, click on an empty area of the publication page.

Figure 4.33
Windowshades and loops indicating two text blocks

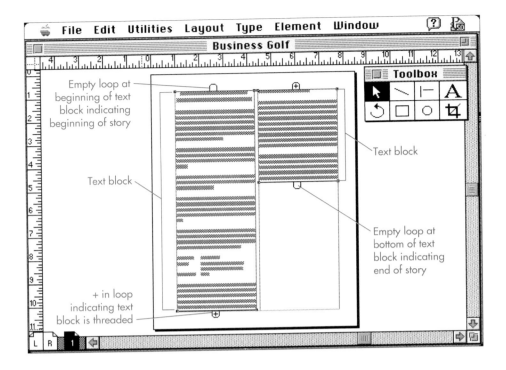

Empty loop at beginning of text block indicating beginning of story

Text block

Text block

Empty loop at bottom of text block indicating end of story

+ in loop indicating text block is threaded

2. **Move the pointer to an empty area.**

3. **Click the mouse button.**

Flowing Text from One Text Block to Another and Dividing Text Blocks

First, you will shorten the text block in the left column. The process is to select the text block, point to the bottom loop, and drag up the windowshade. Figure 4.34 shows this process. *Note:* If you make a mistake while working with text blocks and want to start over from this point, you can choose Revert from the File menu. Choosing Revert is the same as closing your publication without saving any changes and reopening the original publication.

1. **Click on the text in the left column.**

2. **Point to the + in the lower loop (see Figure 4.34).**

3. **Hold down the mouse button. When the double arrow appears, drag the windowshade up to the 9" mark on the ruler (see Figure 4.34).**

4. **Release the mouse button.**

Notice that the text below the windowshade has moved to the next text block. Now you will divide the text in the left column into two text blocks. The process is to move a windowshade to the desired dividing line, then click on the windowshade loop. An icon appears, representing text covered by moving the windowshade. You place the icon in the desired location and click the mouse button to have the text appear as a text block. Figures 4.35 and 4.36 illustrate this process. (This is tricky; before starting, read through the following six steps, referring to the figures. Then go slowly.)

Figure 4.34
Shortening a text block

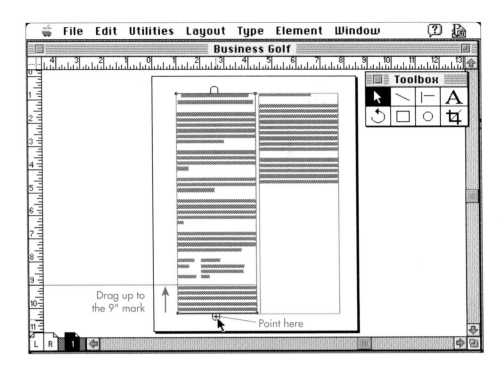

Figure 4.35
Process for dividing
text blocks

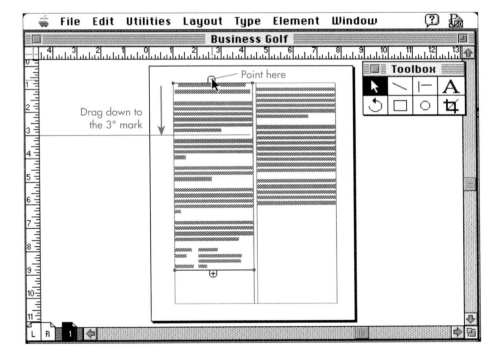

1. **Point to the loop in the top windowshade (see Figure 4.35).**

2. **Hold down the mouse button. When the double arrow appears, drag the windowshade down to the 3" mark (see Figure 4.35).**

3. **Release the mouse button.**

The amount of text covered by the windowshade flows to the next text block. In addition, the text covered by the windowshade can be placed as a separate text block.

4. Click on the loop in the top windowshade.

A text icon appears, representing the text covered by the windowshade.

5. Move the text icon to the upper-left corner of the page (see Figure 4.36).

6. Click the mouse button.

The text flows back as a text block. Now the document has three text blocks.

Moving Text Blocks

Your next step is to move the two large text blocks down the column. The process is to select a text block, hold down the mouse button, and drag the text block to the desired location.

1. Point to the text block in the right column.

2. Hold down the mouse button and wait until you see the four arrows.

3. Drag the text down to the 3¼" mark.

4. Release the mouse button.

5. Repeat the process for the large text block in the left column.

Flowing Text Across Columns

Next you will change the shape of the small text block at the top of the page so text flows across both columns.

1. Click on the small text block.

Notice the corner handles. You will use the lower-right handle to drag the text block across the two columns, as illustrated in Figures 4.37 and 4.38.

2. Point to the lower-right handle (see Figure 4.37).

3. Hold down the mouse button and wait until you see the double arrow.

4. Drag the handle across the page to the right margin of the second column at the 2" mark (see Figure 4.38).

5. Release the mouse button.

The text, an introductory paragraph, flows across the page to fill the new text block shape. Now move this text block down.

6. Point to the text block.

7. Hold down the mouse button and wait until the four arrows appear.

Figure 4.36
Placing the text icon

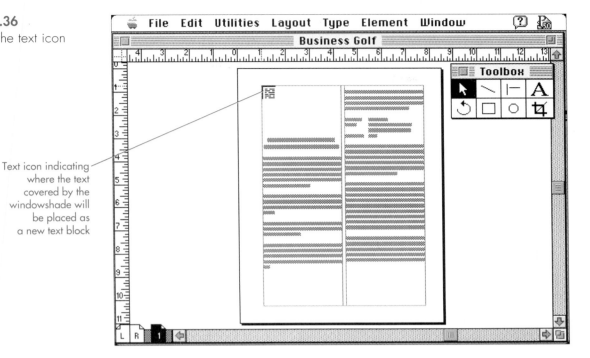

Text icon indicating where the text covered by the windowshade will be placed as a new text block

Figure 4.37
Flowing text across columns

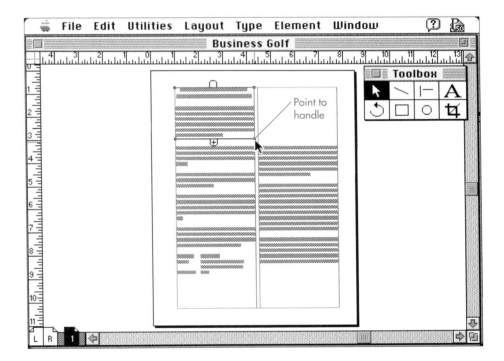

Point to handle

8. Drag the text block down to the 1¾" mark.

9. Release the mouse button.

10. Click on an empty area.

With the changes you have made, there is now room at the top of the document for the resort's logo and room at the bottom for placing a

Figure 4.38
Flowing text across
columns *(continued)*

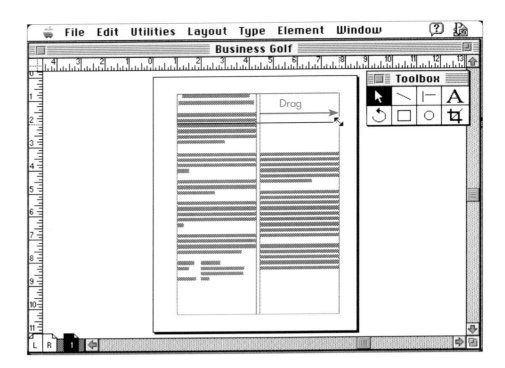

graphic or other text. This section has dealt with rearranging text using text blocks. The document could be further enhanced by changing the type size of the heading and emphasizing the first paragraph with bold, italic, or another type style.

Combining Text Blocks

In the previous section you divided a text block into two text blocks. In this section you will combine two text blocks. The advantage of combining two text blocks is that the text is easier to work with. For example, you may want to combine two adjacent text blocks so that you can move the text as a single block. The process is to select a text block and use the Cut command. Then, using the text tool, click an insertion point inside the other text block. Finally, use the Paste command to place the cut text onto the page.

To practice combining text blocks, you will first type a line of text at the end of the document. This text will be a separate text block that you will combine with the text block above it. Figure 4.39 shows the sentence you will add.

1. Use the Layout menu to change the view to Actual size.

2. Use the scroll bars to display the end of the document.

3. Select the text tool.

4. Select Size from the Type menu and choose 14.

5. Click an insertion point below the end of the document.

Figure 4.39
Sentence to be added

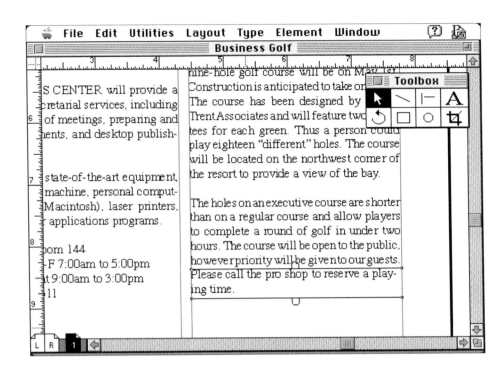

Note: Clicking an insertion point outside of any text block and typing text creates a new text block.

6. **Type the sentence shown in Figure 4.39.**

7. **Use the pointer tool to select the sentence.**

Your screen should resemble Figure 4.39. Notice the empty loops in the windowshades, indicating that this is a separate story as well as a text block.

8. **Select Cut from the Edit menu (⌘-X).**

Now use the text tool to set an insertion point as shown in Figure 4.40.

9. **Select the text tool.**

10. **Click an insertion point (see Figure 4.40).**

11. **Select Paste from the Edit menu (⌘-V).**

12. **Click an insertion point before the *P* in *Please*.**

13. **Press (RETURN) twice.**

14. **Select the pointer tool.**

15. **Click on the new sentence.**

16. **Use the Layout menu to change the view to Fit in window (⌘-W).**

The screen now shows the sentence as part of the larger text block.

Text blocks, like paragraphs, can be copied, moved, and cleared using the Edit menu options. This completes the section on text blocks.

Figure 4.40
Setting an insertion
point

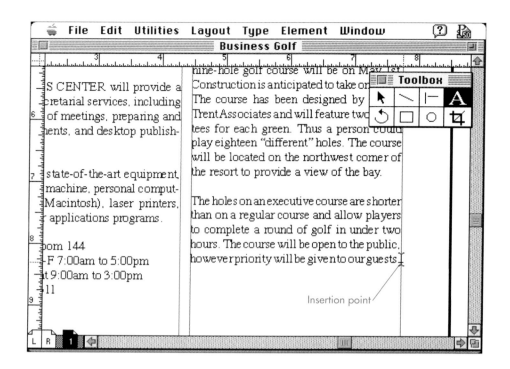

If your study time is up, use the File menu to close the publication without saving.

17. **Close but do not save the publication.**

USING THE CONTROL PALETTE

In this and previous chapters you have been learning how to use the Type menu and the Paragraph specifications dialog box to change the appearance of text and paragraphs by using formatting attributes such as bold and indents. PageMaker provides a shortcut when formatting text and paragraphs called the **Control palette**. In this section you will use the Control palette to make changes in the Business Center document you used earlier. Start by opening a new publication page and placing the Business Center document.

1. **Choose New... from the File menu (⌘-N).**

2. **Click on OK.**

3. **Use the File menu Place... command to import the Business Center document.**

4. **Change the view to 75% and scroll the window to view the top of the publication (see Figure 4.41).**

5. **Click on the text tool.**

6. **Highlight the words** *Business Center* **at the beginning of the document.**

7. **Choose Control palette from the Window menu (⌘-').**

Figure 4.41
Control palette in
character view

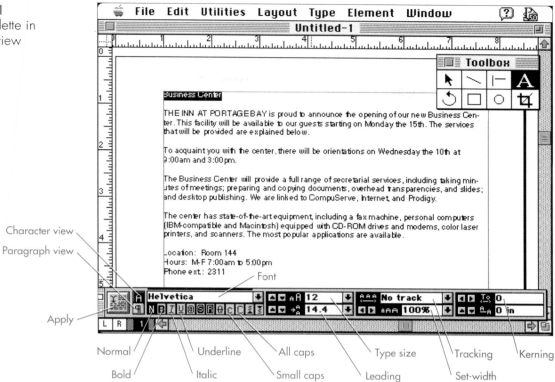

Character view

Paragraph view

Font

Apply

Normal

Bold

Underline

Italic

All caps

Small caps

Type size

Leading

Tracking

Set-width

Kerning

The Control palette appears at the bottom of the screen, as shown in Figure 4.41. There are two views, character and paragraph, that are used when working with text. The **character view** allows you to modify the appearance of text, such as by changing type styles (bold, italic, et cetera), sizes, and fonts; and by changing character spacing (kerning and tracking). Figure 4.41 labels many of the buttons in the character view. The **paragraph view** allows you to align paragraphs, set indents, and specify spacing. Figure 4.42 labels many of the paragraph-view buttons; it also shows the two buttons used to switch between these views. Currently, you should be in character view.

8. Click on the paragraph-view button to change to paragraph view.

9. Click on the character-view button to return to character view.

You will use the Control palette to make several changes in the Business Center publication. Start by changing the *Business Center* heading to Times font, 18 point.

10. Point to the down arrow next to the font box.

11. Hold down the mouse button to display the list of fonts.

12. Drag the pointer to highlight Times, and release the mouse button.

13. Point to the down arrow next to the size box.

14. Hold down the mouse button to display the list of font sizes.

15. Choose 18.

Figure 4.42
Control palette in
paragraph view

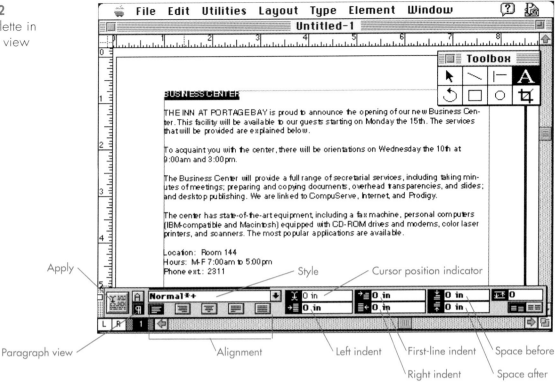

Now use the type style options. After making each change, notice the affect on the heading. With the *Business Center* heading still selected:

16. Click on the bold button.

17. Click on the italic button.

18. Click on the underline button.

19. Click on the small caps button.

20. Click on the all caps button.

21. Click on the normal button.

The spacing options in the Control palette include set-width, kerning, tracking, and leading. The set-width option allows you to adjust the horizontal shape of characters in the selected text. You can use the **nudge buttons** to change the width in increments of 1%, type in a percentage, or use the scroll list to choose a preset percentage. Start by using the nudge buttons.

1. Point to the right arrow next to the set-width option (see Figure 4.43).

2. Click the mouse button.

Notice that the percentage changes to 101%.

3. Continue clicking on the nudge button and viewing the changes to the *BUSINESS CENTER* heading until 110% is displayed.

4. Use the left-arrow nudge button to return the width to 100%.

Now use the scroll list to change the width.

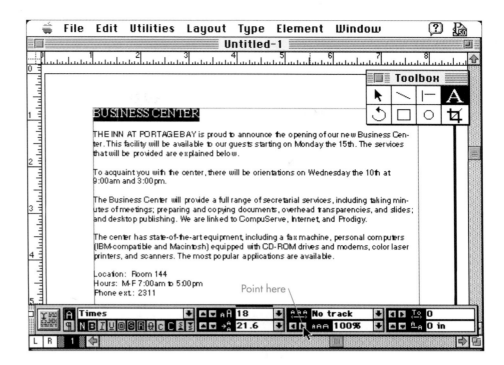

Figure 4.43
Pointing to the nudge button for the set-width option

5. Point to the down arrow next to 100% and hold down the mouse button.

6. Choose 80% and notice the change in the heading.

7. Use the scroll list to change the width to 130% and view the change.

8. Use the scroll list to return the width to normal.

Next use the kerning button to change the spacing between the *A* and *Y* in *BAY*.

9. Click an insertion point between the *A* and *Y* in *BAY*.

10. Click five times on the left-arrow nudge button for the kerning option.

Notice that the setting changes to –0.05, indicating that the spacing has been reduced. For the next two options, tracking and leading, you will need to select a paragraph.

11. Triple-click on the second paragraph to select it.

12. Point to the down arrow for the tracking option and hold down the mouse button.

13. Choose Very loose and notice the result.

14. Choose Very tight from the tracking options.

The character and word spacing is decreased in the paragraph. However, the words are more difficult to read.

15. Change the tracking back to normal.

Now use the leading option to change the line spacing.

16. Point to the down arrow next to the leading option and hold down the mouse button.

17. Choose 11.

Notice that the lines run together because the leading is less than the font size (12 point). The paragraph you are working with may be displayed in Greeked text. If so, you could change the view to Actual size to see how the lines run together.

18. Change the leading to 18.

19. Change the leading to Auto.

Now you will use the paragraph view to make changes in the publication. Start by centering the heading.

1. Click on the paragraph-view button.

2. Select the heading *BUSINESS CENTER*.

3. Click on the center-align button.

Next indent the first line of the first paragraph. There are no nudge buttons or scroll lists for the indent button, so you will need to drag the mouse pointer to select the option and then type in a new setting.

4. Click on the first paragraph.

5. Drag the mouse pointer to select 0, displayed in the first-line indent box (see Figure 4.44).

6. Type *.3*.

7. Click on the Apply button.

The first line of the first paragraph is indented .3 inch. Figure 4.45 shows several changes to the second paragraph. The left and right margins of

Figure 4.44
Selecting the 0 in the first-line indent box

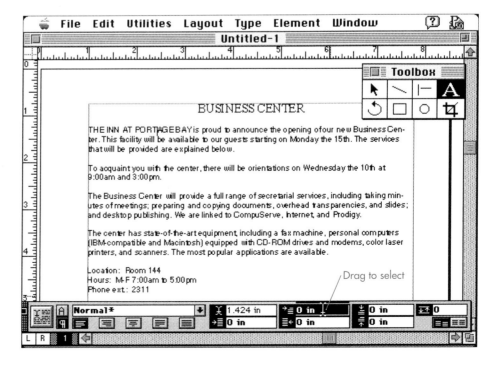

Figure 4.45
Control palette with
several changes

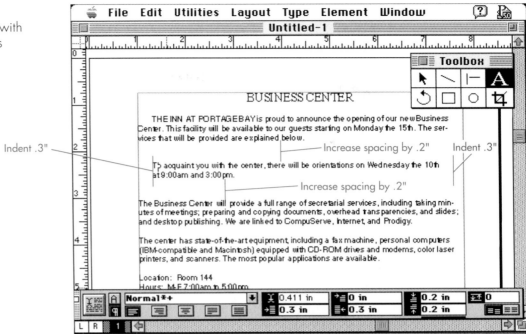

the paragraph are indented .3 inch and the spacing above and below the paragraph has been increased by .2 inch.

8. **Click on the word *To* in the second paragraph.**

9. **On your own, change the settings in the Control palette to duplicate Figure 4.45. Click on the Apply button after each change.**

As you can see, the Control palette is a quick way to make several changes to the text in the publication and to view the results immediately. Continue by removing the Control palette from the Pasteboard and closing the publication.

10. **Choose Control palette from the Window menu (⌘-').**

11. **Use the File menu to close the publication without saving.**

SPECIAL TEXT FEATURES

In this section you will learn how to create four special text features: drop caps, and rotated, flipped, and skewed text.

Creating Drop Caps

A **drop cap** is the first letter in a paragraph which has been enlarged and dropped below the baseline of the first line of the paragraph. A drop cap, as shown in Figure 4.46, helps draw the reader's attention to a particular paragraph. Drop caps are often used at the beginning of a section of a document, such as the beginning of a chapter. You will use a publication called Drop Cap to create the drop cap shown in Figure 4.46.

Figure 4.46
A drop cap

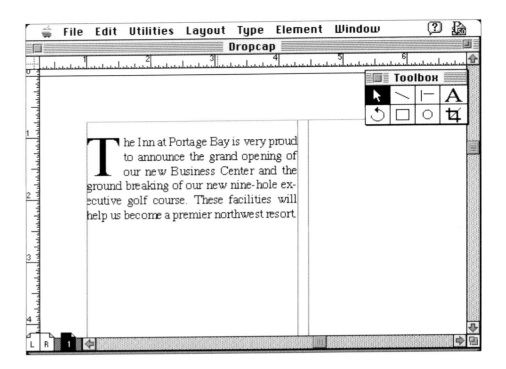

1. **Open Drop Cap.**

The easiest way to create a drop cap is to use the Aldus Additions. These are programs that allow you to automate and enhance many of the PageMaker features. They are found in the Utilities menu. Start by selecting the letter to be changed to a drop cap.

2. **Click on the text tool.**

3. **Drag the I-beam to select the *T* in *The*.**

4. **Choose Aldus Additions from the Utilities menu.**

A list of additions is displayed.

5. **Choose Drop cap...**

The Drop cap dialog box appears. You can drag the dialog box to the bottom of the screen to view the text on the publication page.

6. **Point to the title bar of the dialog box.**

7. **Hold down the mouse button and drag the dialog box down.**

8. **Release the mouse button.**

The dialog box allows you to specify the number of lines for the drop cap and to apply the change without leaving the dialog box. Currently, the size is set to 3. *Note:* Your dialog box may be set to a size other than 3.

9. **If necessary, change the size to 3.**

10. **Click on the Apply button.**

The drop cap is created. To change the size, you must first remove the current drop cap.

11. Click on the Remove button.

12. Change the size to 2.

13. Click on the Apply button.

14. Click on Close to leave the dialog box.

15. Click on a blank area to remove the highlight.

16. Close the publication without saving.

Creating Rotated Text

PageMaker allows you to rotate selected text at any angle. This can create interesting effects for your publication. **Rotated text** is often used along the borders of a publication, as shown in Figure 4.47. In this figure, the resort's name has been rotated 90 degrees and placed along the left side of the page. To rotate text, the text must be a separate text block. Depending on the configuration of your computer and your printer type, the screen display and printed copy of your publication may vary in quality. The following steps lead you through the process of rotating a text block (a heading in this case) that you will create.

1. Choose New... from the File menu (⌘-N).

2. Click on OK.

3. Change the page view to 75% (⌘-7).

4. Scroll the window to view the upper-left corner of the page.

5. Select the text tool.

6. Click an insertion line in the upper-left corner of the page.

Figure 4.47
Example of rotated text

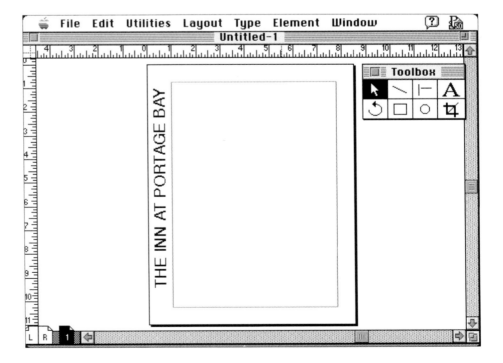

Figure 4.48
Dragging the boundary handle to reduce the size of the text boundary

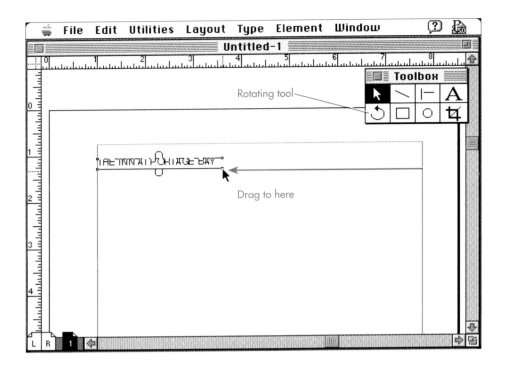

7. Use the Type menu to change the font to Helvetica and the size to 14.

8. Type *THE INN AT PORTAGE BAY.*

9. Select the pointer tool.

10. Click on the text to display the windowshades.

11. Drag the lower-right boundary handle to reduce the size of the text boundary (see Figure 4.48).

The process to rotate text is to select the rotating tool from the Toolbox and point to the text block. Then, hold down the mouse button and slowly move the pointer to create the desired rotation.

12. Click on the rotating tool (see Figure 4.48).

13. Point to the *Y* in *BAY.*

Notice that the pointer changes to a star. The location of the pointer indicates the reference point around which the text rotates.

14. Hold down the mouse button and slowly drag the pointer down a few inches.

Notice that a line follows the pointer.

15. Slowly rotate the line counterclockwise. When the line is at the desired rotation, release the mouse button.

The Undo command can be used to return the text to the original orientation.

16. Choose Undo rotate from the Edit menu.

The Control palette can be used to rotate text more precisely.

17. **With the text block still selected, choose Control palette from the Window menu (⌘-').**

Because a text block is selected, the Control palette displays options that allow you to work with objects (text blocks and graphics). Figure 4.49 labels several of these options. When rotating an object, you need to be concerned with the reference point; that is, the point around which the object rotates. The proxy button displays the reference point and allows you to change it. Figure 4.49 shows the reference point for the text block. Figure 4.50 shows the result of rotating the text block 30 degrees using the rotation option. Complete the following to duplicate Figure 4.50.

18. **Select the 0 in the rotation option box.**

19. **Type 30.**

20. **Click on the Apply button.**

The text block rotates 30 degrees around the reference point. Use the Undo command to return the text block to its original orientation. Then, change the reference point and rotate the object again.

21. **Choose Undo apply from the Edit menu.**

22. **Click on the upper-right corner of the proxy button to change the reference point.**

23. **Change the rotation to 30.**

24. **Click on the Apply button.**

Notice how the text block rotates around the new reference point.

25. **Undo the rotation.**

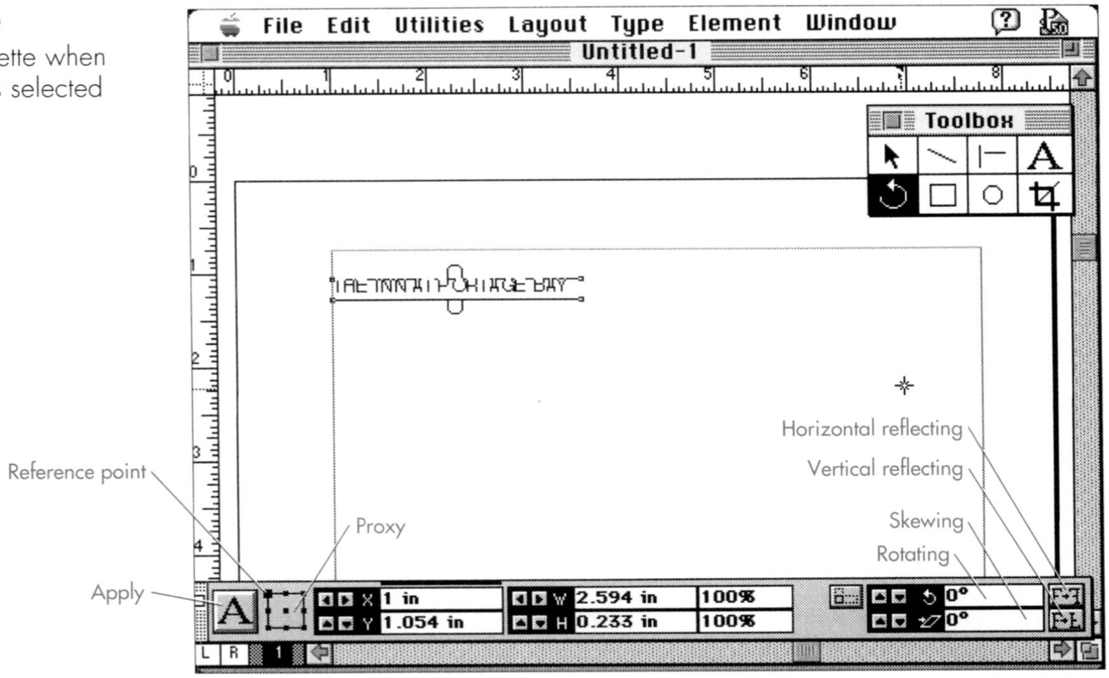

Figure 4.49
Control palette when an object is selected

Figure 4.50
Rotating the text block
30 degrees

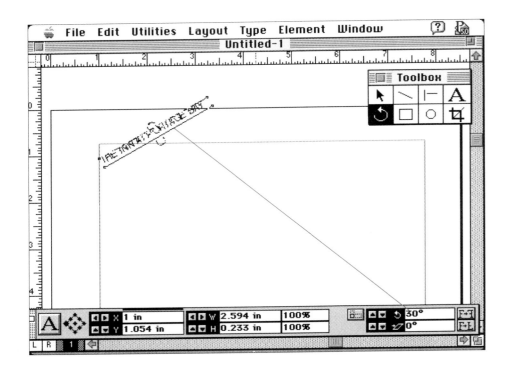

Flipping Text

Two other Control palette options for objects are vertical and horizontal reflecting. These options flip the object vertically and horizontally. **Flipped text** can be used to create mirror images of words. Flipping can also be used with graphics.

1. With the text block selected, click on the horizontal-reflecting button.

2. Click on the button again to reverse the effect.

3. Click on the vertical-reflecting button.

4. Click on the button again to reverse the effect.

Skewing Text

In addition to rotation and flipping objects, you can slant them with the skewing option. **Skewed text** can be used to draw attention to a word or phrase. Skewing can also be used to suggest movement in a graphic. Skewing and flipping together can create shadow effects for characters, words, and graphics.

1. With the text block selected, select the 0 in the skewing option box.

2. Type *36.*

3. Click on the Apply button.

The text is slanted 36 degrees.

4. Change the skew to −20 degrees.

5. Click on the Apply button.

A negative number slants the text in the opposite direction. The rotation and skewing options have nudge buttons so that you can select very fine increments and immediately view the results. This completes the section on special text features. Use the File menu to close the publication.

6. **Close the publication without saving.**

SUMMARY

In this chapter you have learned how to place text into a publication and how to use the pointer and text tools to select a portion of text. You now know how to move, copy, and delete text, and how to work with text blocks. You have also learned how to work with spacing, hyphenation, paragraph alignment, paragraph indentation, and special text features.

KEY TERMS

Clipboard	indents	character view
text tool	tabs	paragraph view
pointer tool	leader	nudge buttons
cut	hyphenation	drop cap
paste	track kerning	rotated text
copy	text block	flipped text
clear	story	skewed text
leading	windowshades	
kerning	Control palette	

QUESTIONS

1. List and explain the three ways to add text to a page.

2. Explain how the Clipboard is used.

3. Describe three ways to select text using the text tool.

4. Explain the process for moving text.

5. Define *leading*. What is its default value?

6. Why would you want to change the leading value?

7. Define *kerning*.

8. PageMaker provides five ways to align paragraphs. List and explain them.

9. List and distinguish between the four types of tabs.

10. When working with paragraphs, why is it important to understand the relationship between spacing and hyphenation?

11. What is a text block; how can it be used?

12. A text block loop can be empty or contain a + or ▼. What does each signify?

13. When would you use the text tool to select text? The pointer tool?

14. What is the value of using the Control palette?

15. What are nudge buttons?

PROJECTS

1. On your data disk is a file called Attractions, developed using Word for Windows. Start a new PageMaker publication, place this document on the page, and edit it to duplicate Figure 4.51. This process involves:

   - using the Control palette to change the heading *AREA ATTRACTIONS* to Helvetica font, size 18, all caps

   - centering the heading

   - justify-aligning all paragraphs

   - setting a left and right indent for the second and third paragraphs at .75 inch

   - inserting tabs (including a decimal tab) below the third paragraph and typing in the admission prices

Figure 4.51
Completed Attractions
publication

AREA ATTRACTIONS

Following is a sample of the most popular seasonal attractions found in our area. There is a comprehensive brochure listing all of the parks, museums, tourist attractions, and tours available in our lobby. Tours of the first two attractions can be arranged at the information desk.

The Skagit Valley Tulip Festival is held early in April. Thousands of visitors flock to the Skagit Valley to enjoy the miles and miles of tulips as they bloom into a dazzling array of colors. Hundreds of varieties of daffodils, tulips, and other spring flowers make this a photographer's and artist's paradise. The climate, soil, and rain combined with the care of the Dutch settlers make the bulb and cut-flower industry one of the most important in the region, with sales estimated at over $14 million. After touring the valley, visitors can enjoy a salmon barbecue, patterned after the native Indian recipes, at the nearby town of La Conner. The Skagit Valley is located on Interstate 5 at Mt. Vernon. The drive takes about one hour and 20 minutes from The Inn at Portage Bay.

The Suquamish Museum is dedicated to the study of the Puget Sound Salish Indians, who were the original inhabitants of this area. Chief Seattle, for whom the City of Seattle is named, was from the Suquamish Tribe. The museum's exhibition, which has toured in Europe, depicts the lines of the Puget Sound Indians prior to and after white settlement through photographs, artifacts, and interviews with tribal elders. The Suquamish Museum is located in one of the most beautiful settings in the Northwest, on the shores of Agate Pass, six miles north of Winslow on Highway 305. The hours are Monday through Thursday 10am - 5pm and Friday through Sunday 10am - 8pm. The admission is:

Adults	2.50
Senior Citizens	2.00
Children	.50

Located on the United States and Canadian border, this park is dedicated to the friendship of the two countries. The park was opened in 1921 and was built with contributions from the schoolchildren in Washington and British Columbia. The Arch monument, which divides the highway, is a symbolic portal for the citizens who visit each country. The beautifully landscaped park provides a serene setting from which to view nearby Birch Bay. The Peace Arch State Park is located on Interstate 5 at the Canadian border. The drive takes about 45 minutes from The Inn at Portage Bay.

Figure 4.52
Edited Contest
publication

THE INN AT PORTAGE BAY
EMPLOYEES' ANNUAL CHILI COOKOFF

As our annual Chili Cookoff approaches you might be interested in the following, which was excerpted from a fact sheet distributed by the International Chili Society.

Chili has long been regarded as America's only original food, having been invented during the Spanish American War by the "Chili Queens" of San Antonio as a way of using old, tough meat in an edible form. No other food in America has developed the passionate following that chili has. Everyone has their favorite chili recipe, generally one made by their mother.

Although chili should be a spicy food, the cartoon ideal of a dish so hot it makes steam come out of your ears is neither realistic nor desirable. Chili should be a spicy, beefy, good-tasting food that everyone can enjoy.

There are no beans in competition chili for severeal reasons. First off, it would make the judging area intolerable. True chili is defined as meat and sauce. Beans made their first appearance in chili courtesy of the Texas prison system, which used beans as filler to stretch out the portions of chili when hoof-and-mouth disease reduced the cattle population one year.

Chili lore includes quotes from Billy the Kid, who refused to rob banks in two Texas towns because they served great chili and he wanted to go there and eat without being disturbed. Heart specialists have long noted that chili made with lean beef or chicken is excellent for your heart due to a special enzyme in the chili powder which serves to assist in the removal of plaque buildup on the artery walls.

The International Chili Society held its first championship in 1967 in Terlingua, Texas, when H.W. Smith of the *New York Times* wrote an article entitled "No One Knows More About Chili Than I Do!" When local Texas author Frank X. Tolbert heard of this, he challenged Smith to a cookoff. Tolbert was so outraged that someone from New York thought they knew more about chili than a Texan, he took ill. His lifelong friend Wick Fowler agreed to defend the Texan. This encounter led to the development of the World Championship Chili Cookoff, for years held in Terlingua.

2. On your data disk is a PageMaker document called Contest. Open this document and, using text blocks, edit it to duplicate Figure 4.52. (This exercise is similar to one you completed earlier in this chapter.) This process involves:

- shortening the text block in the left column
- dividing the text block in the left column into two text blocks
- moving the large text blocks down each column
- flowing the small text block across both columns
- moving the small text block down the page

Figure 4.53
Edited Sites publication

TOURIST SITES

THE INN AT PORTAGE BAY

Following is a sample of the most popular seasonal attractions found in our area. There is a comprehensive brochure listing all of the parks, museums, tourist attractions, and tours available in our lobby.

The Suquamish Museum

The Suquamish Museum is dedicated to the study of the Puget Sound Salish Indians, who were the original inhabitants of this area. Chief Seattle, for whom the City of Seattle is named, was from the Suquamish Tribe. The museum's exhibition, which has toured in Europe, depicts the lines of the Puget Sound Indians prior to and after white settlement through photographs, artifacts, and interviews with tribal elders. The Suquamish Museum is located in one of the most beautiful settings in the Northwest, on the shores of Agate Pass, six miles north of Winslow on Highway 305. The hours are Monday through Thursday 10am - 5pm and Friday through Sunday 10am - 8pm. The admission is $2.50 for adults; $2.00 for senior citizens and $0.50 for children under 12. Special arrangements are available for group or educational tours.

Whale Watching

Each summer visitors are treated to an amazing spectacle as orca whales migrate from the Gulf of California to the waters of Alaska. Their path takes them through the San Juan Islands and provides a rare opportunity to see these beautiful creatures from a respectful distance.

The Tulip Festival

Early in April thousands of visitors flock to the Skagit Valley to enjoy the miles and miles of tulips as they bloom into a dazzling array of colors. Hundreds of varieties of daffodils, tulips, and other spring flowers make this a photographer's and artist's paradise. The climate, soil, and rain combined with the care of the Dutch settlers make the bulb and cut-flower industry one of the most important in the region, with sales estimated at over $14 million. After touring the valley, visitors can enjoy a salmon barbecue, patterned after the native Indian recipes, at the nearby town of La Conner. The Skagit Valley is located on Interstate 5 at Mt. Vernon. The drive takes about one hour and 20 minutes from The Inn at Portage Bay.

The Peace Arch

Located on the United States and Canadian border, this park is dedicated to the friendship of the two countries. The park was opened in 1921 and was built with contributions from school-children in Washington and British Columbia. The Arch monument, which divides the highway, is a symbolic portal for the citizens who visit each country. The beautifully landscaped park provides a serene setting from which to view nearby Birch Bay. The Peace Arch State Park is located on Interstate 5 at the Canadian border. This is a spectacular park and one site that you will not want to miss. The drive takes about 45 minutes from The Inn at Portage Bay.

3. On your data disk is a file called Sites. Open this publication and edit it to duplicate Figure 4.53. This process involves:

- creating a drop cap for the first letter of the first paragraph
- typing *THE INN AT PORTAGE BAY*
- rotating *THE INN AT PORTAGE BAY* text block
- moving the text block to the left side of the page
- increasing the type size
- skewing the heading *TOURIST SITES* by 30 degrees

Figure 4.54
Creating a special
effect

THE INN AT PORTAGE BAY

4. Figure 4.54 shows a special effect created using the skewing process. Create this publication as follows:

- Start a new publication.
- Change the view to Actual size.
- If necessary, change the font to Helvetica.
- Change the font size to 30.
- Type the words *THE INN AT PORTAGE BAY*.
- Copy the text block.
- Position one of the text blocks below the other.
- Flip the bottom text block vertically.
- Skew the bottom text block 50 degrees.
- Align the text blocks as shown in Figure 4.54.
- Experiment by changing the:

(a) nonslanted text to bold

(b) space between characters (with the spacebar and the kerning nudge buttons)

(c) font and font size

(d) skewing degrees

(e) position of the text blocks

Save the publication as Logo.

5. Use the Help function to display the Help window called CONTROL PALETTE: MANIPULATING TEXT. Scroll the window and read the information, then close the Help window.

Upon completion of this chapter you will be able to:

- Distinguish between graphics and text as used in PageMaker

- Distinguish between the types of graphic images used in PageMaker

- Use the PageMaker drawing tools

- Place graphics created using another program

- Modify graphic images

- Work with text and graphics

Working with Graphics

The ability to merge text and graphics and to use them in performing sophisticated design functions separates a desktop publishing program from other software programs. Graphic images are thought of as charts, pictures, drawings, and so on. In a document they attract attention, enhance readability, and make a point. In this chapter you will learn how PageMaker works with graphics as well as how to merge text and graphics.

INDEPENDENT AND INLINE GRAPHICS

PageMaker treats each graphic as an object in the publication. **Graphic objects** are either independent or inline. **Independent graphics** are not part of the text block that surrounds the graphic. Once you have placed an independent graphic, it stays in position until you move it. It can be placed apart from the text, or the text can flow through the graphic, wrap around it, or jump over it. **Inline graphics** are part of the text block that surrounds the graphic. If the text moves, the graphic moves along with it. Inline graphics are useful when you want to embed an illustration in a specific paragraph of a publication and ensure that the illustration will remain in the same position within the paragraph, no matter how the publication is changed. Both independent and inline graphics have a boundary box with handles that are used to resize the graphic.

You determine whether a graphic object is independent or inline by the way you place or paste it. If you have clicked an insertion point on the page using the text tool, the graphic can be placed as an inline graphic. Otherwise it will be placed as an independent graphic.

PageMaker provides three ways to add graphics to a publication. First, you can draw the graphic using one or more of PageMaker's four drawing tools, shown in Figure 5.1. The **drawing tools** allow you to use rectangles, circles, ovals, and straight lines to create graphics. However, none of the tools allow you to make freehand drawings. Second, you can paste a graphic from the Clipboard to the publication page. The graphic can be either one created using another program or one that comes from another PageMaker publication. Third, you can **import** (place) a graphics file created with a program specifically designed to create graphics. Two common graphics programs are paint-type and draw-type programs.

A **paint-type graphic** represents the image as an array of dots, also called pixels. Paint-type images are also referred to as bitmap images. The paint programs used to create these graphics are flexible: They allow you to do freehand drawings, much like an artist would. Paint-type graphics can also be created using a scanner, a machine that converts printed images (such as artwork drawn on paper) or photographs into a graphics file that can be imported into PageMaker.

A **draw-type graphic** represents an image as a geometric shape. That is, each part of the graphic has a precise relationship to the other parts, for example, a pie chart. Each slice or part of the pie makes up an exact percentage of the pie in relationship to all the other slices. Programs that create draw-type graphics include business (charts) and engineering (computer-aided design) as well as illustration programs.

Figure 5.1
PageMaker
drawing tools

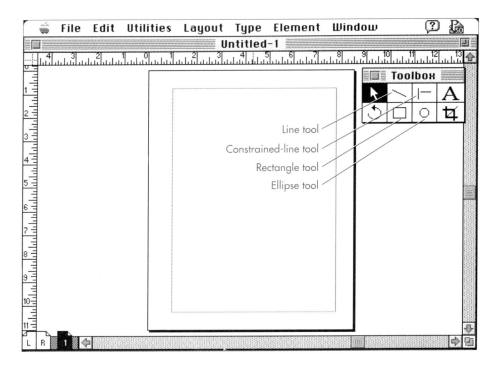

L   R   1

Graphics files created with graphics programs may have an extension identifying the type of file (paint, draw, and so on). For example, a .tiff file name extension identifies the file as a paint-type file in a **tagged image file format (TIFF)**. The icons representing different graphics files as they are imported into PageMaker are:

for a paint-type graphic

for a draw-type graphic

for a scanned image in a tagged image file format (TIFF)

for an image in Encapsulated PostScript (EPS) format

Note: A separate TIFF icon exists even though it is a paint-type file, and a separate PS icon exists even though it is a draw-type file.

WORKING WITH IMPORTED GRAPHICS

In this section you will learn how to import a graphic object created using another program. Then you will learn how to move, resize, and crop the graphic. Last, you will learn how to work with text and graphics.

Placing Graphics

On your data disk is file Fort.tiff, containing a drawing of a historical building, Fort Worden, located near The Inn at Portage Bay. The drawing was scanned and saved as a TIFF file. This paint-type graphic can be imported directly into PageMaker using the Place option from the File menu. To place this graphic on a new PageMaker publication page:

1. Start the PageMaker program.

2. Select New... from the File menu and click on OK in the Page setup dialog box.

With your data disk inserted in the drive:

3. Select Place... from the File menu (⌘-D).

The Place document dialog box appears (see Figure 5.2).

4. If necessary, select the data disk to display a list of the files.

5. If needed, scroll the file names to display Fort.tiff.

6. Click once on Fort.tiff.

Notice that the Place option shows that this graphic will be placed as an independent graphic (see Figure 5.2).

7. Click on OK.

Figure 5.2
Place document
dialog box

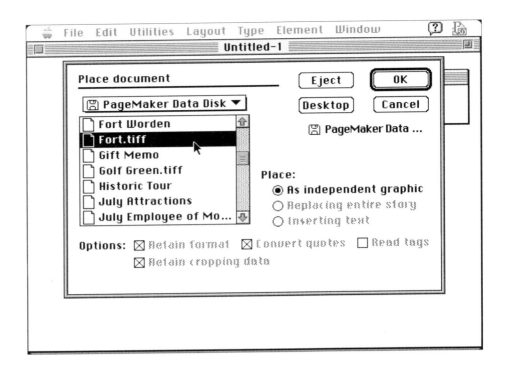

Figure 5.3
Positioning the icon
at the 2" vertical
and horizontal marks

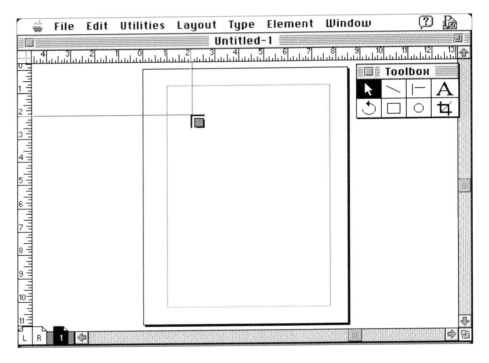

A message may appear, indicating that Fort.tiff was not created with PageMaker 5.0.

8. If the message appears, click on **Open**.

In a few moments the TIFF icon appears.

9. Locate the icon as shown in Figure 5.3, that is, at the 2" vertical and horizontal marks.

10. Click the mouse button to place the graphic.

Figure 5.4
Graphic object with
handles displayed

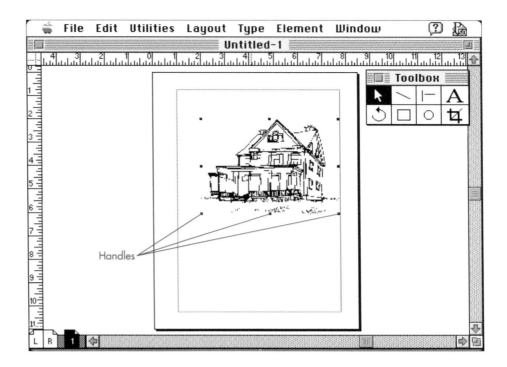

Figure 5.4 shows the graphic object placed on the page. Notice that the object has handles, which indicate it has been selected. You can deselect the object by clicking on a blank area in the publication window or select it by clicking on the object with the pointer or cropping tool. Practice deselecting and selecting the graphic as follows:

11. Point to a blank area.

12. Click the mouse button to deselect the graphic.

13. Point and click on the graphic to select it.

After a graphic object is selected, you can change its lightness as well as copy, move, delete, crop, and resize it.

Changing the Contrast and Lightness of Graphics

PageMaker allows you to change the appearance of a graphic by altering its lightness and contrast with the Image control dialog box. Before using the dialog box, make sure the graphic has been selected (that is, the boundary handles are displayed).

1. Select Image control... from the Element menu.

Figure 5.5 shows the Image control dialog box with the default settings. This dialog box allows you to change the lightness and contrast of the image. The contrast is an adjustment between the image and its background. The shape of the background is outlined by the handles. In this case the background is in the shape of a rectangle. At this point the background is not apparent because it is the same color, white, as the publication page. You can also use the Image control dialog box

Figure 5.5
Image control dialog box with default settings

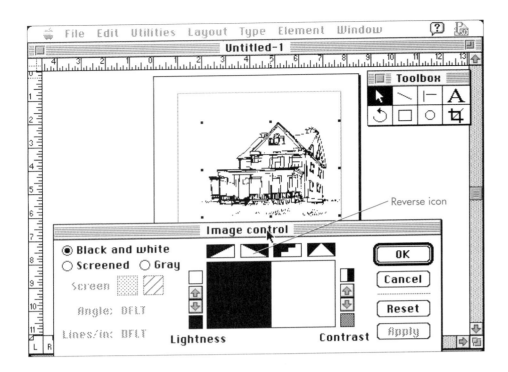

to change the image from black and white to grayscale or screen pattern. A screen pattern will be made up of either dots (the default) or lines.

Notice the Reset button. This button can be used to reset the controls to their default settings. The following steps show you some of the changes you can make to the image using this dialog box. After completing the steps you will use the Reset button to return the settings to their default values. Before making any changes, move the dialog box down to display the image, as shown in Figure 5.5.

1. Point to the word *control* in the title bar of the dialog box.

2. Hold down the mouse button and slowly drag the dialog box to beneath the image.

3. Release the mouse button.

Currently the image is displayed as black lines on a white background. Change the image by reversing the black and white. This can be done with the reverse icon (see Figure 5.5).

4. Click on the reverse icon.

The image is changed to white lines on a black background. Reset the controls, change the image to grayscale, and change the lightness.

5. Click on Reset.

6. Click on Gray.

7. Click on the up arrow above the word *Lightness* to move the slider bar up (see Figure 5.6). *Note:* You can use the mouse pointer to drag the slider bar.

Figure 5.6
Changing the lightness

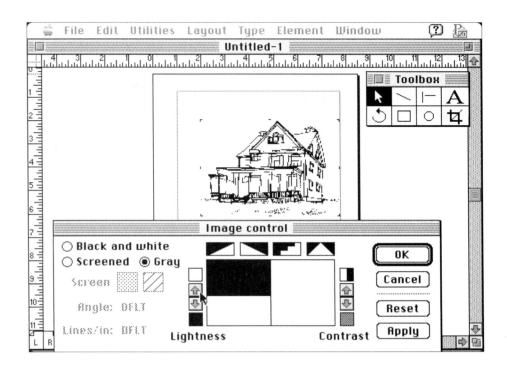

8. Click on Apply.

The image becomes lighter. Now change the grayscale to a screened image.

9. Click on Screened.

The dots making up the image became more visible. You can use the Image control dialog box to experiment with changing the image to obtain the type of effect you desire. For now, reset the controls to their default settings and return to the publication page.

10. Click on Reset.

11. Click on Cancel to remove the dialog box without making any changes to the image.

Resizing a Graphic

To change a graphic's size, you simply drag a handle in the desired direction—toward the graphic to reduce size and away to increase size. When you change the size, the entire graphic stays in view. However, as shown in Figure 5.7, **resizing** the graphic may change its proportions. If you want to maintain the original proportions, hold down (SHIFT) as you resize the graphic. The following steps allow you to duplicate Figure 5.7. Although only one series of steps is needed to duplicate the figure, you will use two series of steps. This will give you practice in reducing and increasing the size of a graphic object.

Start by reducing the size of the graphic object. *Note:* If you make a mistake when working with graphics, you can (in most cases) use the Undo command from the Edit menu to undo the last action.

Figure 5.7
Resizing a graphic

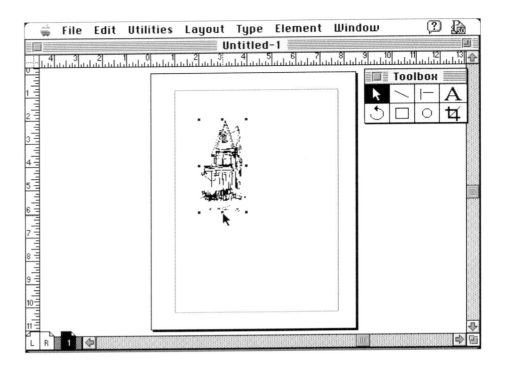

Figure 5.8
Positioning the pointer

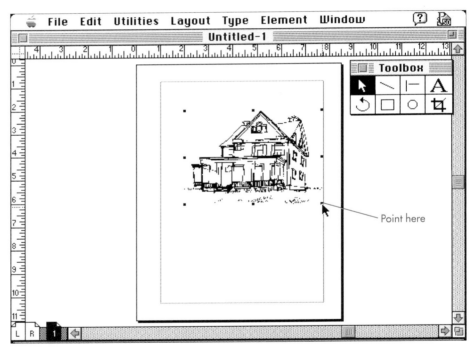

1. Point to the lower-right handle (see Figure 5.8).

2. Hold down the mouse button until the double arrow and a boundary box appear.

3. Drag the handle toward the center of the graphic to the 4" vertical and horizontal marks (see Figure 5.9).

4. Release the mouse button.

Figure 5.9
Dragging the graphic handle toward the center of the graphic

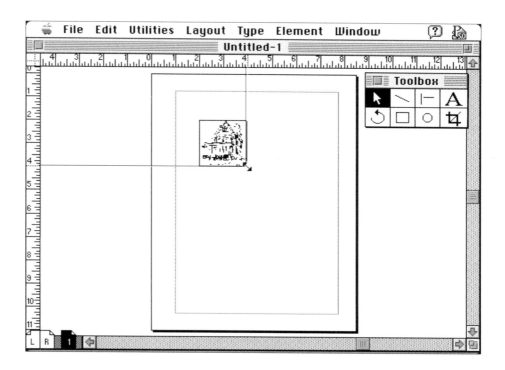

Figure 5.10
Pointing to the middle handle at the bottom of the graphic

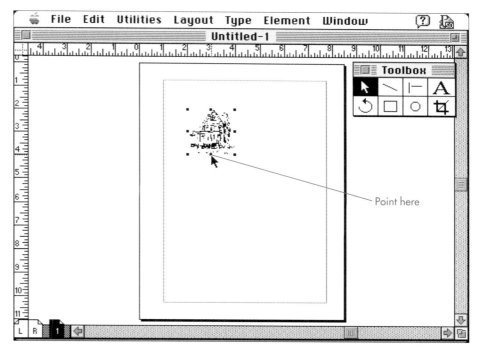

Point here

Now increase the graphic object's size.

5. **Point to the middle handle at the bottom of the graphic (see Figure 5.10).**

6. **Hold down the mouse button until the double arrow appears.**

7. **Drag the handle down to the 6" vertical mark (see Figure 5.7).**

8. **Release the mouse button.**

Figure 5.11
Dragging the handle to the 4" vertical mark

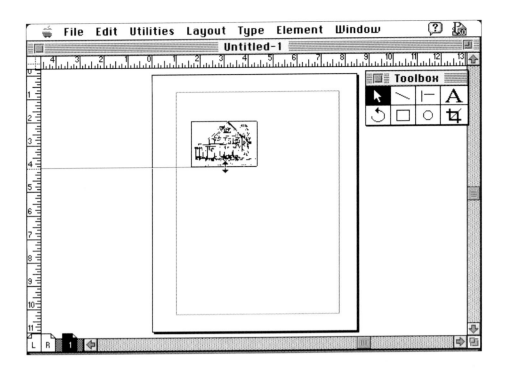

The object's size has been increased, and its proportions have changed. To restore the original proportions, hold down (SHIFT) and press the mouse button.

9. Point to the middle handle at the bottom of the graphic.

10. Hold down (SHIFT).

11. Hold down the mouse button.

The proportions of the original graphic have been restored.

12. Drag the handle up to the 4" vertical mark (see Figure 5.11).

13. Release the mouse button.

14. Release (SHIFT).

Moving, Copying, and Deleting Graphic Objects

The pointer tool can be used to move the graphic object around the page and the Pasteboard. Moving a graphic object does not change its proportions. The process is to point to the graphic (not to a handle), hold down the mouse button until the four arrows appear, drag the graphic to the desired location, and then release the mouse button.

1. Point to the middle of the graphic object.

2. Hold down the mouse button.

3. When the four arrows appear, drag the graphic to the top of the page (see Figure 5.12).

Figure 5.12

Dragging the graphic to the top of the page

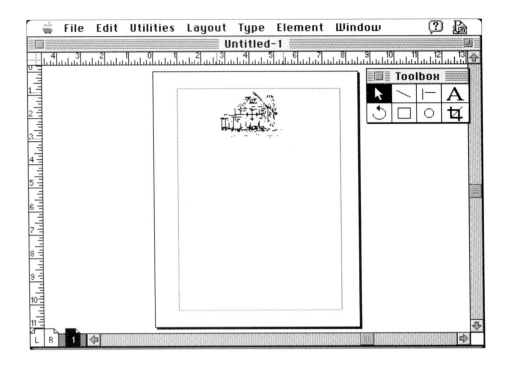

4. **Release the mouse button.**

To copy a graphic, you select the object and choose the Copy option from the Edit menu. Then choose the Paste option from the Edit menu. The graphic object is pasted to a position slightly offset from the original graphic. With the graphic object selected (that is, the handles are visible):

5. **Choose Copy from the Edit menu (⌘-C).**

6. **Choose Paste from the Edit menu (⌘-V).**

The graphic is copied to a position slightly offset from the original. It does not appear that there are two graphics because these graphics overlap. To view both of them, you merely drag one down the page.

7. **Point to the graphic.**

8. **Hold down the mouse button and drag the graphic to the middle of the page (at the 3" horizontal and 4" vertical marks, as shown in Figure 5.13).**

Now both graphics are visible. Only the graphic in the middle of the page displays boundary handles, indicating that it is selected.

To delete a graphic object, select it and then choose Clear from the Edit menu. Delete the graphic at the top of the page as follows:

9. **Click on the graphic at the top of the page to select it.**

10. **Choose Clear from the Edit menu.**

Your page should now resemble Figure 5.14.

Figure 5.13
Dragging the graphic to the middle of the page

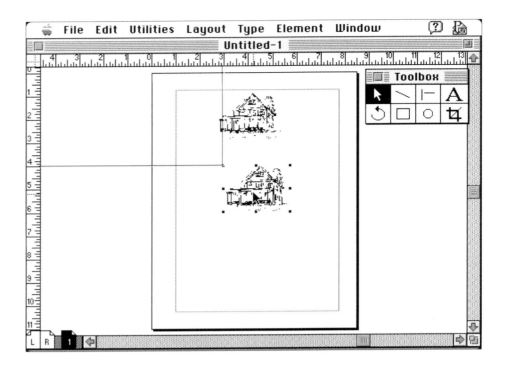

Figure 5.14
Result of deleting one of the graphic objects

Cropping a Graphic PageMaker allows you to crop (trim) an imported graphic. **Cropping** a graphic means changing the amount of the graphic that is visible. To understand cropping, visualize a photograph you want to frame. You decide to try different frame sizes. Say you start out with a frame the same size as the photograph—the entire photo will be in view. As you reduce the frame size (crop), less and less of the photo will be in view. To crop a graphic, you locate the cropping tool on one of the graphic

Figure 5.15
Positioning the
cropping tool

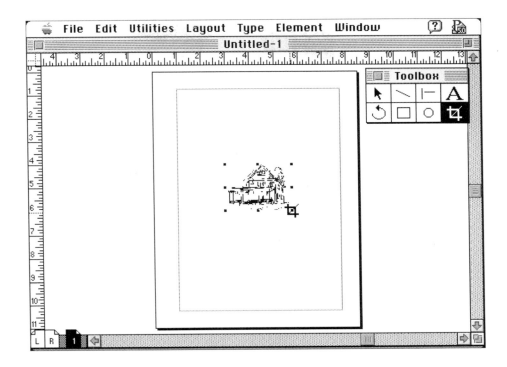

handles and drag the handle to the desired location. When you crop a graphic the part you trimmed off is not deleted; you can use the cropping tool to drag a graphic handle to display the entire graphic again.

1. Click on the cropping tool (⌗) to select it.

2. Position the cropping tool on the graphic image.

3. Click the mouse button to select the graphic object and to display the handles.

4. Position the cropping tool on the lower-right handle (see Figure 5.15).

5. Hold down the mouse button.

6. When the double arrow appears, drag the handle toward the center of the graphic object to the 5" horizontal mark and the 5½" vertical mark (see Figure 5.16).

7. Release the mouse button.

Notice that only part of the graphic is now in view, but, importantly, the entire graphic is still intact. You have changed only the frame size. (Think of the frame as a window through which you view the graphic.) If you wanted to return to the original view, you could use the Undo option from the Edit menu or use the above process to enlarge the frame by dragging away from the graphic rather than toward it. In addition to changing the frame size, you can move the graphic object behind the frame and thus view any part of the graphic. This is done by using the cropping tool to point to the graphic (not a handle), holding down the mouse button, and then moving the graphic as desired.

Figure 5.16
Dragging the handle to the 5" horizontal mark and the 5½" vertical mark

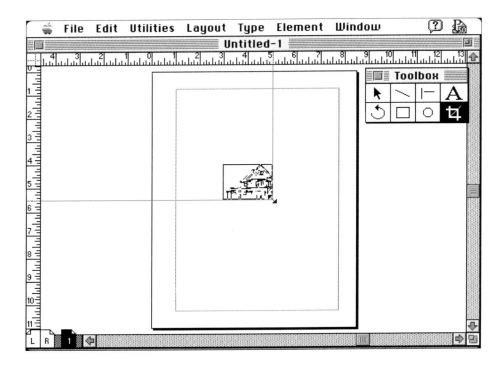

8. Point to the middle of the graphic object.

9. Hold down the mouse button.

10. When the hand icon appears, slowly move it around the frame.

11. Return the graphic to the lower-right corner of the frame (see Figure 5.16).

12. Release the mouse button.

Now return to the original view of the graphic by using the cropping tool to enlarge the frame.

13. Point to the lower-right handle.

14. Drag the handle to enlarge the frame.

The graphic object should resemble Figure 5.14. That is, the entire graphic should be in view and the graphic should be located near the center of the page. The cropping tool is useful because it allows you to select and focus on the part of the graphic most important to you.

WORKING WITH TEXT AND GRAPHICS

Although graphic objects can stand alone on a publication page, they are most often accompanied by text. As mentioned earlier, a graphic object can be either part of the text (inline graphic) or an element separate from the text (independent graphic). An inline graphic becomes a fixed part of a text block. Thus there is little flexibility in how inline graphics and text

Figure 5.17

Integrating text and graphics

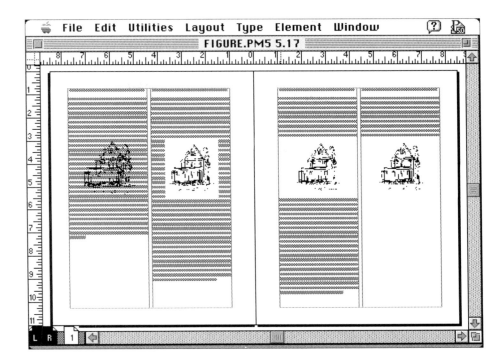

can be manipulated. An independent graphic, however, is separate from the text and can be integrated with text in a variety of ways. In this section you will learn how to work with text and independent graphics.

There are two basic ways to integrate text and graphics. First, you can have the text **flow through** the graphic image—much like superimposing the text on top of the graphic, as shown in Figure 5.17 (left column of left page). Second, you can have the text **wrap around** the graphic. Every graphic object has a border with either a regular (rectangular) or irregular shape. This border determines how close the text will come to the graphic when you specify that text is to wrap around it. There are three ways to flow the text around a graphic, as illustrated in Figure 5.17. You can have the text stop at the top of the graphic and continue to the next column (right column of right page); you can have the text jump over the graphic (left column of right page); and you can have the text flow all around the graphic (right column of left page). To specify the **text wrap**—the wrap and flow options—you use the Text wrap dialog box.

Figure 5.18 shows the Text wrap dialog box. There are three wrap and three text flow options. The first wrap option causes text to flow through the graphic. The second and third wrap options flow text around the graphic, and they represent the graphic object as a regular and irregular shape, respectively. Unless you change it, a graphic object will have a regular (rectangular) border around which text may flow. If you specify that text is to wrap around the graphic, you must also specify how the text will flow, that is, by stopping at the top, jumping over, or flowing completely around the graphic.

Figure 5.18
Text wrap dialog box

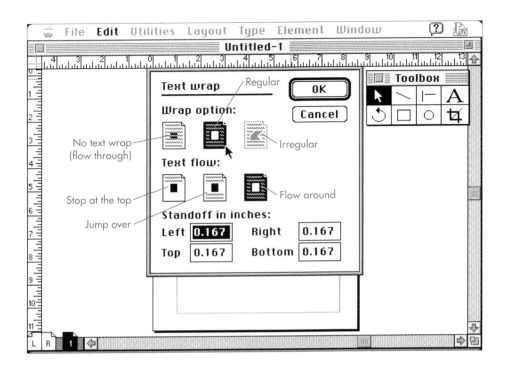

Flowing Text Around a Graphic

On your data disk is file Fort Worden—a one-page, text-only document about Fort Worden created using the word processing program Word for Windows. You will place this document on the publication page and practice flowing text through and around the Fort.tiff graphic with which you've been working. The first step is to move the graphic object to the desired location on the page. (You've just completed this step.) The second step is to specify how you want the text to wrap around the graphic object. Start by making sure the graphic is similar in size and position to the one shown in Figure 5.14. Then complete the following steps to place the text and flow it around the graphic. *Note:* The focus of this section and the comprehensive example later is to study text wrap and text flow techniques. The projects at the end of this chapter, where you will use these techniques, will also address design considerations.

1. **Select the pointer tool.**

2. **Click on the graphic object to select it.**

3. **Select Text wrap... from the Element menu.**

4. **Click on the regular wraparound (middle) icon under Wrap option.**

Notice that the flow-around icon under Text flow is automatically selected and that the Standoff in inches boxes are filled in. The **standoff** is the distance from the graphic to the text.

5. **Click on OK.**

Figure 5.19 shows the boundary box now surrounding the graphic object. When the text flows around the graphic, it stops outside this boundary. Now place the text.

Figure 5.19
Boundary box
surrounding the
graphic object

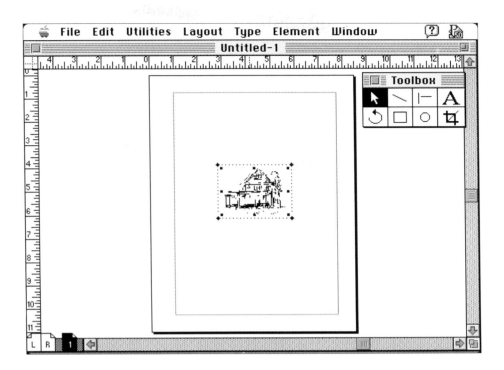

Figure 5.20
Positioning the text icon
at the 3" vertical mark

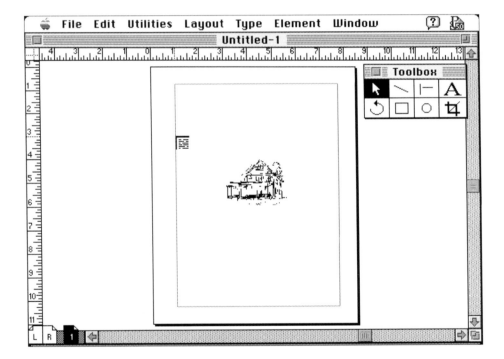

6. Select Place... from the File menu (⌘-D).

7. Select the Fort Worden file from the data disk and click on OK.

8. Position the text icon at the 3" vertical mark (see Figure 5.20).

9. Click the mouse button.

Figure 5.21 shows the text wrapped around the graphic.

Figure 5.21
Text wrapped around
the graphic

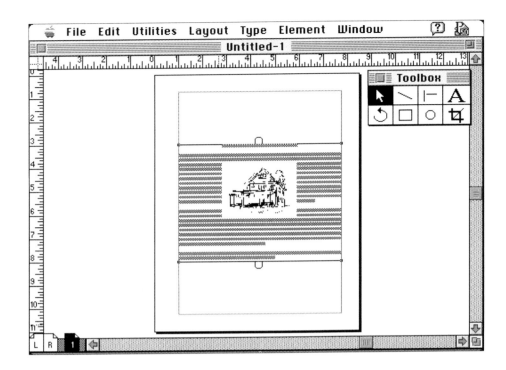

You now have two objects on the page, a graphic and a text block. Each object can be modified, moved, and so on. Remember, always select the object before working with it. Now, select the graphic object and change the text flow.

1. Click on the graphic object to select it.

2. Select Text wrap... from the Element menu.

3. Click on the jump-over (middle) icon under Text flow.

4. Click on OK.

The text now jumps over the graphic.

Flowing Text Through a Graphic

To flow text through a graphic object, select the flow-through icon from the Text wrap dialog box.

1. Choose Text wrap... from the Element menu.

2. Click on the flow-through icon under Wrap option.

3. Click on OK.

The text now flows through the graphic. Before continuing, change the text flow back to wraparound using the following steps.

4. Select Text wrap... from the Element menu.

5. Select the regular wraparound icon under Wrap option.

6. Select the flow-around icon under Text flow.

7. Click on OK.

Changing the Graphic Boundary

You can change the size of a **graphic boundary** by changing the standoff in the Text wrap dialog box or by dragging the boundary lines. You can also change the boundary shape so it is no longer a rectangle. Figure 5.22 shows text flowing around the graphic in an irregular (nonrectangular) shape. To change the boundary, you drag a diamond-shaped boundary handle. (Boundary handles are different from graphic handles.) As you drag a boundary handle, the adjacent handles act as anchors or hinges. Figure 5.22 shows the result of dragging the upper-left handle toward the middle of the graphic. Depending on the desired boundary shape, you may need to add handles. To duplicate Figure 5.22 you need to add two handles. To add a handle, you simply click on the boundary line. To remove a handle, you drag it so that it covers another handle. To make it easier to work with the graphic handles, change the page view to 75% size.

1. Change the page view to 75% (⌘-7).

2. If necessary, use the scroll bars to position the graphic in the middle of the screen.

3. Point to the boundary line at the position shown in Figure 5.23.

4. Click the mouse button to add a handle.

5. Point to the boundary line at the position shown in Figure 5.24.

6. Click the mouse button to add a handle.

Now these two new handles will act as anchors as you drag the upper-left handle to create the new boundary.

7. Point to the upper-left handle on the boundary line.

Figure 5.22
Text flowing around the graphic in an irregular shape

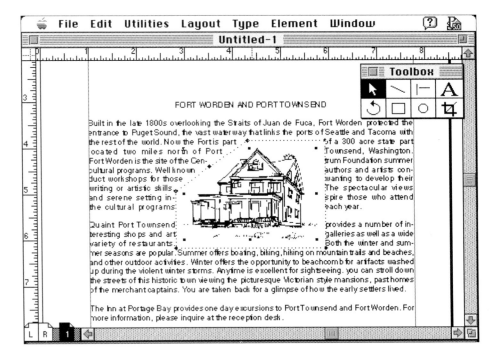

Figure 5.23
Pointing at the boundary line prior to adding a handle

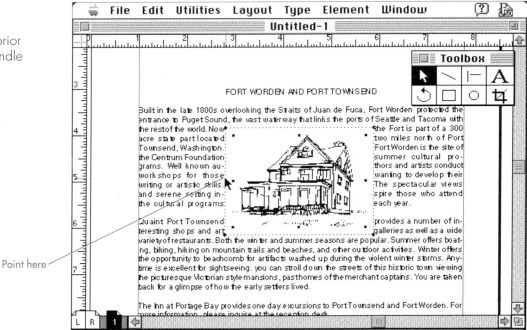

Point here

Figure 5.24
Pointing at the boundary line and clicking to add a handle

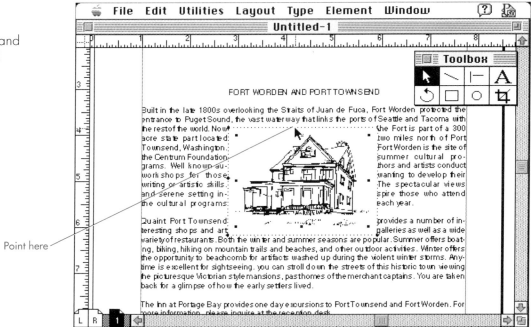

Point here

8. Hold down the mouse button.

9. When the crossbar appears, drag the handle to the position shown in Figure 5.25.

10. Release the mouse button.

The text flows around the graphic object according to the new boundary.

11. Change the page view to Fit in window (⌘-W).

Figure 5.25
Dragging the handle to
create a new boundary

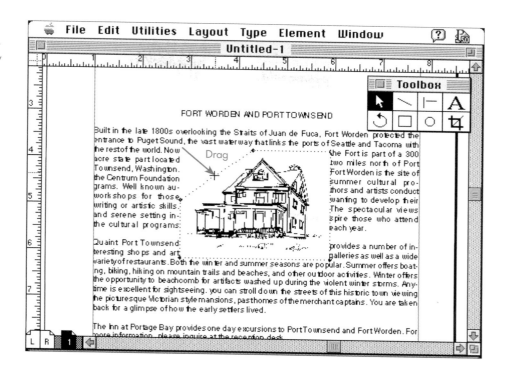

This document is not complete. Later, after you learn to use the drawing tools, you will enhance it to make it more presentable. For now, save the document as file Ft Worden.

12. Select Save as... from the File menu.

Make sure the data disk is selected.

13. Type *Ft Worden*.

14. Click on OK.

15. Select Close from the File menu.

This completes the section on working with text and graphics. If your study time is up, use the File menu to quit PageMaker.

CREATING GRAPHICS USING THE DRAWING TOOLS

In this section you will learn how to use PageMaker's drawing tools to create graphic objects. The process will be to start a new publication, select the desired tool, and draw the graphic. These tools are located in the Toolbox, and to select one you merely click on it. The pointer changes to a **crossbar** (+). Position the crossbar on the page and drag it to draw the graphic. The drawing tools allow you to create rectangles, squares, ovals, circles, and straight lines at any angle. Alone, these tools can create simple shapes; in combination, they can create complex graphics with different fills (shadings) and line types to enhance PageMaker publications.

Below is a brief description of each drawing tool as shown in Figure 5.1.

- The **line tool** draws straight lines at any angle. (Hold down (SHIFT) while drawing the line to draw lines at 45° angles.)

- The **constrained-line tool** draws lines at 45° angles.
- The **rectangle tool** draws rectangles with square corners. (You can select Rounded corners from the Element menu and change the type of corners to rounded. Also, if you hold down (SHIFT) when using the rectangle tool, square shapes are drawn.)
- The **ellipse tool** draws ovals and, when (SHIFT) is held down, circles.

To practice using these tools, you will use the rectangle, ellipse, constrained-line, and line drawing tools to create various graphic objects. Then you will modify, move, and delete the objects.

Drawing Rectangles and Squares

Figure 5.26 shows a graphic object created using the rectangle drawing tool. Complete the following steps to duplicate this figure.

1. Start a new publication.

2. Click on the rectangle tool.

3. Move the pointer to the publication page.

Notice that the pointer changes to a crossbar.

4. Locate the crossbar at the 2" vertical and horizontal marks (see Figure 5.27).

5. Hold down the mouse button and slowly drag the crossbar diagonally (see Figure 5.28).

Figure 5.26
Graphic object created using the rectangle drawing tool

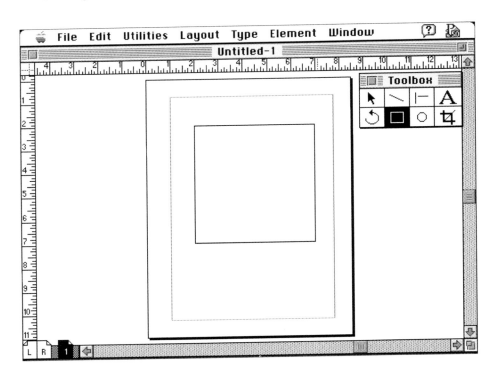

Figure 5.27
Positioning the crossbar at the 2" vertical and horizontal marks

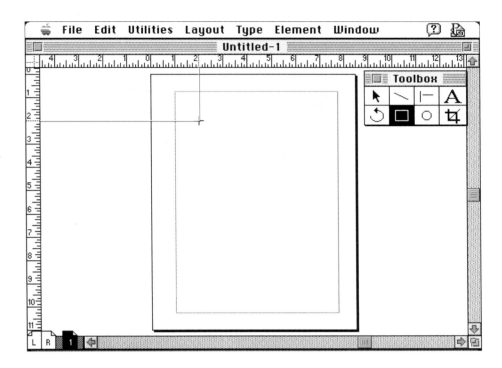

Figure 5.28
Diagonally dragging the crossbar to create the graphic

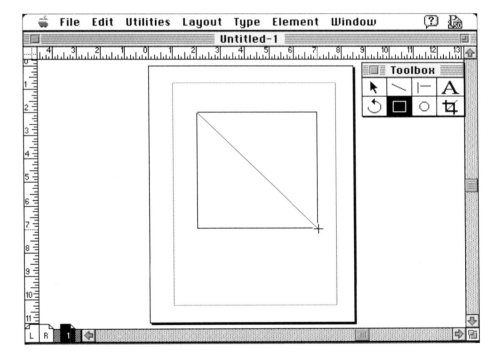

6. **Position the crossbar at the 7" vertical and horizontal marks.**

7. **Release the mouse button.**

The graphic object has been drawn and now can be selected, deselected, resized, moved, enhanced (by changing the lines used for the border and the shading within the graphic), or deleted. Notice the handles on the graphic, indicating that it is selected. You can deselect the graphic by clicking on a blank area.

8. Move the crossbar to a blank area on the publication page.

9. Click the mouse button to deselect the graphic object.

To select the graphic, use the pointer tool.

10. Click on the pointer tool.

11. Point to any border of the graphic.

12. Click the mouse button to select the graphic object.

Now practice resizing and moving the graphic. To resize a graphic, point to any handle and drag the handle to the desired location.

13. Point to the lower-right handle.

14. Hold down the mouse button and drag the handle toward the middle of the graphic.

15. Release the mouse button when the handle is at the 5" vertical and horizontal marks.

16. Point to the middle handle at the bottom of the graphic.

17. Drag the handle down to the 7" vertical mark.

18. Release the mouse button.

PageMaker allows you to reshape a rectangle into a square by holding down (SHIFT) while you drag a handle.

19. Point to the middle handle at the bottom of the graphic.

20. Hold down (SHIFT).

21. Hold down the mouse button.

The rectangle changes to a square. If you drag the handle, the square shape is retained.

22. Drag the handle up 1".

23. Release the mouse button.

24. Release (SHIFT).

To move a PageMaker-drawn graphic, you point to any border (but not to a handle), wait for the pointer to change to four arrows, and drag the graphic to the desired location.

25. Point to any border of the graphic.

26. Hold down the mouse button until the four arrows appear.

27. Drag the graphic to the bottom of the page.

28. Release the mouse button.

29. Now drag the graphic to the middle of the screen.

Two further graphic modifications you can make are to change the width of the borderline and the shading within the border. For rectangular graphic objects, you can also change the shape of the corners. Figure 5.29 shows modifications to the graphic object: The corners have been rounded, the border is thicker, and the graphic is shaded. (Whenever you change the corners, borders, or shading, you must first select the desired graphic object.) With the graphic object selected:

1. Display the Element menu.

2. Choose Rounded corners...

Figure 5.30 shows the Rounded corners dialog box with six choices. The square-corner option is highlighted.

3. Click on the lower-right box.

4. Click on OK.

5. Click on a blank area to remove the handles.

The graphic now appears with rounded corners. Next, change the borderlines and the shading.

6. Click on the graphic to select it.

7. Choose Line from the Element menu.

8. Choose 12 pt.

9. Choose Fill from the Element menu.

10. Choose 20%.

Figure 5.29
Modifications to the graphic object

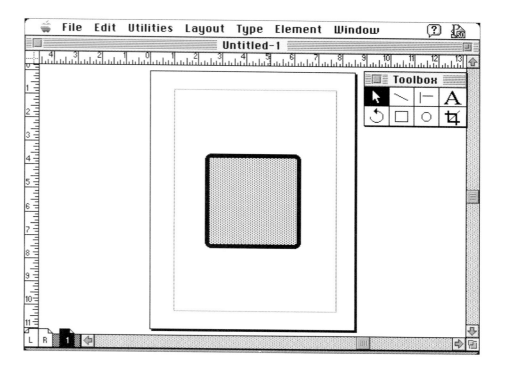

Figure 5.30
Rounded corners
dialog box

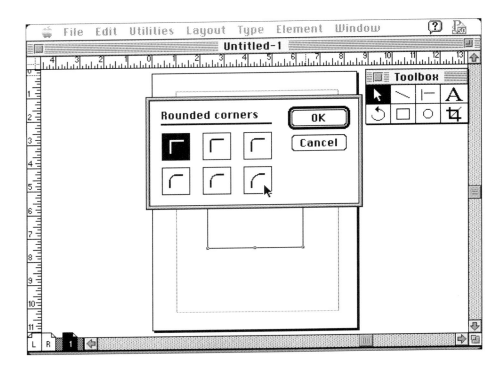

11. Choose Fill and line... from the Element menu.

12. Point to Black in the Color box in the Fill section of the dialog box.

13. Hold down the mouse button and choose Blue.

14. Click on OK.

15. Click on a blank area to remove the handles.

The fill changes to blue.

Your graphic should now resemble Figure 5.29. The Fill and line dialog box can be used to change the fill, line, and color of a graphic. Before continuing, delete this graphic. After a graphic object is selected, it can be deleted with (DELETE) or by choosing Clear from the Edit menu.

16. Click on the graphic to select it.

17. Choose Clear from the Edit menu.

Drawing Ovals and Circles

The process for drawing ovals and circles is the same as for drawing rectangles and squares. You select the drawing tool, position the crossbar on the publication page, and drag the crossbar to create the desired graphic. With the ellipse tool selected, if you hold down (SHIFT) while you drag the crossbar, the graphic will take the shape of a circle. After creating the graphic, you can modify, move, resize, or delete it. Figure 5.31 shows a graphic object created using the ellipse drawing tool. Complete the following steps to draw a graphic similar to the one in Figure 5.31.

Figure 5.31
Graphic object created using the ellipse tool

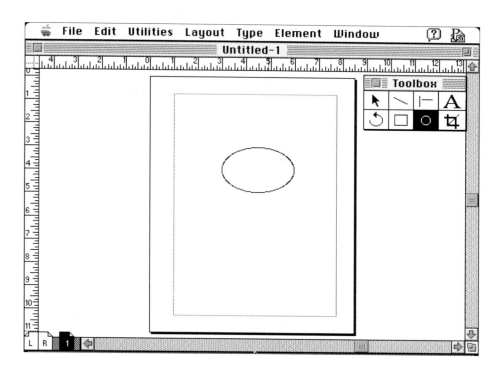

Figure 5.32
Resizing the graphic

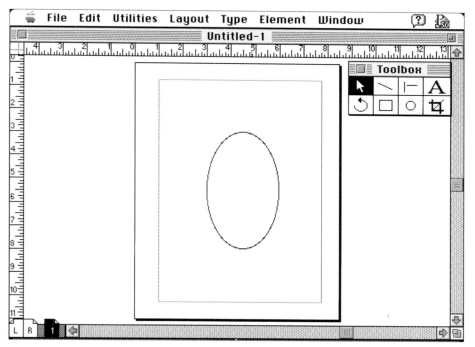

1. **Click on the ellipse tool.**

2. **Position the crossbar at the 3" vertical and horizontal marks.**

3. **Drag the crossbar to the 5" vertical and 6" horizontal marks to approximate the graphic (see Figure 5.31).**

4. **Release the mouse button.**

Notice that there are eight handles with which to resize the graphic. Use the lower-middle handle to resize the graphic to resemble Figure 5.32.

5. Choose the pointer tool.

6. Click on the border of the graphic to display the handles.

7. Point to the lower-middle handle.

8. Drag the handle to the 8" vertical mark to approximate Figure 5.32.

9. Release the mouse button.

Now use (SHIFT) to change the oval to a circle.

10. Point to the lower-middle handle.

11. Hold down (SHIFT) and the mouse button.

12. After the oval changes to a circle, release the mouse button.

13. Release (SHIFT).

Drawing Lines

PageMaker provides two line-drawing tools, the line and the constrained-line. Both allow you to draw straight lines. The difference between them is that the constrained-line tool draws lines only at 45° and 90° angles as measured from the crossbar's arm. The line tool can work like the constrained-line tool if you hold down (SHIFT) as you drag one end of the line.

Practice using the constrained-line tool by drawing lines inside the circle graphic you have just created. Figure 5.33 shows the circle with two lines, one wider than the other. Complete the following steps to duplicate this figure.

Figure 5.33
Circle with two lines, one wider than the other

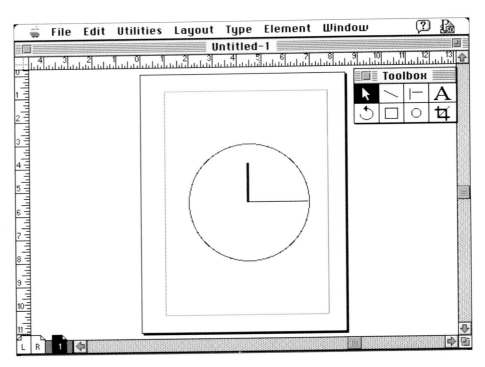

Figure 5.34

Dragging the crossbar across the page to the edge of the circle

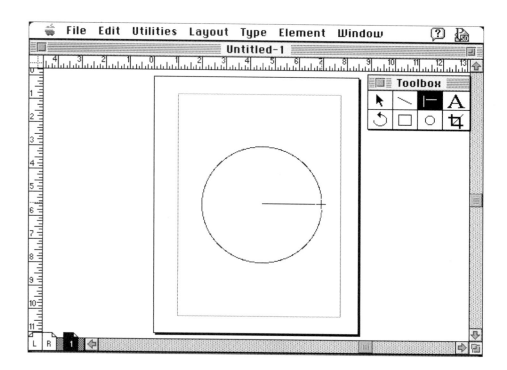

1. Click on the constrained-line tool.

2. Position the crossbar in the middle of the circle.

3. Hold down the mouse button and drag the crossbar across the page to the edge of the circle (see Figure 5.34).

4. Release the mouse button.

The line is a separate graphic object which you can select, deselect, modify, resize, move, and delete. To change the line, you will rotate one end of it around the inside of the circle as though it were the second hand on a clock.

5. Choose the pointer tool.

6. Click on the line to select it and display the handles.

7. Point to the handle at the end of the line (see Figure 5.35).

8. Hold down the mouse button and drag the handle around the inside of the circle.

9. When the handle returns to the starting point, release the mouse button.

Now draw the other line and change its width. To draw a more precise line, change the page view to 50% size.

10. Change the page view to 50% (⌘-5).

11. Use the scroll bars to center the circle on the screen.

12. Choose the constrained-line tool.

Figure 5.35
Pointing to the handle
at the end of the line

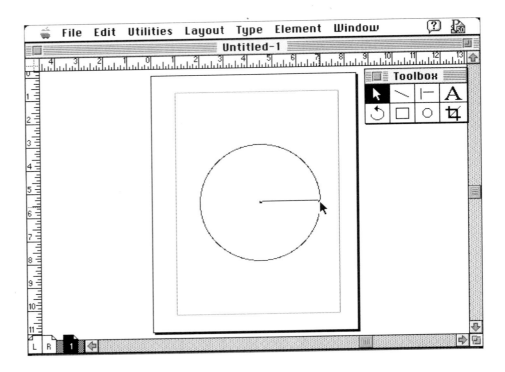

13. Point to the middle of the graphic.

14. Hold down the mouse button and drag the crossbar to the point shown in Figure 5.33.

15. Release the mouse button.

16. Choose Line from the Element menu.

17. Choose 8 pt.

18. Click on a blank area to deselect the graphic.

Your publication page now has three graphic objects, two lines and a circle. You can use the Select all command to select all objects on a publication page. Before continuing, clear the publication page as follows:

19. Choose Select all from the Edit menu (⌘-A).

Notice how all the objects display handles.

20. Choose Clear from the Edit menu (DELETE).

21. Close the publication without saving.

This completes the section on using the drawing tools. If your practice time is up, use the File menu to quit PageMaker.

USING SPECIAL FEATURES

In this section you will learn how to use several special graphics and text features, such as working with multiple graphic objects, using different lines and **fills** (or shades), creating drop shadows, reversing lines, and

Figure 5.36

Three different text and graphic combinations

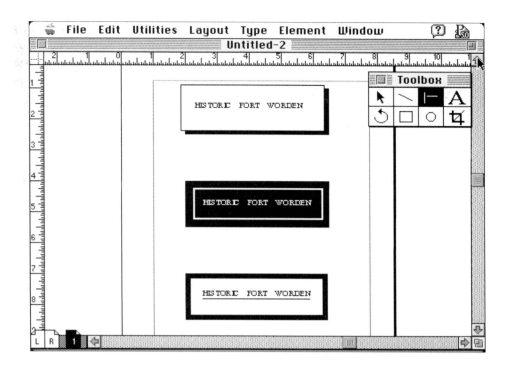

reversing type. Figure 5.36 shows three different text and graphic combinations. Each is a variation of a heading made up of graphic objects created using the drawing tools and the text *HISTORIC FORT WORDEN* placed on top of the graphic objects.

The first heading has a **drop shadow**. Drop shadows are used to give the graphic an illusion of depth. They are created by drawing two identical boxes, one with a **solid shade** for the background and the other with a **paper shade** for the foreground. The paper-shaded graphic is placed over and slightly above and to the left of the solid box. The process is to select the Solid option from the Element Fill menu and draw the first box. Then copy the box so the shapes are identical. Finally, change the shade of the second box to Paper and superimpose it over the first box. The paper shade is the same shade as the publication page. Therefore when you choose this shade, only the border is visible. Complete the following steps to duplicate the first heading.

1. Start a new publication.

2. Select the Fill option from the Element menu and choose Solid.

3. Select the rectangle tool.

4. Position the crossbar at the 1" mark on the vertical ruler and the 2" mark on the horizontal ruler.

5. Drag the crossbar to the 2½" vertical and the 6½" horizontal marks.

6. Release the mouse button.

Now copy the graphic.

7. Select the pointer tool.

8. Select the graphic.

9. Select Copy from the Edit menu (⌘-C).

10. Select Paste from the Edit menu (⌘-V).

The graphic is copied to a position slightly offset from the original. Now change the shade of the copied graphic to Paper and reposition it.

11. Select the Fill option from the Element menu and choose Paper.

12. Point to the middle of the paper-shaded graphic.

13. Hold down the mouse button.

14. When the four arrows appear, drag the box up and to the left and position it on top of the solid graphic (see Figure 5.37).

15. Release the mouse button.

16. Click on a blank area to deselect the graphic.

You now have two graphic objects on the page, one **stacked** on top of the other. You can stack several objects and change the order of the stack. That is, in this example, you can have the solid-shaded graphic placed on top of the paper-shaded graphic. When you stack graphic and text objects, you need to know how to select each object and how to change the order of the stack. To select one of the objects, click on it with the pointer tool. You can also hold down ⌘ while clicking on the objects. As you continue to click, each object in the stack will be selected in turn. To select more than one object at a time, hold down (SHIFT) and click on each object. This procedure is useful for selecting more than one graphic to move. For example, to move the heading

Figure 5.37

Dragging the box to position it on top of the solid graphic

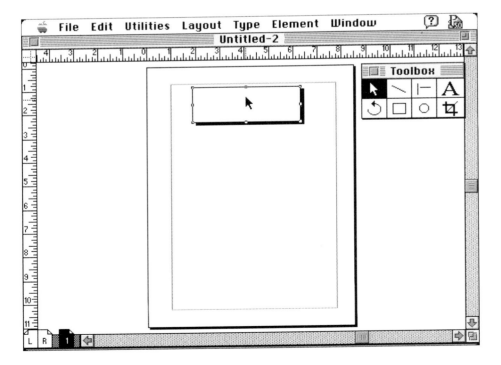

box you have created, you need to select both graphic objects. Practice selecting and moving the heading.

1. Click on the solid-shaded graphic to select it.

2. Hold down (SHIFT) and click on the paper-shaded graphic.

3. Release (SHIFT).

4. Point to the middle of the graphic.

5. Hold down the mouse button until the four arrows appear.

6. Drag the graphic objects down the page.

7. Drag the graphic objects back to the original location.

8. Click on a blank area to deselect the graphic objects.

Now use the Element menu to change the order of the stacked objects. There are two choices in the Element menu used to change this order: Bring to front and Send to back. Because the paper-shaded graphic is on top, you will choose it and send it to the back.

9. Click on the paper-shaded graphic to select it.

10. Display the Element menu.

11. Choose Send to back (⌘-B).

The paper-shaded graphic is placed behind the solid-shaded graphic. Now return to the original stacking order. With the paper-shaded graphic still selected:

12. Choose Bring to front from the Element menu (⌘-F).

Placing Text on a Graphic

Next you will place the title *HISTORIC FORT WORDEN* on the graphic. Use the text tool to type this title on the Pasteboard. Then copy it to the heading. Start by using the Type specifications dialog box to select a large type.

1. Choose Type specs... from the Type menu (⌘-T).

2. Change the point size to 18 and click on OK.

3. Select the text tool.

4. Position the I-beam as shown in Figure 5.38.

5. Click the mouse button to set an insertion point.

6. Change the view to Actual size and scroll the window to view the insertion point.

7. Type *HISTORIC   FORT   WORDEN* (type four spaces between each word).

Figure 5.38
Positioning the I-beam

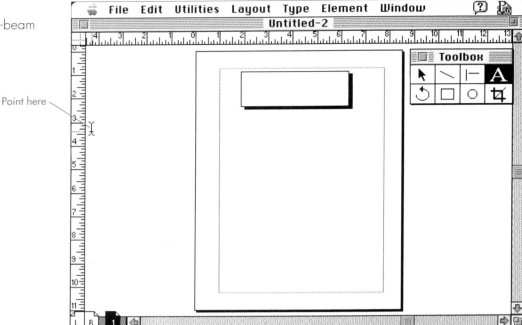

Point here

Figure 5.39
Pointing to a handle

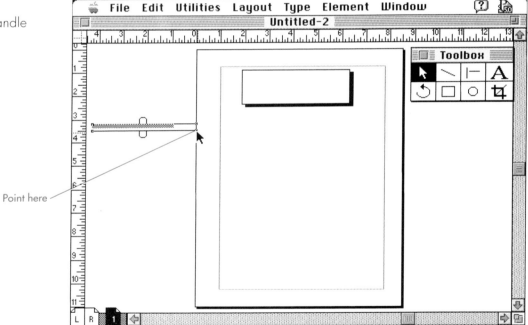

Point here

8. Change the view to Fit in window (⌘-W).

Now, using the pointer tool reduce the size of the text block boundary and drag the text to the graphic.

9. Select the pointer tool.

10. Click on the text to select it.

11. Point to a handle on the right side (see Figure 5.39).

Figure 5.40
Dragging the handle to
reduce the text block
boundary to the same
size as the text

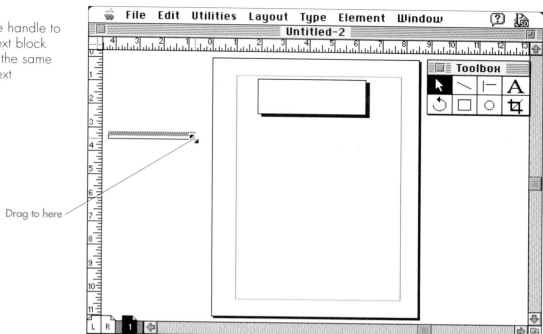

12. **Hold down the mouse button and drag the handle to reduce the text block boundary to the same size as the text (see Figure 5.40).**

13. **Release the mouse button.**

14. **Point to the text and hold down the mouse button.**

15. **When the four arrows appear, drag the text to the center of the graphic.**

16. **Release the mouse button.**

17. **Click on a blank area.**

Now view the text at the actual size.

18. **Change the view to Actual size (⌘-1).**

19. **Scroll the window to view the text.**

The heading should resemble the first graphic object in Figure 5.36.

20. **After viewing the heading, return to the Fit in window view (⌘-W).**

This completes the first heading. The second heading uses two graphic objects and the text title. The same solid-shaded graphic is used as a background. The graphic on top of it is a thin-line rectangle, created using the rectangle drawing tool and selecting Reverse from the Line option of the Element menu. Selecting Reverse changes the line from solid to paper. The text is also reversed so that it appears as a paper image on the solid background. This is done by selecting Reverse from the Type menu Type style option. Start by copying the solid-shaded graphic and drawing the rectangle as a **reverse** line. Then copy the text title and reverse the text type.

1. Click on the solid-shaded graphic to select it.

2. Select Copy from the Edit menu (⌘-C).

3. Select Paste from the Edit menu (⌘-V).

A copy of the graphic appears. Move it to just below the first heading, as shown in Figure 5.36.

4. Point to the graphic.

5. Hold down the mouse button and drag the graphic to just below the first heading.

6. Release the mouse button.

7. Click on a blank area to deselect the graphic.

8. Select 4 pt from the Line option in the Element menu.

9. Select Reverse from the Line option in the Element menu.

10. Select the rectangle tool.

11. Position the crossbar within the graphic (see Figure 5.41).

12. Drag the crossbar to draw the rectangle.

13. Release the mouse button.

Now copy the title from the first heading.

14. Select the pointer tool.

15. Click on the text in the first heading.

16. Select Copy from the Edit menu (⌘-C).

Figure 5.41
Positioning the crossbar within the graphic

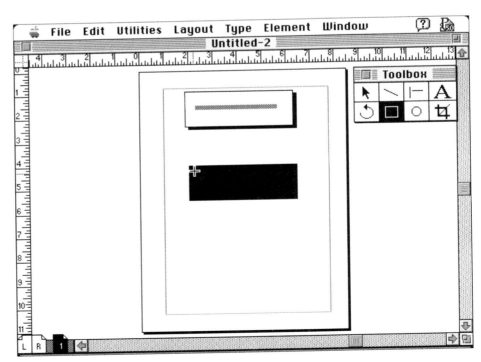

Figure 5.42
Positioning the I-beam

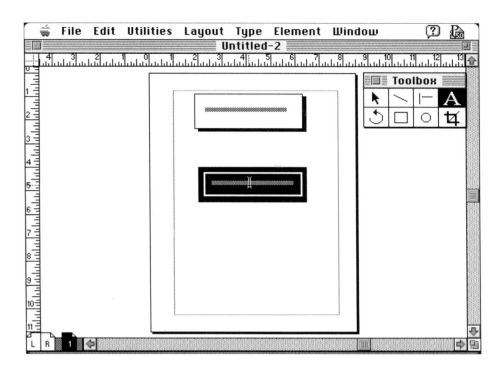

17. Select Paste from the Edit menu (⌘-V).

The title is copied to the page. Now move the title to the heading box and reverse the text.

18. Drag the title to the heading box.

19. Select the text tool.

20. Point to the text with the I-beam (see Figure 5.42).

21. Triple-click the mouse button to select the text.

22. Select Type style from the Type menu.

23. Choose Reverse.

24. Click on a blank area to deselect the text.

25. Click on the pointer tool.

26. Choose Reverse from the Line option in the Element menu to deselect it.

Take a moment to view this new heading.

27. Change the view to Actual size (⌘-1).

28. If necessary, scroll the window to view the heading.

29. Return to the Fit in window view (⌘-W).

This completes the second heading. The third heading is composed of a box drawn with a 12-point, paper-shaded line, and the title with a 2-point underline. To complete this heading:

1. Select 12 pt from the Line option in the Element menu.

2. Select Paper from the Fill option in the Element menu.

3. Select the rectangle tool.

4. Draw the box as shown in Figure 5.36.

Now copy the text from the first heading.

5. Select the pointer tool.

6. On your own, copy the text in the first heading.

7. Drag the text into the bottom heading box.

8. Click on a blank area to deselect the text.

Now draw the underline. First, change the view to Actual size.

9. Change the view to Actual size (⌘-1).

10. Scroll the window to display the bottom heading.

11. Select 2 pt from the Line option in the Element menu.

12. Select the constrained-line tool.

13. Position the crossbar underneath the text.

14. Hold down the mouse button and drag the crossbar to draw the underline.

15. Change the view to Fit in window.

16. Click on a blank area to remove the handles.

17. Change the view to 50% (⌘-5).

18. Use the scroll bars to view all of the headings.

This completes the section on using special features. Only a few of the line and fill options were demonstrated. Several others can be used to enhance the appearance of documents and create special effects when working with graphic objects. (*Note:* Some printers will not print reverse text.)

Before continuing, clear the publication page as follows:

19. Choose Select all from the Edit menu (⌘-A).

20. Choose Clear from the Edit menu (DELETE).

21. Close the publication without saving.

If your practice time is up, use the File menu to quit PageMaker.

TRANSFORMING A GRAPHIC

In Chapter 4 you learned how to create special effects by rotating, reflecting, and skewing text. These effects can also be applied to graphic

Figure 5.43

Graphic transformed by rotating, reflecting, and skewing

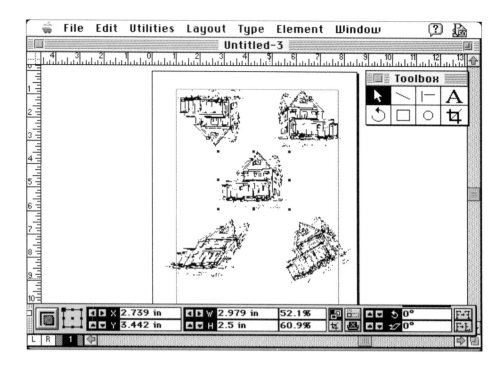

objects. Complete the following to individually create the effects shown in Figure 5.43.

1. **Start a new publication and place the Fort.tiff graphic.**

2. **Change the size of the graphic to approximately half of its original size.**

3. **Display the Window menu.**

4. **Choose Control palette (⌘-').**

Your screen should resemble Figure 5.44. Now use the Control palette to change the appearance of the graphic.

5. **Click on the horizontal-reflecting button (see Figure 5.44).**

6. **Click on the horizontal-reflecting button again.**

7. **Click on the vertical-reflecting button.**

8. **Click on the vertical-reflecting button again.**

9. **Change the rotation to 30 degrees.**

10. **Click on the Apply button.**

11. **Change the rotation to 45, 90, and 180 degrees, clicking on the Apply button each time.**

12. **Change the rotation to 0 degrees and click on the Apply button.**

13. **Change the skew to 30 degrees and click on the Apply button.**

14. **Change the skew to –30 degrees and click on the Apply button.**

Figure 5.44
Graphic after the
contrast has been
changed

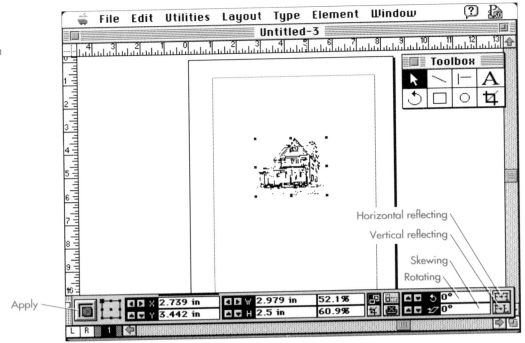

15. Change the rotation and the skew to 40 degrees and click on the Apply button.

16. Change the rotation and skew to 0 degrees and click on the Apply button.

As you can see, there is quite a variety of special effects and combinations of special effects that can be created.

17. Close the Control palette.

18. Close the publication without saving.

A COMPREHENSIVE EXERCISE

In this final section you will use the techniques you have learned in this chapter to enhance the Ft Worden document. Figure 5.45 shows the document with the changes you will make. They are:

- moving the text and graphic up the page
- changing the upper-right boundary
- creating a shaded boundary around the entire document
- creating a box at the bottom of the document
- inserting text into the box

1. Open Ft Worden.

2. If necessary, change the view to Fit in window (⌘-W).

Figure 5.45
Changes to the
Ft Worden publication

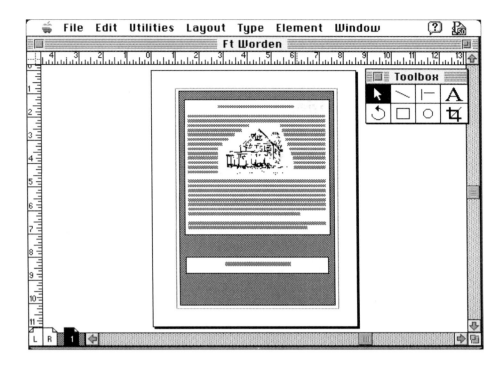

The first step is to move the text and the graphic object up the page. The process is to select both the text and the graphic. Then, using the pointer tool, drag them up the page together.

3. Click on the text to select it.

4. Hold down (SHIFT) and click on the graphic to select it.

5. Release (SHIFT).

6. Point to the graphic.

7. Hold down the mouse button.

8. When the four arrows appear, drag the objects up to the 1½" vertical mark (see Figure 5.46).

9. Release the mouse button.

10. Click on a blank area to deselect the objects.

Now change the upper-right graphic boundary. The process is to click on the boundary at either side of the upper-right corner to set anchor points. Then drag the corner in to create the new boundary. (This is the same process you carried out earlier in the chapter when you changed the upper-left side boundary.)

1. Change the page view to 75% (⌘-7).

2. If necessary, use the scroll bars to center the graphic onscreen.

3. Click on the graphic to select it.

4. Point to the top boundary line (see Figure 5.47).

Figure 5.46
Dragging the objects to
the 1½" vertical mark

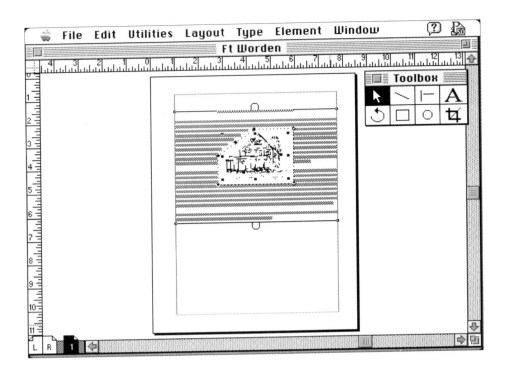

Figure 5.47
Pointing to the top
boundary line

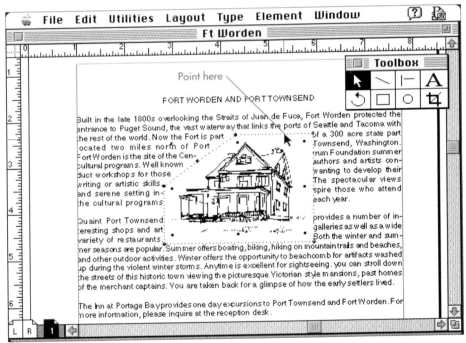

5. **Click the mouse button to set an anchor point.**

6. **Point to the right boundary line (see Figure 5.48).**

7. **Click the mouse button to set an anchor point.**

8. **Point to the upper-right boundary and drag the handle
   (see Figure 5.49).**

9. **Release the mouse button.**

Figure 5.48
Pointing to the right
boundary line

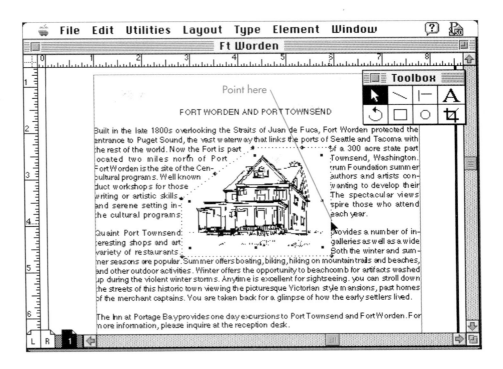

Figure 5.49
Dragging the handle

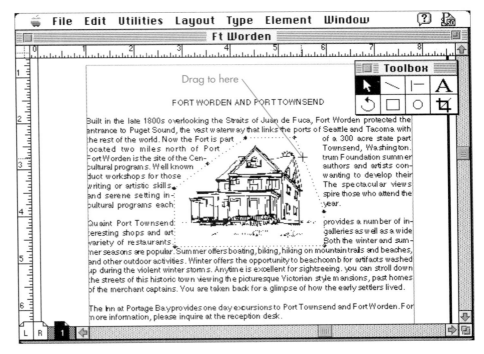

The text flows around the new boundary line.

10. Change the page view to Fit in window (⌘-W).

Next you will create a shaded border around the document, which requires resizing the text to allow for the border.

1. Click on the text to select it.

2. Point to the lower-right handle of the text block.

Figure 5.50
Dragging the handle
to the 7¼" mark

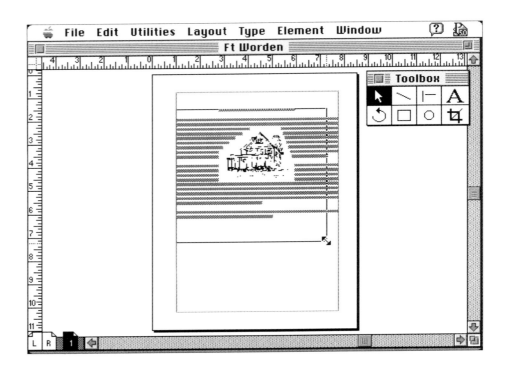

3. Hold down the mouse button and drag the handle to the 7¼" mark on the horizontal and vertical rulers (see Figure 5.50).

4. Release the mouse button.

5. Point to the lower-left handle.

6. Hold down the mouse button and drag the handle to the 1½" mark on the horizontal ruler and the 7¼" mark on the vertical ruler (see Figure 5.51).

7. Release the mouse button.

Now create the shaded border around the text, which requires drawing two rectangles—one, paper shaded, the other, 40% shaded. The stacking order will be, from front to back: the text, the graphic object, the paper-shaded drawing, and the 40%-shaded drawing.

1. Click on a blank area to deselect the text.

2. Select Paper from the Fill option in the Element menu.

3. Select the rectangle tool.

4. Draw a rectangle around the text as shown in Figure 5.52.

5. Select Send to back from the Element menu (⌘-B).

6. Click on a blank area to deselect the rectangle.

7. Select 40% from the Fill option in the Element menu.

8. Draw another rectangle just inside the margin guides (see Figure 5.53).

9. Select Send to back from the Element menu (⌘-B).

Figure 5.51
Dragging the handle
to the 1½" mark

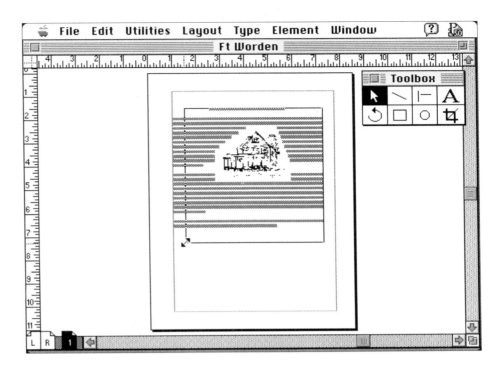

Figure 5.52
Rectangle drawn
around the text

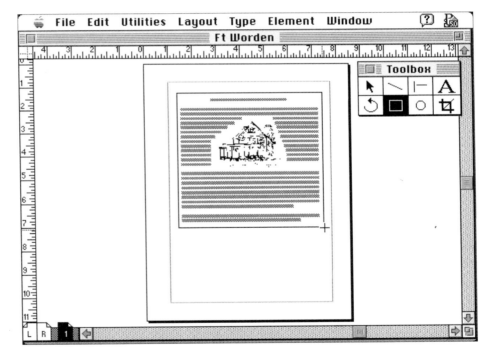

10. Click on a blank area to deselect the rectangle.

Now create the box at the bottom of the document.

1. Select Paper from the Fill option in the Element menu.

2. Draw the box as shown in Figure 5.45.

Finally, type the text on the Pasteboard and move it into the box.

Figure 5.53

Rectangle drawn just inside the margin guides

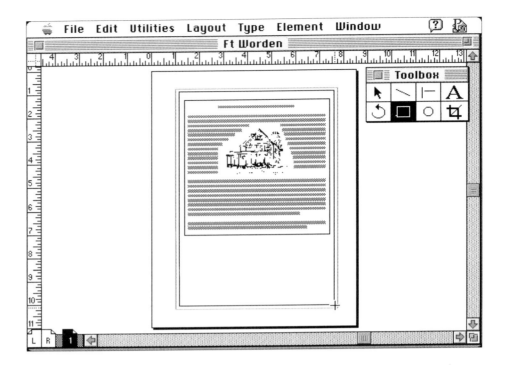

3. Select the text tool.

4. Select Size from the Type menu.

5. Choose 18 point.

6. Position the I-beam on the Pasteboard outside the page.

7. Click the mouse button to set an insertion point.

8. Change the view to Actual size (⌘-1).

9. Type *HISTORICAL   REGISTRY* (type four spaces between the words).

10. Change the view to Fit in window (⌘-W).

11. Select the pointer tool.

Now reduce the text block to fit it within the box.

12. Click on the text to select it.

13. Point to a right handle of the text block boundary.

14. Hold down the mouse button and drag the handle to reduce the text block boundary to the same size as the text.

15. Release the mouse button.

Now move the text block to the center of the box.

16. Drag the text to the center of the box.

17. Click on a blank area to deselect the text.

18. Change the page view to 75% and use the scroll bars to view the document.

19. Save the publication as Ft Worden 2.

20. Close the publication.

This completes the comprehensive example. If your practice time is up, use the File menu to quit PageMaker.

SUMMARY

You have learned one of the most important and powerful features of PageMaker—how to work with graphics. You know how to import graphics developed with another program and how to use the drawing tools to create graphics and enhance PageMaker documents. You have also learned how to resize, crop, move, and delete graphics as well as how to integrate graphics and text.

KEY TERMS

graphic objects	resizing	constrained-line tool
independent graphics	cropping	rectangle tool
inline graphics	flow through	ellipse tool
drawing tools	wrap around	fill
import	text wrap	drop shadow
paint-type graphic	standoff	solid shade
draw-type graphic	graphic boundary	paper shade
tagged image file format (TIFF)	crossbar	stacked
	line tool	reverse

QUESTIONS

1. Distinguish between independent and inline graphics.

2. Describe the three ways to add graphics to a publication.

3. Distinguish between a paint-type and a draw-type graphic.

4. What are the steps for importing a graphic?

5. How do you resize a graphic?

6. Explain what is meant by cropping a graphic.

7. List and briefly explain the use of each PageMaker drawing tool.

8. List and briefly explain the three ways to wrap text around a graphic.

9. What is the process for changing a graphic boundary?

10. What is meant by *standoff*?

11. How do you (1) individually select graphic objects that are stacked, (2) have more than one graphic object selected at a time, and (3) select all graphic objects on a page?

12. Explain how the Line and Fill options might be used to enhance a graphic object.

PROJECTS

1. To practice the skills you have learned in Chapter 5, you will create the publication shown in Figure 5.54, a flyer used to promote the Portage Bay Golf Club. On your data disk are two files you will use. Bay Golf Club is a text file created using Microsoft Word. Ninth Green is a file containing a graphic, the ninth green. You will start a new publication, place these two files, and edit the document to duplicate Figure 5.54. Depending on the font you use and the placement of the graphic on the page, your finished document may not match the figure exactly. The steps are:

   ■ Start a new publication.

   ■ Place the Ninth Green graphic in the middle of the page.

   ■ Select the regular wraparound option from the Text wrap dialog box.

   ■ Place the Bay Golf Club text file.

   ■ Use the text tool to highlight all the text; change the type to Helvetica 12 or a similar font.

   ■ Move the text down the page to allow room for a heading.

   ■ Change the type to a larger size, such as 24 point.

   ■ On the Pasteboard, type the heading *PORTAGE BAY GOLF CLUB* with three spaces between each word.

   ■ On another area of the Pasteboard, draw a drop-shadow box large enough to surround the heading.

   ■ Place the heading over the box.

   ■ Move the heading and box to the top of the page. *Hint:* Use (SHIFT) and the pointer tool to select all three components of the heading.

   ■ Change the boundary lines of the graphic to create the irregular shape. *Hint:* Change the page view to Actual size. You will need to set anchors and move the boundary line at several points. Again, it is not necessary to duplicate the figure exactly.

Figure 5.54
Project 5.1—
Golf Club flyer

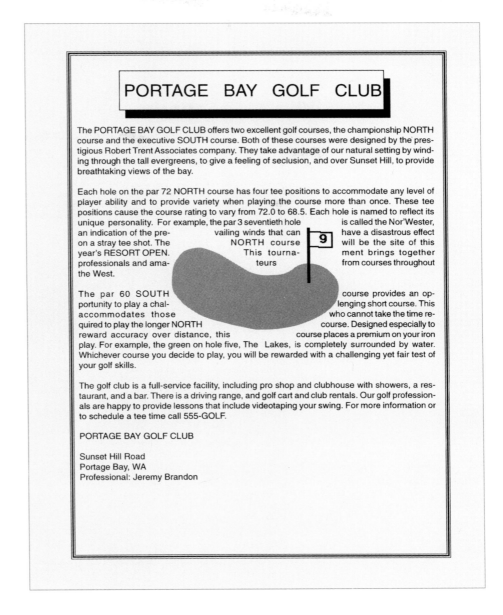

PORTAGE BAY GOLF CLUB

The PORTAGE BAY GOLF CLUB offers two excellent golf courses, the championship NORTH course and the executive SOUTH course. Both of these courses were designed by the prestigious Robert Trent Associates company. They take advantage of our natural setting by winding through the tall evergreens, to give a feeling of seclusion, and over Sunset Hill, to provide breathtaking views of the bay.

Each hole on the par 72 NORTH course has four tee positions to accommodate any level of player ability and to provide variety when playing the course more than once. These tee positions cause the course rating to vary from 72.0 to 68.5. Each hole is named to reflect its unique personality. For example, the par 3 seventieth hole is called the Nor'Wester, an indication of the pre- vailing winds that can have a disastrous effect on a stray tee shot. The NORTH course will be the site of this year's RESORT OPEN. This tourna- ment brings together professionals and ama- teurs from courses throughout the West.

The par 60 SOUTH course provides an op- portunity to play a chal- lenging short course. This accommodates those who cannot take the time re- quired to play the longer NORTH course. Designed especially to reward accuracy over distance, this course places a premium on your iron play. For example, the green on hole five, The Lakes, is completely surrounded by water. Whichever course you decide to play, you will be rewarded with a challenging yet fair test of your golf skills.

The golf club is a full-service facility, including pro shop and clubhouse with showers, a restaurant, and a bar. There is a driving range, and golf cart and club rentals. Our golf professionals are happy to provide lessons that include videotaping your swing. For more information or to schedule a tee time call 555-GOLF.

PORTAGE BAY GOLF CLUB

Sunset Hill Road
Portage Bay, WA
Professional: Jeremy Brandon

- Draw a triple-line border slightly larger than the margin guides.
- Print the publication.
- Save the publication as Golf Club Flyer.

2. Project 1 let you practice the skills you have learned in this chapter. You may have noticed that when you wrap text around a graphic, the text may become difficult to read. Figure 5.55 shows the same graphic and text as in Project 1 but with the following changes:

- The publication is two-column.
- The graphic is placed over both columns.
- The text is wrapped around a graphic shape.

Figure 5.55
Project 5.2—Revised
Golf Club flyer

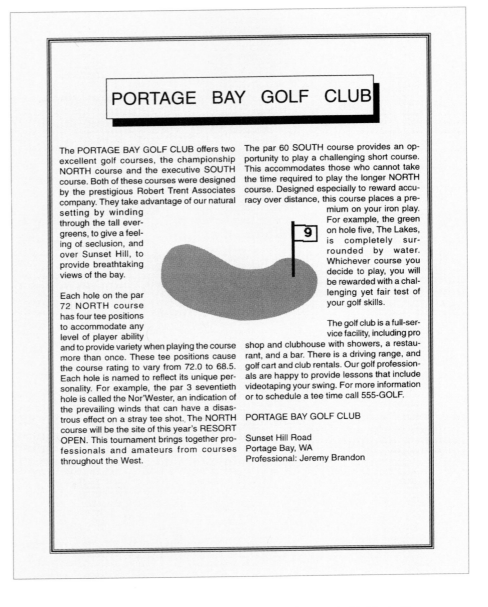

On your own, using the Ninth Green and Bay Golf Club files, create a new publication that resembles Figure 5.55. Save the publication as Golf Club Flyer 2 and print it.

3. Using the Fort Worden and Fort.tiff files, create a publication that is similar to the comprehensive exercise in the last section of Chapter 5. Change the layout to two columns and change the graphic boundaries so that the text is easier to read. (See Project 2 for ideas.) Save the publication as Ft Worden 3 and print the document.

4. Use the Help function to display the Help window called CONTROL PALETTE: MANIPULATING AN OBJECT. Scroll the window and read the information, then close the Help window.

Upon completion of this chapter you will be able to:

- Explain how master pages differ from publication pages

- Move between master pages and publication pages and among publication pages

- Use master pages and a template to create a publication

- Place text and graphics in a publication

- Use a style sheet to format text

CHAPTER 6

Placing Text Using Master Pages, Templates, and Style Sheets

T his chapter has two parts. The first introduces you to master pages, templates, and style sheets by letting you create a set of master pages and explore a template and its style sheet. In the second part, you will create a newsletter for The Inn at Portage Bay, using a newsletter template previously designed and saved on the data disk provided with this book. In Chapter 7 you will create the master pages, template, and style sheet yourself.

MASTER PAGES

PageMaker has two kinds of pages: master pages and publication pages. **Master pages** are like an outline, a plan for what the publication pages will look like—in other words, the format of a particular publication. They may contain headers and footers that will appear on every page as well as nonprinting guides. Using master pages allows you to specify the format for a publication's left- and right-hand pages one time and then reuse the format for each page spread in the publication. Master pages save time when you are setting up a publication.

Anything you put on master pages will appear on the publication pages. Master pages would include such things as:

- a nonprinting layout grid, including margin guides, column guides, and horizontal and vertical ruler guides

- text and graphics that appear on every page, such as company logo, page number, name of publication, issue, and date

A **publication page** is a page of your document. It contains the elements from the master pages as well as the text and graphics that are unique to that page. It may also contain text and graphics placeholders to show how the publication will look when completed. Publication page icons appear in the lower left of your Pasteboard and contain numbers. Master page icons contain an *L* and *R*.

Elements that are part of a master page cannot be changed or deleted while you are on a publication page, even though you can see them. You must first move to the master page to change them. The maximum number of master pages is two—one for the left and one for the right. If your publication does not differentiate between left and right, there is only one master page.

Visualize your publication as made up of two layers of transparent paper. When you create a page of your publication, you start with a layer of master page. Then you place another transparent piece of paper on top of the master page—the publication page. On the publication page you place articles and graphics. Printing the publication page captures the elements on both the master page and the publication page.

Understanding Master Pages

In this first section you will create a new publication and change various master page settings to understand how master pages correspond to publication pages. Pay attention to what happens as you change the settings and click between the various pages. Completing this exercise will help you create a newsletter using master pages and a template later in this chapter.

1. Open PageMaker.

2. Select New... from the File menu (⌘-N).

3. In the Page setup dialog box, enter the following values:

Number of pages: 4

Inside (margin in inches):   3

Verify that Double-sided and Facing pages have an ×.

4. If your Page setup dialog box matches Figure 6.1, click on OK. If not, make the necessary changes.

The value 3 inches was selected for the inside margin so it will be easy for you to see the difference between inside and outside margins. Notice the page icons in the lower-left corner of your publication window (see Figure 6.2). The *L* and *R* are for the left and right master pages. The *1* through *4* are the four publication pages you specified in the Page setup dialog box.

When you first see the publication window, the page 1 icon is highlighted, and one sheet of paper, corresponding to page 1, is on your screen. Look carefully at the page in the publication window. Recall that the inside margin is 3 inches and the outside margin is 0.75 inch. Note for page 1 that the inside margin is on the left and the outside margin is on the right.

Figure 6.1
Page setup dialog box

Verify that Double-sided and
Facing pages have an ×

Set Number
of pages to 4

Change Inside
margin to 3 inches

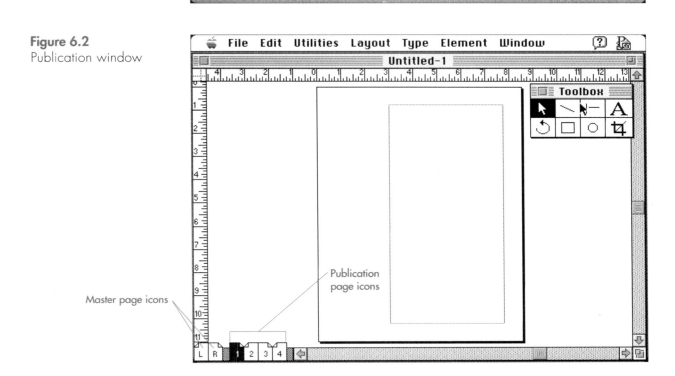

Figure 6.2
Publication window

Master page icons

Publication
page icons

1. Click on the page 2 icon.

Now you should have pages 2 and 3 in the publication window. Look at the publication page icons in the lower-left corner of the screen. Pages 2 and 3 are highlighted. You see two pages in the publication window because **Facing pages** was selected in the Page setup dialog box (refer to Figure 6.1). The Facing pages option allows you to design two pages simultaneously, a left and a right, and to see an open publication just as your readers will see it.

Next, notice the margins in the pages on the Pasteboard—3 inches and 0.75 inch. For a left-hand page, the inside margin is on the right; for a right-hand page, it is on the left.

To clarify this arrangement, take a piece of paper from a notebook or pad. Fold it in half as if it were going to be a birthday card. Number the surfaces front-to-back from 1 to 4. Draw a box in the area that will contain text, using 3 inches and 0.75 inch for the margins. On each of the four surfaces, write *left* or *right*, beginning with right on page 1.

Thus, page 1 is a right-hand page, page 2 a left-hand page, and so on. The master page corresponding to page 1 carries the R icon. In fact, every odd-numbered page is a right-hand page and every even-numbered page is a left-hand page. Looking at your publication window, notice how the L master page icon corresponds to the even-numbered page icons, and the R icon corresponds to the odd-numbered icons.

So when creating a master page for page 1, start with the R not the L master page. It may seem backward, but only because logic would seem to dictate that left should come first. Now that you understand how left and right master pages correspond to publication pages, click on each page icon and look at the publication window.

1. **Click on L. You'll see both the left and right master pages (see Figure 6.3).**

2. **Click on 1.**

3. **Click on 2. You see pages 2 and 3.**

4. **Click on 4.**

Figure 6.3
Master pages displayed

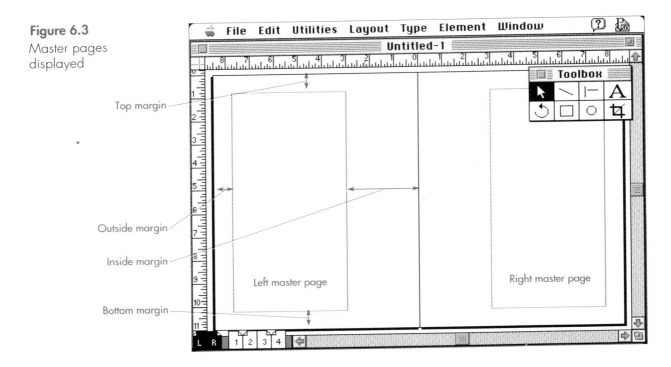

Top margin

Outside margin

Inside margin

Bottom margin

As you've just seen, in a four-page document, pages 2 and 3 are facing pages; pages 1 and 4 do not have a facing page. That is why you see only one page when you click on pages 1 and 4.

Setting Columns on Master Pages

In this practice you will set two columns for the left master page and three columns for the right master page. This step will let you see how left and right master pages correspond to publication pages.

1. Click on L.

This step tells PageMaker you will be working on the master pages.

2. Select Column guides... from the Layout menu.

Figure 6.4 shows the Column guides dialog box after you make the following changes.

3. Click on the box labeled Set left and right pages separately.

You should now see an × in the box, which allows you to have a different number of columns on the left and right master pages.

4. Type 2 for Left.

5. Press (TAB) once.

6. Type 3 for Right.

7. Click on OK.

Figure 6.4
Column guides
dialog box

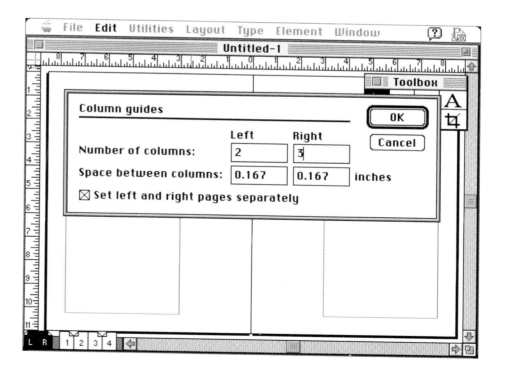

Figure 6.5
Publication window: two columns on left page, three columns on right page

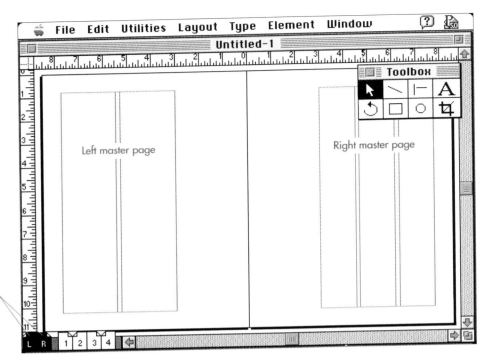

Master page icons highlighted

Your view should be the same as Figure 6.5, with two columns on the left master page and three columns on the right. You have not changed the inside and outside margins.

Columns evenly divide a page's available width. When you specify the number of columns, PageMaker calculates the width of each, given the width of the page, and reserves space, called a **gutter**, between columns. PageMaker's default gutter is ⅙ inch or 0.167 inch. PageMaker also allows you to customize your page and have columns of unequal width, as you will see later in this chapter.

Click on the publication page icons in the lower-left corner of the screen and notice the page layout.

1. **Click on 1.**

2. **Click on 2.**

Again, you see pages 2 and 3 together and can note the differences between them.

3. **Click on 4.**

Double-Sided and Facing Pages

You select **Double-sided** in the Page setup dialog box when you want to create a publication whose pages will be printed back-to-back. Inside and outside margins may be set separately to allow for binding or punching holes in the inside margin. Odd- and even-page layouts are mirror images of each other.

Figure 6.6
Page setup with
Facing pages off

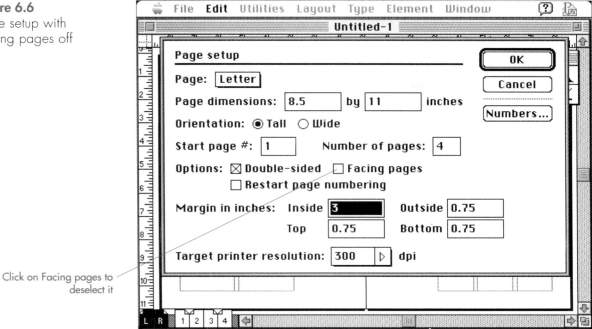

Click on Facing pages to
deselect it

When Double-sided is not selected (no × is in the box), the publication is single-sided, wherein odd and even pages have the same layout. When you create a new publication, the Page setup dialog box within the File pull-down menu allows you to select between double- and single-sided pages and to indicate facing pages. Use facing pages when you want to create a double-sided publication whose pages will be printed back-to-back (such as this book) and when you want to work with two pages at once.

Turn off Facing pages by doing the following, as shown in Figure 6.6.

1. **Select Page setup... from the File menu.**

2. **Click on Facing pages to remove the ×.**

3. **Click on OK.**

The result is shown in Figure 6.7. Left and right master pages still occur, but only one page at a time appears onscreen. Look at each page, noting that the number of columns (two or three) corresponds to the left and right master pages. Also note that the inside and outside margins still correspond to the master pages.

4. **Click on L.**

5. **Click on R.**

6. **Click on 1.**

7. **Click on 2.**

8. **Click on 3.**

9. **Click on 4.**

Figure 6.7
Publication with
Facing pages off

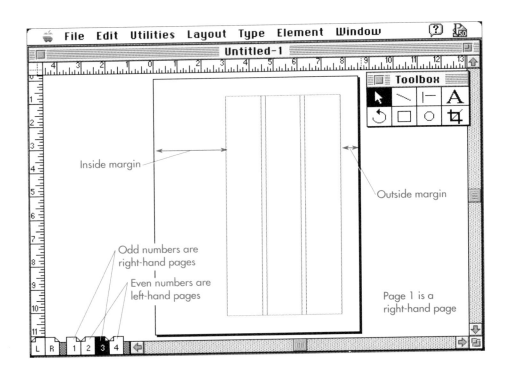

To change from double-sided to single-sided pages:

1. Select Page setup... from the File menu.

2. Click on Double-sided to remove the ×.

Notice that the words *Inside* and *Outside* within the Margin in inches area have changed to *Left* and *Right*. Because this publication is now single-sided, left and right margins make more sense than inside and outside margins.

3. Click on OK.

Look at the master page and publication page icons in the lower-left portion of the publication window (see Figure 6.8). All the page icons are now right-sided pages because just one kind of page occurs.

Next click through the master and publication pages.

4. Click on R.

5. Click on 1.

6. Click on 2.

7. Click on 3.

8. Click on 4.

Every view is the same: When Double-sided pages is deselected, only one kind of page occurs.

Now clear the Pasteboard of this publication.

1. Select Close from the File menu.

Figure 6.8
Publication with
Double-sided pages
deselected

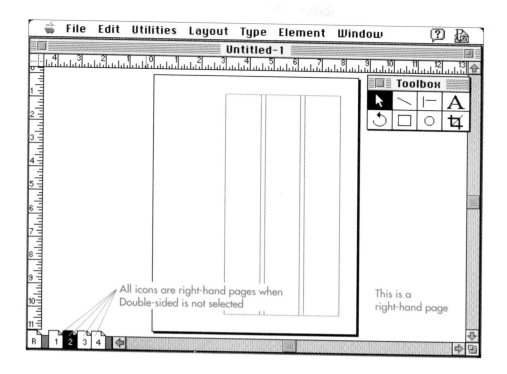

All icons are right-hand pages when
Double-sided is not selected

This is a
right-hand page

2. When PageMaker asks if you want to save, select No.

Now that you've explored master pages—learned why page 1 of a
publication corresponds to a right, not left, master page; experimented
with setting columns on master pages; selected double-sided and single-
sided pages; and viewed the difference between facing and nonfacing
pages—it's time to explore templates.

TEMPLATES

PageMaker creates two kinds of files that can be saved: publications and
templates. When you open a publication, the default is Original, and you
see the publication's name in the title bar. When you open a template, the
default is Copy. This forces you to name the file when saving, so you
don't override the empty template. You may create your own template,
or use ones available commercially from other companies. As you already
know, publications are newsletters, advertisements, brochures, and so on
(in short, something created within PageMaker).

Understanding Templates

Templates are the outline of how the entire publication will look.
They are created once, saved, and used frequently. Templates contain
master pages, style sheets, and the publication's layout grid. Creating a
template allows you to reuse the format for each version of a publication.
With a template you can have a standard layout for your company's
product brochures. For example, in the template you can specify the size
of the brochure, include a company logo and name, and set up a **Style**

palette that defines all the fonts that may be used. In this way, you save time and ensure a consistent style, or look, for the brochures. Creating and reusing a template allows you to direct your energies to the content. Thus the greatest advantages of templates are that they save time and provide design consistency.

Templates are created by outlining the publication's format. You begin as you would with any publication. You create a new publication, specify the number and size of pages, set up columns, make ruler guides, and type information, such as headings, that would appear whenever the template is used. You may choose to include dummy text or graphics, to show how your publication will look. Then you save it as a template. What is missing from a template is text specific to any particular issue of the newsletter, annual report, product brochure, or whatever publication the template is set up for.

To create a publication from a template, open the file containing it, then create your publication. Finally, save it as a publication.

Exploring the Template for the Inn's Newsletter

First you will open a template stored on the data disk that came with this book and explore its style sheet. Insert the disk into the drive. Use Figure 6.9 as a guide as you proceed. With PageMaker started, do the following:

1. Select Open... from the File menu (⌘-O).

2. Single-click on Portage Newsletter Template. PageMaker will automatically select Copy.

3. Click on OK.

Figure 6.9
Opening the newsletter template

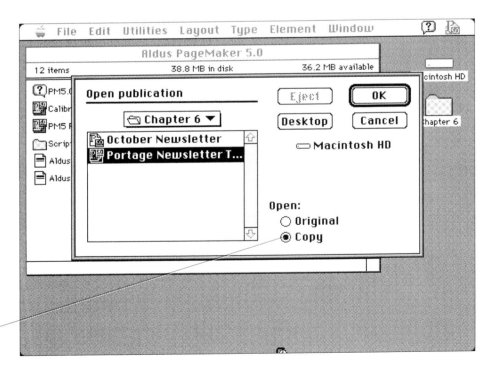

PageMaker automatically selects Copy

Figure 6.10
Portage Inn Soundings
newsletter template

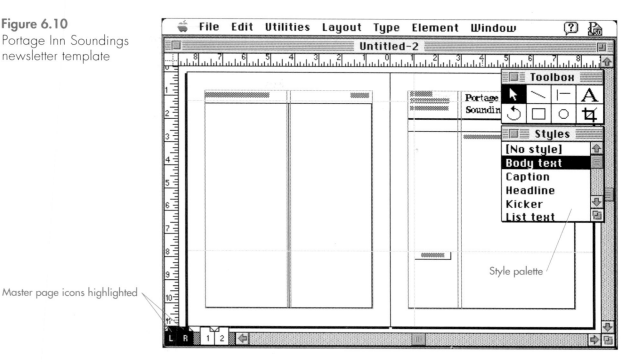

Master page icons highlighted

Style palette

Figure 6.10 shows the newsletter template on the Pasteboard. Look at the title bar and notice the word *Untitled-2*. When you select Copy, you are given a copy of the file to work with, not the original. An advantage of selecting Copy is that when you save the publication, you will be prompted for a name. Thus there is less danger of altering your original template with changes or text. A second advantage to using Copy is that any changes are made faster. When you select Original, every time you make a change, the computer accesses the file. This takes considerable time and noticeably slows down operations.

In Figure 6.10, note two special items in the publication window. First, the master page icons are highlighted, which means you are looking at master pages rather than publication pages. Second, the Style palette appears below the Toolbox.

STYLE SHEETS

Style sheets include the type, margins, column widths, and other variables in a publication's format. The Style palette contains the list of type styles and sizes used in the publication's style sheet.

Exploring the Style Palette

In this section you will explore the styles in the Style palette to gain an understanding of what is behind it. Although you will merely be looking in this chapter, in the next chapter you will create the Style palette. As you explore, be careful not to make changes. But if you inadvertently do, start over by reopening the template. Look at the Headline style by doing the following:

1. **Make sure the master page icons are highlighted.**

2. **Point to Headline in the Style palette.**

3. **Hold down ⌘ and click the mouse button.**

Your screen should look like Figure 6.11. The Headline style is completely defined here. Type selection, indentation, tab stops, and hyphenation control can be examined or changed by selecting the appropriate button.

To look at each part of the Headline style:

4. **Click on Type...**

Note that the dialog box is the Type specifications dialog box.

5. **Click on Cancel.**

Cancel is faster than OK. Cancel returns you immediately to the previous screen; OK updates the style sheet whether you have made changes or not.

6. **On your own, click on the Para..., Tabs..., and Hyph... buttons and examine the corresponding dialog boxes. When finished:**

7. **Click on Cancel.**

For each style listed in the Style palette, press the Command key while clicking on the style. The styles used in this publication are summarized in the following table.

Figure 6.11
Headline style from the Style palette

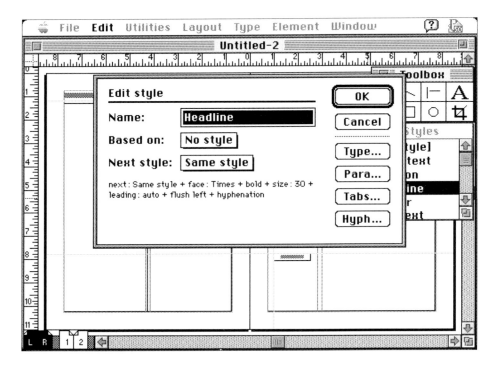

Name of style	Font	Size	Indents		
			Left	First	Right
Body text	Times	11	.1	.2	.1
Caption	Based on Body text + italic	11	.1	.2	.1
Headline	Times + bold	30	0	0	0
Kicker	Based on Subhead 1 – bold + italic	12	0	.1	.1
List text	Based on Body text	11	.05	.05	.1
Subhead 1	Based on Headline	18	0	.1	.1

Determining Text Style on Master Pages

The styles in the Style palette were used to create the master pages for the Portage Inn Soundings newsletter. The highlighted choices in the Style palette change as you move around the text already on the page.

1. Verify that the master page icons are selected.

2. From the Toolbox, select the text tool.

3. Position the I-beam on the right master page within the masthead *Portage Inn Soundings*.

4. Click.

The Style palette should have Headline selected because you have positioned the I-beam within text using the Headline style. Thus, it is not critical for you to know the font for a text section as you can always use PageMaker to tell you its style.

For each of the following, notice what is selected from the Style palette.

5. Position the I-beam within *Manager's Monthly Message* (Greeked text below the masthead).

6. Click.

7. Position the I-beam within *Monthly Newsmemo for Inn Employees* (Greeked text to the left of the masthead).

8. Click.

9. Position the I-beam within *In this issue* (boxed text).

10. Click.

11. Position the I-beam within *Portage Inn Soundings* on page 2.

12. Click.

What you have been discovering is that when the I-beam is positioned within text, the Style palette highlights the type style of that text.

Comparing Text on Master Pages to Text on Numbered Pages

To further understand how master pages relate to publication (or numbered) pages, move to page 1 and repeat the exploration you did on the master pages. As you position the I-beam within the text on the numbered pages, observe what happens to the Style palette.

1. Click on the page 1 icon.

2. Position the I-beam within *Portage Inn Soundings*; click.

3. Position the I-beam within *Manager's Monthly Message*; click.

With the page 1 icon selected, what happened when you moved around the text? Did the highlighted style in the Style palette change as you moved from one text area to another? The answer is no. Why not? Because the text was created on the master pages. As stated earlier, although it will print on the publication pages, text created on the master pages cannot be accessed or changed from within a publication page.

CREATING A NEWSLETTER FOR THE INN

In this section you will create a newsletter using a template that accompanied this book. You will place some text, type other text, and place a graphic. The finished newsletter you will create is shown in Figure 6.12.

The Inn at Portage Bay produces a monthly two-page newsletter, Portage Inn Soundings, for its employees. One of its purposes is to keep employees informed of factors that affect them, such as employment policies. A second purpose is to inform employees of local events, both at the Inn and in nearby communities, so employees can share this information with Inn guests. Finally, the newsletter highlights Inn achievements, such as when the Inn won an award for the Spinnaker Restaurant cuisine, and it also highlights employees and their achievements.

As you work on the newsletter, save it often. Choose a name and make sure you save it as a publication file.

Placing the Text Files in the Newsletter

The October issue of Portage Inn Soundings has six articles and one graphic (see the following table for a list). All six articles were written using Microsoft Word. The graphic was drawn, scanned, and saved as a TIFF file.

Figure 6.12
The finished newsletter

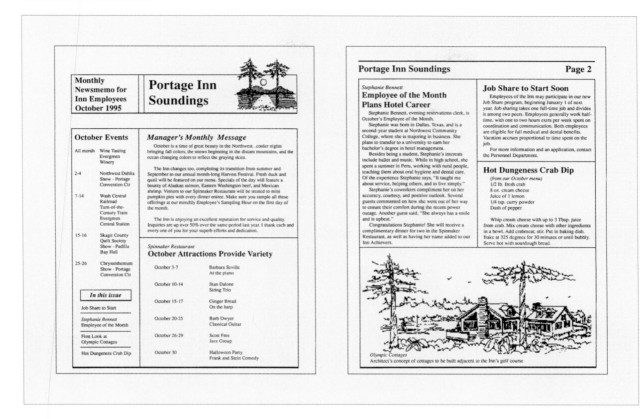

You will place each article using a style from the Style palette and, in some cases, make minor adjustments to the headline or text alignment.

Contents	Stored on disk as:	Placement
Manager's Monthly Message	Oct Message	Page 1, column 2
October Attractions	Oct Attractions	Page 1, column 2
October Events	Oct Event	Page 1, column 1
Employee of the Month	Oct Employee of Month	Page 2, column 1
Job Share	Oct Job Share	Page 2, column 2
Dungeness Crab Recipe	Oct Recipe (Crab Dip)	Page 2, column 2
Olympic Cottages	Cottages.tiff	Page 2, bottom

Before continuing, check the following:

- data disk is in drive

- page view is 50% or 75% size and page shows space where Manager's Monthly Message article will be placed, which is below the heading *Manager's Monthly Message* in the second column

Placing the Manager's Monthly Message

The Manager's Monthly Message is a short article that allows the manager to communicate with employees. It was written using Microsoft Word. The original article in Word format is shown in Figure 6.13. Notice the format of the article—it has no paragraph indentation.

When PageMaker imports a file from another word processor, it puts the text through a filter. A **filter** allows PageMaker to interpret special codes saved with a document, such as Tab and Enter and the codes for bold and underline. Because each word processing program has its own special codes, PageMaker comes with filters for widely used word processors. PageMaker does not have a filter for every word processor sold, nor does it have a filter for versions of word processors released after PageMaker's version was released.

All files are imported and placed using filters. There are filters for text, spreadsheet, database, and graphics files. PageMaker has both import and export filters. The person who installed PageMaker on your computer either installed all the filters or selected only some to install. Because each filter requires space on the hard drive, it is not practical to install filters you won't use. To see the list of filters installed on your computer, do question 13 at the end of this chapter.

When importing text, font selection and size, paragraph indentation, and other choices are applied to the text file based on the style selected from the Style palette. If no style is selected, the text will be placed using the

Figure 6.13
Manager's Monthly Message article in Word format

October is a time of great beauty in the Northwest...cooler nights bringing fall colors, the snows beginning in the distant mountains, and the ocean changing colors to reflect the graying skies.

The Inn changes too, completing its transition from summer and September to our annual month-long Harvest Festival. Fresh duck and quail will be featured on our menu. Specials of the day will feature a bounty of Alaskan salmon, Eastern Washington beef, and Mexican shrimp. Visitors to our Spinnaker Restaurant will be treated to mini pumpkin pies with every dinner entree. Make sure you sample all these offerings at our monthly Employee's Sampling Hour on the first day of the month.

The Inn is enjoying an excellent reputation for service and quality. Inquiries are up more than 50% over the same period last year. I thank each and every one of you for your superb efforts and dedication.

publication's default style. This style can be seen when you open a new publication and specify Style palette.

To place the Manager's Monthly Message article:

1. **Verify that the page 1 icon is highlighted.**

2. **Select the pointer tool (if necessary).**

3. **Click on Body text in the Style palette.**

This step tells PageMaker that the text you are placing will be in Body text style.

4. **Select Place... from the File menu (⌘-D).**

5. **Select the appropriate directory if it is not already selected.**

6. **Click on Oct Message.**

7. **Click on Retain format to remove the ×.**

8. **Verify the following:**

As new story is selected.

Retain format is not selected.

Convert quotes is selected.

Read tags is not selected.

Compare your screen to Figure 6.14. If your screen does not match, make the necessary changes.

9. **Click on OK.**

Figure 6.14
Selecting Oct Message
to place

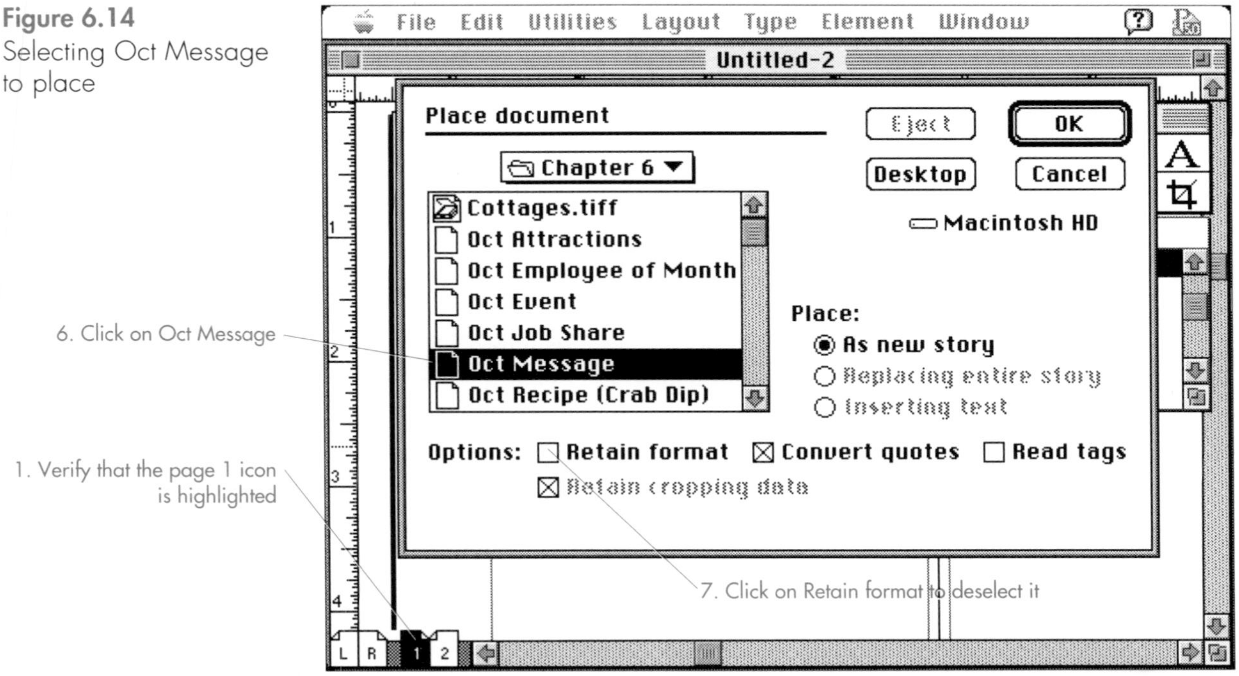

6. Click on Oct Message

1. Verify that the page 1 icon
is highlighted

7. Click on Retain format to deselect it

Figure 6.15
Placing the text
below the heading

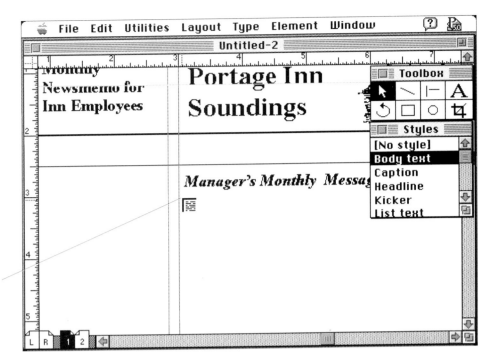

10. Move the loaded text icon
below the heading

Many of the choices in Figure 6.14 are new choices and require some explanation. Retain format tells PageMaker to import the document's character and paragraph formatting and the style sheet along with the document. Some word processors (for example, Microsoft Word) have style sheets. Convert quotes causes PageMaker to translate ordinary quotation marks (") into typographer's quote marks (" "). Read tags tells PageMaker to look for style names inside brackets within the imported text. PageMaker will apply the style to that paragraph. For example,

<Headline> President Declares Tax Cut

will cause PageMaker to import that paragraph with Headline style as specified in the Style palette. A paragraph ends when there is a hard return, that is, (RETURN) had been pressed. As new story indicates that the imported text will not be replacing any other text that has been used as a placeholder on a template. Retain format (off), Convert quotes (on), and As new story (on) are the options you want for this article.

Your screen should look like Figure 6.15, showing the loaded text icon which has replaced the mouse pointer.

10. Move the icon below the *Manager's Monthly Message* heading.

11. Click.

Your screen should look like Figure 6.16. If you could see the entire article, you would see the top and bottom windowshades bracketing the text. As you learned in Chapter 4, these, along with the square handles in the corners, allow you to move or delete text blocks.

Figure 6.16
Manager's Monthly
Message article

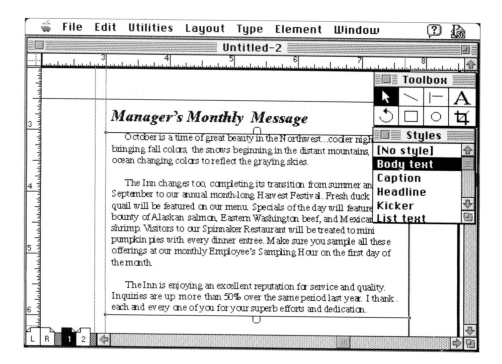

The text, defined as Body text in the Style palette, has been placed within the margins of the new publication. PageMaker changed the paragraph indentation in the source file to reflect specifications in Body text.

Draw a 1-point line under the Manager's Monthly Message article to separate it from the article that will appear below it.

1. Turn off the column guides by selecting Guides and rulers from the Layout menu and clicking on Guides (⌘-J).

2. Select Line from the Element menu.

3. Click on 1 pt.

4. Select the constrained-line tool from the Toolbox.

5. Adjust the view so you can see the complete area where the line will be placed.

6. Draw a line across the column under the article (see Figure 6.17).

Placing the October Attractions Article

In this section you will place the October Attractions article and change the style of two headlines, *Spinnaker Restaurant* and *October Attractions Provide Variety*.

Spinnaker Restaurant uses 12-point italic; *October Attractions Provide Variety* uses 18-point normal type. The real headline is *October Attractions*

Figure 6.17
Placing a line
under the article

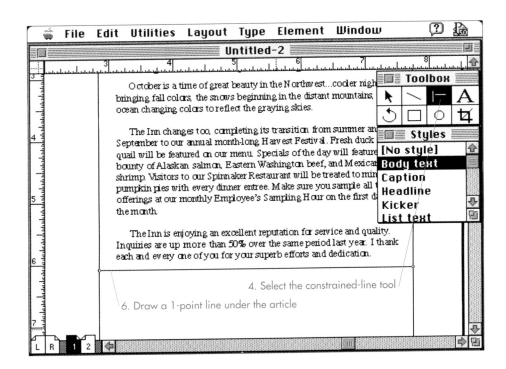

Provide Variety, whereas the use of the restaurant name above is called either a kicker or an eyebrow. A **kicker** or **eyebrow** appears above the headline in a different type style. Its purpose is to attract attention, provide information, and draw readers to the article. Often it is in smaller type, say 12 point over an 18-point headline. Figure 6.23 shows the use of an eyebrow over a headline.

To place the October Attractions article:

1. Replace the column guides by selecting Guides and rulers from the Layout menu and clicking on Guides (⌘-J).

2. Click on Body text in the Style palette.

3. Select Place... from the File menu (⌘-D).

4. Click on Oct Attractions.

5. Click on Retain format to deselect it (if necessary).

6. Click on OK. The loaded text icon appears.

7. Click to place the story below the Manager's Monthly Message article (see Figure 6.18).

8. Click outside the windowshades to remove them.

To change the style of *Spinnaker Restaurant:*

1. Click on the text tool in the Toolbox.

2. Place the I-beam to the left of the words *Spinnaker Restaurant.* Click and drag over the words to select them (see Figure 6.19).

Figure 6.18
October Attractions
article placed

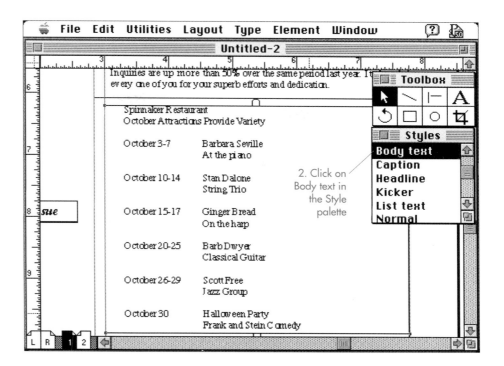

Figure 6.19
Spinnaker Restaurant
heading selected

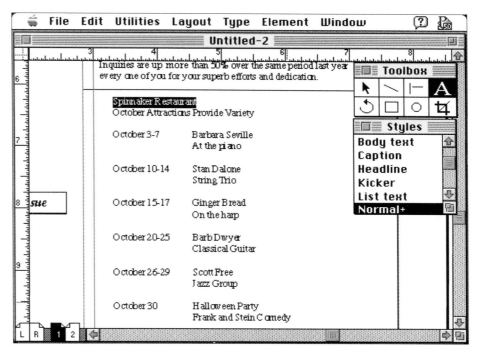

3. **Click on Kicker in the Style palette. This changes the type to Times 12 italic (see Figure 6.20).**

To change the style of *October Attractions Provide Variety*:

1. **Place the I-beam to the left of the word *October*. Click and drag over the line to select the title (see Figure 6.21).**

2. **Click on Subhead 1.**

Figure 6.20
Heading changed
to 12-point italic

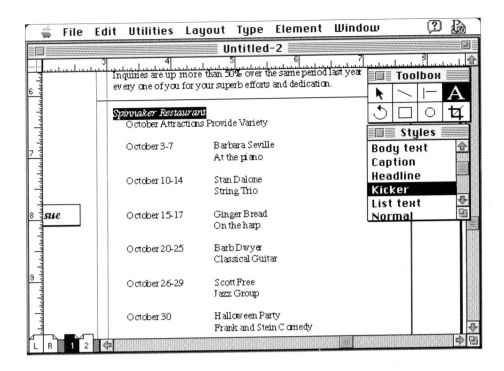

Figure 6.21
Selecting the
second headline

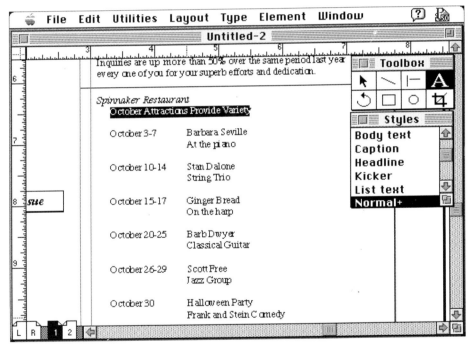

Your screen should now look like Figure 6.22.

Before placing the next article, make sure everything you have placed so far looks correct. Move around the publication's second column and compare your page to Figure 6.23. If you need to redo a part, select and delete it. Then redo the steps. When you are satisfied that your newsletter looks correct, proceed to the next section.

Figure 6.22
Both headlines with
the new styles

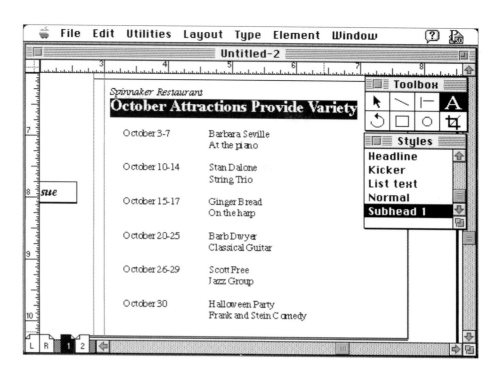

Figure 6.23
Page 1 after placing
two articles

Kicker

Subhead 1

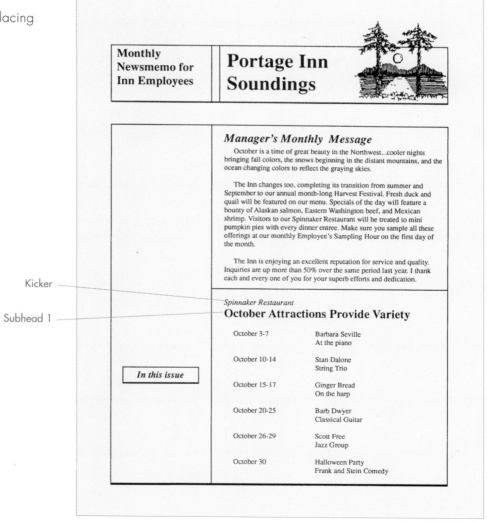

Placing the October Events List

October Events is a listing of local activities in and around the Inn. This feature goes in the upper-left column of page 1, to the left of the Manager's Monthly Message. To change your page view so you have the target area in the center of the Pasteboard:

1. Hold down (OPTION) and ⌘ and click the mouse button to change the view so that the entire page appears on the Pasteboard (Fit in window).

2. Point to the top center of page 1's left column.

3. Hold down (OPTION) and ⌘ and click the mouse button to change the page view.

The process for placing the October Events listing is similar to that for the other two articles. Use either the specifications listed below or the set of steps to place the article.

Style: List text

Name of article on disk: Oct Event

Change headline style to: Subhead 1

First you will import and place Oct Event using List text from the Style palette. Next you will change the headline style to Subhead 1. Finally, you will make sure all the text is properly lined up.

To place the October Events article:

1. Select the pointer tool from the Toolbox.

2. Select List text from the Style palette.

3. Select Place... from the File menu (⌘-D).

4. Select Oct Event.

5. Click on Retain format to deselect it (if necessary).

6. Click on OK.

The mouse pointer has been replaced with the loaded text icon.

7. Place the article by pressing the mouse button and dragging to fill the space (see Figure 6.24).

To change the style of the headline:

1. Click on the text tool in the Toolbox.

2. Place the I-beam to the left of the words *October Events*. Click and drag the I-beam over the words to select them.

3. Click on Subhead 1.

Your publication page should now look like Figure 6.25. If any of the text is misaligned, insert or delete tabs or spaces as necessary so your publication matches Figure 6.25.

Figure 6.24
Placing the article
by dragging to fill
the space

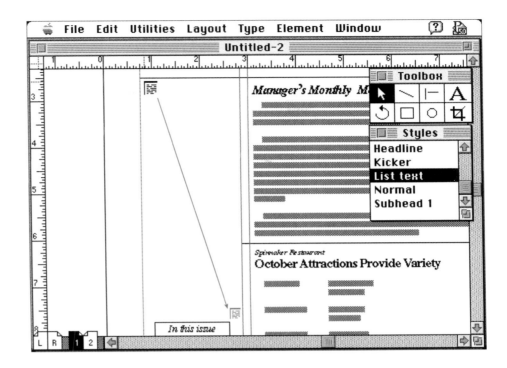

Figure 6.25
Page 1 after placing
three articles

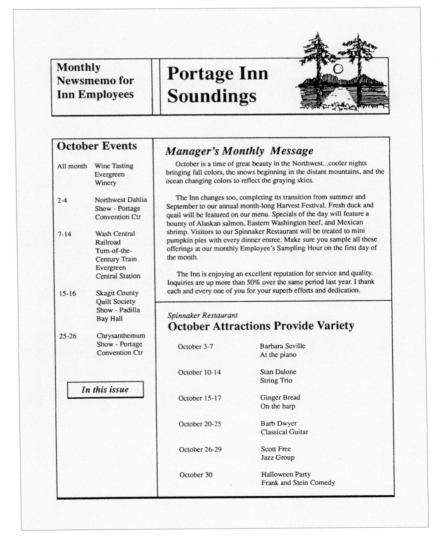

Your next task for page 1 is to list the newsletter articles under the In this issue box. First, you will type each line of text; then you will use the constrained-line tool to add three lines to separate the four listed items. This part of the newsletter will look like Figure 6.26.

To type the list of newsletter articles:

1. Make sure the text tool is selected in the Toolbox.

2. Change the page view to show the area below the In this issue box.

3. Position the I-beam under the In this issue box; click.

4. Select Body text from the Style palette.

5. Change the indentation for where text will appear: Select Paragraph... from the Type menu (⌘-M).

6. Type *0.18* next to First (see Figure 6.27).

7. Click on OK.

8. Type *Job Share to Start.*

9. Press (RETURN) twice to double-space.

To type the employee's name in italic, press the shortcut keys ⌘-(SHIFT)-I or:

10. Select Type style from the Type menu.

11. Click on Italic.

12. Type *Stephanie Bennett.*

13. Press (RETURN) once to single-space.

Figure 6.26
Listing of articles
in newsletter

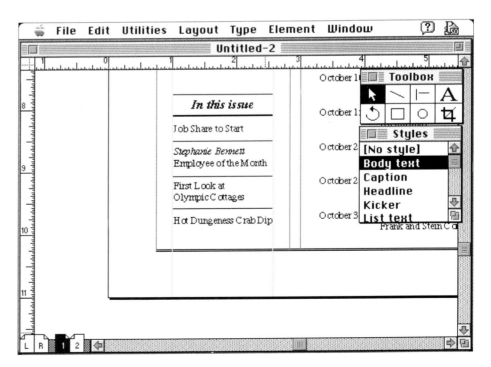

Figure 6.27
Changing first indent
of Body text

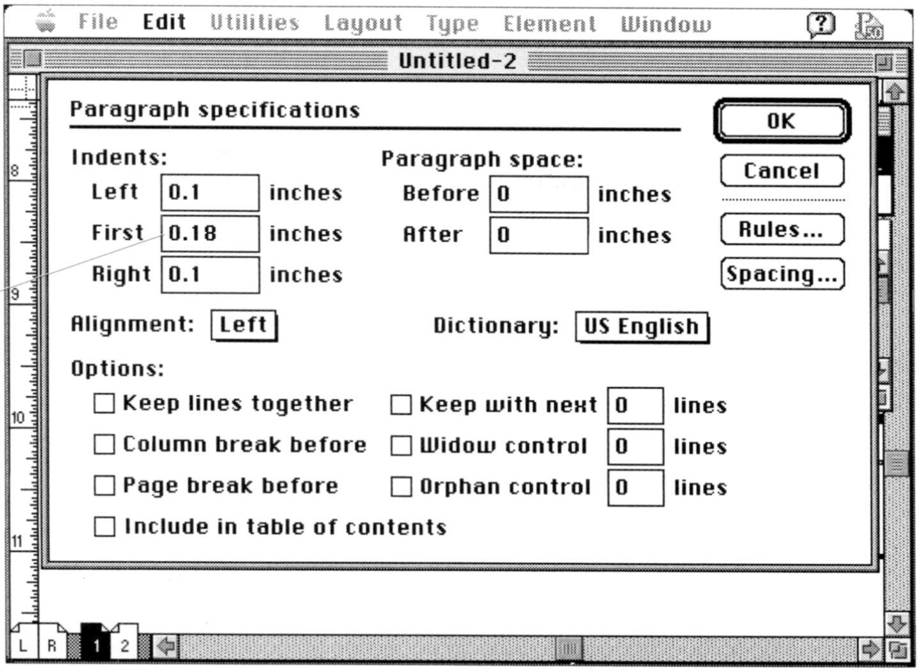

Change First indent
to 0.18 inches

Turn off italic so that the next line will be normal. Use the shortcut keys ⌘-SHIFT-I or:

14. Select Type style from the Type menu.

15. Click on Normal.

16. Type *Employee of the Month.*

17. Press RETURN twice to double-space.

18. Type *First Look at* RETURN *Olympic Cottages.*

19. Press RETURN twice to double-space.

20. Type *Hot Dungeness Crab Dip.*

Now you will add three lines to separate the four items. To do this you will draw one line and copy it once to the Clipboard. Then you will paste it twice so that all three lines are the same length.

To draw and copy the line:

1. Select the constrained-line tool in the Toolbox.

2. Select Line from the Element menu and verify that 1 pt is selected.

3. Create two column guides on the edges of the In this issue box (see Figure 6.28).

4. Using Figure 6.28 as a guide, draw a line under *Job Share to Start.*

With the line still selected, copy it once:

5. Select Copy from the Edit menu (⌘-C).

Figure 6.28
Drawing the line

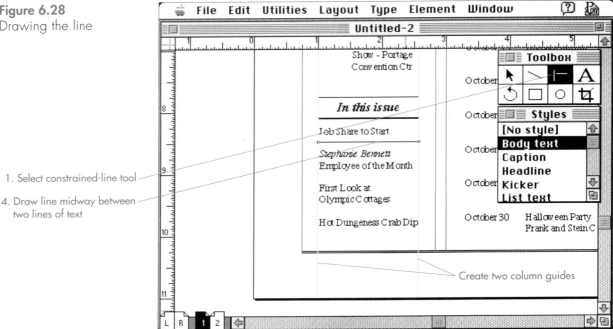

1. Select constrained-line tool

4. Draw line midway between
   two lines of text

Create two column guides

This copies the line to the Clipboard, erasing any contents of the Clipboard. To paste the line:

6. **Select Paste from the Edit menu (⌘-V).**

The pasted line will have handles. To position it under the text:

7. **Point to the line, being careful not to point to a handle. Press the mouse button and drag the line, positioning it under *Employee of the Month*.**

8. **Release the mouse button.**

9. **Repeat steps 6, 7, and 8 to paste and position a line under the remaining text.**

Adding the Month and Year to the Masthead

Your final task for page 1 is to type the month and year near the top of the publication, as shown in Figure 6.29. In order to get the text to line up properly, you must type it on the master page.

1. **Click on the master page icon.**

2. **Change the page view to highlight the left part of the masthead.**

3. **Select the text tool from the Toolbox.**

4. **Position the I-beam after the word *Employees;* click an insertion point. Notice that the style in the Style palette changes to Subhead 1.**

5. **Press (RETURN).**

6. **Type *October* and the current year.**

Figure 6.29
Typing the month
and year

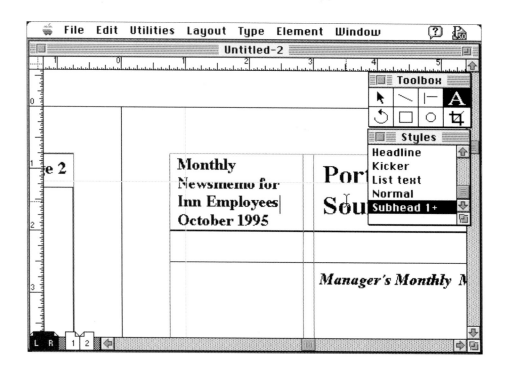

Page 1 is complete! (See Figure 6.30.) Now you will use some of the skills you've learned to place three articles on page 2. Finally, you will place a graphic at the bottom of page 2.

Completing Page 2 of the Newsletter

Figure 6.31 shows the final layout of page 2 with all the specifications. To reproduce page 2, use either the specifications in Figure 6.31, the following steps, or a combination of the two.

Placing the Employee of the Month Article

The Employee of the Month article was written using Word for Windows. Style tags at the beginning of each paragraph name the style that PageMaker should apply when importing the text. Recall that a paragraph ends when (RETURN) is pressed. Figure 6.32 shows the Employee of the Month article in Word for Windows format.

To place the article:

1. Click on the page 2 icon.

2. Select the pointer tool from the Toolbox.

3. Change the page view so you see the upper-left corner of the publication page.

4. Select Place... from the File menu (⌘-D).

5. Click on Oct Employee of Month.

6. Click on Retain format to deselect it (if necessary).

7. Click on Read tags to select it.

Figure 6.30
Completed page 1

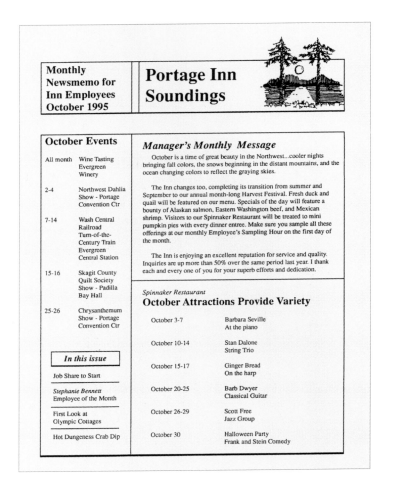

Compare your screen to Figure 6.33. If it doesn't match, make the necessary changes.

8. Click on OK.

9. Click to place the article.

Using style tags makes formatting an article very simple.

Placing the Job Share Article

This article goes at the top of the right-hand column on page 2. First you will place the article. Then you will change the headline style to Subhead 1. Finally, you will draw a line under the article.

Move your page view to the top of column 2 and select Body text from the Style palette. The specifications you will need to complete this task are:

		Place document dialog box options:
Text style:	Body text	
Headline style:	Subhead 1	☐ Retain format (off)
Article:	Oct Job Share	☒ Convert quotes (on)
Line under article:	1 point	☐ Read tags (off)

Figure 6.31
Page 2 of the newsletter

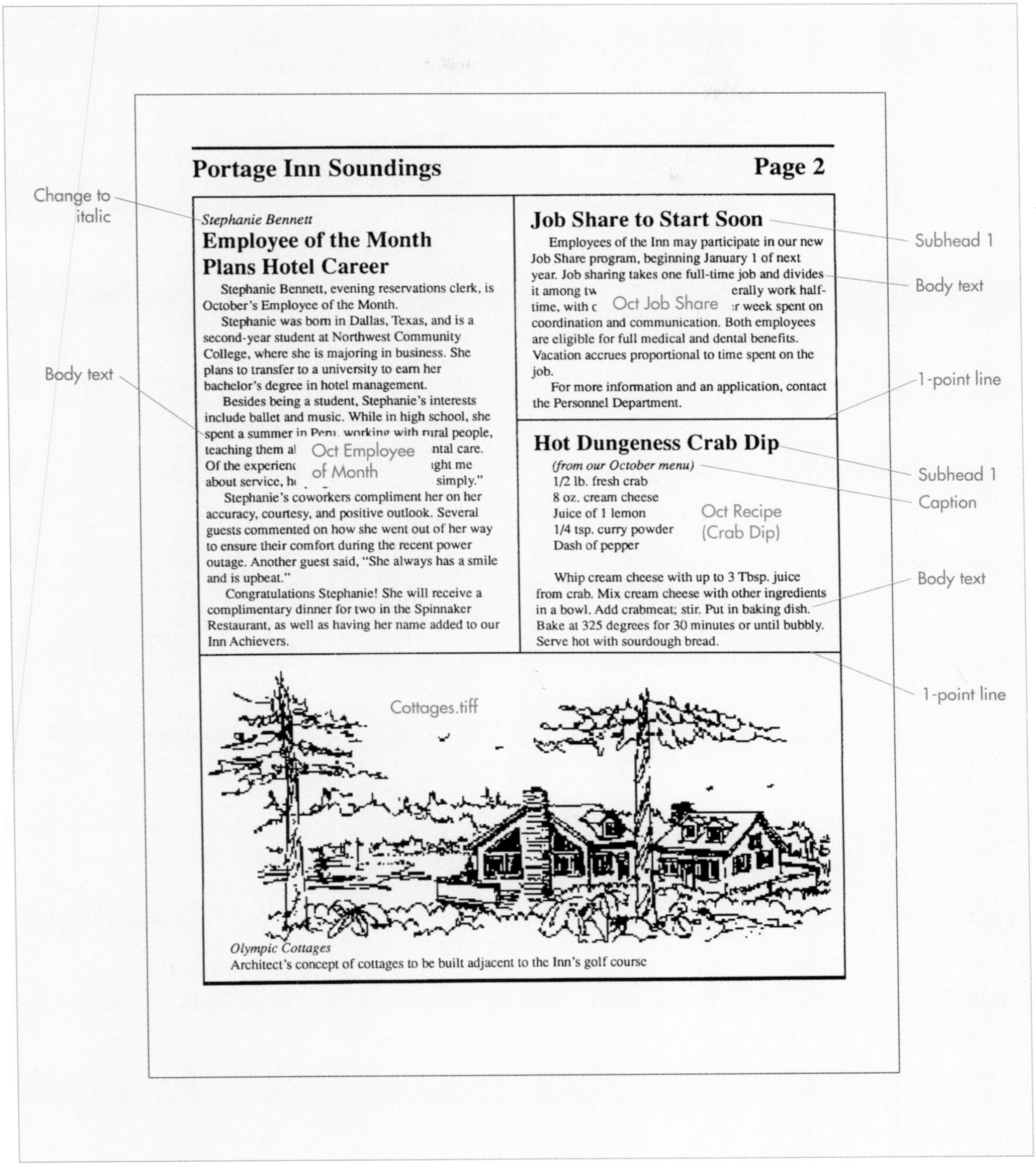

Change to italic

Portage Inn Soundings Page 2

Stephanie Bennett

Employee of the Month Plans Hotel Career

Body text

Stephanie Bennett, evening reservations clerk, is October's Employee of the Month.

Stephanie was born in Dallas, Texas, and is a second-year student at Northwest Community College, where she is majoring in business. She plans to transfer to a university to earn her bachelor's degree in hotel management.

Besides being a student, Stephanie's interests include ballet and music. While in high school, she spent a summer in Peru, working with rural people, teaching them al Oct Employee ntal care. Of the experienc of Month ught me about service, he simply."

Stephanie's coworkers compliment her on her accuracy, courtesy, and positive outlook. Several guests commented on how she went out of her way to ensure their comfort during the recent power outage. Another guest said, "She always has a smile and is upbeat."

Congratulations Stephanie! She will receive a complimentary dinner for two in the Spinnaker Restaurant, as well as having her name added to our Inn Achievers.

Job Share to Start Soon

Subhead 1

Body text

Employees of the Inn may participate in our new Job Share program, beginning January 1 of next year. Job sharing takes one full-time job and divides it among tw erally work half-time, with c Oct Job Share r week spent on coordination and communication. Both employees are eligible for full medical and dental benefits. Vacation accrues proportional to time spent on the job.

For more information and an application, contact the Personnel Department.

1-point line

Hot Dungeness Crab Dip

Subhead 1
Caption

(from our October menu)
1/2 lb. fresh crab
8 oz. cream cheese
Juice of 1 lemon   Oct Recipe
1/4 tsp. curry powder   (Crab Dip)
Dash of pepper

Body text

Whip cream cheese with up to 3 Tbsp. juice from crab. Mix cream cheese with other ingredients in a bowl. Add crabmeat; stir. Put in baking dish. Bake at 325 degrees for 30 minutes or until bubbly. Serve hot with sourdough bread.

1-point line

Cottages.tiff

Olympic Cottages
Architect's concept of cottages to be built adjacent to the Inn's golf course

Figure 6.32
Oct Employee of Month in Word format

A paragraph ends when (RETURN) is pressed

Style tags

<Kicker>Stephanie Bennett
<Subhead 1>Employee of the Month
<Subhead 1>Plans Hotel Career
<Body text>Stephanie Bennett, evening reservations clerk, is October's Employee of the Month.
<Body text>Stephanie was born in Dallas, Texas, and is a second-year student at Northwest Community College, where she is majoring in business. She plans to transfer to a university to earn her bachelor's degree in hotel management.
<Body text>Besides being a student, Stephanie's interests include ballet and music. While in high school, she spent a summer in Peru, working with rural people, teaching them about oral hygiene and dental care. Of the experience Stephanie says, "It taught me about service, helping others, and to live simply."
<Body text>Stephanie's coworkers compliment her on her accuracy, courtesy, and positive outlook. Several guests commented on how she went out of her way to ensure their comfort during the recent power outage. Another guest said, "She always has a smile and is upbeat."
<Body text>Congratulations Stephanie! She will receive a complimentary dinner for two in the Spinnaker Restaurant, as well as having her name added to our Inn Achievers.

Selecting Read tags in the Place document dialog box instructs PageMaker to apply the style tag to that paragraph

Figure 6.33
Place document
dialog box

5. Click on Oct Employee of Month

6. Click on Retain format to deselect it

7. Click on Read tags to select it

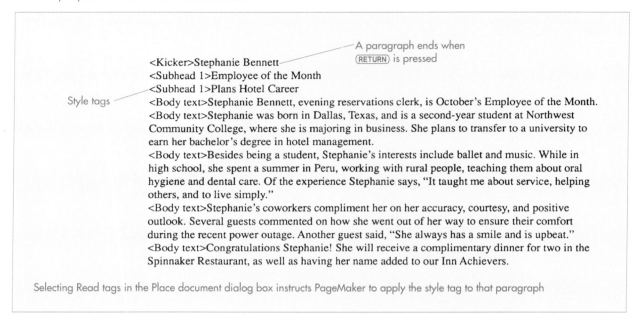

When this article is correctly placed with a line drawn under it, proceed to the next section.

Placing the Dungeness Crab Dip Recipe

This article goes under the Job Share article that you just placed. First you will place the recipe. Then you will change the headline style to Subhead 1 and the subheading to Caption. Next you will adjust the placement of the recipe so that its last line is flush with that of the article in the first column. Finally, you will draw a line across both columns. The specifications you will need to complete this task are:

		Place document dialog box options:
Text style:	Body text	
Headline style:	Subhead 1	☐ Retain format (off)
Subheading style:	Caption	☒ Convert quotes (on)
Article:	Oct Recipe (Crab Dip)	☐ Read tags (off)
Line under article:	1 point	

Place the recipe and make changes to the headline and subheading. To adjust the recipe so that it lines up with the end of the Employee of the Month article:

1. Select the pointer tool.

2. Adjust the page view so you can see where both columns end.

3. Click on the recipe to select it.

4. Pointing to the middle of the selected text block, press the mouse button and move the text block so that the ends of the articles in the two columns are aligned. If you need a ruler guide to assist you, pull one down from the ruler.

Now draw a line below both articles across both columns.

Placing the Graphic

Your last task in creating this newsletter is to place the graphic, a drawing that was scanned and saved as a TIFF file. It is stored on your disk as Cottages.tiff.

The first step will be to draw a box that fills the entire unused portion of the page, covering the column line that separates the two columns. The process you will use will be to paste a piece of paper over the bottom third of the page, place the graphic, and fit it onto the pasted paper.

To paste a piece of paper over the bottom third of the page:

1. Select Fill from the Element menu.

2. Click on Paper.

3. Verify that 1 pt is selected in Line from the Element menu.

4. Select the rectangle tool.

5. Draw a rectangle from the left as shown in Figure 6.34. Be sure the rectangle fits the existing lines. It does so when its border erases the drawn outline on the newsletter.

You should now have a white box covering the unused space at the bottom of page 2.

Figure 6.34
Drawing a rectangle
for the graphic

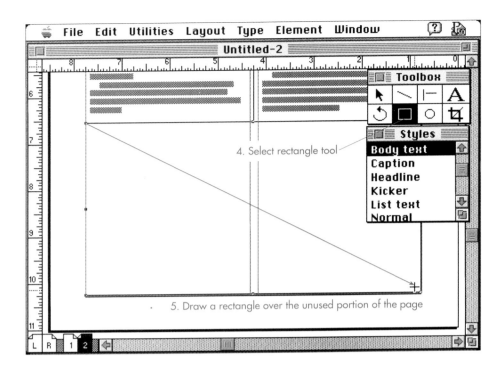

To place the graphic:

1. Select Place... from the File menu (⌘-D).

2. Select Cottages.tiff.

3. Click on OK.

Notice that the mouse pointer has changed to a place-tiff icon (▓), as shown in Figure 6.35.

4. Position the icon as shown in Figure 6.35.

5. Drag the mouse diagonally from the top-left corner to the lower-right corner (see Figure 6.36).

6. Release the mouse button.

If you don't like what you've done, either delete the graphic and place it again or resize it using techniques described in Chapter 5.

To type the caption:

1. Select the text tool.

2. Click on Body text.

3. Click an insertion point under the graphic.

4. Type: *Olympic Cottages* (RETURN)
   Architect's concept of cottages to be built adjacent to the Inn's golf course.

5. Select the text *Olympic Cottages* and change it to italic.

6. Expand the text block over the two columns.

Figure 6.35
Initial position of icon for placing Cottages.tiff

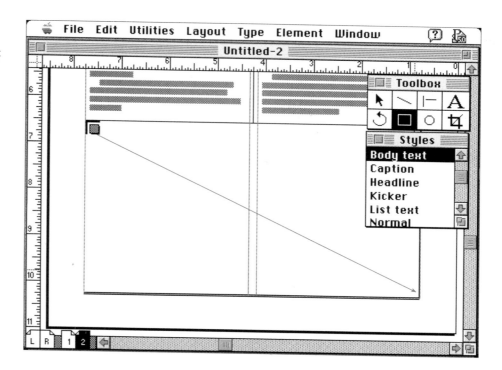

Figure 6.36
Boundaries of graphic

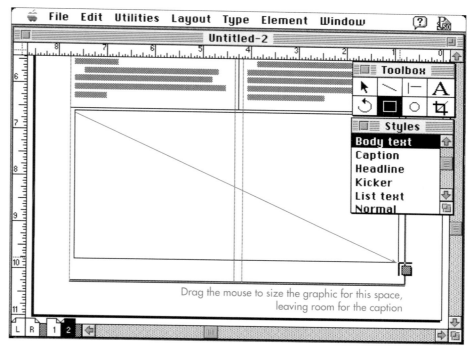

Drag the mouse to size the graphic for this space, leaving room for the caption

The bottom of the newletter page should look like Figure 6.37. Save the newsletter as a publication. The steps are:

1. Select Save from the File menu (⌘-S).

2. Select Publication, if necessary (see Figure 6.38).

3. Type a name for the newsletter.

4. Click on OK.

Figure 6.37
The graphic with the caption added

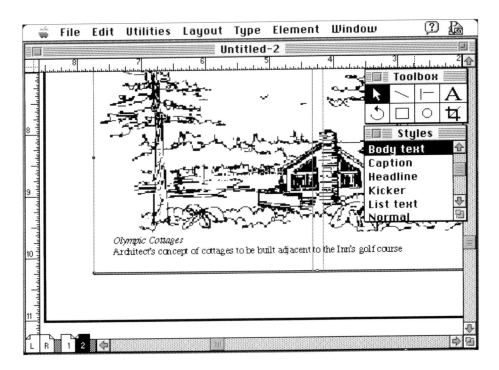

Figure 6.38
Saving the newsletter

Make sure Publication is selected

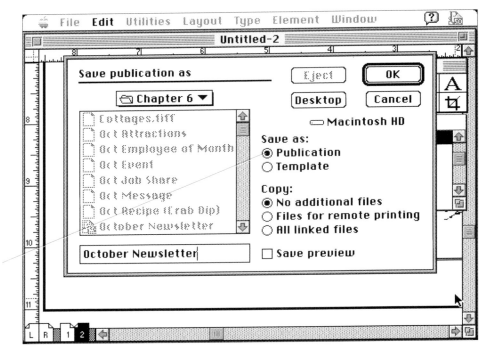

Finally, print the newsletter.

Project 1 at the end of this chapter directs you to create a July issue for the Portage Inn Soundings. You may want to complete that project now, while all the steps are fresh, rather than waiting until you complete the chapter.

The PageMaker package contains almost 20 templates with sample brochures, a calendar, manual, newsletters, and various types of labels. The templates may be used as they are, or they may serve as starting points from which you customize and create your own.

Many templates contain text and graphics placeholders. **Text placeholders** reserve space on the page for various kinds of text, including headlines and body text. Filler text appears throughout template files to hold the place of body text. **Graphics placeholders** are suggested locations for various types of graphics, such as drawings, photographs, and logos.

In this section you will open a PageMaker newsletter template, explore it, place an article with style tags on the first page, and place a graphics file. The text and graphic will replace the placeholders on the template. In working through this section, you will review several skills you learned in Chapter 4. Figure 6.39(a) shows the first page of the PageMaker template, and Figure 6.39(b) shows what the newsletter will look like after you complete this practice.

Figure 6.39(a)
Page 1 of Newsletter 1 template

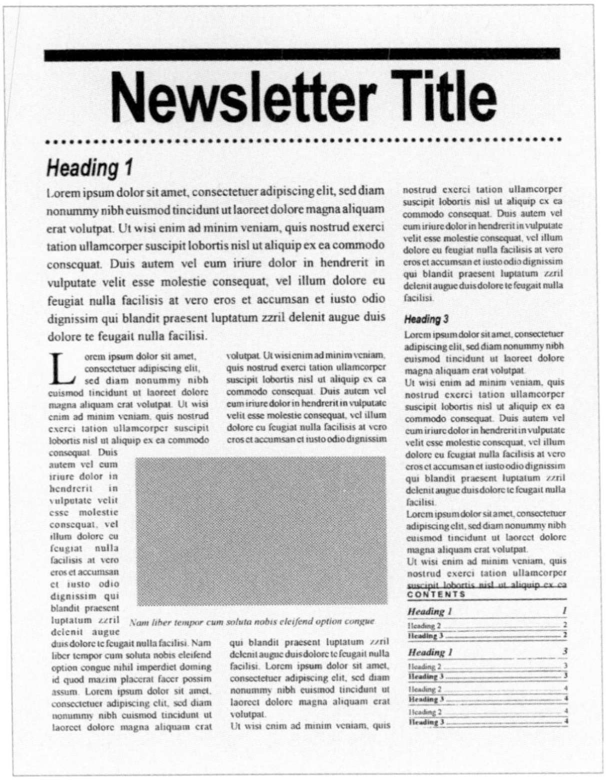

Newsletter Title

Heading 1

Lorem ipsum dolor sit amet, consectetuer adipiscing elit, sed diam nonummy nibh euismod tincidunt ut laoreet dolore magna aliquam erat volutpat. Ut wisi enim ad minim veniam, quis nostrud exerci tation ullamcorper suscipit lobortis nisl ut aliquip ex ea commodo consequat. Duis autem vel eum iriure dolor in hendrerit in vulputate velit esse molestie consequat, vel illum dolore eu feugiat nulla facilisis at vero eros et accumsan et iusto odio dignissim qui blandit praesent luptatum zzril delenit augue duis dolore te feugait nulla facilisi.

Lorem ipsum dolor sit amet, consectetuer adipiscing elit, sed diam nonummy nibh euismod tincidunt ut laoreet dolore magna aliquam erat volutpat. Ut wisi enim ad minim veniam, quis nostrud exerci tation ullamcorper suscipit lobortis nisl ut aliquip ex ea commodo consequat. Duis autem vel eum iriure dolor in hendrerit in vulputate velit esse molestie consequat, vel illum dolore eu feugiat nulla facilisis at vero eros et accumsan et iusto odio dignissim qui blandit praesent luptatum zzril delenit augue duis dolore te feugait nulla facilisi. Nam liber tempor cum soluta nobis eleifend option congue nihil imperdiet doming id quod mazim placerat facer possim assum. Lorem ipsum dolor sit amet, consectetuer adipiscing elit, sed diam nonummy nibh euismod tincidunt ut laoreet dolore magna aliquam erat volutpat. Ut wisi enim ad minim veniam, quis nostrud exerci tation ullamcorper suscipit lobortis nisl ut aliquip ex ea commodo consequat. Duis autem vel eum iriure dolor in hendrerit in vulputate velit esse molestie consequat, vel illum dolore eu feugiat nulla facilisis at vero eros et accumsan et iusto odio dignissim qui blandit praesent luptatum zzril delenit augue duis dolore te feugait nulla facilisi. Lorem ipsum dolor sit amet, consectetuer adipiscing elit, sed diam nonummy nibh euismod tincidunt ut laoreet dolore magna aliquam erat volutpat.

Ut wisi enim ad minim veniam, quis nostrud exerci tation ullamcorper suscipit lobortis nisl ut aliquip ex ea commodo consequat. Duis autem vel eum iriure dolor in hendrerit in vulputate velit esse molestie consequat, vel illum dolore eu feugiat nulla facilisis at vero eros et accumsan et iusto odio dignissim qui blandit praesent luptatum zzril delenit augue duis dolore te feugait nulla facilisi.

Nam liber tempor cum soluta nobis eleifend option congue.

Heading 3

Lorem ipsum dolor sit amet, consectetuer adipiscing elit, sed diam nonummy nibh euismod tincidunt ut laoreet dolore magna aliquam erat volutpat.

Ut wisi enim ad minim veniam, quis nostrud exerci tation ullamcorper suscipit lobortis nisl ut aliquip ex ea commodo consequat. Duis autem vel eum iriure dolor in hendrerit in vulputate velit esse molestie consequat, vel illum dolore eu feugiat nulla facilisis at vero eros et accumsan et iusto odio dignissim qui blandit praesent luptatum zzril delenit augue duis dolore te feugait nulla facilisi.

Lorem ipsum dolor sit amet, consectetuer adipiscing elit, sed diam nonummy nibh euismod tincidunt ut laoreet dolore magna aliquam erat volutpat.

Ut wisi enim ad minim veniam, quis nostrud exerci tation ullamcorper suscipit lobortis nisl ut aliquip ex ea

CONTENTS

Figure 6.39(b)
Page 1 at end of this practice

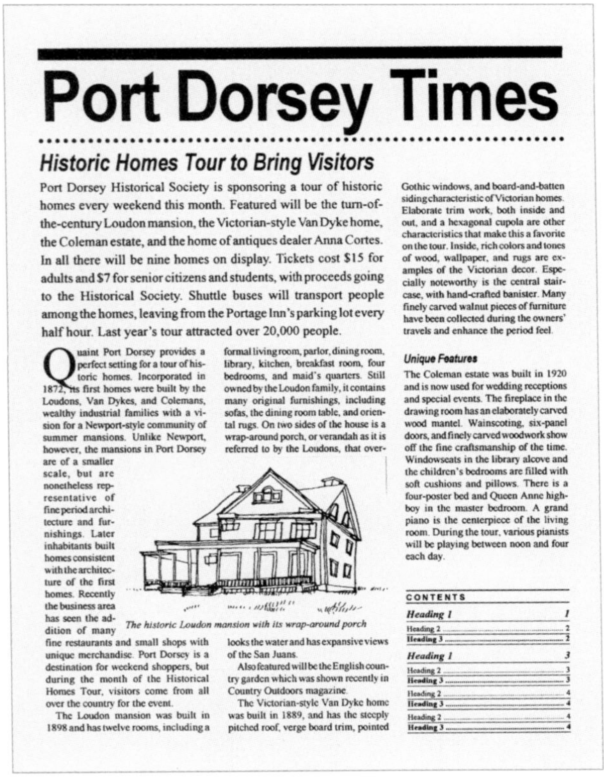

Port Dorsey Times

Historic Homes Tour to Bring Visitors

Port Dorsey Historical Society is sponsoring a tour of historic homes every weekend this month. Featured will be the turn-of-the-century Loudon mansion, the Victorian-style Van Dyke home, the Coleman estate, and the home of antiques dealer Anna Cortes. In all there will be nine homes on display. Tickets cost $15 for adults and $7 for senior citizens and students, with proceeds going to the Historical Society. Shuttle buses will transport people among the homes, leaving from the Portage Inn's parking lot every half hour. Last year's tour attracted over 20,000 people.

Quaint Port Dorsey provides a perfect setting for a tour of historic homes. Incorporated in 1872, its first homes were built by the Loudons, Van Dykes, and Colemans, wealthy industrial families with a vision for a Newport-style community of summer mansions. Unlike Newport, however, the mansions in Port Dorsey are of a smaller scale, but are nonetheless representative of fine period architecture and furnishings. Later inhabitants built homes consistent with the architecture of the first homes. Recently the business area has seen the addition of many fine restaurants and small shops with unique merchandise. Port Dorsey is a destination for weekend shoppers, but during the month of the Historical Homes Tour, visitors come from all over the country for the event.

The Loudon mansion was built in 1898 and has twelve rooms, including a formal living room, parlor, dining room, library, kitchen, breakfast room, four bedrooms, and maid's quarters. Still owned by the Loudon family, it contains many original furnishings, including sofas, the dining room table, and oriental rugs. On two sides of the house is a wrap-around porch, or verandah as it is referred to by the Loudons, that overlooks the water and has expansive views of the San Juans.

The historic Loudon mansion with its wrap-around porch

Also featured will be the English country garden which was shown recently in Country Outdoors magazine.

The Victorian-style Van Dyke home was built in 1889, and has the steeply pitched roof, verge board trim, pointed Gothic windows, and board-and-batten siding characteristic of Victorian homes. Elaborate trim work, both inside and out, and a hexagonal cupola are other characteristics that make this a favorite on the tour. Inside, rich colors and tones of wood, wallpaper, and rugs are examples of the Victorian decor. Especially noteworthy is the central staircase, with hand-crafted banister. Many finely carved walnut pieces of furniture have been collected during the owners' travels and enhance the period feel.

Unique Features

The Coleman estate was built in 1920 and is now used for wedding receptions and special events. The fireplace in the drawing room has an elaborately carved wood mantel. Wainscoting, six-panel doors, and finely carved woodwork show off the fine craftsmanship of the time. Windowseats in the library alcove and the children's bedrooms are filled with soft cushions and pillows. There is a four-poster bed and Queen Anne highboy in the master bedroom. A grand piano is the centerpiece of the living room. During the tour, various pianists will be playing between noon and four each day.

CONTENTS

Opening a PageMaker Template

The template shown in Figure 6.39(a) is named Newsletter 1. It is a four-page newsletter included in the Aldus Additions. In this section you will transform the template into the newsletter shown in Figure 6.39(b). To open the Newsletter 1 template:

1. Select Utilities, Aldus Additions, Open template...

2. Double-click on Newsletter 1.

Be patient, as it takes several minutes to open the template.

Exploring the Newsletter Template

Explore the template by adjusting the page view so you can see more detail. Click on each page icon and look at the pages. In the steps that follow, you will look at the following:

- the text placeholders
- the number of text blocks
- the text styles

First, look closely at the text placeholders.

1. Adjust the page view so you can read the text.

Notice the text in Latin. PageMaker calls this text "Lorem ipsum" after the first two words in the file and uses it for all text placeholders. It is meant to show you how a publication will look with text.

Next, look at the stories on the page and determine how many text blocks there are.

2. Using the pointer tool, point and click on the story under *Heading 1*. Notice the plus sign (+) in the bottom windowshade loop, which means there is more (hidden) text in the text block.

Additional information about the text block may be found by looking at Display textblock info in Aldus Additions.

3. Select Utilities, Aldus Additions, Display textblock info...

After looking at the information:

4. Click on OK.

When composing newsletters, you need to fit articles or stories to the space. The information available in Display textblock info provides valuable information to help you do this.

5. Using the pointer tool, select the text in the bottom half of the first column.

Again, notice the plus sign at the bottom of the column.

Figure 6.40
Dragging the
windowshade to
reveal more text

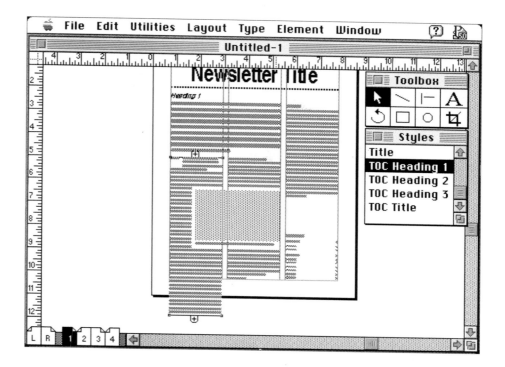

6. Pointing to the plus sign, click and drag the windowshade down to reveal more text (see Figure 6.40).

7. Point and click on the text in the second column above the graphics placeholder.

Notice the plus sign in the top windowshade loop, meaning the block is threaded to a previous block.

8. Click on the third column.

Notice the plus sign in the top windowshade loop and the empty windowshade loop at the end of the block. The empty loop signifies the end of the text block.

Finally, you will explore the text styles on the first page.

Using the text tool, click on different parts of the page and look at which style in the Style palette becomes highlighted. Click within:

- Newsletter Title

- Heading 1

- paragraph after Heading 1

- text in column 1

- caption under the graphics placeholder

- Heading 3 in the third column

Figure 6.41
Type styles for page 1

Figure 6.41 summarizes the styles on the first page. Recall that to find out more about a particular style you can press ⌘ while clicking on the style name in the Style palette.

Creating the Newsletter Using a PageMaker Template

The Inn at Portage Bay is near Port Dorsey, a resort town of historic homes. The Inn sponsors a tour of the historic homes, raising money for the Historical Society and generating tourist traffic for the area. The Inn's desktop publishing staff produces a newsletter describing the homes on the tour.

There are two elements to place in the newsletter: a text file named Historic Tour and a graphics file named Fort.tiff. The newsletter title must be changed to *Port Dorsey Times* and the caption under the drawing will be replaced. A drop cap will be created. The Contents section in the third column will be left as it is. The word *HEADER* must be removed from the line above the newsletter title. Figure 6.42 summarizes the changes.

Figure 6.42
Changes to the newsletter

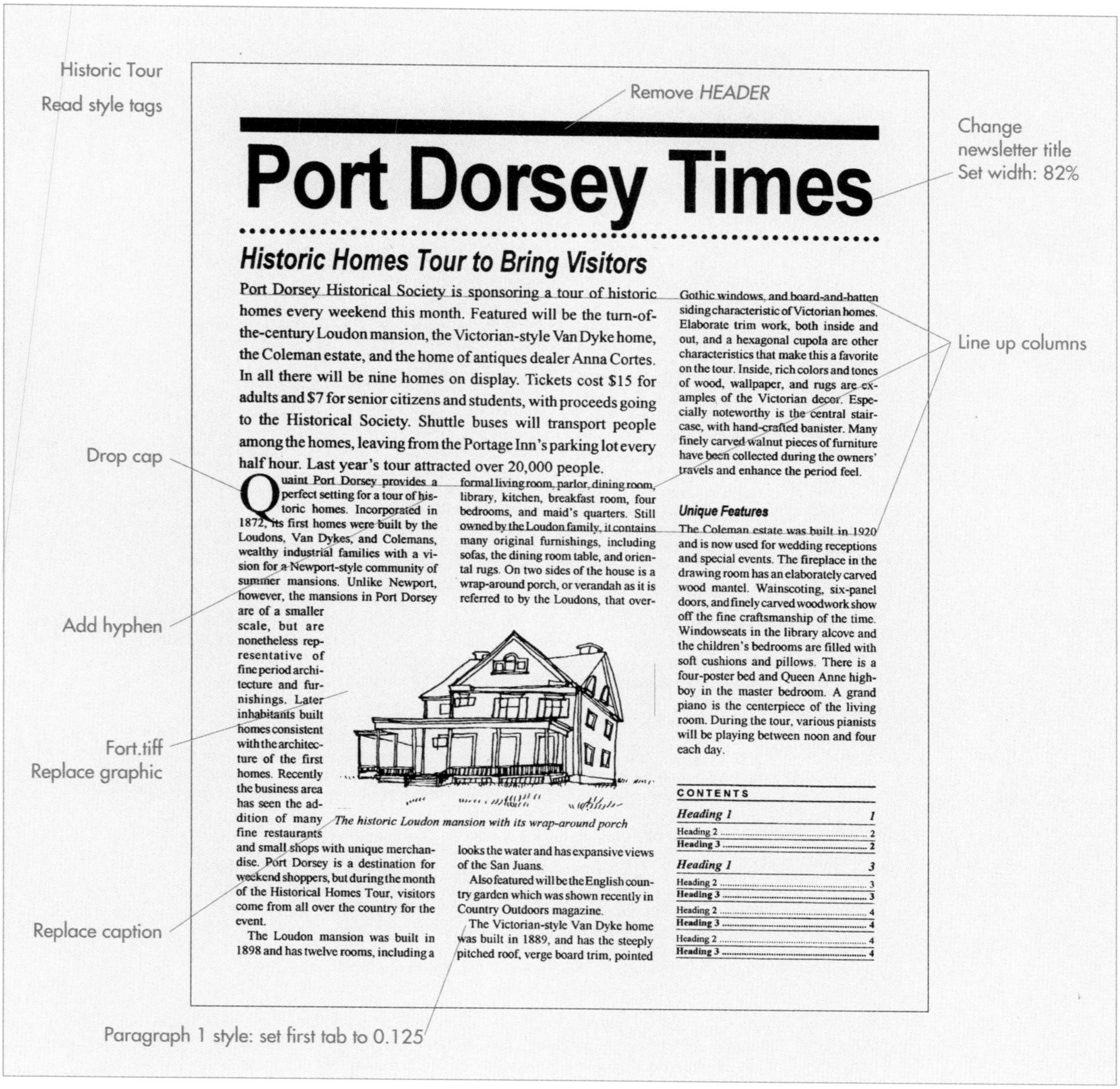

Historic Tour
Read style tags

Remove *HEADER*

Change newsletter title
Set width: 82%

Port Dorsey Times

Historic Homes Tour to Bring Visitors

Port Dorsey Historical Society is sponsoring a tour of historic homes every weekend this month. Featured will be the turn-of-the-century Loudon mansion, the Victorian-style Van Dyke home, the Coleman estate, and the home of antiques dealer Anna Cortes. In all there will be nine homes on display. Tickets cost $15 for adults and $7 for senior citizens and students, with proceeds going to the Historical Society. Shuttle buses will transport people among the homes, leaving from the Portage Inn's parking lot every half hour. Last year's tour attracted over 20,000 people.

Drop cap

Add hyphen

Quaint Port Dorsey provides a perfect setting for a tour of historic homes. Incorporated in 1872, its first homes were built by the Loudons, Van Dykes, and Colemans, wealthy industrial families with a vision for a Newport-style community of summer mansions. Unlike Newport, however, the mansions in Port Dorsey are of a smaller scale, but are nonetheless representative of fine period architecture and furnishings. Later inhabitants built homes consistent with the architecture of the first homes. Recently the business area has seen the addition of many fine restaurants and small shops with unique merchandise. Port Dorsey is a destination for weekend shoppers, but during the month of the Historical Homes Tour, visitors come from all over the country for the event.

The Loudon mansion was built in 1898 and has twelve rooms, including a formal living room, parlor, dining room, library, kitchen, breakfast room, four bedrooms, and maid's quarters. Still owned by the Loudon family, it contains many original furnishings, including sofas, the dining room table, and oriental rugs. On two sides of the house is a wrap-around porch, or verandah as it is referred to by the Loudons, that over-

Fort.tiff
Replace graphic

Replace caption

The historic Loudon mansion with its wrap-around porch

looks the water and has expansive views of the San Juans.

Also featured will be the English country garden which was shown recently in Country Outdoors magazine.

The Victorian-style Van Dyke home was built in 1889, and has the steeply pitched roof, verge board trim, pointed

Line up columns

Gothic windows, and board-and-batten siding characteristic of Victorian homes. Elaborate trim work, both inside and out, and a hexagonal cupola are other characteristics that make this a favorite on the tour. Inside, rich colors and tones of wood, wallpaper, and rugs are examples of the Victorian decor. Especially noteworthy is the central staircase, with hand-crafted banister. Many finely carved walnut pieces of furniture have been collected during the owners' travels and enhance the period feel.

Unique Features

The Coleman estate was built in 1920 and is now used for wedding receptions and special events. The fireplace in the drawing room has an elaborately carved wood mantel. Wainscoting, six-panel doors, and finely carved woodwork show off the fine craftsmanship of the time. Windowseats in the library alcove and the children's bedrooms are filled with soft cushions and pillows. There is a four-poster bed and Queen Anne highboy in the master bedroom. A grand piano is the centerpiece of the living room. During the tour, various pianists will be playing between noon and four each day.

CONTENTS

Heading 1 1
Heading 2 2
Heading 3 2

Heading 1 3
Heading 2 3
Heading 3 3
Heading 2 4
Heading 3 4
Heading 2 4
Heading 3 4

Paragraph 1 style: set first tab to 0.125

Changing the Newsletter Title

To change the newsletter title:

1. Use the text tool to highlight *Newsletter Title*.

2. Type *Port Dorsey Times*.

The newsletter title does not fill the masthead space. Change the width of the title.

3. Use the text tool to highlight the new title.

4. Select Set width from the Type menu.

5. Click on Other.

6. Type *82*.

7. Click on OK or press (RETURN).

Placing the Text

The text you will place is a file named Historic Tour. It was created in Microsoft Word and has style tags. Figure 6.43 shows the file.

Figure 6.43
Historic Tour file in
Word format

<Heading 1>Historic Homes Tour to Bring Visitors
<Paragraph 2>Port Dorsey Historical Society is sponsoring a tour of historic homes every weekend this month. Featured will be the turn-of-the-century Loudon mansion, the Victorian-style Van Dyke home, the Coleman estate, and the home of antiques dealer Anna Cortes. In all there will be nine homes on display. Tickets cost $15 for adults and $7 for senior citizens and students, with proceeds going to the Historical Society. Shuttle buses will transport people among the homes, leaving from the Portage Inn's parking lot every half hour. Last year's tour attracted over 20,000 people.
<Paragraph 1>Quaint Port Dorsey provides a perfect setting for a tour of historic homes. Incorporated in 1872, its first homes were built by the Loudons, Van Dykes, and Colemans, wealthy industrial families with a vision for a Newport-style community of summer mansions. Unlike Newport, however, the mansions in Port Dorsey are of a smaller scale, but are nonetheless representative of fine period architecture and furnishings. Later inhabitants built homes consistent with the architecture of the first homes. Recently the business area has seen the addition of many fine restaurants and small shops with unique merchandise. Port Dorsey is a destination for weekend shoppers, but during the month of the Historical Homes Tour, visitors come from all over the country for the event.
    The Loudon mansion was built in 1898 and has twelve rooms, including a formal living room, parlor, dining room, library, kitchen, breakfast room, four bedrooms, and maid's quarters. Still owned by the Loudon family, it contains many original furnishings, including sofas, the dining room table, and oriental rugs. On two sides of the house is a wrap-around porch, or verandah as it is referred to by the Loudons, that overlooks the water and has expansive views of the San Juans.
    Also featured will be the English country garden which was shown recently in Country Outdoors magazine.
    The Victorian-style Van Dyke home was built in 1889, and has the steeply pitched roof, verge board trim, pointed Gothic windows, and board-and-batten siding characteristic of Victorian homes. Elaborate trim work, both inside and out, and a hexagonal cupola are other characteristics that make this a favorite on the tour. Inside, rich colors and tones of wood, wallpaper, and rugs are examples of the Victorian decor. Especially noteworthy is the central staircase, with hand-crafted banister. Many finely carved walnut pieces of furniture have been collected during the owners' travels and enhance the period feel.
<Heading 3>Unique Features
<Paragraph 1>The Coleman estate was built in 1920 and is now used for wedding receptions and special events. The fireplace in the drawing room has an elaborately carved wood mantel. Wainscoting, six-panel doors, and finely carved woodwork show off the fine craftsmanship of the time. Windowseats in the library alcove and the children's bedrooms are filled with soft cushions and pillows. There is a four-poster bed and Queen Anne highboy in the master bedroom. A grand piano is the centerpiece of the living room. During the tour, various pianists will be playing between noon and four each day.

To place the file you will first delete the four text blocks on the newsletter. If the newsletter had one text block instead of four, you could use the Replacing entire story option in the Place document dialog box. But since there are four text blocks, it is easier to delete them first and use the As new story option.

After placing the file, you will create a drop cap. Finally, you will make sure the text is properly aligned across the columns.

To delete the text blocks:

1. **Using the pointer tool, select a text block.**

2. **Press** (DELETE).

3. **Repeat steps 1 and 2 for each of the other three text blocks.**

At this point, your publication should look like Figure 6.44. To place Historic Tour, verify that the pointer tool is selected, then:

1. **Select Place... from the File menu (⌘-D).**

2. **Single-click on Historic Tour.**

3. **Click on Retain format to deselect it (if necessary).**

4. **Click on Read tags to select it.**

5. **Click on OK.**

6. **Position the loaded text icon at the top of column 1. Click to place the text.**

The first part of the story must be stretched over two columns.

Figure 6.44
Newsletter after deleting the text blocks

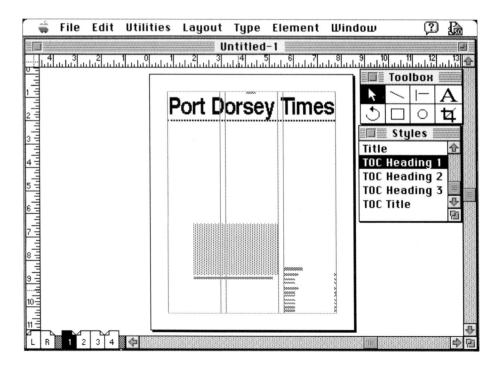

7. Using the handle at the top-right corner of the text block, drag it to fill two columns, as shown in Figure 6.45.

After the first paragraph, which fills two columns, the rest of the story is one column wide. To adjust the rest of the story to fit into one column:

8. Point to the red triangle at the bottom of the page.

9. Drag it up until it is below the end of the first paragraph. Release the mouse button (see Figure 6.46).

Figure 6.45
Dragging to place the text over two columns

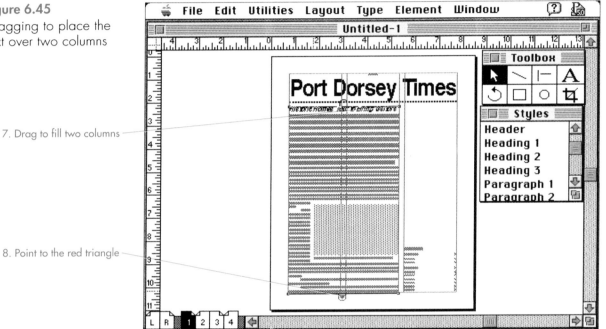

7. Drag to fill two columns

8. Point to the red triangle

Figure 6.46
Adjusting remainder of text to fit into one column

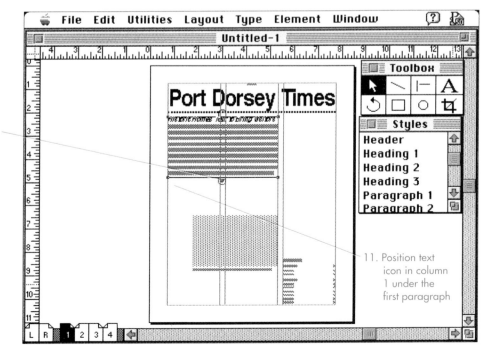

10. Click on the red triangle

11. Position text icon in column 1 under the first paragraph

Figure 6.47
Continuing the story
into the third column

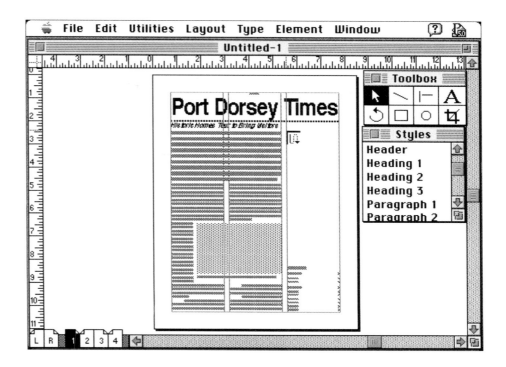

10. Click on the red triangle to get the text icon.

11. Position the text icon in column 1 under the first paragraph. Click to place the text.

12. Click on the red triangle at the bottom of the column to get the text icon.

13. Place the text in column 2 under the first paragraph.

14. Repeat steps 12 and 13 to continue the story into the third column, placing the text next to the top of the first paragraph, as shown in Figure 6.47.

To create a drop cap at the beginning of the second paragraph:

15. Using the text tool, position the I-beam before the *Q* in *Quaint*.

16. Select Utilities, Aldus Additions, Drop cap...

17. Click on OK to accept the default (3 lines).

To align the text between columns:

18. Using at least 200% size, adjust the page view so you can see the top of the two-column story, as shown in Figure 6.48.

19. Pull a ruler guide from the horizontal ruler and place it under the first line of text in column 1.

20. Adjust the alignment of the text in column 2 to match column 1. (Using the pointer tool, click on the text in either column; move the text block so that it lines up with the text in the adjacent column.)

Figure 6.48
Aligning the text in columns 1 and 2

19. Pull a ruler guide from the horizontal ruler

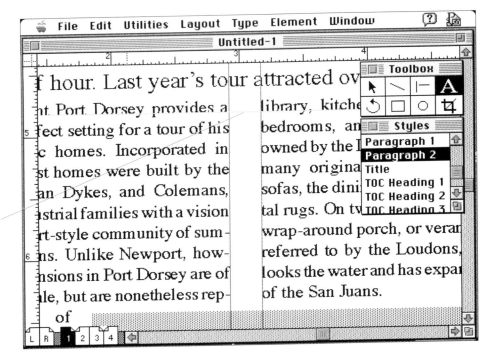

Figure 6.49
Aligning column 3 with columns 1 and 2

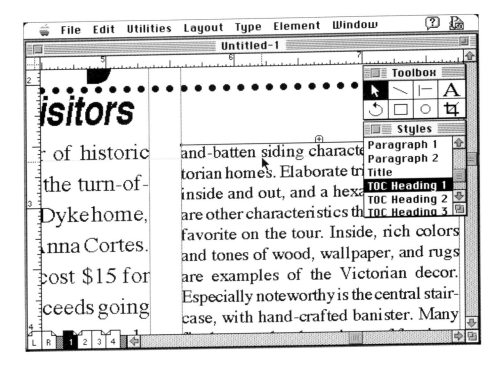

21. Look at the bottom of column 2. Make sure that columns 1 and 2 line up at the end of the page. Adjust the number of lines if necessary.

22. Adjust column 3 so the first line of text lines up with that in columns 1 and 2, as shown in Figure 6.49.

At this point only the top of column 3 matches the alignment of column 2. You will adjust the rest of column 3 later in this chapter.

Placing the Graphics File

The next step is to place Fort.tiff in the graphics placeholder.

1. Using the pointer tool, click on the gray box.
2. Select Place... from the File menu (⌘-D).
3. Single-click on Fort.tiff.
4. Select Replacing entire graphic.
5. Click on OK.

To replace the caption:

1. Use the text tool to highlight the caption.
2. Type *The historic Loudon mansion with its wrap-around porch.*

There are four other tasks to do in order to get your publication to match Figure 6.39(b). These are:

- Add a hyphen to the word break in *historic*.
- Set the first tab in Paragraph 1 style at 0.125.
- Align the lower part of the third column to the text in the second column.
- Remove the word *HEADER* from the line above *Port Dorsey Times*.

The reason you need to add a hyphen is that when you set the drop cap to three lines, PageMaker does not automatically hyphenate the text. Setting the first tab at 0.125 makes the paragraph breaks more distinct. Aligning column 3 to column 2 at the top leaves the bottom unaligned, and it looks awkward as it is. Finally, removing the word *HEADER* will eliminate this text placeholder we won't be needing.

Completing the first two items on the list is straightforward and will be left to you. To align the bottom of columns 2 and 3, use a technique similar to the one you used to change the text from two columns to one column.

1. With the pointer tool selected, click on the text in the third column.
2. Move the bottom windowshade to just above the heading *Unique Features*.
3. Click on the red triangle.
4. Place the text icon below the paragraph that ends with *period feel*.
5. Click the mouse button.

You now have a separate text block for the Unique Features paragraph.

6. Pull a horizontal ruler guide down to below the fourth line in column 2 to use as an alignment guide.

7. Align the Unique Features paragraph to the text in column 2.

The word *HEADER* is on the right master page. To remove it:

1. Click on the master page icons.

2. With the text tool selected, highlight *HEADER*.

3. Press (DELETE).

Refer to Figure 6.42 to make sure you have made all the changes. If you are done, remove pages 2, 3, and 4 (select Remove pages from the Layout menu), save your file, and print it.

You may choose to change the font of the drop cap. The Q in *Quaint* "crashes" with the word *its* in the fourth line of the paragraph. Figure 6.50 shows the publication with the Q changed to Helvetica. The graphic has also been flipped 180 degrees, which tends to draw the reader's eye onto the page, rather than directing it to the left edge.

Figure 6.50
Newsletter with different drop cap and the graphic flipped

Port Dorsey Times

Historic Homes Tour to Bring Visitors

Port Dorsey Historical Society is sponsoring a tour of historic homes every weekend this month. Featured will be the turn-of-the-century Loudon mansion, the Victorian-style Van Dyke home, the Coleman estate, and the home of antiques dealer Anna Cortes. In all there will be nine homes on display. Tickets cost $15 for adults and $7 for senior citizens and students, with proceeds going to the Historical Society. Shuttle buses will transport people among the homes, leaving from the Portage Inn's parking lot every half hour. Last year's tour attracted over 20,000 people.

Quaint Port Dorsey provides a perfect setting for a tour of historic homes. Incorporated in 1872, its first homes were built by the Loudons, Van Dykes, and Colemans, wealthy industrial families with a vision for a Newport-style community of summer mansions. Unlike Newport, however, the mansions in Port Dorsey are of a smaller scale, but are nonetheless representative of fine period architecture and furnishings. Later inhabitants built homes consistent with the architecture of the first homes. Recently the business area has seen the addition of many fine restaurants and small shops with unique merchandise. Port Dorsey is a destination for weekend shoppers, but during the month of the Historical Homes Tour, visitors come from all over the country for the event.

The Loudon mansion was built in 1898 and has twelve rooms, including a formal living room, parlor, dining room, library, kitchen, breakfast room, four bedrooms, and maid's quarters. Still owned by the Loudon family, it contains many original furnishings, including sofas, the dining room table, and oriental rugs. On two sides of the house is a wrap-around porch, or verandah as it is referred to by the Loudons, that overlooks the water and has expansive views of the San Juans.

The historic Loundon mansion with its wrap-around porch

Also featured will be the English country garden which was shown recently in Country Outdoors magazine.

The Victorian-style Van Dyke home was built in 1889, and has the steeply pitched roof, verge board trim, pointed Gothic windows, and board-and-batten siding characteristic of Victorian homes. Elaborate trim work, both inside and out, and a hexagonal cupola are other characteristics that make this a favorite on the tour. Inside, rich colors and tones of wood, wallpaper, and rugs are examples of the Victorian decor. Especially noteworthy is the central staircase, with hand-crafted banister. Many finely carved walnut pieces of furniture have been collected during the owners' travels and enhance the period feel.

Unique Features

The Coleman estate was built in 1920 and is now used for wedding receptions and special events. The fireplace in the drawing room has an elaborately carved wood mantel. Wainscoting, six-panel doors, and finely carved woodwork show off the fine craftsmanship of the time. Windowseats in the library alcove and the children's bedrooms are filled with soft cushions and pillows. There is a four-poster bed and Queen Anne highboy in the master bedroom. A grand piano is the centerpiece of the living room. During the tour, various pianists will be playing between noon and four each day.

CONTENTS

SUMMARY

You have created two newsletters using templates. One template was created by the authors and saved on your disk. The other is part of the PageMaker package and can be found in the Aldus Additions.

Templates are valuable design tools and timesavers. They allow you to quickly produce quality documents. In this chapter you learned about templates, master pages, the Style palette, placing text and graphics, resizing graphics, and using placeholders. You used style tags to format text. In the next chapter you will create a template for the Inn's Annual Report.

KEY TERMS

master pages	template	kicker
publication pages	Style palette	eyebrow
facing pages	style sheets	text placeholder
gutter	filter	graphics placeholder
double-sided		

QUESTIONS

1. What is a master page? What kinds of items appear on master pages?

2. State the advantages of using master pages.

3. What is the advantage of working with facing pages?

4. Is page 1 of a publication a left or right master page? Explain your answer.

5. Does page 1 of a publication have a facing page? Explain.

6. For each of the following, state whether you would put it on a master page or a publication page.

   (a) column guides

   (b) page number

   (c) grid

   (d) table of contents for a newsletter

   (e) masthead

   (f) company logo

7. What is a template? What is included in it?

8. State the advantages of working with templates.

9. What are the advantages of working with a copy of a template or publication rather than the original?

10. What is a gutter? How does it differ from a margin?

11. Compare and contrast templates and master pages.

12. What are the advantages and disadvantages of using style tags in a word processing file?

13. Make a list of the filters installed on your computer. To do this, look in the Aldus filters folder. Use Finder and type filter.

14. Using Help, make a list of the information you can learn about a text block.

15. Using Help, list the two ways to display master pages.

16. Using Help, determine the graphics filters available for your version of PageMaker.

17. Using Help, explain how you hide some master page elements on a publication page.

PROJECTS

1. Use the Portage Newsletter template to create a July issue for the Portage Inn Soundings newsletter. Refer to Figure 6.51 for article names and placement. Make sure you start with the template and not your finished publication.

2. Use PageMaker templates to create the following:
   - Fax cover sheet (Figure 6.52)
   - Purchase order (Figure 6.53)
   - Invoice (Figure 6.54)

   Replace the logo box with Portage.tiff and type the correct address and phone number for the Inn.

3. Use either newsletter template to create your own newsletter for The Inn at Portage Bay. Write the articles using a word processing program compatible with PageMaker.

Figure 6.51
July newsletter specifications

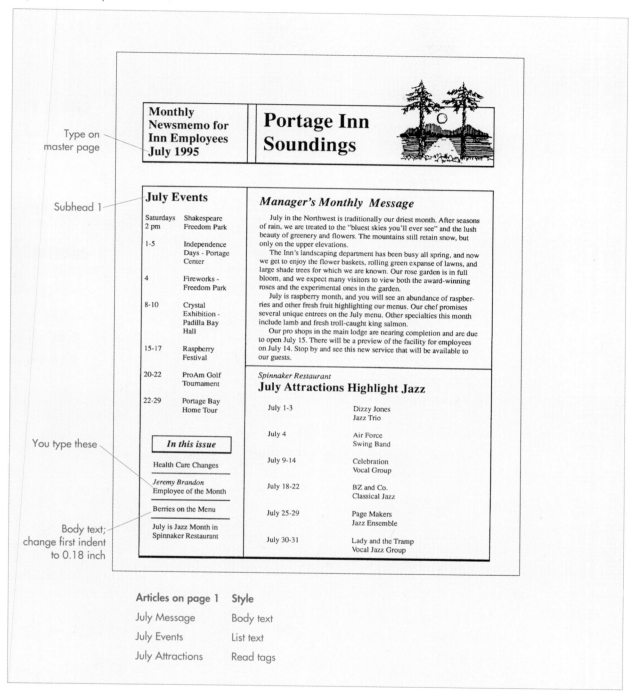

Type on master page

Monthly Newsmemo for Inn Employees July 1995

Portage Inn Soundings

Subhead 1

July Events

Saturdays 2 pm	Shakespeare Freedom Park
1-5	Independence Days - Portage Center
4	Fireworks - Freedom Park
8-10	Crystal Exhibition - Padilla Bay Hall
15-17	Raspberry Festival
20-22	ProAm Golf Tournament
22-29	Portage Bay Home Tour

In this issue

You type these

Health Care Changes

Jeremy Brandon
Employee of the Month

Berries on the Menu

July is Jazz Month in Spinnaker Restaurant

Body text; change first indent to 0.18 inch

Manager's Monthly Message

July in the Northwest is traditionally our driest month. After seasons of rain, we are treated to the "bluest skies you'll ever see" and the lush beauty of greenery and flowers. The mountains still retain snow, but only on the upper elevations.

The Inn's landscaping department has been busy all spring, and now we get to enjoy the flower baskets, rolling green expanse of lawns, and large shade trees for which we are known. Our rose garden is in full bloom, and we expect many visitors to view both the award-winning roses and the experimental ones in the garden.

July is raspberry month, and you will see an abundance of raspberries and other fresh fruit highlighting our menus. Our chef promises several unique entrees on the July menu. Other specialties this month include lamb and fresh troll-caught king salmon.

Our pro shops in the main lodge are nearing completion and are due to open July 15. There will be a preview of the facility for employees on July 14. Stop by and see this new service that will be available to our guests.

Spinnaker Restaurant
July Attractions Highlight Jazz

July 1-3	Dizzy Jones Jazz Trio
July 4	Air Force Swing Band
July 9-14	Celebration Vocal Group
July 18-22	BZ and Co. Classical Jazz
July 25-29	Page Makers Jazz Ensemble
July 30-31	Lady and the Tramp Vocal Jazz Group

Articles on page 1	Style
July Message	Body text
July Events	List text
July Attractions	Read tags

Figure 6.51
July newsletter specifications *(continued)*

July Employee of Month

July Health Read style tags

Read style tags

July Raspberries Read style tags

You type this

Golf Green.tiff

Body text

Portage Inn Soundings　　　　　　　　　　　**Page 2**

Jeremy Brandon

Employee of the Month Loves Golf, All Sports

Jeremy Brandon, our golf pro, is July's Employee of the Month.

Jeremy was born in Olympia, Washington, and has lived in the Northwest all his life. He is a graduate of Arizona State University, where he majored in Engineering and English. Attending on a golf scholarship, he won several NCAA titles and was ranked 23rd nationally for collegiate golfers.

Jeremy started playing golf with his parents when he was about 7. "I could barely hit the side of a barn at 50 feet when I first started," he said recently. But after many lessons, and watching golfers as a caddy for what seemed like forever, Jeremy began placing in tournaments. First there were local ones, where he admits, with characteristic understatement, "My play was a bit uneven." In high school, by his sophomore year, he started to place in every competition he entered. "At that time, things began to click and I had a good senior year." Good indeed, as Jeremy capped the individual state title and led his team to be Conference Champs.

Jeremy has been the golf pro here since the Inn opened. His responsibilities include lessons, and he has organized the golf mini vacations that have brought groups of visitors to our resort.

Congratulations to Jeremy! He will receive a complimentary dinner for two in the Spinnaker Restaurant as well as having his name added to our list of Inn Achievers.

Health Care Changes

July is open enrollment month. If you wish to change your health care coverage, this is the time to do it. Barbara Van Dyke in Payroll has forms and can answer your questions about coverage plans.

Non-smokers may reduce the cost of their health care by signing and returning the Non-Smoker Statement that accompanied your June paycheck. If you and your spouse have not used tobacco products in the past 12 months, sign the form and bring it to Payroll. The deadline is July 15.

It's the Berries!!!

Our July menu will include these raspberry delights. Make sure you sample each during our Employee Sampling Hour on the first day of the month.

　Raspberry ice cream and sorbet
　Cantaloupe and raspberry salad
　Raspberry pie
　Haddock with raspberry puree sauce
　Raspberry bombe
　Raspberry pudding
　Raspberry cranberry muffins
　Cold raspberry soup
　Raspberry scones

Portage Inn
ProAm Golf Tournament
July 20 - 22

At last year's ProAm Tournament, only 20 percent of the entrants shot par on the fifteenth hole.

Articles on page 2	Style
July Employee of Month	Read tags
July Health	Read tags
July Raspberries	Read tags
Golf Green.tiff	

Figure 6.52
Project 6.2—
Fax cover sheet

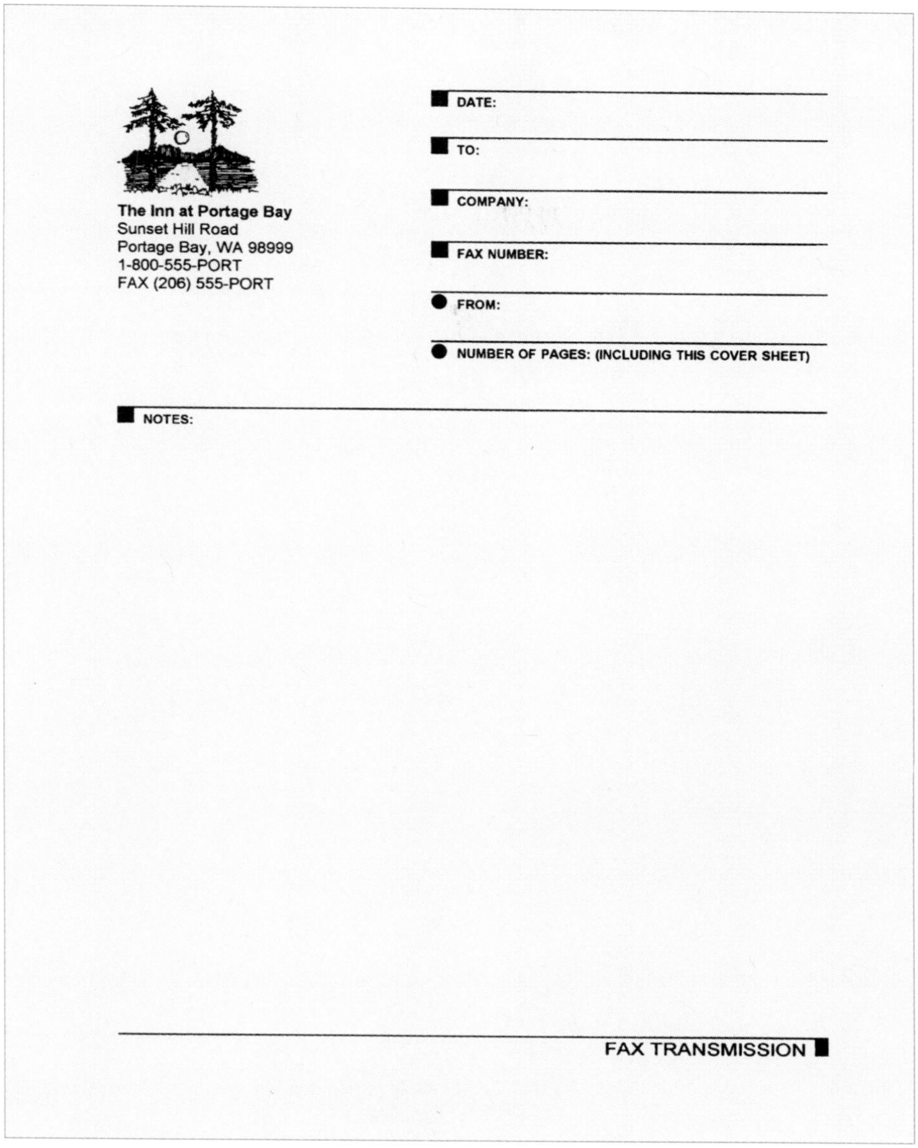

The Inn at Portage Bay
Sunset Hill Road
Portage Bay, WA 98999
1-800-555-PORT
FAX (206) 555-PORT

■ DATE:

■ TO:

■ COMPANY:

■ FAX NUMBER:

● FROM:

● NUMBER OF PAGES: (INCLUDING THIS COVER SHEET)

■ NOTES:

FAX TRANSMISSION ■

Figure 6.53
Project 6.2—
Purchase order

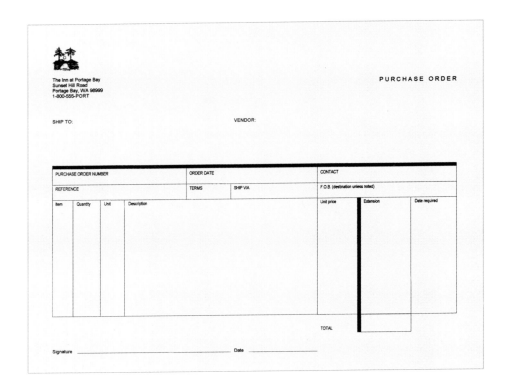

Figure 6.54
Project 6.2—Invoice

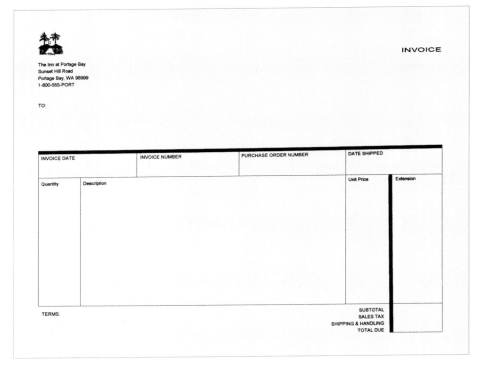

Upon completion of this chapter you will be able to:

- Define *grid system,* explain its purpose, and create one

- Define *style sheet;* explain its purpose; and modify, add, and delete styles in the Style palette

- Define *master pages,* explain their purpose, and create them

- Define *template,* explain its purpose, and create one

- Create automatic page numbers

CHAPTER 7

Creating Grids, Style Sheets, Master Pages, and Templates

In Chapter 6 you created a newsletter using a template stored on the disk accompanying this book. The template contained the layout, or underlying structure, for the newsletter. In this chapter you will learn how to create that underlying structure for PageMaker documents and be introduced to some design concepts.

There are four components to the structure of documents: grids, style sheets, master pages, and templates. You will learn about each of the four and use them to create an Annual Report for the Inn at Portage Bay. The template you will complete in this chapter is shown in Figure 7.1.

Several skills are needed to produce any desktop-published document. These include knowing how to use the software, identifying the document's objective, creating the document's copy, and designing the layout.

Personal computer-based software, such as PageMaker, shortens the time between initial concept and final document production. It can mean the software user is the only person involved in all the steps—from the first design through to delivery of camera-ready copy. Although one person *may* possess all the skills necessary to produce a quality document, it does not necessarily follow that knowing PageMaker ensures a well-designed brochure, newsletter, or annual report. Desktop publishing allows us to create well-designed publications, as well as poorly designed ones, much faster than we could before.

Thus it is important to plan a publication before placing text and graphics on the page. This step will lead to (but not guarantee) better design. In this chapter you will learn how to use PageMaker to execute design decisions. In the next chapter you will learn about some of the rules behind page design and have an opportunity to experiment with design concepts.

Figure 7.1
Annual Report finished template, pages 1–3

GRIDS

When building a house, you expect the architect to have a plan before construction begins. It is also reasonable to expect to do some page design before creating a document. The idea behind creating a **grid** is to give the page a structure on which to build publication pages. The grid is actually a set of nonprinting horizontal and vertical lines that divide the page into rectangles and show you where to place headlines, text, graphs, and pictures. To continue the analogy between page design and house design, creating a page grid before creating master pages is like deciding upon the framing interval between wall studs before creating a framing plan for a house. Both are underlying structures on which a product is built, and both require design and planning to succeed.

There are many advantages to using a grid system. A grid gives the publication a unified appearance and reflects the proportions you have used to design a page. A grid system imposes organization on an untrained designer and assists the designer in placing page elements. It makes the publication look planned and helps coordinate team contributions to a project. Readers get used to the grid you present. For all these reasons, it is wise to start with a grid.

Examples of grid systems are shown in Figure 7.2. In addition to the two and three columns dividing the page vertically, horizontal lines complete the grid system. After establishing the grid, articles, pictures, and graphs may be placed. Once the grid system is set up, additional decisions may be made about headers and footers, page numbers, and how to place headlines.

Figure 7.2
Examples of
grid systems

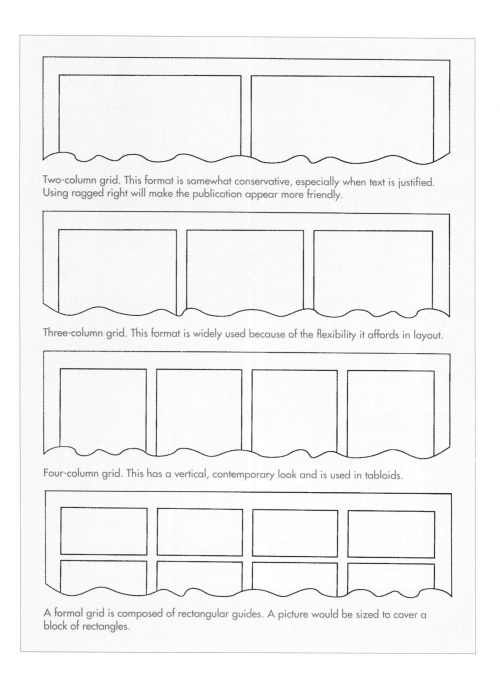

Two-column grid. This format is somewhat conservative, especially when text is justified. Using ragged right will make the publication appear more friendly.

Three-column grid. This format is widely used because of the flexibility it affords in layout.

Four-column grid. This has a vertical, contemporary look and is used in tabloids.

A formal grid is composed of rectangular guides. A picture would be sized to cover a block of rectangles.

Variations on the Grid

Page layout does not always mean staying strictly inside the grid. For example, in a four-column grid, a graph or picture may be placed over three columns, as in Figure 7.3. However, it's rare to use one and a half columns. Using one and a half columns of a four-column grid may imply that underlying the four columns is an eight-column grid.

A second variation of the grid system is to use it to define two columns of unequal width. In this case, there should still be an underlying grid. For example, in a grid system with three columns, the two page columns may be in proportions of one-third and two-thirds. The narrow column may be filled with text, as in the newsletter you created in Chapter 6,

Figure 7.3
Variation on
grid layout

Figure 7.4
Columns of
uneven width

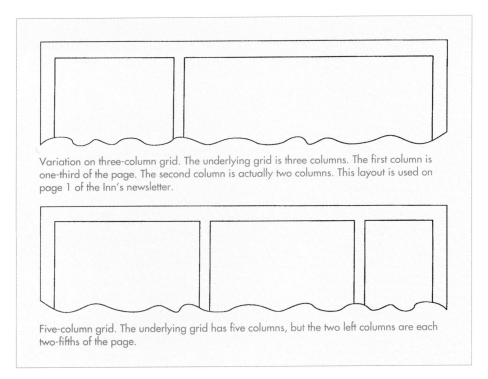

Variation on three-column grid. The underlying grid is three columns. The first column is one-third of the page. The second column is actually two columns. This layout is used on page 1 of the Inn's newsletter.

Five-column grid. The underlying grid has five columns, but the two left columns are each two-fifths of the page.

or be used as a scholar's margin. Figure 7.4 illustrates columns of unequal width.

A **scholar's margin** is a narrow column, typically on the outside edge of a page, that is predominantly white space. Its purpose is to give visual interest to the page, allow for emphasis of key items, and draw the reader into the text. The scholar's margin may contain section headings, boxed items that enhance body text, or pull quotes. A **pull quote** is a quote from the body copy repeated somewhere else for emphasis. In this case, a pull quote may appear in the scholar's margin in the neighborhood of the quote in context. Pull quotes may also appear within the body text in larger print.

A further grid variation is to leave one or more sections without body text across the top of the page, as shown in Figure 7.5. This allows the use of chapter or section headings, lead-in quotes, or other items to enhance interest. The idea is similar to that of the scholar's margin, but the blank space is at the top of the page.

A grid is critical to good page design and layout, but it should be an organizational tool rather than a design prison.

Creating a Grid with PageMaker

A grid system has two components: horizontal lines and vertical lines. Horizontal lines are created by pointing to the top (or horizontal) ruler, pressing the mouse button, and dragging a line to the appropriate place. Vertical lines are done in the same way, except using the left (vertical) ruler. A second method of establishing vertical lines is to let PageMaker create columns using the Column guides dialog box from the Layout pull-down menu. An advantage of this method is that PageMaker divides the page evenly; you don't have to worry about measuring.

Figure 7.5
Creative use of blank space

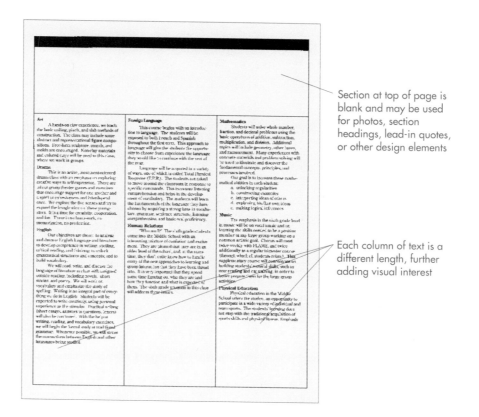

Section at top of page is blank and may be used for photos, section headings, lead-in quotes, or other design elements

Each column of text is a different length, further adding visual interest

Figure 7.6

Completed grid for the Inn's Annual Report

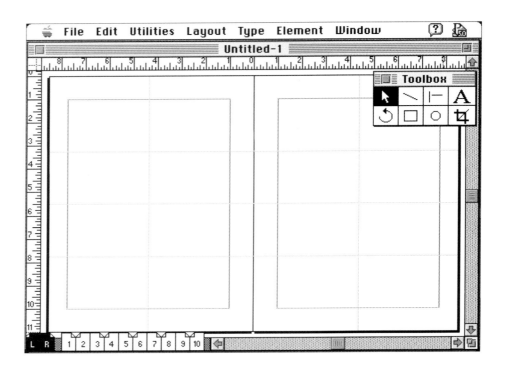

In this practice you will create a new publication and drag lines from the rulers to create a grid with two vertical and four horizontal lines. Then you will use the Column guides dialog box to establish two columns. In this way you will practice both methods of making vertical lines: dragging rulers and making columns. This grid will become the basis for the Annual Report you'll work on later in the chapter. Figure 7.6 shows how the completed practice will look.

Getting Started

In this section you will start PageMaker, create a new publication, verify options, and click on the master page icons.

1. **Open PageMaker.**

2. **Select New... from the File menu (⌘-N).**

3. **In the Page setup dialog box, choose the following options (see Figure 7.7).**

   Number of pages: 10

   Top: 1 (Margin in inches)

   Bottom: 1 (Margin in inches)

4. **Click on OK.**

Verify that the correct options are selected:

5. **Select the Layout menu, then Guides and rulers (see Figure 7.8).**

6. **Verify that both Rulers and Guides are checked.**

7. **Verify that Lock guides is *not* checked.**

Figure 7.7
Page setup dialog
box for the Inn's
Annual Report

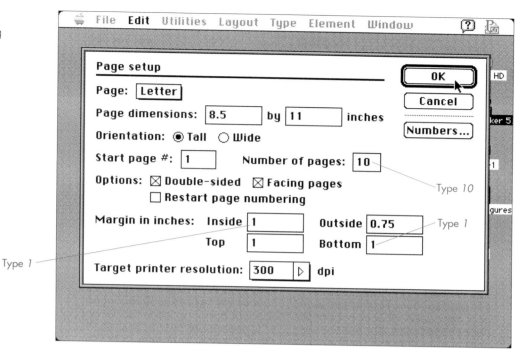

Figure 7.8
Guides and rulers
options from the
Layout menu

Verify that Rulers is checked

Verify that Guides is checked

Verify that Lock guides is
not checked

Click on master page icons

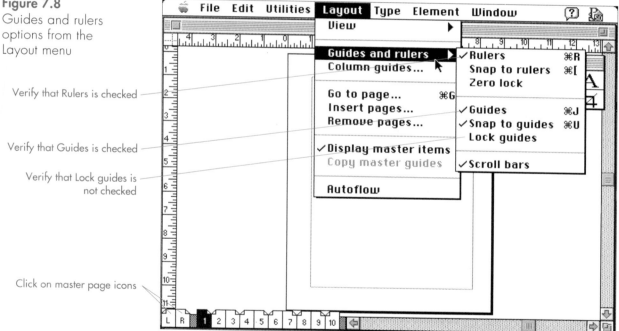

8. **Click on the master page icons (the L and R icons in the lower-left corner) to make sure the grid you create will appear on every page.**

Calculating Where the Lines Are Placed

Drawing the grid requires a bit of planning. This grid will have four rows and two columns in addition to the margins. The page is 8½ × 11 inches. A basic calculator performs the simple arithmetic.

Figure 7.9
Completed grid

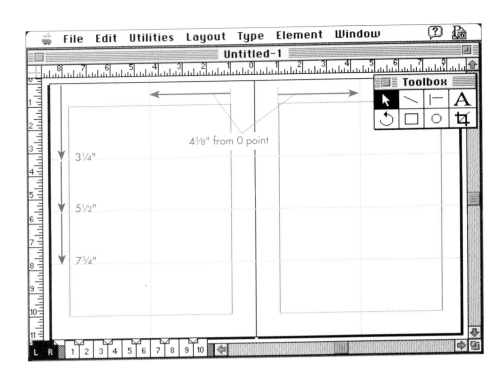

To calculate where to place the vertical line, start with the 8½" width. The 8½" dimension has an outside margin of ¾" and an inside margin of 1". That leaves 6¾" (8.5 − 0.75 − 1) to halve. Dividing 6¾ by 2 gives 3⅜. Thus, place a vertical grid line 3⅜" from either margin line. Measuring in eighths is not difficult because PageMaker's ruler has markings.

To divide the 11" dimension into four equal parts requires three lines. Recall that top and bottom margins are each 1", so the space available is 9" (11 − 2). Dividing 9 by 4 gives 2¼. Thus, the three horizontal lines will be 2¼" apart. With 1" as the starting point, the horizontal lines will cross at 3¼", 5½", and 7¾". All grid dimensions are noted in Figure 7.9.

Drawing the Vertical Lines

You will draw a vertical line in the center of each of the two master pages.

1. Point to the vertical ruler on the left side.

2. Pressing the mouse button, drag a line 4⅜" from the 0 or center point (page fold). Release the mouse. If the guideline is not correctly positioned, point to it and drag it until you are satisfied with its position.

3. Repeat steps 1 and 2 to draw a vertical line in the center of the other master page.

Drawing the Horizontal Lines

You will draw three horizontal lines on each master page.

1. Point to the top ruler.

2. Pressing the mouse button, drag a line 3¼" from the 0 point. Release the mouse.

3. Repeat steps 1 and 2 to create lines 5½" and 7¾" from the top.

You have now positioned several guides on the master pages, creating a grid. After you verify that the lines are in the correct positions, lock the guides so you don't inadvertently move them.

4. Select Layout.

5. Select Guides and rulers, Lock guides.

Creating Columns

The columns you created with the vertical guidelines are not recognized by PageMaker when working with text. To create actual columns:

1. Select Column guides... from the Layout menu.

2. Type 2 for the number of columns.

3. Click on OK.

Now PageMaker will be able to place text in a two-column format.

You have created the underlying grid for the Annual Report. In the next section you will create the Style palette for this publication.

STYLE SHEETS

Graphic designers create a style sheet for each publication. A **style sheet** is a list of type styles and sizes for the publication, such as Headline, Caption, and Body text styles. Each style is a set of instructions for formatting text. A **style** includes a font and size; a choice of normal, bold, or italic; and paragraph characteristics, such as indentation and margins.

Instead of naming it a style sheet, PageMaker calls this tool a **Style palette**. Within each style is a font description, the margins, and indentation for that style. For example, you may use Times 30 bold for a headline, the same size font with italic for a subheading, and Times 10 for body text. Indentation for each of the three styles may be different, as may be the left and right margins. In PageMaker terms, all the styles for one publication make up a Style palette. A graphic designer would call this a style sheet.

The Window pull-down menu allows you to specify whether you want the Style palette to appear on the Pasteboard. If you select Style palette, a box will appear at the right side of the Pasteboard. The Style palette will list the styles defined for that publication. PageMaker has seven default styles: [No style], Body text, Caption, Hanging indent, Headline, Subhead 1, and Subhead 2. The styles may be modified or deleted, and other styles may be added through the Define styles dialog box in the Type pull-down menu. In this way, each publication may be customized.

When creating style sheets for a client, it's a good practice to keep a notebook and include in it each publication and its style sheet. You may even want to annotate a document with respect to which style was used for each of its parts.

Creating the Style Palette for the Inn's Annual Report

In this section you will tell PageMaker to display the Style palette on the Pasteboard. Starting with the default Style palette, you will modify four styles, delete two styles, and create one style for the Inn's Annual Report. In this way you will have the opportunity to work with adding, changing, and deleting styles.

The Inn's Annual Report will use five different styles: Body text, Headline, Subhead 1, Subhead 2, and Pull quote. The first four are part of the default Style palette and will require modification. You will create Pull quote. Finally, you will delete Caption and Hanging indent, two default styles.

The styles for this project will use the Times and Helvetica typefaces. Their specifications are summarized in the following table.

Name of style	Specifications
Body text	Times + size 11 + leading auto + flush left + first indent 0.3333 + hyphenation
Headline	Helvetica + bold + size 30 + leading auto + flush left + incl TOC
Subhead 1	Headline + italic + size 18
Subhead 2	Subhead 1 – bold – italic + centered
Pull quote	Subhead 1 – bold – italic

Getting Started

Prior to creating and manipulating styles, you need to make sure the Style palette appears on the Pasteboard.

1. Select Window.

2. If there is no check next to Style palette, click on Style palette (⌘-Y) (use Figure 7.10 as a guide).

Modifying Styles

To change the Body text style:

1. In the Style palette, click on Body text.

Clicking on Body text in step 1 is not essential in this process, but it is a good practice. At times, having the style selected before looking at its specifications will make your task simpler.

Step 2 allows you to look at and change specifications for Body text.

Figure 7.10
Window pull-down menu

Click on Style palette

Style palette lists the
styles for a publication

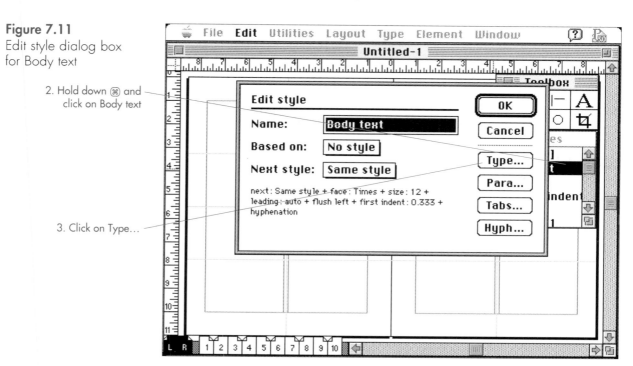

2. Hold down ⌘ and click on Body text.

You should see the Edit style dialog box onscreen, as shown in Figure 7.11. The Edit style dialog box describes the features of the selected style. You need to change Body text to meet the specifications for the Annual Report. To change the font:

3. Click on Type...

4. Click on the arrow to the right of the Size value.

Figure 7.11
Edit style dialog box
for Body text

2. Hold down ⌘ and
click on Body text

3. Click on Type...

5. Select 11 points.

6. Verify that your screen matches Figure 7.12.

7. Click on OK.

Look at your screen. It should match Figure 7.13. Below Next style are the specifications for the typeface and the leading. Flush left means the text will be flush to the left margin. First indent refers to how far the next line will be indented after you press (RETURN). The specifications also

Figure 7.12
Type specifications dialog box for Body text after selecting point size

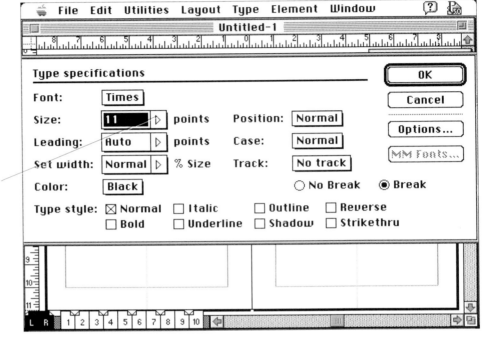

Clicking on the arrows lets you view and select other options

Figure 7.13
Edit style dialog box after changing specifications for Body text

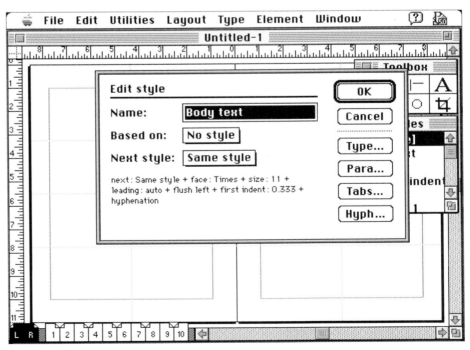

show the selection of hyphenation. The Edit style dialog box describes
the features of the selected style.

8. Click on OK.

To change the Headline style:

1. Click on Headline.

2. Hold down ⌘ and click on Headline.

3. Click on Type...

4. Press the mouse button on the font name.

5. Scroll up and click on Helvetica.

6. Click on OK (compare your screen with Figure 7.14).

7. Click on OK to return to the Pasteboard.

To change Subhead 1 style:

1. Click on Subhead 1.

2. Hold down ⌘ and click on Subhead 1.

Notice that Subhead 1 is based on Headline, so its specifications are the
same as those of Headline except for changes noted below the Next style
line. These changes are noted with a + when the change is an addition
and a – when it is a deletion. The changes shown with the + and – remain
changes to the Headline style, and you will also make additional changes.

3. Click on Type...

4. Verify that Bold is selected.

Figure 7.14
Edit style dialog box
after specifications
for Headline

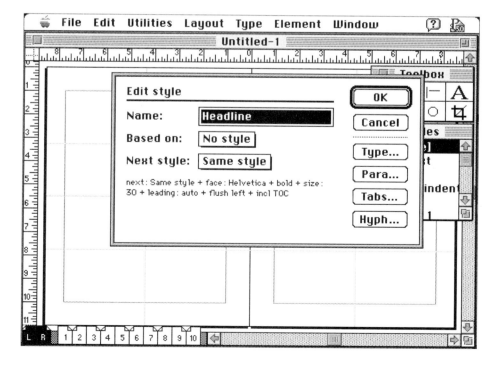

Figure 7.15
Subhead 1
specifications

6. Verify that 18 is selected

5. Click on Italic

4. Verify that bold is selected

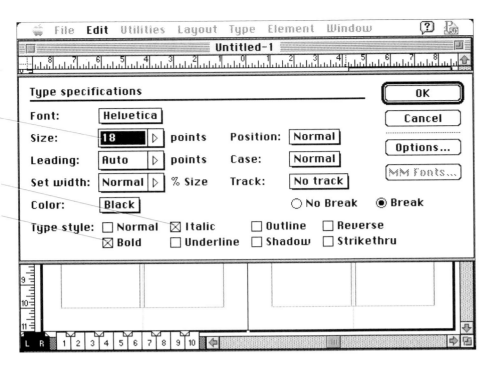

5. Click on Italic.

6. Verify that 18 is selected (compare your screen with Figure 7.15).

7. Click on OK.

8. Click on OK.

To change Subhead 2 style:

1. Scroll down to Subhead 2.

2. Click on Subhead 2.

3. Hold down ⌘ and click on Subhead 2.

4. Click on Type...

5. Verify that Helvetica is selected.

6. Click on Normal (next to Type style).

7. Select 18 points.

8. Click on OK.

For Subhead 2 you will also make a minor change in the paragraph specifications. The default alignment for all the styles is flush left. You will change Subhead 2's alignment to Center.

9. Click on Para...

10. Press the mouse button on Left in the Alignment box.

11. Select Center. The Paragraph specifications dialog box should match Figure 7.16.

12. Click on OK. The Edit style dialog box should match Figure 7.17.

Figure 7.16
Paragraph
specifications for
Subhead 2

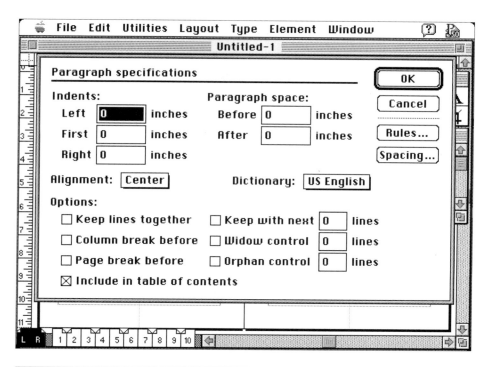

Figure 7.17
Complete specifications
for Subhead 2 after
changing paragraph
alignment

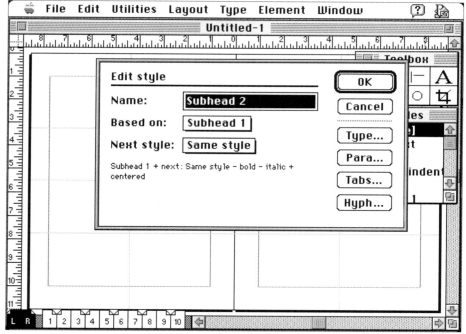

13. **Click on OK.**

Adding a New Style

The Annual Report designers want to use pull quotes, which, as you recall, are short quotes selected to stimulate interest and transform people who would scan an article into people who will read an article. This design element will require a style to be added. Because the style will be used for pull quotes, its name will be "Pull quote." Its style will be based on Subhead 1, with a font specification of Helvetica 18 Normal.

To define a new style, you select the Define styles option from the Type pull-down menu. You will see the same Edit style dialog box you worked with when you modified styles in the previous section.

Because you are going to base Pull quote on Subhead 1, start by selecting Subhead 1.

1. **Click on Subhead 1 in the Style palette.**

2. **Select Define styles... from the Type menu (⌘-3).**

The Define styles dialog box should match Figure 7.18.

3. **Select New...**

4. **In the Name box, type *Pull quote* (*do not* press RETURN).**

5. **Click on Type...**

6. **Verify that Helvetica is selected.**

7. **Verify that 18 is selected.**

8. **Select Normal (next to Type style).**

The Type specifications dialog box should look like Figure 7.19.

9. **Click on OK.**

   Returns you to the Edit style dialog box.

The Edit style dialog box should match Figure 7.20.

10. **Click on OK.**

    Returns you to the Define styles dialog box.

Figure 7.18
Define styles
dialog box

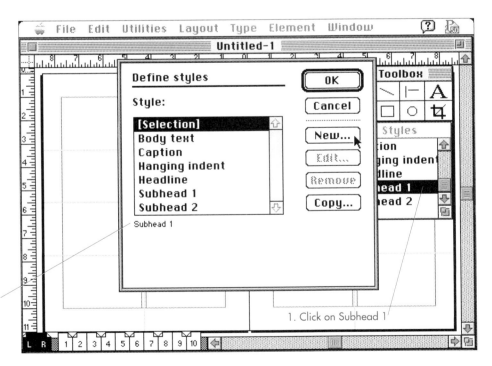

Note that Subhead 1 is
shown (because you
clicked on it prior to
selecting Define styles)

Figure 7.19
Type specifications
for Pull quote

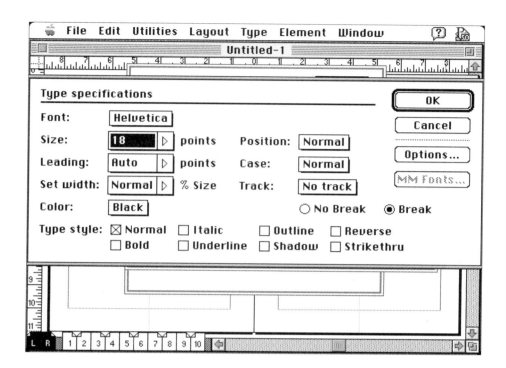

Figure 7.20
Pull quote
specifications

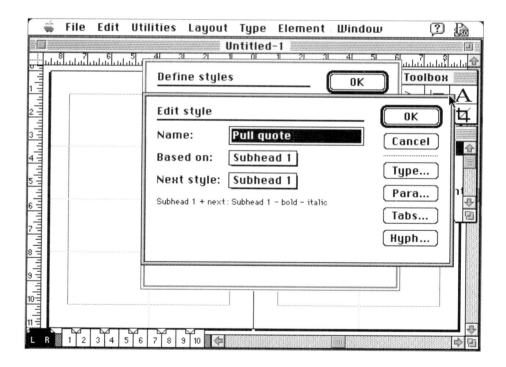

Deleting a Style

The last step is to delete the Caption and Hanging indent styles. The Remove option deletes the selected style. First select the style you wish to delete, then remove it. If you don't do these steps in this order, you will remove whichever style is already selected. While still in the Define styles dialog box:

1. Click on Caption.

Figure 7.21
Define styles
dialog box with
Caption selected

1. Select Caption

2. Click to remove

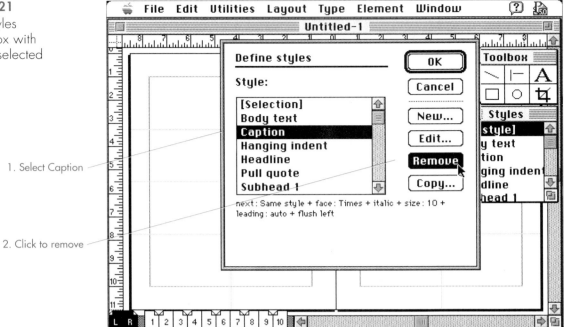

The Define styles dialog box should match Figure 7.21.

2. Click on Remove.

3. Select Hanging indent (if necessary).

4. Click on Remove.

5. Click on OK.

The Style palette should now have six styles: [No style], Body text, Headline, Pull quote, Subhead 1, and Subhead 2.

You have set up your first style sheet by defining the styles for the Inn's Annual Report. In the next sections you will use them to create the master pages and the template.

MASTER PAGES

There are two master pages, a left and a right. As you recall from Chapter 6, anything you put on the left master page appears on every even-numbered page; anything on the right, on every odd-numbered page. **Master pages** are a blueprint of what all the left and right pages will look like.

Remember, left master pages are even numbered—2, 4, 6, et cetera. Right master pages are odd numbered—1, 3, 5, and so on. At first glance, this relationship (left/even, right/odd) seems backward until you reason it out. Page 1 of a double-sided document is always a right-hand page. When you turn page 1, you see facing pages 2 and 3, a pair of left and right pages. Remembering this concept is easier when you visualize a publication's pages rather than memorizing the first two sentences of this paragraph.

You need to consider carefully what you want to put on the master pages. The important question to ask is: Which items appear on every left page and which on every right page? Some possible items are the grid, page numbers, document title, and horizontal and/or vertical grid lines. Not everything needs to be placed on master pages. Some items may be better placed on the numbered pages and saved as part of a template. Perhaps, for example, a financial statement always goes on page 1 of the Annual Report. In that case, you would put the permanent elements of the financial statement on a numbered page. Remember, master pages define all left and all right pages.

Creating Master Pages for the Inn's Annual Report

For The Inn at Portage Bay's Annual Report, the master pages will contain the following items:

- grid (already created in the first section)
- 1-point line at the top of each page across both columns
- 12-point line at the top of each page across one column
- *The Inn at Portage Bay* on each left-hand page
- *Annual Report* on each right-hand page
- page number on odd-numbered pages only

By the end of this section you will have a set of master pages containing everything on this list. The master pages will look like Figure 7.22, but will have page-number markers instead of actual page numbers.

Figure 7.22
Annual Report pages 1–3

Figure 7.23
Drawing the
1-point line

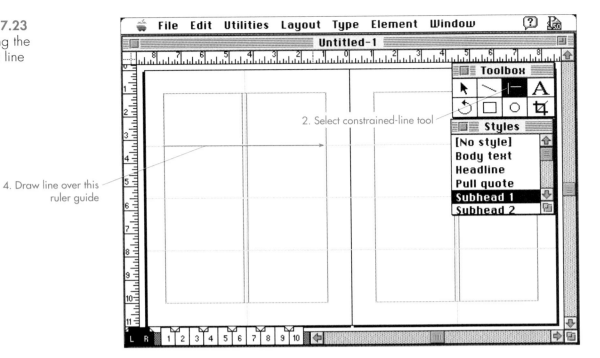

2. Select constrained-line tool

4. Draw line over this
ruler guide

Creating the 1-point Line

The master pages for the Annual Report have two lines: one with a width of 1 point across each page and a second 12-point line spanning the outside column on each page. Each line could be created twice, but it's better to create the two different lines once and then copy each to the other master page. Copying a line or other graphic guarantees that each figure has the same dimensions. Creating an item twice does not guarantee identical dimensions. It's also quicker and easier to copy than to re-create something.

Start by creating and copying the 1-point line, then the 12-point line.

1. Select Element, Line, and select 1 pt.

2. In the Toolbox, select the constrained-line tool.

3. Point to the left-hand starting position for the line (see Figure 7.23).

4. Press and drag the mouse to the page's right margin.

5. Release the mouse button.

Copying the Line

Recall that objects must be selected (have handles) to be copied. Make sure the line is still selected before proceeding. If it does not have handles, select the pointer tool in the Toolbox and point to the line.

1. Select Copy from the Edit menu (⌘-C).

2. Select Paste from the Edit menu (⌘-V).

Figure 7.24
1-point lines drawn at top of master pages

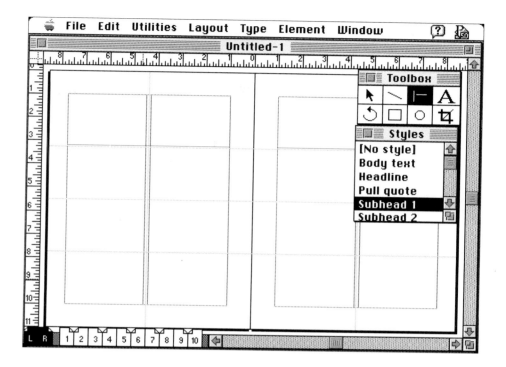

The copied line now appears near the original, with handles. You want to move the line without changing its length or angle. To do this, point anywhere on the line but a handle.

3. Point to the new line; do not point to a handle.

4. Press and drag the line to the corresponding location on the right master page; release the mouse button (see Figure 7.24).

5. When you are satisfied that the line is correctly placed, click to deselect.

Creating the 12-point Line

The 12-point line will appear in the outside column of each page and hang below the 1-point line. Before starting this section, verify that the line you just moved is not selected.

1. Select Element, Line, 12 pt.

2. Select the constrained-line tool from the Toolbox (if necessary).

3. Draw the line in the outside column, as shown in Figure 7.25.

Now change the page view to look at these lines up close (point to a spot you want to be in the center of the screen and press (OPTION) + ⌘ and click the mouse button). If you are not satisfied with the placement of the 12-point line, you may either move it (using the pointer tool in the Toolbox) or delete it (press (DELETE)) and start again.

4. When you are satisfied with the line placement, copy it to the other master page (refer to Figure 7.1 if necessary).

Figure 7.25
12-point line drawn
on left master page

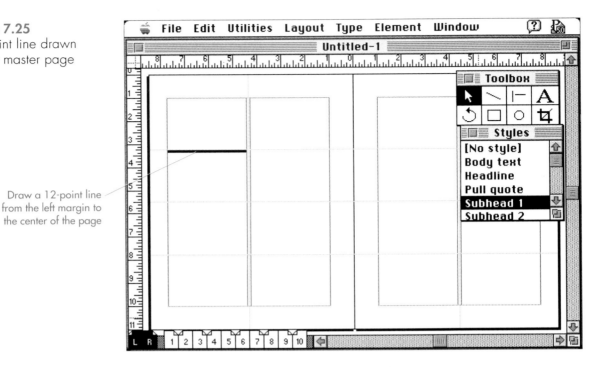

Draw a 12-point line
from the left margin to
the center of the page

Writing Above the Lines

In this section you will type *The Inn at Portage Bay* aligned left on the left master page and *Annual Report* aligned right on the right master page. You will use the Subhead 1 style from the Style palette. Throughout this set of directions, adjust the page view as needed.

1. Click on Subhead 1, if necessary.

2. Select the text tool from the Toolbox.

3. Position the I-beam over the 12-point line on the left master page; click an insertion point.

4. Type *The Inn at Portage Bay.*

5. Position the I-beam over the 12-point line on the right master page; click an insertion point.

6. Select Type, Alignment, Align right (⌘-SHIFT-R).

Notice the + after Subhead 1 in the Style palette, which indicates you have temporarily altered Subhead 1. When you select another style in the Style palette, the plus sign will disappear.

7. Type *Annual Report.*

Creating Page Numbers

There are two methods to number pages in a PageMaker document: (1) type a page number on every numbered page or (2) create a page-number marker on a master page. A **page-number marker** is a placeholder for your page number. PageMaker will automatically place the correct page number on each page once you put the page-number marker on the master page. For the Inn's Annual Report, you will establish a page-number marker for right-hand pages only. Thus, odd-numbered pages will be numbered, even-numbered pages will not. ⌘, (OPTION), and P are pressed at the same time to insert a page-number marker.

1. **Position the I-beam above the words** *Annual Report;* **click an insertion point.**

2. **Verify that Subhead 1 is selected.**

3. **Select Type, Alignment, Align right (⌘-(SHIFT)-R).**

4. **Hold down ⌘ and (OPTION) and press P.**

At this point, you should see RM, which is the page-number marker. RM means Right Master. Had you placed it on the left master page, you would have seen LM. As you move through the numbered pages, you will see the odd page numbers replace the page-number marker. To verify:

5. **Click on the publication page icons in the lower-left corner.**

You have now created the master pages for The Inn at Portage Bay's Annual Report. To summarize, you have drawn a grid and created lines and headings on each page. You reviewed the process of copying a graphic, learned how to create page-number markers, and used the Style palette to type some text on the master pages.

In the next section you will create a template and add items to the numbered pages to complete the template. Now save your master pages as a template. If you need to end your session, close the publication and quit PageMaker; otherwise, proceed to the next section. To save:

1. **Select File, Save as...**

2. **In the File name box, type** *Annual Report.*

3. **Click on Template.**

4. **Click on OK.**

TEMPLATES

As has previously been stated, a **template** is the framework for a publication. It contains master pages, a grid, and a Style palette. Templates are files that can be used repeatedly and doing so speeds up the creation of documents. Templates, if carefully designed, add continuity to the whole family of a business's publications by duplicating Style palettes and basing every publication on the same grid.

Every time you open a template, PageMaker automatically selects the Copy option, as shown in Figure 7.26. This means you get an untitled copy of the template. After opening a template, typically you would

Figure 7.26
Open publication
dialog box

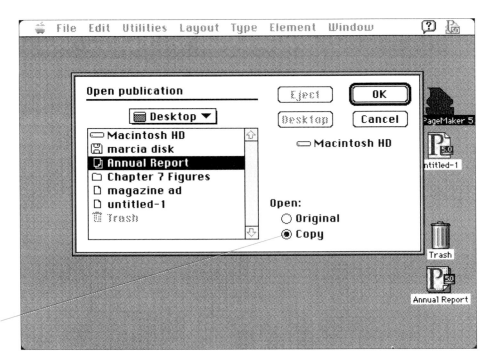

When you open a
template, PageMaker
selects the Copy option

place text, graphs, and pictures. Then you would save it as a publication. But there are times that you want to open a template, make changes to it, and save it with the same name. In that case, in the Open publication dialog box you would click on Original.

PageMaker comes with a variety of templates to help you in publication layout. There are templates for creating a brochure, calendar, manual, newsletter, invoice, and envelope, as well as templates for labels for diskettes, cassettes, CDs, and videotapes—to name but a few. A complete list of templates is available in the PageMaker documentation or by selecting Open template from the Aldus Additions option in the Utilities menu.

Comparing Master Pages and Templates

Some of the same terms can be used to describe both master pages and templates. Both describe the document's underlying structure. Both give the publication consistency and allow layout to be done faster. In some cases, no difference exists between a particular set of master pages and a template for a publication.

But these terms cannot be used interchangeably. Master pages are merely one aspect of templates, which may also contain individual page layouts and Style palettes. Master pages are a pair of left and right pages, whereas a template can have a different layout for every page in the publication.

For the Inn's Annual Report, you will create a unique layout for page 1, Financial Highlights. In this way you will see how master pages can be used with special layouts to produce part of a template.

Creating the Financial Highlights Page

The Financial Highlights section of the Inn's Annual Report is a spreadsheet with various financial categories in the left-hand column and the numbers for the current and previous years to the right. Financial Highlights will appear on page 1 of the Annual Report. You will type the list and a heading. The money figures will be part of the publication but not part of the template. Your final copy should look like Figure 7.27. The type specifications are:

Financial Highlights	Helvetica 18 point, Bold	Subhead 2 + Align left
List of items	Times 11 point, Normal	Body text

Use Figure 7.27 as a guide to create the Financial Highlights page, then save the document as a template.

Figure 7.27
Annual Report page 1 with Financial Highlights

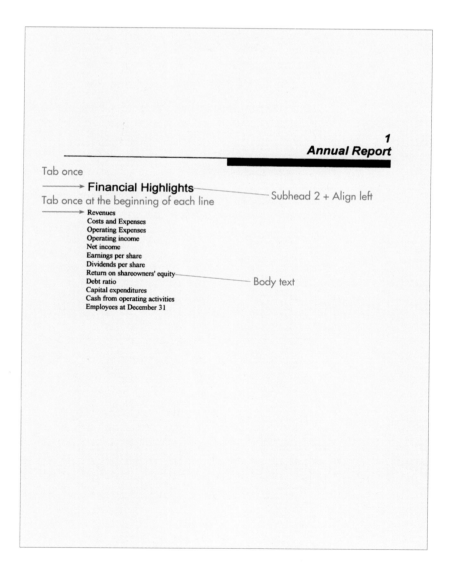

To create the Financial Highlights page:

1. Click on the page 1 icon.

2. Adjust the page view so you can see the left column of page 1.

3. Click on Subhead 2 in the Style palette.

4. Click on the text tool.

5. Select Type, Alignment, Align left (⌘-SHIFT-L). This temporarily changes the alignment of Subhead 2 from center to left.

6. Click an insertion point for the heading.

7. Press TAB once.

8. Type *Financial Highlights.*

9. Press RETURN twice to put space between the heading and the body of the report.

10. Click on Body text.

11. Using Figure 7.27 as a guide, type the list, pressing TAB once at the beginning of each line.

12. Print pages 1 through 3 of the template to show the layout.

13. Save the template. Make sure that Template is selected in the Save publication dialog box. Select Yes to replace existing file, and exit PageMaker.

You have now finished a complete template. You have created an underlying grid, a Style palette, and master pages; you have numbered your pages, and created a special layout for Financial Highlights.

SUMMARY

If this project were for a client, you would now use this template to place articles, pictures, graphs, and financial data. By starting with the same template each time, you would be assured of consistency and quality.

KEY TERMS

grid

scholar's margin

pull quote

style sheet

style

Style palette

master pages

page-number marker

template

QUESTIONS

1. What are the advantages to using a grid system?

2. List several items that might be found in a scholar's margin. How does the use of a scholar's margin improve a publication's appearance?

3. What is the difference between creating columns by dragging lines from the left vertical ruler and creating them using the Column guides dialog box?

4. What does it mean when a type style choice is *based on* another style choice? How does *based on* affect what appears in the Edit style dialog box?

5. What is contained in the Style palette list?

6. What elements are part of a style?

7. When a page design calls for a line, circle, or box to appear twice, why should you copy the graphic rather than create it twice?

8. What are the components of a template?

9. Make the argument for why you should create a template. Why do you suppose some people create documents without making templates?

Using Help, answer the following questions.

10. How do you place a graphic in a template placeholder?

11. In which menu do you find the Copy option for copying a style sheet from another publication?

1. Choose a magazine. Determine its grid. Guess at the different styles it has in its Style palette. Critique the design. Do you like it? Why or why not?

2. Create the template for the newsletter from Chapter 6. Use Figure 7.28 as a guide. Refer to the table on page 213 for the summary of the styles used in the template.

3. Create the template for a menu for the Inn's Spinnaker Restaurant. Use Figure 7.29 as a guide.

4. Create a template of your own design for the Inn's Spinnaker Restaurant. Before designing the menu, study various menus.

Figure 7.28
Project 7.2—Template for Portage Bay Soundings

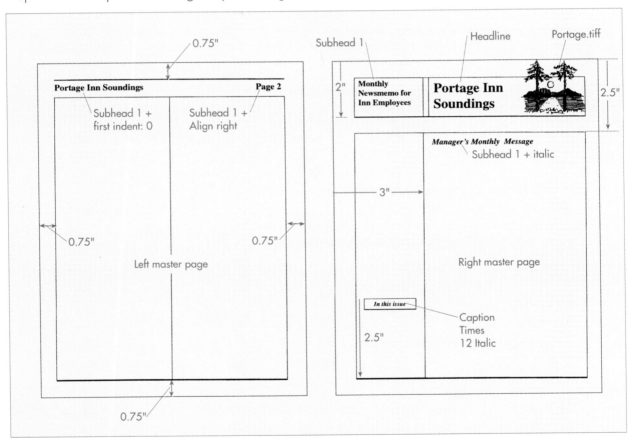

Figure 7.29
Project 7.3—Menu template

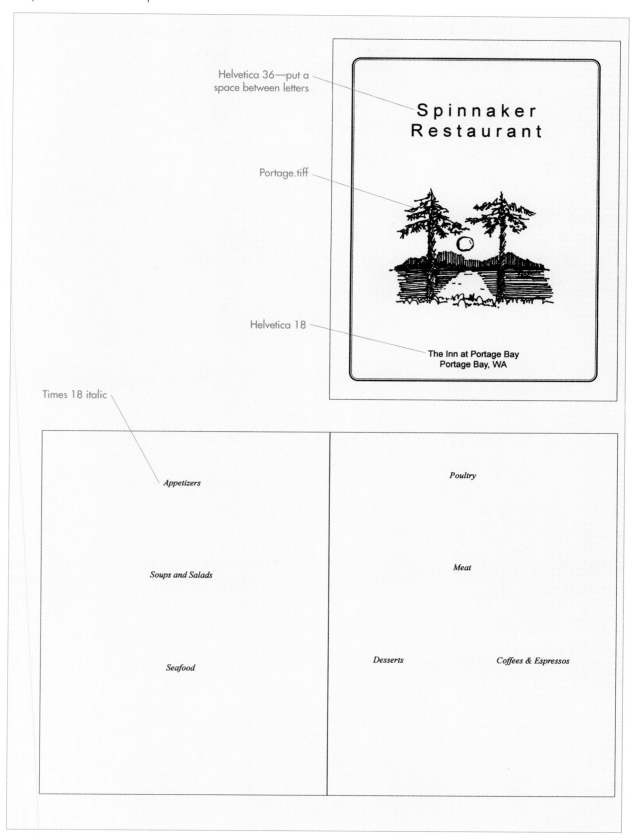

Helvetica 36—put a
space between letters

Spinnaker
Restaurant

Portage.tiff

Helvetica 18

The Inn at Portage Bay
Portage Bay, WA

Times 18 italic

Appetizers

Poultry

Soups and Salads

Meat

Seafood

Desserts

Coffees & Espressos

Figure 7.30
Project 7.5—Daily
Activities Schedule

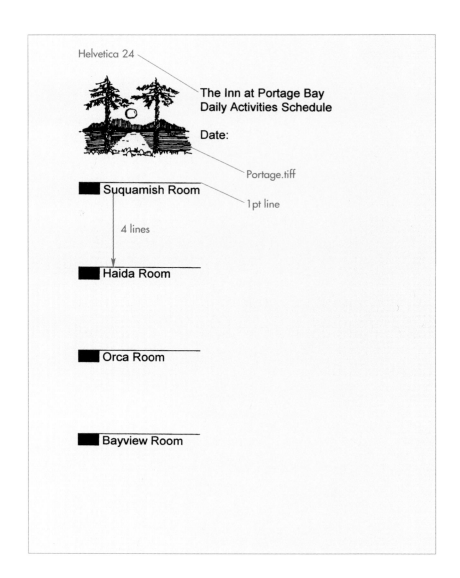

5. The Inn produces a Daily Activities Schedule for its conference rooms. Create a template for the rooms. Copy and paste the lines and filled boxes so they are all the same size. Use Figure 7.30 as a guide.

Figure 7.31
Project 7.6—Template
for Daily Specials

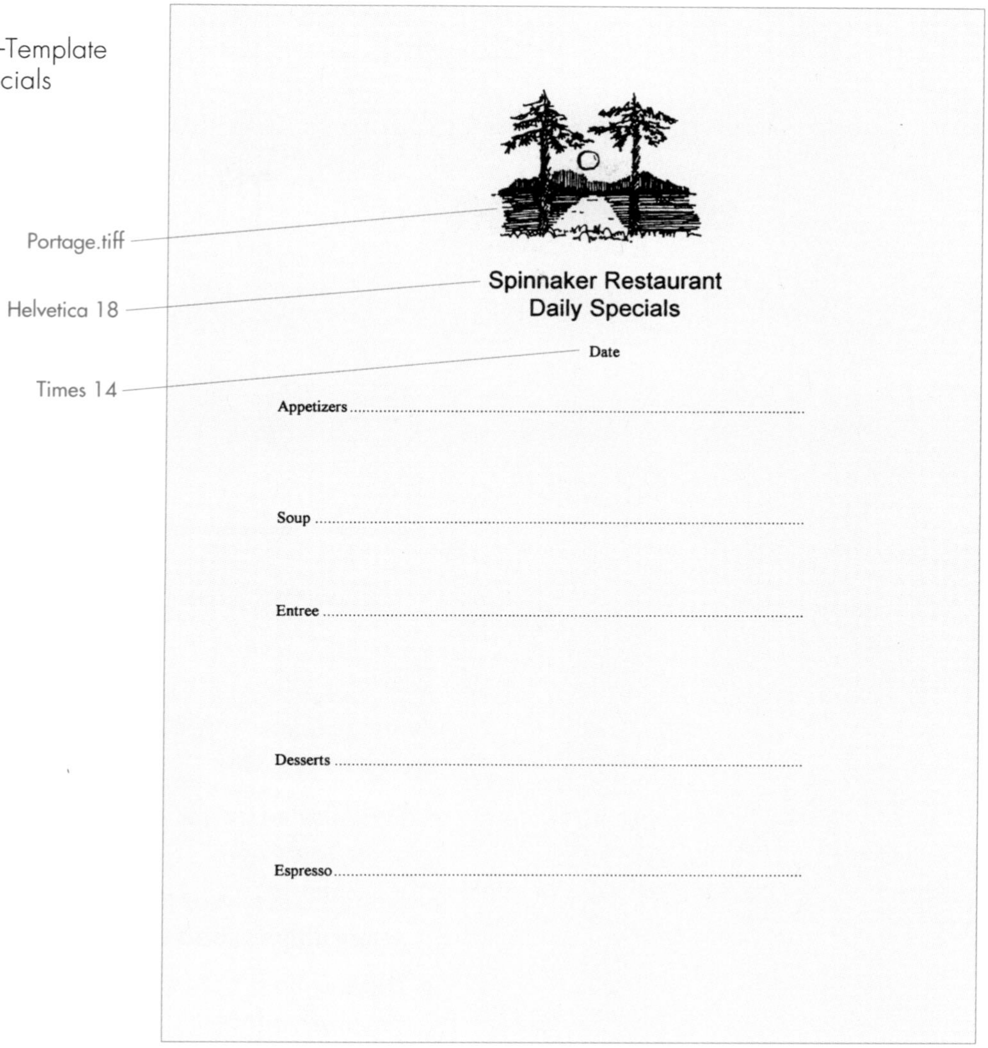

Portage.tiff

Helvetica 18

Times 14

**Spinnaker Restaurant
Daily Specials**

Date

Appetizers ....

Soup ....

Entree ....

Desserts ....

Espresso ....

6. The Spinnaker Restaurant has different daily specials. Create a template for the Daily Specials. Use the word *Date* as a placeholder. Use tabs and leaders next to each category. See Figure 7.31.

7. The Inn has a portfolio of services that is left in every room. The different sections include a page for breakfast, lunch, dinner (room service); telephone information; directory of services; entertainment; and club facilities. Design a style sheet for this portfolio and create the template.

Upon completion of this chapter you will be able to:

- Describe what decisions you must make prior to design

- Describe the impact of font choice on a publication's readability

- Differentiate between serif, sans serif, and decorative fonts

- Know when to use bold and italic for emphasis

- Describe when to choose justified rather than nonjustified text

- Consider and resolve hyphenation issues

- Design headlines that will draw readers to an article

- Define the terms *optical center* and *eye dwell* and explain their importance to design

- Evaluate layout with respect to symmetry and asymmetry

- Understand the principles of graphic placement

- Recognize components that contribute to or detract from page layout

Design Concepts

Desktop publishing is more than learning keystrokes to use PageMaker or a comparable software package. Desktop publishing integrates graphic design with the productivity of a computer to give the user two advantages unavailable before: speed in producing camera-ready material and the ability to experiment and play "what if" with publication page layout.

PageMaker has many operational rules. Design, on the other hand, has few rules. There is no formula or set of steps you can follow to produce a good design. There is no right or wrong design; rather, design is described using qualitative words such as *poor, good,* and *better.*

There are, however, principles to guide design considerations; and research, mostly out of the advertising industry, can set you on the path to creating professional-looking designs. But there are times when you deliberately go against the guidelines and accepted practices to achieve emphasis.

A willingness to experiment is critical to the design process. PageMaker allows you to experiment with different type fonts and layouts with relative ease. Commercially available packages of fonts and clip art increase the design choices available to you. Scanners allow you to import photos and artwork. Draw programs make it easy for an artist to quickly create artwork. With so many possibilities, it is easy to understand why the words *right* and *wrong* do not apply to design.

Now, a caution: Design cannot be taught completely in one short chapter. Indeed, entire courses of study are devoted to design concepts and practices. This chapter will introduce and describe some design guidelines, show examples, allow you to critique layouts, increase your awareness of design, and give you the opportunity to begin gaining experience.

You may not agree with every guideline presented here. In fact, any two designers may have three different opinions with respect to many of the ideas put forth in this chapter. Also, what works in one publication with one audience will not necessarily work in a different setting. That's why there are few rules but lots of guidelines and examples. Even going against the guidelines may yield positive results.

This chapter is organized into four sections. First, a short discussion of general considerations will create a context in which basic design decisions can be made. Next is a discussion about choosing typefaces and related issues. Third, concepts of page layout and design are presented. Finally, some comments about applying these ideas and integrating them with restraint complete the chapter.

GENERAL CONSIDERATIONS

When designing any publication, first identify the publication's objectives and intended audience. With respect to objectives, ask questions such as: What is the purpose of this catalog, brochure, or newsletter? Is it to inform, sell, or increase name familiarity? What, if any, change of behavior do you expect after a person sees the publication? Do you want or expect a response? Will the person know more technical or financial information after reading the piece? Is the objective to increase the public's positive feelings about the company? What image should the publication project: formal, friendly, or other?

Audience is another consideration. Who will receive the advertisement, flyer, or prospectus? What is the age and education level of the audience? How familiar is the audience with the source of the publication?

Answering these questions first helps determine some design decisions. For example, do the objectives and audience require high quality, average quality, or low quality of production? What works well for one audience may fall flat with a different group. Design is driven by a publication's purpose and objectives as well as by knowing and understanding the target audience.

CHOOSING TYPEFACES AND RELATED ISSUES

Typefaces, or fonts, can be categorized as serif and sans serif. A **serif** is a line or curve extending from the end of a letter, such as on the typeface for this text. The French word *sans* means without, so a **sans serif** typeface is one without extensions at the end of the letter, such as that for the headings on this page. A third category of fonts is decorative fonts. Examples of different typefaces are shown in Figure 8.1.

Figure 8.1
Serif, sans serif, and
decorative fonts

Bodoni
ABCDEFGHIJKLMNOPQRSTUVWXYZ
abcdefghijklmnopqrstuvwxyz

Avant Garde
ABCDEFGHIJKLMNOPQRSTUVWXYZ
abcdefghijklmnopqrstuvwxyz

Arnold Böcklin
ABCDEFGHIJKLMNOPQRSTUVWXYZ
abcdefghijklmnopqrstuvwxyz

PageMaker does not contain fonts. The Macintosh operating system includes Times (a serif font) and Helvetica (a sans serif font). Several companies have font packages that can be used with PageMaker to increase the options available—examples include Adobe, Bitstream, Microsoft, and Agfa Compugraphic. Some packages are compatible with the IBM-PC whereas others are compatible with Macintosh. Some font packages require PostScript printers; others work well in PCL (Printer Command Language) and dot-matrix printers. More font packages that interface with PageMaker continue to become available.

Fonts have names such as Helvetica, Times Roman, or Futura, to name a few. Some font names are company specific. Two typefaces may resemble one another when placed side by side on a page but will have minor design distinctions and different names because the fonts were developed by different designers and published by different companies.

The origins of fonts are as varied as their appearance. Times Roman was designed by Stanley Morison in 1931 for the *London Times* newspaper. German type designer Paul Renner created Futura in 1928. Futura is an example of the Bauhaus principle of functionalism, in which form follows function. It is a sans serif font with letterforms having only their bare essentials. Sumner Stone designed three integrated type families for Adobe: Stone Informal, Stone Sans, and Stone Serif. Stone Informal was developed specifically for desktop publishing and laser printer technology. When used in the same publication, the three Stone typefaces work together to provide an integrated look. Figure 8.2 shows the five fonts mentioned here.

Bitstream's Charter was the first typeface specifically developed for digital electronic typesetting. Its serifs are square and easily digitized, and it looks good on low-resolution laser printers and high-resolution

Figure 8.2
Five fonts

Times Roman
ABCDEFGHIJKLMNOPQRSTUVWXYZ
abcdefghijklmnopqrstuvwxyz

Futura
ABCDEFGHIJKLMNOPQRSTUVWXYZ
abcdefghijklmnopqrstuvwxyz

Stone Informal
ABCDEFGHIJKLMNOPQRSTUVWXYZ
abcdefghijklmnopqrstuvwxyz

Stone Sans
ABCDEFGHIJKLMNOPQRSTUVWXYZ
abcdefghijklmnopqrstuvwxyz

Stone Serif
ABCDEFGHIJKLMNOPQRSTUVWXYZ
abcdefghijklmnopqrstuvwxyz

typesetters. It is similar to Adobe's Times Roman font. Compare the appearance of the serif fonts in Figure 8.3. In particular, compare the upper- and lowercase Gs in each typeface.

Sans serif text is clean, simple, and projects rationality and objectivity (although not always readability). An example is Helvetica, named after the Latin word for Switzerland, designed by Max Miedinger, a Swiss, in 1957. Compare the different sans serif fonts in Figure 8.4. Again, compare the Gs.

All the fonts in Figures 8.3 and 8.4 are the same point size. Notice, however, how two fonts of equal point size use different amounts of space on the page.

Serifs create a line at the top and bottom of a text line and guide the eye across the page. Sans serif text does not have that line, and the eye has difficulty reading, wanting instead to leave the text line and wander through the body of the text.

For body text, a serif font is preferred for readability. Research has shown that comprehension of text blocks with serifs is 75%–80% whereas comprehension of text blocks set in a sans serif typeface is 20%–30%. Serif text is described as old-fashioned, friendly, and easy to read. Sans serif text is described as clean, sleek, modern, and not as easy to read. Figure 8.5 shows paragraphs set in serif and sans serif

Figure 8.3
Various serif fonts

Baskerville
ABCDEFGHIJKLMNOPQRSTUVWXYZ
abcdefghijklmnopqrstuvwxyz

Bookman
ABCDEFGHIJKLMNOPQRSTUVWXYZ
abcdefghijklmnopqrstuvwxyz

Clarendon
ABCDEFGHIJKLMNOPQRSTUVWXYZ
abcdefghijklmnopqrstuvwxyz

Garamond
ABCDEFGHIJKLMNOPQRSTUVWXYZ
abcdefghijklmnopqrstuvwxyz

Goudy
ABCDEFGHIJKLMNOPQRSTUVWXYZ
abcdefghijklmnopqrstuvwxyz

Lubalin Graph
ABCDEFGHIJKLMNOPQRSTUVWXYZ
abcdefghijklmnopqrstuvwxyz

Palatino
ABCDEFGHIJKLMNOPQRSTUVWXYZ
abcdefghijklmnopqrstuvwxyz

Souvenir
ABCDEFGHIJKLMNOPQRSTUVWXYZ
abcdefghijklmnopqrstuvwxyz

Tiffany
ABCDEFGHIJKLMNOPQRSTUVWXYZ
abcdefghijklmnopqrstuvwxyz

fonts to illustrate this point. Notice in the sans serif text how each stroke of every letter has the same width. Contrast this with serif text, where each letter has thicks and thins. This contributes to a serif font's readibility.

Figure 8.4
Various sans serif fonts

Bauhaus
ABCDEFGHIJKLMNOPQRSTUVWXYZ
abcdefghijklmnopqrstuvwxyz

Eras
ABCDEFGHIJKLMNOPQRSTUVWXYZ
abcdefghijklmnopqrstuvwxyz

Eurostile
ABCDEFGHIJKLMNOPQRSTUVWXYZ
abcdefghijklmnopqrstuvwxyz

Franklin Gothic
ABCDEFGHIJKLMNOPQRSTUVWXYZ
abcdefghijklmnopqrstuvwxyz

Helvetica
ABCDEFGHIJKLMNOPQRSTUVWXYZ
abcdefghijklmnopqrstuvwxyz

Helvetica Condensed
ABCDEFGHIJKLMNOPQRSTUVWXYZ
abcdefghijklmnopqrstuvwxyz

Letter Gothic
ABCDEFGHIJKLMNOPQRSTUVWXYZ
abcdefghijklmnopqrstuvwxyz

Optima
ABCDEFGHIJKLMNOPQRSTUVWXYZ
abcdefghijklmnopqrstuvwxyz

Univers 55
ABCDEFGHIJKLMNOPQRSTUVWXYZ
abcdefghijklmnopqrstuvwxyz

Figure 8.5
Compare readability of
serif and sans serif fonts

Sans serif type

Serif type

Fourscore and seven years ago our fathers brought forth on this continent a new nation, conceived in Liberty, and dedicated to the proposition that all men are created equal.

Now we are engaged in a great civil war, testing whether that nation, or any nation so conceived and so dedicated, can long endure. We are met on a great battlefield of that war. We have come to dedicate a portion of that field, as a final resting-place for those who here gave their lives that that nation might live. It is altogether fitting and proper that we should do this.

But, in a larger sense, we cannot dedicate, we cannot consecrate, we cannot hallow this ground. The brave men, living and dead, who struggled here, have consecrated it far above our poor power to add or detract. The world will little note nor long remember what we say here, but it can never forget what they did here. It is for us, the living, rather, to be dedicated here to the unfinished work which they who fought here have thus far so nobly advanced. It is rather for us to be here dedicated to the

Fourscore and seven years ago our fathers brought forth on this continent a new nation, conceived in Liberty, and dedicated to the proposition that all men are created equal.

Now we are engaged in a great civil war, testing whether that nation, or any nation so conceived and so dedicated, can long endure. We are met on a great battlefield of that war. We have come to dedicate a portion of that field, as a final resting-place for those who here gave their lives that that nation might live. It is altogether fitting and proper that we should do this.

But, in a larger sense, we cannot dedicate, we cannot consecrate, we cannot hallow this ground. The brave men, living and dead, who struggled here, have consecrated it far above our poor power to add or detract. The world will little note nor long remember what we say here, but it can never forget what they did here. It is for us, the living, rather, to be dedicated here to the unfinished work which they who fought here have thus far so nobly advanced. It is rather for us to be here dedicated to the great task remaining before us -

Figure 8.6
Serif text with sans
serif headline

Lincoln Dedicates Penn Battlefield

Fourscore and seven years ago our fathers brought forth on this continent a new nation, conceived in Liberty, and dedicated to the proposition that all men are created equal.

Now we are engaged in a great civil war, testing whether that nation, or any nation so conceived and so dedicated, can long endure. We are met on a great battlefield of that war. We have come to dedicate a portion of that field, as a final resting-place for those who here gave their lives that that nation might live. It is altogether fitting and proper that we should do this.

A sans serif font may be used for headlines, providing contrast with a serif font for text. Figure 8.6 shows a sans serif headline with serif text. Sans serif may also be used for publications where there is not much text, such as announcements and advertisements.

A third category of fonts is decorative fonts. In the past few years, font publishers have created a variety of decorative fonts. These are best used for emphasis in a publication, or for an invitation or announcement. Figure 8.7 shows several examples of decorative fonts, and Figure 8.8 is an invitation that uses two decorative fonts appropriately.

Figure 8.7
Decorative fonts

BANCO
ABCDEFGHIJKLMNOPQRSTUVWXYZ

Brush Script
ABCDEFGHIJKLMNOP2RSTUVWXYZ
abcdefghijklmnopqrstuvwxyz

MACHINE
ABCDEFGHIJKLMNOPQRSTUVWXYZ

Psychadelic Smoke
ABCDEFGHIJKLMNOPQRSTUVWXYZ
abcdefghijklmnopqrstuvwxyz

Snell Roundhand
ABCDEFGHIJKLMNOP2RSTUVWXY
abcdefghijklmnopqrstuvwxyz

TRIBECA
ABCDEFGHIJKLMNOPQRSTUVWXYZ

Figure 8.8
Using decorative fonts

You are invited To Suzy Wilcox's 7Th

BiRTHDAY PARTY

Eraser Dust 30 point

Suzy's House
529 Kecker STreeT
MonTocs, New York
May 4 1:00-4:30
Please respond To Suzy's Mom by April 31
847-7349

Lefty Casual 14 point

Font Size

Again, there are guidelines to help you choose the appropriate size of type for different applications. Suggestions are:

Use	Point Size
Headlines	48 maximum, 14 minimum
Subheads	half of headline size; 20 minimum recommended
Body copy	6–13; 10 point is a good choice

Use larger headlines for important messages and smaller headlines for messages of less importance. Medium-sized headlines range from 24 to 36 point. A headline set in 24 point should not have a subhead because half of 24 is 12, less than the minimum of 14 for a subhead.

Body copy point sizes traditionally range between 6 and 13 point, with 8 to 12 point most common. Research has shown 10 point to be most readable to general audiences. Children and young adults do better with 11 point. With 12 point, it is difficult to get enough text within the area of eye focus. Fourteen point and larger is used for text other than text blocks, such as for flyers, and is called **display type** (see Figure 8.9).

Figure 8.9
Different point sizes in different fonts

Folio Bold 36
Century Oldstyle 36
Eurostile Bold 24
Garamond Bold 24

Important headlines should be set in 24- to 36-point type

Univers 18
Univers Extended 18
Univers Condensed 18

Sabon 12   **Futura Bold 12**
Sabon 10   **Futura Bold 10**

Body copy is best in the 10- to 12-point range

There is a trend to set an oversized initial capital letter, called a **drop cap**, to begin the first paragraph. Guidelines for this include using a type size three to four times the size of the body copy. In other words, if the body copy size is 10 point, the initial cap should be 30 to 40 point. The initial cap can be linked with three to four or more lines of body text. *Time* magazine sometimes uses drop caps eight lines in height. Readership of paragraphs with oversized initial caps will be about 15% greater than paragraphs without them.

PageMaker 5.0 makes using drop caps easy. The Drop cap option in the Aldus Additions will automatically size and place an oversized cap. In the Drop cap dialog box, the user specifies the size in terms of number of lines.

Use a readable font for the oversized cap. Another idea is to use a very ornate font, such as Augsburger Initials or Old English Text. Use it once, or perhaps twice, per page in a diagonal line to unify the page and facing pages. A capital letter may also hang in the margin or be boxed for added emphasis. Be careful when using several drop caps that they do not spell anything. Figure 8.10 shows many of these concepts.

Figure 8.10
Using drop caps

Spacing Between Lines, Words, Letters, and Paragraphs

Leading, the vertical spacing between lines of type, can be adjusted to improve the readability and appearance of a publication. Recall from Chapter 4 that "automatic" leading is 120% of type size. For 10-point type, the default is 12-point leading. Although it is easy to use automatic leading, some designers always select a specific leading to give the look they want. For headlines, reduced leading helps a headline appear as a cohesive unit. Increasing leading in body copy lightens up the appearance and makes the text block less gray. Figure 8.11 illustrates some of these concepts.

Figure 8.11(a) Headline layouts with different leading values

Lincoln Dedicates
Sacred Battlefield

Century, 30-point type with Auto leading
(120% of 30 is 36)

Lincoln Dedicates
Sacred Battlefield

Century, 30-point type with 33.5-point leading

Lincoln Dedicates
Sacred Battlefield

Century, 30-point type with 30.5-point leading

Figure 8.11(b) Body text with two leading values

Lorem ipsum dolor sit amet, consectetuer adipiscing elit, sed diam nonummy nibh euismod tincidunt ut laoreet dolore magna aliquam erat volutpat. Ut wisi enim ad minim veniam, quis nostrud exerci tation

12-point type with Auto leading

Lorem ipsum dolor sit amet, consectetuer adipiscing elit, sed diam nonummy nibh euismod tincidunt ut laoreet dolore magna aliquam erat volutpat. Ut wisi enim ad minim veniam, quis nostrud exerci tation

12-point type with 18-point leading (150%)

Letterspacing is controlled by **kerning**. As stated in Chapter 4, PageMaker has an automatic pair-kerning function. Desktop publishers can override the results through manual kerning. In Figure 8.11, manual kerning was used for the *fi* in *Battlefield* because the top of the *f* covered the dot over the *i*. When two or more characters are united and appear as one, it is called a **ligature**. Examples are fi, fl, and œ. The Matthew Carter/Cherie Cone version of Galliard includes ligatures as part of its base font set, adding a sense of style to typeset publications.

Force justify may be used to space a word across a column. By expanding the space between the letters, the word or words become a design element. In Figure 8.12, *The Inn at Portage Bay* has been force-justified across a column to produce an interesting visual effect.

Figure 8.12
Using words as a design element

Using extra space between paragraphs adds lightness to a publication's appearance and diminishes the gray. Figure 8.13 contrasts two columns with different paragraph spacing.

Figure 8.13
Two columns with different paragraph spacing

Lorem ipsum dolor sit amet, consectetuer adipiscing elit, sed diam nonummy nibh euismod tincidunt ut laoreet dolore magna aliquam erat volutpat. Ut wisi enim ad minim veniam, quis nostrud exerci tation ullamcorper suscipit lobortis nisl ut aliquip ex ea commodo consequat.

Duis autem vel eum iriure dolor in hendrerit in vulputate velit esse molestie consequat, vel illum dolore eu feugiat nulla facilisis at vero eros et accumsan et iusto odio dignissim qui blandit praesent luptatum zzril delenit augue duis dolore te feugait nulla facilisi.

Ut wisi enim ad minim veniam, quis nostrud exerci tation ullamcorper suscipit lobortis nisl ut aliquip ex ea commodo consequat, vel illum dolore eu feugiat nulla facilisis at vero eros et accumsan et iusto odio dignissim qui blandit praesent luptatum zzril delenit augue duis dolore te feugait nulla facilisi.

Lorem ipsum dolor sit amet, consectetuer adipiscing elit, sed diam nonummy nibh euismod tincidunt ut laoreet dolore magna aliquam erat volutpat. Ut wisi enim ad minim veniam, quis nostrud exerci tation ullamcorper suscipit lobortis nisl ut aliquip ex ea commodo consequat.

Duis autem vel eum iriure dolor in hendrerit in vulputate velit esse molestie consequat, vel illum dolore eu feugiat nulla facilisis at vero eros et accumsan et iusto odio dignissim qui blandit praesent luptatum zzril delenit augue duis dolore te feugait nulla facilisi.

Ut wisi enim ad minim veniam, quis nostrud exerci tation ullamcorper suscipit lobortis nisl ut aliquip ex ea commodo consequat, vel illum dolore eu feugiat nulla facilisis at vero eros et accumsan et iusto odio dignissim qui blandit praesent luptatum zzril delenit augue duis dolore te feugait nulla facilisi.

Headline Creation

The purpose of a headline is to "grab" the reader, to get her or him to read the article. Two factors contribute to how successfully you grab a reader. First is the content of the headline and the general interest of the story to the reader. Second is the font and type size.

As stated previously, headlines provide contrast to body text when a font different from the body text and neighboring headlines is used. Recall that 14- to 48-point type is recommended for headlines, with subheads half that size. Subheads should be a minimum of 20 point, and thus are used with headlines of 40 point or more.

Some publications, such as *The New York Times*, set headlines as titles, with most words capitalized. Other publications set headlines in the form of a sentence and capitalize accordingly. Headlines can be one to three lines, with two lines optimal. Avoid separating the headline and body copy with a line or bar.

Another technique that works well to increase readership is to use an **eyebrow**, or **kicker**, above a headline. An eyebrow is a few words above the headline, in smaller type, used to arouse interest. Eyebrows, headlines, and subheads for one article should be in the same typeface, but with variations. For example, a headline may be Helvetica 40 bold with a subhead in Helvetica 20 italic. Figure 8.14 shows some headline layouts.

Figure 8.14
Headline layouts

Consumer Prices Increase 4.8%

President Sets Budget Meeting; Congress Divided on Capital Gains

An eyebrow, or kicker, above the headline can bring readers into the text

President Sets Budget Meeting
Congress Divided on Capital Gains Tax

Headlines and subheads should be in different type sizes

Considerations for headlines include: whether to use left, right, or center alignment; leading so letterspacing and word spacing are appropriate; and weight of typeface. Experiment with the options available and, through trial and error, critiques, and finally experience, you will eventually develop a feel for what works.

The key concern in all decisions with respect to typeface is communication. Which combination of typeface, size, leading, and layout of text block best communicates to the reader?

Emphasis

Italic and bold type may be used for emphasis, but body text in all italic is difficult to read, as is text set completely in bold or capitals. Use italic for mild emphasis within text or for contrast in headlines. Use bold for stronger emphasis and for headlines that shout the message. Figures 8.15(a) and 8.15(b) illustrate these ideas.

Figure 8.15(a)
Using too much italic and bold type

Fourscore and seven years ago our fathers brought forth on this continent a new nation, conceived in Liberty, and dedicated to the proposition that all men are created equal.

Now we are engaged in a great civil war, testing whether that nation, or any nation so conceived and so dedicated, can long endure. We are met on a great battlefield of that war. We have come to dedicate a portion of that field, as a final resting-place for those who here gave their lives that that nation might live. It is altogether fitting and proper that we should do this.

But, in a larger sense, we cannot dedicate, we cannot consecrate, we cannot hallow this ground. The brave men, living and dead, who struggled here, have consecrated it far above our poor power to add or detract. The world will little note nor long remember what we say here, but it can never forget what they did

Fourscore and seven years ago our fathers brought forth on this continent a new nation, conceived in Liberty, and dedicated to the proposition that all men are created equal.

Now we are engaged in a great civil war, testing whether that nation, or any nation so conceived and so dedicated, can long endure. We are met on a great battlefield of that war. We have come to dedicate a portion of that field, as a final resting-place for those who here gave their lives that that nation might live. It is altogether fitting and proper that we should do this.

But, in a larger sense, we cannot dedicate, we cannot consecrate, we cannot hallow this ground. The brave men, living and dead, who struggled here, have consecrated it far above our poor power to add or detract. The world will little note nor long remember what

Figure 8.15(b)
Using italic and bold for emphasis

Fourscore and seven years ago our fathers brought forth on this continent a new nation, conceived in Liberty, and dedicated to the proposition that all men are created equal.

Now we are engaged in a great civil war, testing whether that nation, or any nation so conceived and so dedicated, can long endure. We are met on a great battlefield of that war. We have come to dedicate a portion of that field, as a final resting-place for those who here gave their lives that that nation might live. *It is altogether fitting and proper that we should do this.*

Fourscore and seven years ago our fathers brought forth on this continent a new nation, conceived in Liberty, and dedicated to the proposition that all men are created equal.

Now we are engaged in a great civil war, testing whether that nation, or any nation so conceived and so dedicated, can long endure. We are met on a great battlefield of that war. We have come to dedicate a portion of that field, as a final resting-place for those who here gave their lives that that nation might live. **It is altogether fitting and proper that we should do this.**

Avoid underlining for emphasis. The reader's eyes have difficulty distinguishing between the words and the underline. Also, descenders are obscured by the line, which also inhibits readability.

Some people overuse all caps in text; this gives a telegram-like appearance. It is difficult to read because all the letters are of similar shape and size. Ascenders and descenders differentiate letters, increase comprehension, and add visual interest.

Using all caps and underlining is reminiscent of how we emphasized words on a typewriter. Then, it was our only option; now, however, we can easily use bold and italic, among other design variables. Figure 8.16 gives an example of underlining and all caps.

Figure 8.16
Overuse of underlining and all caps makes body copy difficult to read

Fourscore and seven years ago our fathers brought forth on this continent a new nation, conceived in Liberty, and dedicated to the proposition that all men are created equal.

Now we are engaged in a great civil war, testing whether that nation, or any nation so conceived and so dedicated, can long endure. We are met on a great battlefield of that war. We have come to dedicate a portion of that field, as a final resting-place for those who here gave their lives that that nation might live. It is altogether fitting and proper that we should do this.

FOURSCORE AND SEVEN YEARS AGO OUR FATHERS BROUGHT FORTH ON THIS CONTINENT A NEW NATION, CONCEIVED IN LIBERTY, AND DEDICATED TO THE PROPOSITION THAT ALL MEN ARE CREATED EQUAL.

NOW WE ARE ENGAGED IN A GREAT CIVIL WAR, TESTING WHETHER THAT NATION, OR ANY NATION SO CONCEIVED AND SO DEDICATED, CAN LONG ENDURE. WE ARE MET ON A GREAT BATTLEFIELD OF THAT WAR. WE HAVE COME TO DEDICATE A PORTION OF THAT FIELD, AS A FINAL RESTING-PLACE FOR THOSE WHO HERE GAVE THEIR LIVES THAT THAT NATION MIGHT LIVE. IT IS ALTOGETHER FITTING AND PROPER THAT WE SHOULD DO THIS.

Justified and Nonjustified Text

When you **justify** text, the text lines up on both the right- and the left-hand margins. Nonjustified text with an uneven right margin is called **ragged** right; on the left, ragged left. Text may be wrapped around graphics. Still another alternative is to center text. PageMaker gives you all these options.

Justified text gives a publication a formal feel. When specifying justified text, PageMaker determines how many words can fit on a line, then uses proportional spacing to evenly distribute the characters and word spaces on the line. Manual kerning can be used to override some spacing, but it is not practical to use manual kerning throughout a long document.

Ragged-right text has a more casual appearance. Not justifying text is appropriate for some newsletters, in catalogs for particular products, and for some companies trying to project a friendly, rather than formal, image. Figure 8.17 shows how the same paragraph appears with a ragged right margin and with full justification.

There are also times when you will want to have ragged-left text—for example, on a page having an irregular graphic. Text in the lower right-hand quadrant of a page may need to be finished on the outside column and "unfinished" on the inside. This may appear unsettling or disorganized, so use this technique deliberately, for special emphasis.

There are possible problems with justified text. Depending on leading and kerning, justified text may have patches of white space that appear as "rivers" and "lakes" when you view the publication from a distance, as shown in Figure 8.18. Experimenting with the leading and kerning can solve the problem and give the publication a more even look.

Figure 8.17
Ragged-right and
justified text

Left aligned (ragged right)

Fourscore and seven years ago our
fathers brought forth on this continent a new
nation, conceived in Liberty, and dedicated
to the proposition that all men are created
equal.

Now we are engaged in a great civil war,
testing whether that nation, or any nation so
conceived and so dedicated, can long endure.
We are met on a great battlefield of that war.
We have come to dedicate a portion of that
field, as a final resting place for those who
here gave their lives that that nation might
live. It is altogether fitting and proper that we
should do this.

Justified text

Fourscore and seven years ago our fathers
brought forth on this continent a new nation,
conceived in Liberty, and dedicated to the
proposition that all men are created equal.

Now we are engaged in a great civil war,
testing whether that nation, or any nation so
conceived and so dedicated, can long endure.
We are met on a great battlefield of that war.
We have come to dedicate a portion of that
field, as a final resting place for those who here
gave their lives that that nation might live. It is
altogether fitting and proper that we should do
this.

Figure 8.18
Effects of leading
and tracking, or
letterspacing, on
justified text

Normal leading (120% of point size),
no tracking

But, in a larger sense, we cannot dedicate, we
cannot consecrate, we cannot hallow this ground.
The brave men, living and dead, who struggled here,
have consecrated it far above our poor power to add
or detract. The world will little note nor long remember what we say here, but it can never forget what they
did here. It is for us, the living, rather, to be dedicated
here to the unfinished work which they who fought
here have thus far so nobly advanced. It is rather for
us to be here dedicated to the great task remaining
before us - that from these honored dead we take
increased devotion to that cause for which they gave
the last full measure of devotion - that we here highly
resolve that these dead shall not have died in vain;
that this nation, under God, shall have a new birth of
freedom; and that government of the people, by the
people, for the people, shall not perish from the earth.

Extra leading (150% of point size),
very loose tracking

But, in a larger sense, we cannot dedicate,
we cannot consecrate, we cannot hallow this
ground. The brave men, living and dead, who
struggled here, have consecrated it far above
our poor power to add or detract. The world will
little note nor long remember what we say here,
but it can never forget what they did here. It is
for us, the living, rather, to be dedicated here to
the unfinished work which they who fought
here have thus far so nobly advanced. It is
rather for us to be here dedicated to the great
task remaining before us - that from these
honored dead we take increased devotion to
that cause for which they gave the last full
measure of devotion - that we here highly resolve that these dead shall not have died in vain;
that this nation, under God, shall have a new
birth of freedom; and that government of the
people, by the people, for the people, shall not
perish from the earth.

Rivers caused by alignment of
spaces running through text

Hyphenation in Ragged-right Text

Hyphenation is separating a word between two syllables, putting
part of the word on one line, and moving the remainder to the next line.
PageMaker allows you to turn automatic hyphenation on or off in the
Hyphenation dialog box from the Type pull-down menu. You may
specify Manual only, Manual plus dictionary, or Manual plus algorithm.
For a description of these options, look in Help under Hyphenation.

A **hyphenation zone** may also be specified in the Hyphenation dialog
box. The hyphenation zone is an acceptable area in a line of text for
breaking the text, either with hyphenation or by moving the word that
doesn't fit onto the next line. Hyphenation zones apply only to text that
is not justified.

Changing the width of the hyphenation zone has an impact on the text
block's visual appearance. Figure 8.19 shows the same text with two

Figure 8.19
Hyphenation zones

0.8-inch hyphenation zone—more ragged appearance, fewer hyphens

0.2-inch hyphenation zone—less ragged right margin, more hyphens

Fourscore and seven years ago our fathers brought forth on this continent a new nation, conceived in Liberty, and dedicated to the proposition that all men are created equal.

Now we are engaged in a great civil war, testing whether that nation, or any nation so conceived and so dedicated, can long endure. We are met on a great battlefield of that war. We have come to dedicate a portion of that field, as a final resting place for those who here gave their lives that that nation might live. It is altogether fitting and proper that we should do this.

Fourscore and seven years ago our fathers brought forth on this continent a new nation, conceived in Liberty, and dedicated to the proposition that all men are created equal.

Now we are engaged in a great civil war, testing whether that nation, or any nation so conceived and so dedicated, can long endure. We are met on a great battlefield of that war. We have come to dedicate a portion of that field, as a final resting place for those who here gave their lives that that nation might live. It is altogether fitting and proper that we should do this.

different hyphenation zones. In general, the smaller the hyphenation zone you specify, the closer each line will come to the right margin. Also, a small hyphenation zone creates more two- and three-letter word divisions. A larger hyphenation zone creates a more ragged appearance, with fewer small word divisions.

Hyphenation slows you down when you are reading text because you have to read a portion of the word, look to the next line for the remainder of the word, and put the two pieces together. A guideline is that hyphenation should occur in no more than 3% of the lines, and never allow more than three consecutive hyphens to occur.

PAGE LAYOUT AND DESIGN

The purpose of the layout is to draw the reader into the publication and create readers out of people who would just as soon scan pages. Creating an area of visual interest on every page promotes readership. A graphic or picture will draw the eye to the page (see Figure 8.20).

Another principle of page layout is to use white space to enhance readability. Avoid the temptation to fill every part of the page with text. Wide margins, indentation, and drawings can increase readability. Too much type looks dense and heavy on the page and does not invite the reader into the publication. White space, used properly, makes documents easier to read [compare Figures 8.21(a) and (b)].

Figure 8.20
Using graphics to increase visual interest

Courtesy of Ken Trimpe, The Creative Dept.

Figure 8.21(a)
Type filling entire page

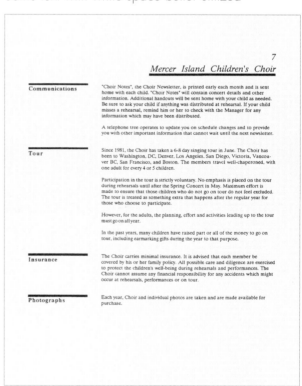

Figure 8.21(b)
Same text with white space better utilized

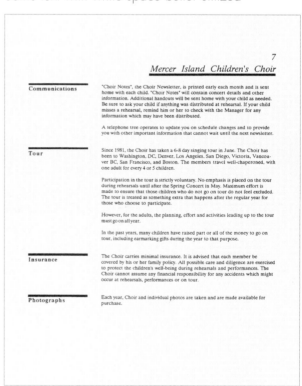

Understanding five design principles will assist you in designing the page: optical center and eye flow, eye dwell, balance, optical weight, and graphic orientation and placement. Let's consider each of them separately.

Optical Center and Eye Flow

When first viewing a page, the eye focuses on the **optical center** of the page. This is slightly above and to the left of the physical center of the page. Then the eye traces a *z*-like pattern—called **eye flow**—from left to right and top to bottom on the page, as shown in Figure 8.22.

The **terminal area** is in the lower-right quadrant of the page. To keep interest on the page, place a strong graphic in this area. The terminal area is where the eye ends and leaves the page. When designing a page, ask: What is the last image you want the reader to have? It could be the company logo, a coupon, or a telephone number. Avoid the mistake of the cigarette ad that has the Surgeon General's warning in the terminal area of the page.

Eye Dwell

Research has shown that the eye spends a different amount of time in different quadrants of the page. The top half of the page keeps the eye for 60% of the time; the bottom half for 40% (see Figure 8.23). You can improve **eye dwell** by placing a photo or other attention getter in a lower eye-dwell quadrant to focus attention on another area of the publication.

Figure 8.22
Optical center, eye flow

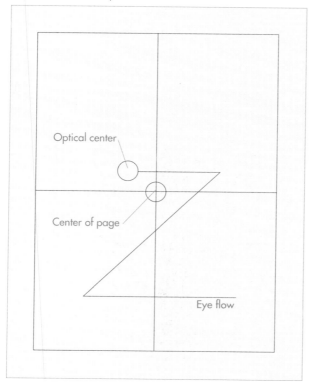

Figure 8.23
Eye dwell

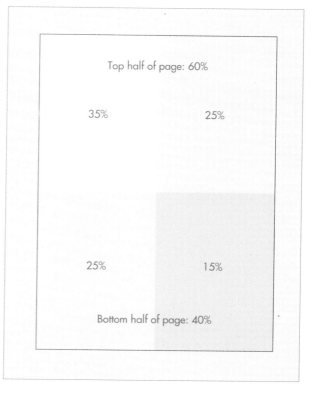

Look at the four-panel brochure in Figure 8.24. Notice that each panel has balance, and there is overall balance when the four panels are viewed at the same time. The large picture in the first panel balances the two smaller pictures in the fourth panel. The optical center of the brochure is probably in the second panel. By using the biggest picture in panel one, your eye is drawn to the first panel and you are more likely to read the entire brochure. Finally, notice how there is a good mix of pictures with apples, people, and apples and people. This also adds to the visual interest.

Figure 8.24
Four-panel brochure

Courtesy of Ken Trimpe, The Creative Dept.

Balance

There are two different approaches to page layout: **symmetric** and **asymmetric**. In symmetrical layout, elements such as text and graphics are balanced across a horizontal, vertical, or diagonal line. The image is conservative, orderly, and formal. Examples are shown in Figure 8.25.

In asymmetrical layout, text and graphics are balanced with optical weight. Asymmetrical layouts are more energetic and dynamic. An example is shown in Figure 8.26. For this type of effect, designers use an odd number of visuals in page layout.

Optical Weight

Optical weight is the ability of a graphic component to attract the reader's eye. Some guidelines for understanding optical weight are:

Higher Optical Weight	*Lower Optical Weight*
Large	Small
Dark	Light
Color	Black, white, gray
Irregular shape	Regular shape

Figure 8.25
Symmetrical layouts

Courtesy of Ken Trimpe, The Creative Dept.

Courtesy of Dorothy Mulligan,
American Association of School Administrators

Courtesy of Sheila Hoffman, Newsletters and More

Figure 8.26
Asymmetrical layout

Courtesy of Ken Trimpe, The Creative Dept.

Figure 8.27
Using a small, dark shape to balance the optical weight of a large, lighter shape

Courtesy of Overlake Hospital Medical Center

This means a small, dark shape can balance a larger, light shape. Figure 8.27 illustrates this principle.

Another critical layout concern is keeping track of the overall design. When you have facing pages, you are constantly going back and forth between the detail of a particular section and the overall look of the two-page spread. Layout that looks good on two individual pages can appear disorganized when the pages are placed side by side. Look at two facing pages and be aware of how they work, or do not work, together.

Additionally, you can go outside the grid to enhance interest and provide visual surprise. Pulling a picture or other visual into a wide margin or using a large drop cap for a paragraph are two ways to accomplish this (see Figure 8.28).

Figure 8.28
Pulling a picture into a wide margin

Courtesy of Ken Shafer, Ken Shafer Design

Graphic Orientation and Placement

When choosing a graphic, consider its orientation and placement. The graphic should bring the reader *into* the publication, rather than direct the reader's focus outward. Notice in Figure 8.29 how the chair and sculpture both face inward, toward the text.

Another consideration is **word wrap,** or **runaround.** Allowing a graphic to "intrude" a column of text gives a less formal and more artistic feel. Figure 8.29 illustrates both orientation and word wrap.

Look again at the Port Dorsey Times (Figure 8.30), a newsletter you created in Chapter 6. The orientation of the house directs your eye out of

Figure 8.29
Graphic orientation directs the reader's eye inward; word wrap increases visual interest

Fine WOODWORKS

Women in Wood
May 1 – July 29 at Gilman Village

Fine woodworking includes the use of many very sharp tools and potentially dangerous high speed lathes and saws. To say nothing of constantly having to lift heavy planks of wood and finished furniture. For these reasons, it perhaps is not surprising that the stereotypical image of a fine woodworker is male.

How wrong such images can be, as today there are many women fine woodworkers. To illustrate the incredible diversity of talent and skills amongst women woodworkers, we are providing a complete list of the women taking part in a show currently on display at our Gilman Village gallery and the pieces each have featured.

Judith Ames
Shell bed and end tables
Stephanie Baillie
Carved salmon & bass fish sculptures
Mercedes Brown
Ikebana stands & spinning tops
Lynn Buss
Marquetry wall hangings
Martha Collins
Cribbage boards, jewelry box, candlesticks & bracelets with intricate inlays
Virginia Dotson
Turning in Finnish birch & ebony
Connie Ewing
Screen
Kay Kammerzell
Rustic furniture in hazel branches, burnished copper & sheep wool
Lynn Louise
Sculptural bench
Norma Pizzaro
Full length mirror in wenge, sweet gum and maple
Alice Porembski
Table and mirror
Julene Schlack
Napkin rings
Jennifer Schwarz
Coffee table and sculptured wall cabinet with glass
Rita Stochosky
Letter openers
Helga Winter
Turnings in big leaf maple ▪

Turning
by Helga Winter

Rustic furniture
by Kay Kammerzell

Fine WOODWORKS

Northwest woodworkers in the news

Two Northwest woodworkers have made the news in recent months. Judith Ames' *Cloud chair*, made from fiddleback western maple, was shown in the May 1993 *Fine WoodWorking* magazine. This piece was originally built for the 1992 "Environmentally Friendly" show. Tom Stangeland had an entire article devoted to his work in the May 30 issue of *the Seattle Times Pacific* magazine. It featured a Greene and Greene style dining room from a San Juan home, made of certified sustained-yield mahogany from Belize. ▪

Michael Davock
Sculptured Pregnant Torso

The number of skilled wood carvers within our 33 member woodworker cooperative can be counted on less than one hand. Michael is both a very talented and very dedicated artist who often works for months on a single piece. His beautifully carved pregnant torso took three months to complete.

Michael has had to develop his own special carving techniques to complete such intricate carvings. He frequently starts by creating a template of the design concept, made up of multiple slim softwood boards, each held together by dowels and not glued. If something is not quite to Michael's satisfaction he can easily pull apart the many layers of the template reaching the section that needs to be changed. Once the changes have been made the template can be quickly fitted back together and checked to see if yet more adjustments are necessary. A time consuming process, which is repeated as often as necessary until perfect.

Once the softwood template is completed to his satisfaction he knows exactly how and where to start on the final hardwood piece. For his work *Pregnant Torso* Michael carefully selected some exceptional Lacewood with its delicate, intricate grain patterns. ▪

Sculptured Pregnant Torso
by Michael Davock

Northwest Gallery of Fine Woodworking

▪ Pioneer Square Gallery
202 First Ave. S.
Seattle, WA 98104
(206) 625-0542
(206) 382-1965 (FAX)
Hours:
Mon-Sat 10:30-5:30
Sunday 12:00-5:00

▪ Gilman Village Gallery
317 N.W. Gilman Blvd.
Issaquah, WA 98027
(206) 391-4221
Hours:
Mon-Sat 10:00-6:00
Thursday until 8:00
Sunday 12:00-5:00

▪ Sales Associates
Pandora Andre-Beatty
Yodit Assefa Clarke
Andre Diaz
Jennifer Durrie
Katharine McBain
Carol Mirman
Norma Pizzaro

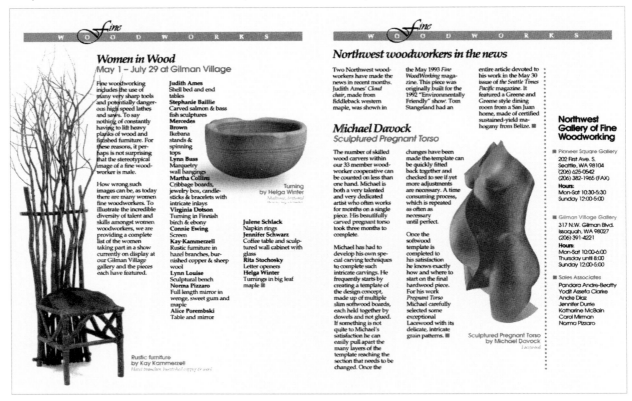

Courtesy of Sheila Hoffman, Newsletters and More

Figure 8.30
(a) Awkward orientation

Port Dorsey Times

Historic Homes Tour to Bring Visitors

Port Dorsey Historical Society is sponsoring a tour of historic homes every weekend this month. Featured will be the turn-of-the-century Loudon mansion, the Victorian-style Van Dyke home, the Coleman estate, and the home of antiques dealer Anna Cortes. In all there will be nine homes on display. Tickets cost $15 for adults and $7 for senior citizens and students, with proceeds going to the Historical Society. Shuttle buses will transport people among the homes, leaving from the Portage Inn's parking lot every half hour. Last year's tour attracted over 20,000 people.

Quaint Port Dorsey provides a perfect setting for a tour of historic homes. Incorporated in 1872, its first homes were built by the Loudons, Van Dykes, and Colemans, wealthy industrial families with a vision for a Newport-style community of summer mansions. Unlike Newport, however, the mansions in Port Dorsey are of a smaller scale, but are nonetheless representative of fine period architecture and furnishings. Later inhabitants built homes consistent with the architecture of the first homes. Recently the business area has seen the addition of many fine restaurants and small shops with unique merchandise. Port Dorsey is a destination for weekend shoppers, but during the month of the Historical Homes Tour, visitors come from all over the country for the event.

The Loudon mansion was built in 1898 and has twelve rooms, including a formal living room, parlor, dining room, library, kitchen, breakfast room, four bedrooms, and maid's quarters. Still owned by the Loudon family, it contains many original furnishings, including sofas, the dining room table, and oriental rugs. On two sides of the house is a wrap-around porch, or verandah as it is referred to by the Loudons, that overlooks the water and has expansive views of the San Juans.

The historic Loudon mansion with its wrap-around porch

Also featured will be the English country garden which was shown recently in Country Outdoors magazine.

The Victorian-style Van Dyke home was built in 1889, and has the steeply pitched roof, verge board trim, pointed Gothic windows, and board-and-batten siding characteristic of Victorian homes. Elaborate trim work, both inside and out, and a hexagonal cupola are other characteristics that make this a favorite on the tour. Inside, rich colors and tones of wood, wallpaper, and rugs are examples of the Victorian decor. Especially noteworthy is the central staircase, with hand-crafted banister. Many finely carved walnut pieces of furniture have been collected during the owners' travels and enhance the period feel.

Unique Features

The Coleman estate was built in 1920 and is now used for wedding receptions and special events. The fireplace in the drawing room has an elaborately carved wood mantel. Wainscoting, six-panel doors, and finely carved woodwork show off the fine craftsmanship of the time. Windowseats in the library alcove and the children's bedrooms are filled with soft cushions and pillows. There is a four-poster bed and Queen Anne highboy in the master bedroom. A grand piano is the centerpiece of the living room. During the tour, various pianists will be playing between noon and four each day.

CONTENTS

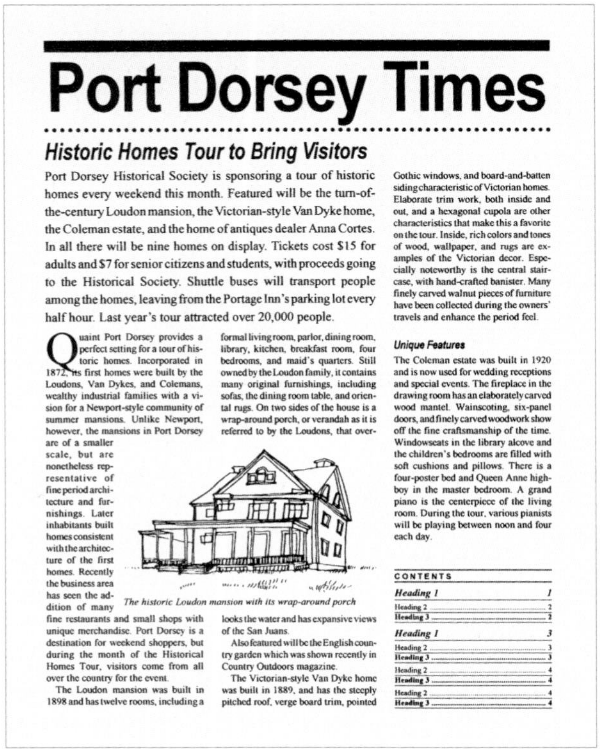

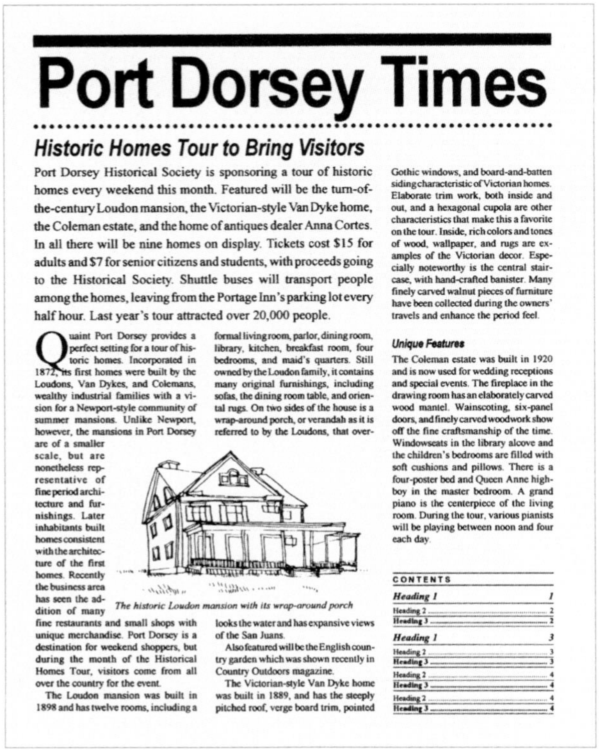

(b) Flipping the house graphic orients the reader toward the interior of the publication

Port Dorsey Times

Historic Homes Tour to Bring Visitors

Port Dorsey Historical Society is sponsoring a tour of historic homes every weekend this month. Featured will be the turn-of-the-century Loudon mansion, the Victorian-style Van Dyke home, the Coleman estate, and the home of antiques dealer Anna Cortes. In all there will be nine homes on display. Tickets cost $15 for adults and $7 for senior citizens and students, with proceeds going to the Historical Society. Shuttle buses will transport people among the homes, leaving from the Portage Inn's parking lot every half hour. Last year's tour attracted over 20,000 people.

Quaint Port Dorsey provides a perfect setting for a tour of historic homes. Incorporated in 1872, its first homes were built by the Loudons, Van Dykes, and Colemans, wealthy industrial families with a vision for a Newport-style community of summer mansions. Unlike Newport, however, the mansions in Port Dorsey are of a smaller scale, but are nonetheless representative of fine period architecture and furnishings. Later inhabitants built homes consistent with the architecture of the first homes. Recently the business area has seen the addition of many fine restaurants and small shops with unique merchandise. Port Dorsey is a destination for weekend shoppers, but during the month of the Historical Homes Tour, visitors come from all over the country for the event.

The Loudon mansion was built in 1898 and has twelve rooms, including a formal living room, parlor, dining room, library, kitchen, breakfast room, four bedrooms, and maid's quarters. Still owned by the Loudon family, it contains many original furnishings, including sofas, the dining room table, and oriental rugs. On two sides of the house is a wrap-around porch, or verandah as it is referred to by the Loudons, that overlooks the water and has expansive views of the San Juans.

The historic Loudon mansion with its wrap-around porch

Also featured will be the English country garden which was shown recently in Country Outdoors magazine.

The Victorian-style Van Dyke home was built in 1889, and has the steeply pitched roof, verge board trim, pointed Gothic windows, and board-and-batten siding characteristic of Victorian homes. Elaborate trim work, both inside and out, and a hexagonal cupola are other characteristics that make this a favorite on the tour. Inside, rich colors and tones of wood, wallpaper, and rugs are examples of the Victorian decor. Especially noteworthy is the central staircase, with hand-crafted banister. Many finely carved walnut pieces of furniture have been collected during the owners' travels and enhance the period feel.

Unique Features

The Coleman estate was built in 1920 and is now used for wedding receptions and special events. The fireplace in the drawing room has an elaborately carved wood mantel. Wainscoting, six-panel doors, and finely carved woodwork show off the fine craftsmanship of the time. Windowseats in the library alcove and the children's bedrooms are filled with soft cushions and pillows. There is a four-poster bed and Queen Anne highboy in the master bedroom. A grand piano is the centerpiece of the living room. During the tour, various pianists will be playing between noon and four each day.

CONTENTS

Heading 1 1
Heading 2 2
Heading 3 2
Heading 1 3
Heading 2 3
Heading 3 3
Heading 2 4
Heading 3 4
Heading 2 4
Heading 3 4

the newsletter. Flipping the graphic changes its orientation and brings the reader into the publication.

ABOUT RESTRAINT

There is common agreement that restraint is important with design. Using every type size available is not advisable (see Figure 8.31). Nor is it a good idea to use too many special effects on a single page, such as drop caps, nonjustified text, and pulling a picture into a margin. The sum of all the special effects can have an overwhelming and cluttered look, as if the designer had a checklist of special effects and all of them had to appear on one page. Restraint is wise advice.

Figure 8.31
A lack of restraint results in a cluttered, haphazard design

Ransom *NOTE* News

Dedicated to the Principle that More is Best   Issue 3275

In this issue
Lorem 1
Ipsum dolor 2
Dolor sit amet 3

Newsletter Surpasses *Old* Font Record

Forty-two styles used in publication

Lorem ipsum dolor sit amet, consectetuer adipiscing elit, sed diam nonummy nibh euismod tincidunt ut laoreet dolore magna aliquam erat volutpat. Ut wisi enim ad minim veniam, quis nostrud exerci tation ullamcorper suscipit lobortis nisl ut aliquip ex ea commodo consequat. Duis autem vel eum iriure dolor in hendrerit in vulputate velit esse molestie consequat, vel illum dolore eu feugiat nulla facilisis at vero eros et accumsan et iusto odio dignissim qui blandit praesent luptatum zzril delenit augue duis dolore te feugait nulla facilisi. Lorem ipsum dolor sit amet, consectetuer adipiscing elit, sed diam nonummy nibh euismod tincidunt ut laoreet dolore magna aliquam erat volutpat. Ut wisi enim ad minim veniam, quis nostrud exerci tation ullamcorper suscipit lobortis nisl ut aliquip ex ea commodo consequat.

Duis autem vel eum iriure dolor in hendrerit in vulputate velit esse molestie consequat, vel illum dolore eu feugiat nulla facilisis at vero eros et accumsan et iusto odio dignissim qui blandit praesent luptatum zzril delenit augue duis dolore te feugait nulla facilisi. Nam liber tempor cum soluta nobis eleifend option congue nihil imperdiet doming id quod mazim placerat facer possim assum.

Lorem ipsum dolor sit amet, consectetuer adipiscing elit, sed diam.

Industry News

Magna aliquam erat volutpat.
Ut wisi enim ad minim veniam, quis nostrud exerci tation ullamcorper. suscipit lobortis nisl ut aliquip ex ea commodo consequat. Duis autem vel eum iriure dolor in hendrerit in vulputate

Velit esse molestie consequat, vel illum

dolore eu feugiat nulla facilisis at vero eros et accumsan et iusto odio dignissim qui blandit praesent luptatum zzril delenit augue duis dolore te feugait nulla facilisi. Lorem ipsum dolor sit amet, consectetuer adipiscing elit, sed diam nonummy nibh euismod tincidunt ut laoreet dolore magna aliquam erat volutpat. Ut wisi enim ad minim veniam, quis nostrud exerci tation.

COMING SOON TO A DESKTOP NEAR YOU
Type Publisher ANNOUNCES 72 New Fonts

Nonummy nibh euismod tincidunt ut laoreet dolore magna aliquam erat volutpat. Ut wisi enim ad minim veniam, quis nostrud exerci tation ullamcorper suscipit lobortis nisl ut aliquip ex ea commodo consequat. Duis autem vel eum iriure dolor in hendrerit in vulputate velit esse molestie consequat, vel illum dolore eu feugiat nulla facilisis at vero eros et accumsa. et iusto odio dignissim qui blandit praesent luptatum zzril delenit augue duis. dolore te feugait nulla facilisi. Lorem ipsum dolor sit amet, consectetuer. Adipiscing elit, sed diam nonummy nibh euismod tincidunt ut laoreet dolore.

SUMMARY

Desktop publishing is the first real creative step forward since the invention of movable type. Now you can speed up the design process and experiment with different fonts, layouts, and techniques with relative ease. Through mastering PageMaker, understanding basic design concepts, and being willing to experiment, you will produce quality documents that communicate your message.

Look again at Figure 8.28. Design techniques used here include italic oversized caps, pull quotes, photo outside grid, different type size in the title, and ragged right. The design works because of generous amounts of white space and the designer's ability to pull together everything into a well-integrated, cohesive layout.

KEY TERMS

serif	kicker	terminal area
sans serif	justify	eye dwell
display type	ragged	symmetric
drop cap	hyphenation	asymmetric
kerning	hyphenation zone	optical weight
ligature	optical center	word wrap
eyebrow	eye flow	runaround

QUESTIONS

1. What are the physical distinctions between serif and sans serif fonts? What reactions do people have to each? Do you agree with the characterizations? When would you use serif fonts? When would you use sans serif fonts?

2. Describe decorative fonts. When would you use one?

3. When should italic and bold be used? When should they not? When should you use underlining and all caps?

4. Explain the difference between justified and nonjustified text. What design considerations influence decisions about when to use each?

5. What is the purpose of a headline? Give examples of headlines that show different design concepts.

6. Define *optical center* and *eye flow*. What is their importance to page layout?

7. Explain the importance of identifying audience and objectives to publication design. What design elements are influenced by your understanding of audience and objectives? Be specific.

8. Explain eye dwell. What is its impact on page design?

9. Give an example of how to use optical weight for balance.

10. Evaluate a magazine, advertisement, brochure, or catalog. Who is the audience? Is the appearance formal or friendly? Look at the fonts. How many are used? What design features are used? How effective is the page layout and overall appearance?

PROJECTS

1. Look at Figure 8.27. Identify the grid. Evaluate the design for font, justification, emphasis, optical center and eye flow, balance, optical weight, graphic placement, and white space. What is your overall response to the spread?

2. Look at Figure 8.32. Answer the same questions as in Project 1.

Figure 8.32
Project 8.2

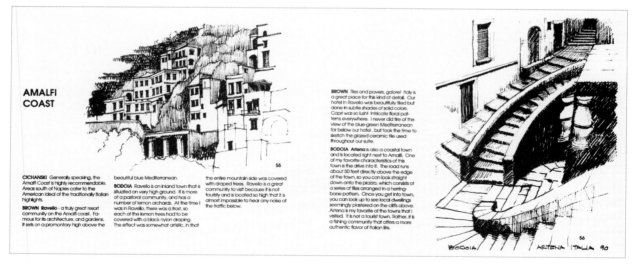

3. Figure 8.33 is from the same publication as Figure 8.32. Is the design consistent? Explain.

4. Look at Figure 8.34. Answer the same questions as in Project 1.

Figure 8.33
Project 8.3

Figure 8.34
Project 8.4

Figure 8.35
Project 8.5

EARTHSAVE SEATTLE: PERSONAL FOOD CHOICES . . . GLOBAL RESULTS   WINTER 1994 VOLUME 4 NUMBER 1

Challenges to change: finding meaning in food

BY LARRY KAPLOWITZ

If people were driven purely by physiological needs, we wouldn't have any trouble choosing and maintaining a wholesome and nutritious diet. You are not likely to find an anteater or a mosquito worrying over what it should eat. What distinguishes human beings from other creatures, however, is our penchant for investing even simple physiological functions with meaning. And there's probably no human activity that we've endowed with a greater complexity of meanings than eating.

I point this out not to suggest that you need extensive psychoanalysis in order to alter your eating habits, but to emphasize that there's more to changing your diet than merely knowing what to buy and how to fix it once you've got it home. Yes, solid practical know-how is an essential element in making a successful transition. However it is equally important to begin to recognize and master the intangible and often unconscious factors that have been influencing your food choices. If you're not conscious of them, they can quickly derail your best intentions.

Throughout most of human history, finding and gathering food was the primary activity of our species. We knew where our food came from and how we fit into the larger food chain of which we were a part. Our food was intrinsically meaningful. Today, hunting and gathering has been replaced by abstract and often meaningless activities (i.e., our jobs) that we engage in primarily to earn money (another abstraction). With this money we purchase food that has been raised, processed, and packaged, often beyond recognition, by people we will never meet in places we will never see. Little

wonder that we must find other ways to make our involvement with food meaningful.

One of the specific ways that we give meaning to food is to endow it with the ability to fulfill our emotional needs, or at least to distract ourselves from them. How many times have you turned to food out of loneliness or despair or anxiety or boredom? Have you ever treated yourself to something rich and decadent to reward yourself for an accomplishment, or to compensate for some setback, or just to make up for having a miserable day? In our unstable and rapidly changing society of transient relationships, jobs, and homes, food may be the one thing in our lives we can count on. That pint of Deep Chocolate Peanut Butter Haagen-Dazs or that Big Mac will always be there for you. You can find them

Our January 13th program, **Challenges to Change,** *will feature a panel of real people from many points on the food-choice continuum. In an "Oprahue" style format, they will share about their challenges and successes and the obstacles they have faced (and are still facing) in changing their diets. There will be ample opportunity for audience questioning and interaction. This promises to be a lively and enlightening evening. See back cover for details.*

Continued on page 5

Courtesy of Sheila Hoffman, Newsletters and More

5. Look at Figure 8.35. Answer the same questions as in Project 1.

6. Create your own issue of Ransom Note News. Use as many poor design elements as you can. In the text of your newsletter, describe each feature and why the design is poor.

7. Find a poorly designed publication. Redesign the document to make the communication more effective.

Upon completion of this chapter you will be able to:

- Describe the differences between layout and story views

- Enter new text in Story Editor

- Use the spelling checker

- Use the Find and Change commands

- Place a word-processed file into a story

- Import a graphic

- Place a story in a publication

Story Editor

In previous chapters you worked with text in the layout view. You created new text for publications by typing paragraphs, and you worked with text blocks. PageMaker 5.0 also has a feature called **Story Editor**, a built-in word processor that provides a faster, more powerful way to edit text. Story Editor gives you a spelling checker and search and replace (Find and Change) capabilities. And it reduces the time between typing text and seeing it onscreen.

In this chapter you will create a publication using Story Editor. The publication is shown in Figure 9.1. You will type the first paragraph and import three other paragraphs as two different stories. You will combine the two stories into one text block using a set of steps first introduced in Chapter 4. The process demonstrated in this chapter to create this four-paragraph publication is not the most straightforward method available; it would be more logical to deal with four paragraphs as one file. This approach was chosen intentionally to illustrate the features of Story Editor using a short publication to lessen your typing time. Thus, do all the parts of this chapter even though you may wonder why a single paragraph is treated as a story. The techniques described here are applicable to longer publications.

LAYOUT VIEW VERSUS STORY VIEW

When you first open a PageMaker publication, you are in **layout view**. The Toolbox appears, and you can work with text and graphics. You enter **story view** from layout view by selecting Edit story from the Edit pull-down menu. This places a text-only window on top of your layout

Figure 9.1
Final publication

view. Within story view, you may work with text only. Text processing is faster because the graphics portion of the program is not available.

Figure 9.2 shows the same publication in layout and story views. In story view, notice the absence of the Toolbox. This is because the only option available to you is text processing. Also notice the title bar, which displays the name of the **story**. Stories are named with the first 20 or so characters of the story because a story is not a complete file, but rather part of a publication. A publication may be made up of one or more stories. Another difference between the two views is the menu bar, as shown in Figure 9.3. Only layout view has Layout and Element pull-down menus. Only story view has a Story pull-down menu. This means that certain commands can be accessed only in layout view while other commands can be accessed in only story view. Still other commands are available in either view.

WORKING IN STORY EDITOR

Do the following to open a new publication and access Story Editor.

1. Start PageMaker.

Figure 9.2(a)
Publication in
layout view

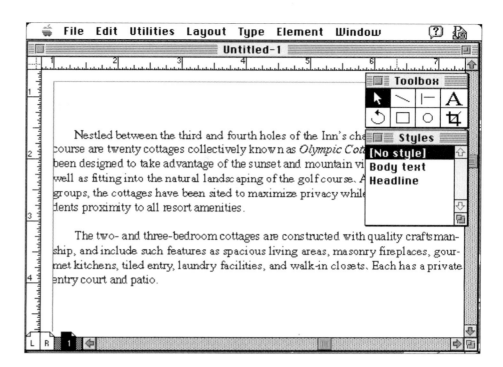

Figure 9.2(b)
Publication in
story view

Title bar shows first
words in story

Toolbox is missing

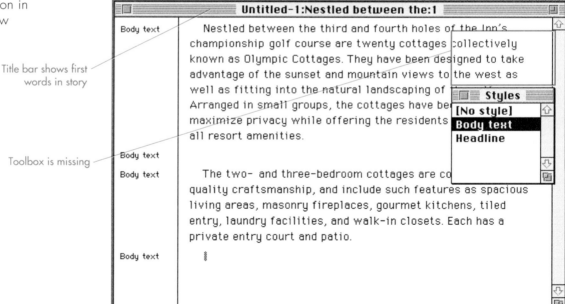

2. Select Open... from the File menu (⌘-O).

3. Select Promo 2 Template.

4. Select Edit story from the Edit menu (⌘-E).

You have entered Story Editor; your screen should look like Figure 9.4.
Take a few moments to look at the story view. Note how it is a window
on top of the layout view.

Figure 9.3
Menu bars in layout
and story views

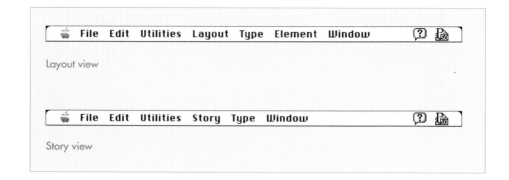

Layout view

Story view

Figure 9.4
Story Editor screen

Story view menu bar

Sidebar displays
paragraph style

Story window title

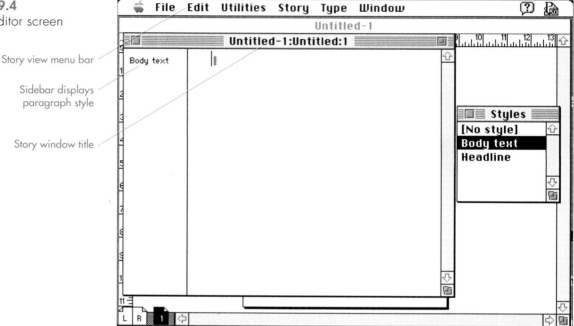

Look at the type in the Style palette. Recall that you can press ⌘ while clicking on the style name. As you look at the type, note that Body text is Times 14 and Headline is Times 30 Bold.

Exploring the Menu Bar in Story Editor

The menu bar in Story Editor is different from that in layout view. Pull down and explore each of the menus in the menu bar. They are shown in Figure 9.5.

The first thing you will do is center and type the title *Olympic Cottages* using the Headline style.

1. Click on Headline in the Style palette.

2. Type *Olympic Cottages.*

3. Press (RETURN) twice.

Figure 9.5
Pull-down menus in story view

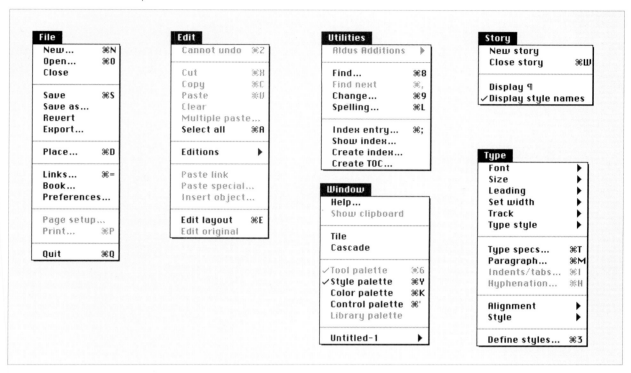

Now you will type the first paragraph of the document, shown in Figure 9.6. Make sure that you make some mistakes so you can use the spelling checker.

1. Click on Body text.

2. Type the paragraph shown in Figure 9.6.

Figure 9.6
First paragraph

Type with at least two errors

Adjacent to the golf course at the Inn at Portage Bay is 40 acres of woods. Alders, cedars, and fir trees abound, reaching to a bluff overlooking Puget Sound. Oanoramic views to the to the west include the San Juan Islands, Olympic Mountains, and Puget Sound. To the east lies Mt. Baker and its foothills. Now this setting has been planned to allow a fortinate few appreciate its beauty and serenity.

Look at the Pasteboard. Notice that the headline and body text appear to be the same size even though the headline is 30 point and the body text is 14 point. This is because you are in Story Editor and not in layout view. All text will be shown the same size. On closer inspection, you should notice that the headline is in bold whereas body text is in normal type.

Using the Spelling Checker

To use the spelling checker:

1. Select Spelling... from the Utilities menu (⌘-L).

Figure 9.7 shows the Spelling dialog box. Notice that Current story is the default selection. It is not necessary to move the cursor to the top of the document as some word processors require. Current story tells Story Editor to check the entire story.

2. Click on Start.

When the spelling checker finds a word that does not match any word in its 100,000-word dictionary, it will highlight the word and list alternatives. You then have three choices: to ignore, replace, or add the word.

Select Ignore when the highlighted word is correct although not in the dictionary and you do not wish to add it to the dictionary. *Puget* is a word that will not be in the dictionary.

Select Replace when the highlighted word is spelled incorrectly, and the list contains a correct spelling.

To replace a word:

1. Move the mouse pointer to your choice.

2. Click on the replacement word.

3. Click on Replace.

An alternate method is to double-click on the replacement word. Figure 9.8 shows both methods.

Figure 9.7
Spelling dialog box

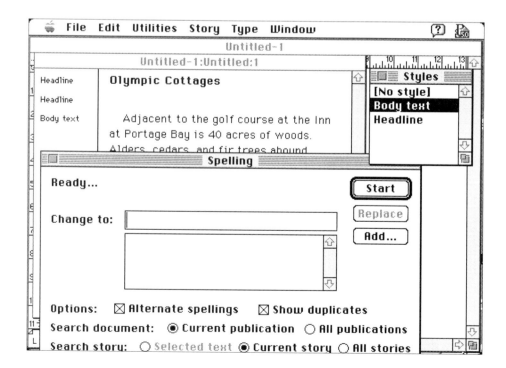

Sometimes a word is misspelled and the computer list does not contain the correct spelling. This can happen when you type something like *Oanoramic* for *Panoramic*.

To type a correction for a misspelled word (see Figure 9.9):

1. **Click an insertion point in the word.**

2. **Use (DELETE) to delete characters.**

Figure 9.8(a)
Replacing a word using the Replace button

2. Click on replacement word

3. Click on Replace

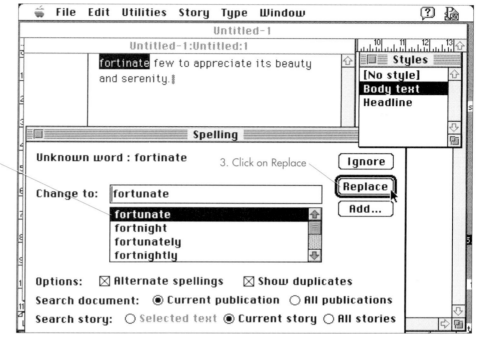

Figure 9.8(b)
Replacing a word by double-clicking

Double-click on the correct word

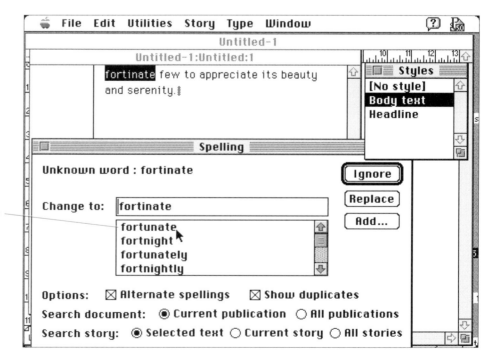

Figure 9.9
Typing a correction

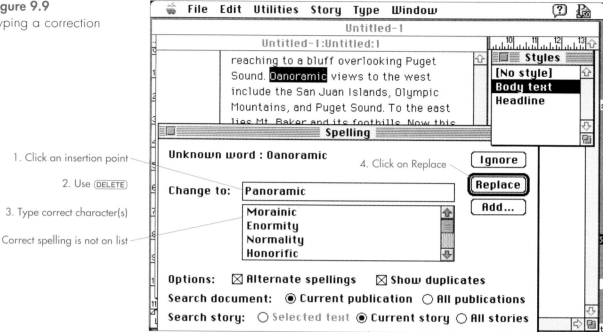

1. Click an insertion point

2. Use (DELETE)

3. Type correct character(s)

Correct spelling is not on list

3. **Type the correct characters.**

4. **Click on Replace.**

To add a word that is spelled correctly but is not in PageMaker's dictionary:

1. **Click on Add.**

The dialog box will tell you when the spelling check is complete. To remove the box from the screen:

1. **Click on the Close box of the Spelling dialog box.**

When you have used the spelling checker on the first paragraph and have removed the Spelling dialog box, continue with the next set of steps.

Importing a Story into Story Editor

The second and third paragraphs are stored in a file called Olympic Cottages 1 on your data disk. This file was created using Word 3.0, and PageMaker has a filter to recognize these files.

Make sure you are in Story Editor and your cursor is at the beginning of the second paragraph. Your screen should match Figure 9.10 before beginning the next set of steps.

To import a text file and append it to the end of another story:

1. **Select Place... from the File menu (⌘-D).**

2. **Click on Olympic Cottages 1 (do not double-click).**

3. **Click on Inserting text (see Figure 9.11).**

Figure 9.10
Getting ready to
import a story

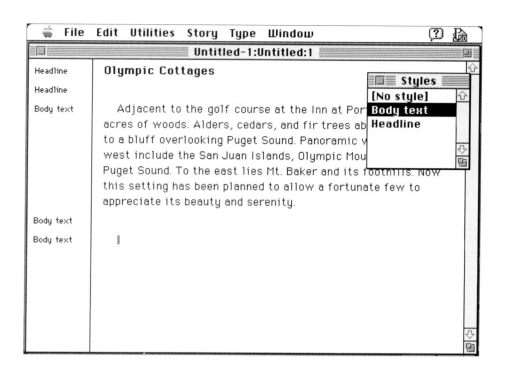

Figure 9.11
Importing a story

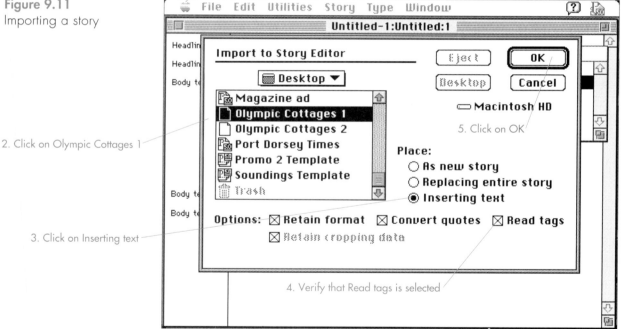

2. Click on Olympic Cottages 1

3. Click on Inserting text

4. Verify that Read tags is selected

5. Click on OK

4. Make sure Read tags is selected.

5. Click on OK.

The publication now contains three paragraphs. These three paragraphs are recognized as a single story because the typing and importing were done in one story window without leaving Story Editor. Recall that when you imported Olympic Cottages 1 you clicked on Inserting text. This added the imported text to the existing story. Thus, you now have one story. This becomes important as you progress through the next set of steps and import another paragraph as a second story.

The fourth and final paragraph is stored as Olympic Cottages 2. You will import it as a new story twice so that you can explore more of the features of Story Editor.

1. **Select Place… from the File menu (⌘-D).**

2. **Click on Olympic Cottages 2.**

   As new story is selected.

3. **Click off Retain format (if necessary).**

4. **Click on Read tags (if necessary).**

5. **Click on OK.**

Notice that a new window appears with a title bar The Olympic Cottage:1 and the new paragraph.

6. **Click on Body text in the Style palette (if necessary).**

Repeat steps 1 through 5 above to import the same story again. Now you have an additional story called The Olympic Cottage:2 on top of your other windows (see Figure 9.12). You can move from one story to another.

1. **Select Untitled-1 from the Window menu.**

You will see a list of the open stories, as well as the Layout option. To select one, move the mouse pointer to it and release. (See Figure 9.13.)

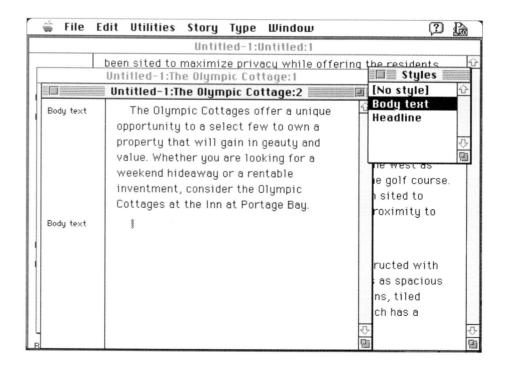

Figure 9.12
Story view after importing paragraph a second time

Figure 9.13
Titles of different
windows in layout
and story views

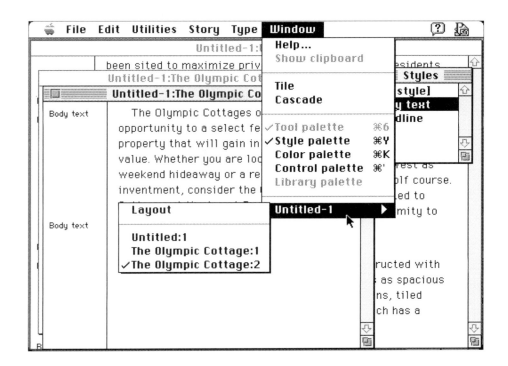

An alternate method to move to another story when several stories are in the window is to point to the story's title bar and click.

To close The Olympic Cottage:1, a duplicate story:

1. **Select The Olympic Cottage:1 from the Window pull-down menu.**

2. **Click on the Close box of The Olympic Cottage:1 window.**

PageMaker will give you a warning message telling you that the story has not been placed.

3. **Click on Discard.**

Now you should have two stories: Untitled:1 and The Olympic Cottage:2. If they are not on your screen, put them there by selecting Window and the name of the story. Your screen should look like Figure 9.14.

Placing Stories in Layout View

The next step is to place the two stories from Story Editor into layout view. First you will place Untitled:1, then you will place The Olympic Cottage:2.

Make sure Untitled:1 is onscreen (see Figure 9.15). If it is not, select it.

To place Untitled:1 in layout view:

1. **Select Edit layout from the Edit menu (⌘-E).**

2. **Place the loaded text icon on the publication page near the top-left corner and click.**

Figure 9.14
Publication
after discarding
duplicate story

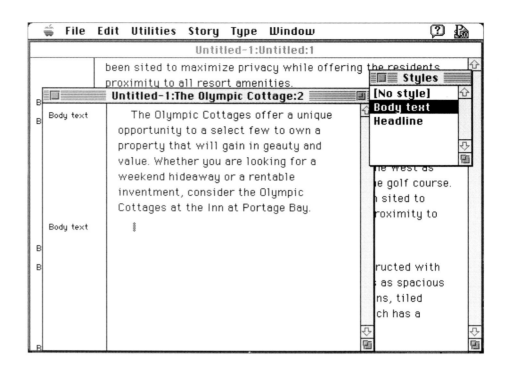

Figure 9.15
Getting ready to place
the story in layout view

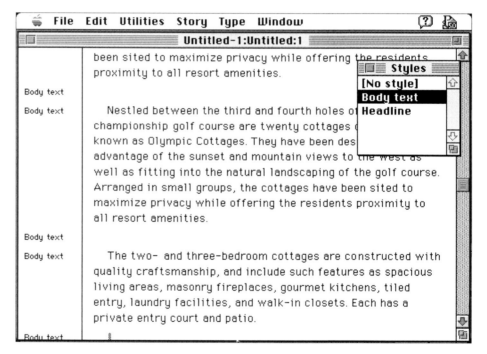

3. Remove the windowshades by clicking outside the text block.

To place The Olympic Cottage:2 as a second story, first select it, then place it.

1. Select Window, Untitled-1: The Olympic Cottage:2.

Figure 9.16
Verifying that
two stories have
been placed

Windowshade loops
identify this as an
independent text block

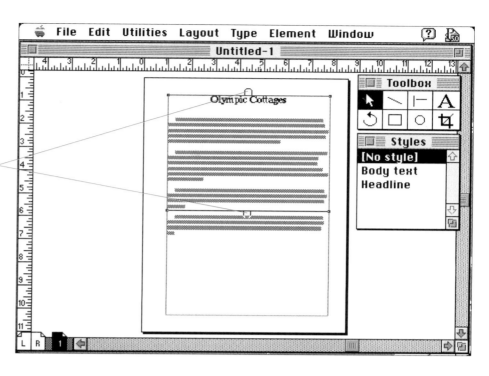

This moves you to Story Editor with The Olympic Cottage:2 selected.

2. Click on Body text (if necessary).

3. Select Edit layout from the Edit menu ((⌘)-E).

4. Place the loaded text icon below the existing text and click.

Now you have placed two stories. To verify that they are indeed two stories and not one, use the pointer tool from the Toolbox. Click on one of the first three paragraphs. Notice how the windowshades define the first three paragraphs of the text as one text block (see Figure 9.16). Click outside the windowshades. Point and click on the last paragraph. In layout view, you have two stories or text blocks.

Earlier in the chapter you used the spelling checker on the paragraph you typed. Since you can't assume that imported text is error-free, put the entire document through a spelling check. The spelling checker is in the Utilities pull-down menu.

1. Select the Utilities menu.

Notice that the Spelling option is gray and unavailable in layout view. The spelling checker is available only in Story Editor. You need to return to Story Editor.

To spell-check the entire document:

1. Select Edit story from the Edit menu ((⌘)-E).

This moves you to Story Editor.

2. Select Spelling... from the Utilities menu ((⌘)-L).

Figure 9.17
Spell-checking the
entire document

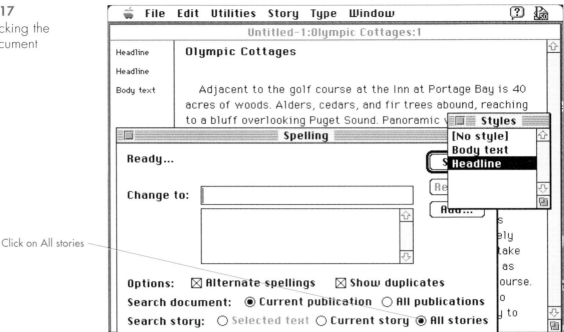

Click on All stories

3. Click on All stories (see Figure 9.17).

4. Click on Start.

It's always a good idea to check imported text for spelling errors rather
than assume it to be error-free.

To return to layout view:

1. Select Edit layout from the Edit menu ((⌘)-E) *or* select Window,
   Untitled-1, Layout.

It may be better to combine the two text blocks (stories) into one for ease
of handling. This set of steps was first introduced in Chapter 4 and is
repeated here. The technique involves first selecting and cutting one of
the text blocks, clicking an insertion point in the other text block, and
pasting the cut text into it. Select the second text block for cutting, and
paste it at the end of the first text block (see Figure 9.18).

To combine two text blocks into one:

1. Adjust the page view so you can see the last paragraph at 75% size.
   You should also be able to see some of the third paragraph
   (see Figure 9.19).

2. Click on the text tool in the Toolbox.

3. Move the I-beam to the beginning of the last paragraph. Click an
   insertion point and drag the mouse over the paragraph to select it.

4. Delete the paragraph by selecting Cut from the Edit menu ((⌘)-X).

Figure 9.18
The two text blocks

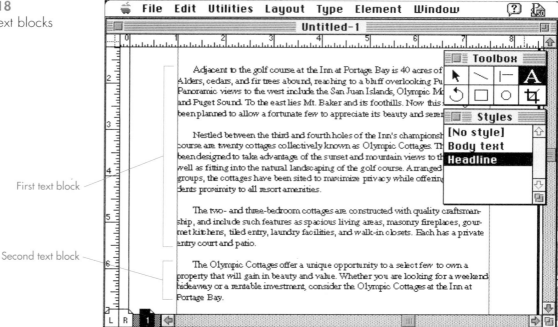

First text block

Second text block

Figure 9.19
Getting ready to
combine text blocks

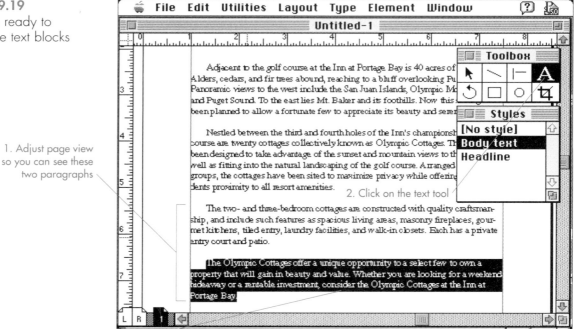

1. Adjust page view
so you can see these
two paragraphs

2. Click on the text tool

3. Select the last paragraph

5. **Move the I-beam to the end of the first text block (see Figure 9.20). Click an insertion point.**

6. **Select Paste from the Edit menu (⌘-V).**

7. **Move the I-beam to a point between the two (now joined) text blocks (that is, after the word *patio*). Click an insertion point (see Figure 9.21).**

8. **Press (RETURN) twice.**

Figure 9.20
Move the I-beam to the
end of the text block

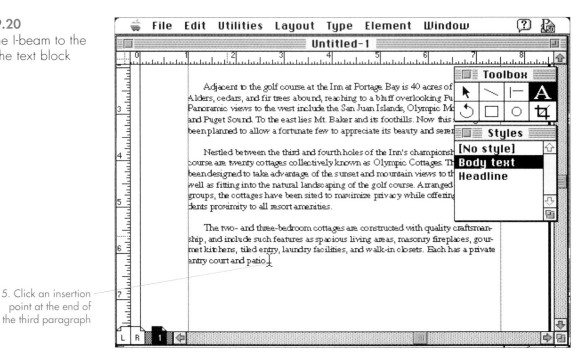

5. Click an insertion
point at the end of
the third paragraph

Figure 9.21
Create an insertion
point after *patio*

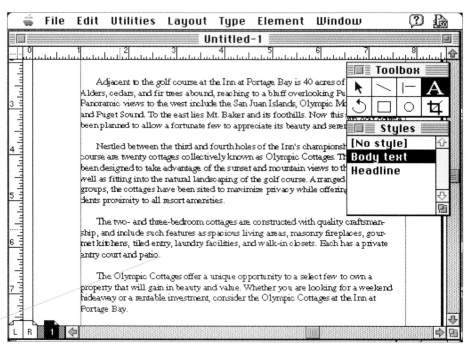

Now you have combined the two text blocks into one and still have four paragraphs. To verify that you have one text block:

1. Select the pointer tool in the Toolbox.

2. Adjust the page view to Fit in window.

3. Point to and click on the Greeked text.

Figure 9.22
One text block

Windowshades indicate
one text block

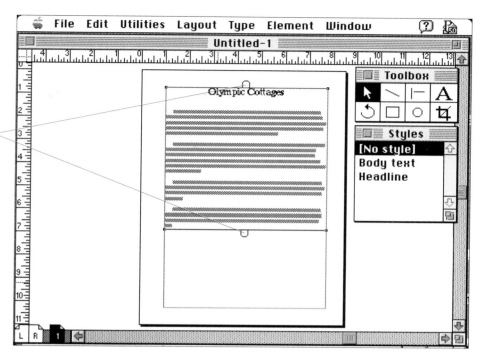

You should see the windowshades around the complete document, as shown in Figure 9.22.

Using Find and Change

Story Editor also has a feature that allows you to find specific text and change it to other text or another style, such as bold or italic. In this section you will direct Story Editor to find every occurrence of *Olympic Cottages* in the body text and change the style to italic. The headline will remain bold and will not be changed to italic.

To change *Olympic Cottages* to italic:

1. **Select Edit story from the Edit menu (⌘-E).**

2. **Select Change... from the Utilities menu (⌘-9).**

   The Change dialog box appears.

3. **Click on Attributes... (see Figure 9.23).**

4. **In the Find section, depress the mouse button on the Size arrow and select 14 (see Figure 9.24).**

5. **Select Normal from Type style.**

6. **In the Change section, select Italic from Type style.**

7. **Click on OK.**

   This returns you to the Change dialog box.

Figure 9.23
Change dialog box

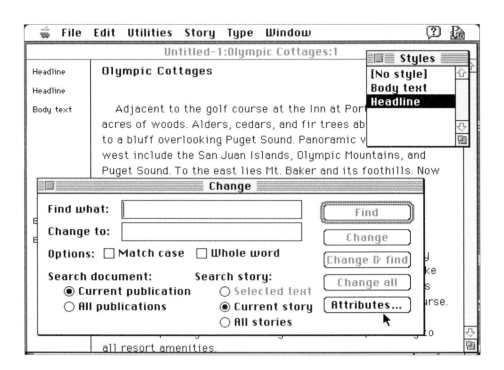

Figure 9.24
Change attributes
dialog box

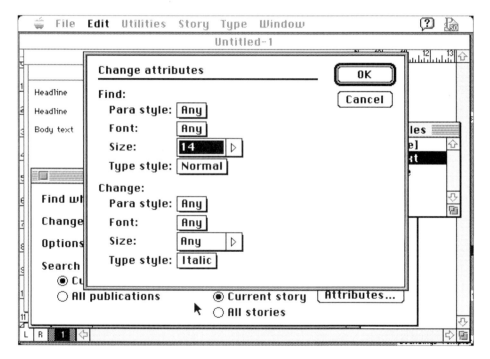

8. Move the pointer to the Find what box and click an insertion point.

9. Type *Olympic Cottages.*

10. Click on Change all (see Figure 9.25).

11. Click the Close button.

12. Return to layout view.

Look at the text to verify that the changes have been made.

Figure 9.25
Changing *Olympic
Cottages* to italic

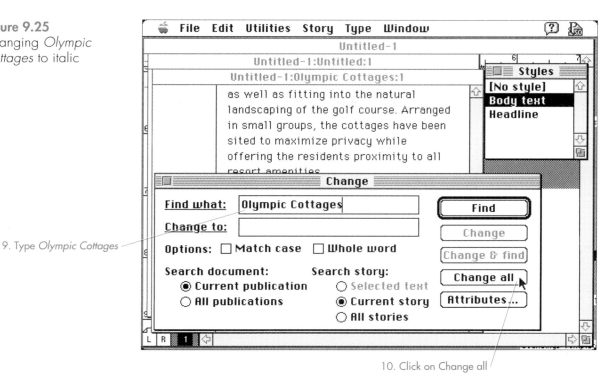

9. Type *Olympic Cottages*

10. Click on Change all

OTHER WORD PROCESSING FEATURES

Cursor-control keys are another feature of word processors. They allow
you to move quickly around the document, up and down a screen, to the
beginning or end of a line or sentence, and to delete characters. Story
Editor's cursor-control keys are summarized in Figure 9.26.

1. Click an insertion point anywhere in the story.

2. Use the cursor-control keys to move around the document.

IMPORTING A TIFF FILE

To complete the publication, you will import a TIFF file and place it at
the bottom of the page. This file, named Cottages.tiff (Figure 9.27), was
drawn and then scanned. The resultant image was digitized and saved as
a TIFF file.

To import and place Cottages.tiff:

1. Select Place... from the File menu (⌘-D).

2. Click on Cottages.tiff.

3. Verify that As independent graphic is selected.

4. Click on OK.

Figure 9.26
Story Editor
cursor-control keys

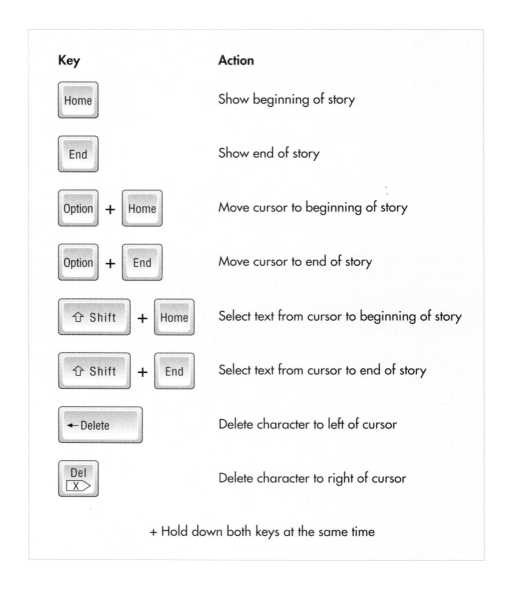

Key	Action
Home	Show beginning of story
End	Show end of story
Option + Home	Move cursor to beginning of story
Option + End	Move cursor to end of story
⇧ Shift + Home	Select text from cursor to beginning of story
⇧ Shift + End	Select text from cursor to end of story
← Delete	Delete character to left of cursor
Del X	Delete character to right of cursor

+ Hold down both keys at the same time

Figure 9.27
Cottages.tiff file

5. When the graphic icon appears, place it below the text. Press and drag the mouse to fill the available space. Use the pointer tool to resize if needed.

Save and print your publication.

SUMMARY

Story Editor gives you a faster, more powerful way to edit text. Within Story Editor you may type text, spell-check, and search and replace. You can also import text from other word processors and format text using the Style palette. Story Editor makes it easier for you to work with text.

KEY TERMS

Story Editor story view story

layout view

QUESTIONS

1. List Story Editor's features.

2. What are the advantages of using Story Editor for text processing rather than using layout view?

3. What can't you do in story view?

4. What can't you do in layout view?

Using Help, answer the following questions.

5. In the Help index, locate Story Editor: Display ¶. Click on Shortcuts. How many buttons are at the bottom of the Shortcuts screen? What characters do you type to produce:

Bullet (•)

Copyright (©)

Paragraph (¶)

Registered trademark (®)

En space

Em space

6. To display a paragraph style in story view, choose _____ from the Story menu. Paragraphs with no style attached are identified with _____.

1. Using Story Editor, type the text in Figure 9.28. Place Conference.eps so that the bottom of the figure aligns with the bottom of the text. Change the Body text style so that there is no first-line indentation. Complete the publication so that it looks like Figure 9.28.

Figure 9.28
Project 9.1—Business Center flyer

Template:
Promo 2 Template

Business Center

The Business Center provides a full range of services and equipment to help you during your stay. Support services include:

Bullets created using
Aldus Additions

- ◆ Note taking during meetings
- ◆ Preparing and copying documents
- ◆ Desktop publishing

The Center has a variety of equipment, including:

- ◆ Computers, both Macintosh and Windows format
- ◆ Laser printer
- ◆ Fax machine
- ◆ Full-page scanner
- ◆ Duplicating machine

The computers have multiple word processing, spreadsheet, and desktop publishing programs already installed. Our software library has a variety of database, drawing, and presentation programs which can be installed within two hours of a request. Each computer has a fax/modem from which you may send or receive electronic mail.

Confernce.eps

Location: Room 144

Hours: M-F 7:00 am to 5:00 pm
             Sat 9:00 am to 3:00 pm
             and by appointment
             Closed Sundays

Phone ext.: 2311

Bottom alignment

Figure 9.29
Project 9.2—Pro Shops flyer

Template:
Promo 2 Template

Portage Pro Shops

The Inn at Portage Bay has a set of Pro Shops designed to meet your needs for tennis, bicycling, swimming, and golf. Our sales staff includes experts who participate in these sports and know the technical specifications of the equipment. They can advise you on sales and help you make your individual, family, or group stay more enjoyable.

In the tennis department the shop carries a selection of rackets, balls, and apparel. We can string your new racket or restring your old racket with your choice of string. You may make reservations for courts, lessons, and the ball machine in the shop. In addition our staff can help you organize a tournament for your group.

Type this in Story Editor

In the bicycle department we have bicycles available for rental. Enjoy the nearby scenic trails at your own pace with complementary map and a box lunch from the Portage Pub. Bicycles may be rented for a half-day or on a daily basis. Discounts are available for rentals of three or more days.

In the swimwear department we carry a full selection of famous-name swimwear for men, women, and children. Also available are goggles, beach towels, and sand toys.

Our golf department has clubs, balls, gloves, and apparel available for purchase. You may rent clubs, arrange for lessons, and make reservations for tee times in the Pro Shop. We can help you organize a golf tournament for your group. Packages are available for golf club rental, lesson, and greens fee.

No matter what your needs, our professional staff can assist you.

Golf Green.tiff

2. Using the same directions as for Project 1, create the publication shown in Figure 9.29.

Upon completion of this chapter you will be able to:

- List the steps necessary to create a book

- Create index entries

- Create cross-references in an index

- Open multiple publications at the same time

- Create an index for a book

- Create a book list

- Create a table of contents

- Print a book

- Discuss the limitations of PageMaker's indexing functions

Assembling Publications into a Book

PageMaker automates much of the work involved in producing the camera-ready copy for a book or other long publication. Simply stated (and for our purposes), a **book** is a series of PageMaker publications. Using the File menu Book command, you assemble a book list. Creating an index and table of contents requires just a few clicks of the mouse. PageMaker makes the tedious tasks of indexing and developing a table of contents far easier.

PLANNING THE BOOK

The most important step in making a book is careful planning. First, plan the overall design and layout of each publication to ensure consistency. Create a set of master pages and a template for the book with design elements common to every page. Next, decide which styles, such as Headline or Subhead 1, will appear in the table of contents. Using the Define styles command, specify Include in TOC for the appropriate styles. Planning will make assembling the book a much simpler process.

CREATING THE BOOK

Creating a book is a multistep process. First, create a publication that will be part of a book using the following steps. Open the common book template, insert or remove pages as needed, create the publication, and save it as a publication file. Repeat this for each publication. Within each publication, use the Index entry command to identify which terms will appear in the index. Second, create an empty table of contents and index. Third, assemble all the publications, including the table of contents and index, into a book list. Fourth, use the Create index and Create TOC commands to automatically build these publications. Finally, print the book. Creating a book is more complex than merely creating a publication but, with careful planning, PageMaker assists in the generation of an index and table of contents, automatic page numbering, and printing.

THE EMPLOYEE BENEFITS BOOK

In this chapter you will create the Employee Benefits book shown in Figure 10.1. This book will contain four publications: a table of contents, a publication with three pages, a publication with two pages, and an index. You will start with two existing publications, explore their Style palettes, and create index entries for them. Next you will use a template to create two empty publications: the index and table of contents. You will assemble a book list in both the index and table of contents, use PageMaker to generate the index and table of contents, and then save these two publications. Finally, you will print the book.

Figure 10.1
Employee Benefits book

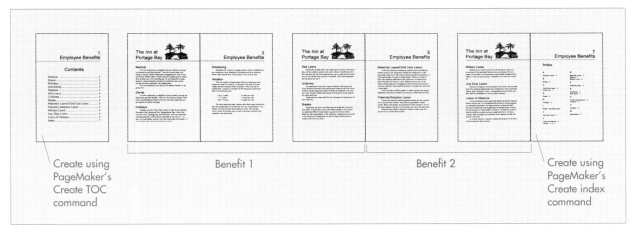

The process and skills presented here may be applied to longer books whose preparation includes publications with multiple writers. Each writer would start with the same template, including master pages and Style palette. An editor would edit the documents for style and consistency. Perhaps one person would take responsibility for indexing the complete publication; good indexing requires special skills. Assembling a long book would follow the same steps, but the project would understandably be more complex.

Exploring the Style Palettes for the Employee Benefits Book Publications

There are two publications for the Benefits book: Benefit 1 and Benefit 2. Both were created using Benefit Template and thus have the same style sheet. You will explore the style sheet for Benefit 1.

1. Start PageMaker.

2. Open Benefit 1.

Figure 10.2 shows the publication.

Figure 10.2
Benefit 1

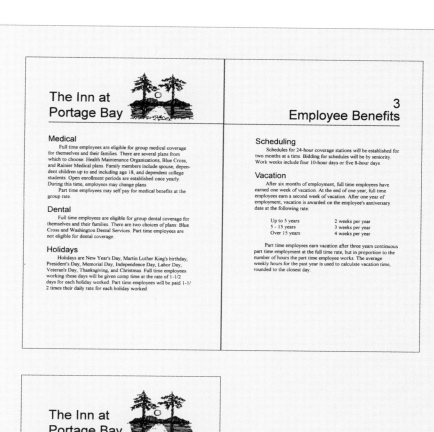

Figure 10.3
Edit style dialog box
for Body text

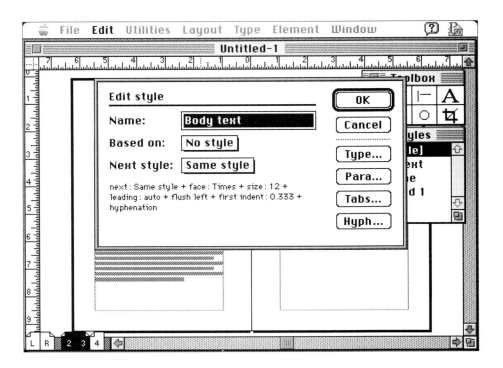

Look at the Pasteboard and notice that the Style palette has three styles: Body text, Headline, and Subhead 1.

To explore Body text style:

1. Press ⌘ and click on Body text.

Figure 10.3 shows the Edit style dialog box.

2. Click on Para...

Figure 10.4 shows the Paragraph specifications dialog box for Body text. Note that the Include in table of contents option is not selected.

3. Click on Cancel to return to the Edit style dialog box.

4. Click on Cancel to return to the Pasteboard.

To explore Headline style:

1. Press ⌘ and click on Headline.

2. Click on Para...

Note that the Include in table of contents option is not selected.

3. Click on Cancel to return to the Edit style dialog box.

4. Click on Cancel to return to the Pasteboard.

To explore Subhead 1 style:

1. Press ⌘ and click on Subhead 1.

2. Click on Para...

Figure 10.4
Paragraph specifi-
cations dialog box
for Body text

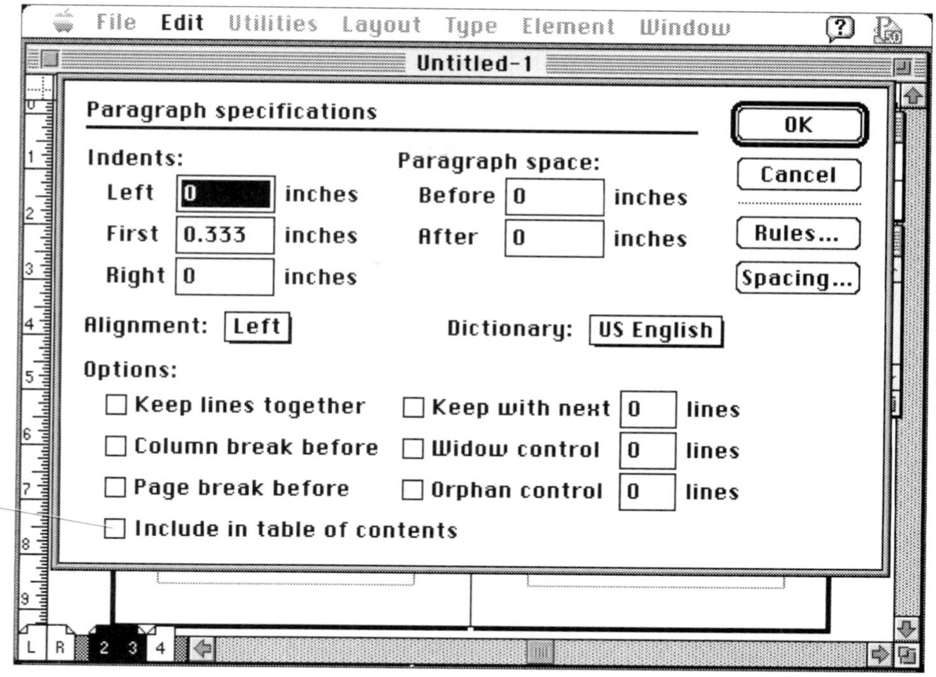

Note that Include in table of
contents is not selected

Figure 10.5
Paragraph specifi-
cations dialog box
for Subhead 1

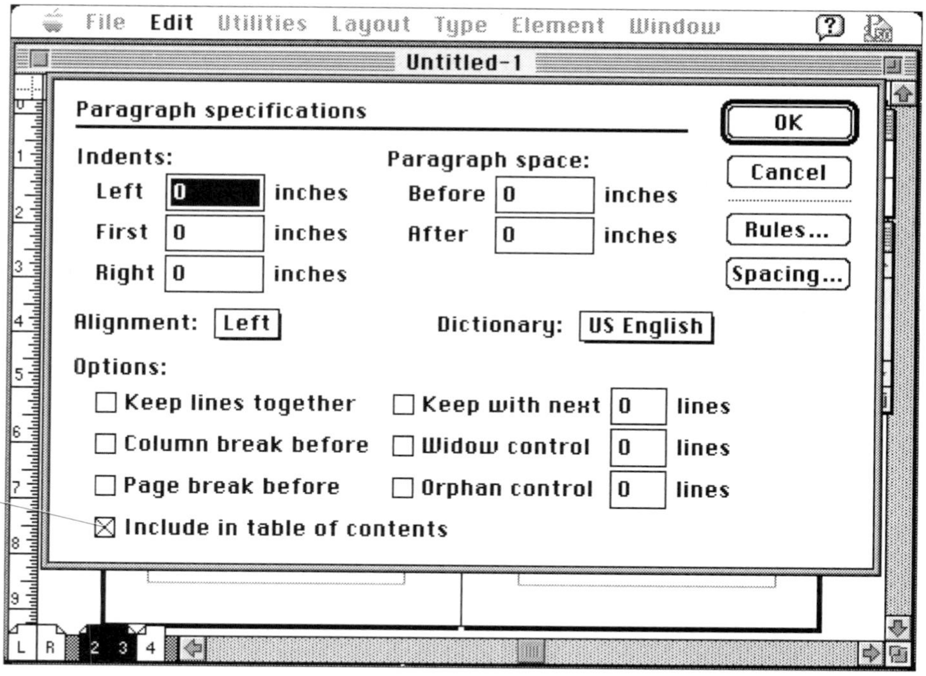

Note that Include in table of
contents is selected

Figure 10.5 shows the Paragraph specifications dialog box for Subhead 1. Note that the Include in table of contents option is selected. This means that any text formatted as Subhead 1 will be included in the table of contents when you create it.

3. Click on Cancel to return to the Edit style dialog box.

4. Click on Cancel to return to the Pasteboard.

Creating Index Entries

PageMaker has a powerful indexing feature that simplifies the process of creating an **index**. You select the parts to index and give each a name. PageMaker keeps track of page references and assembles the index for you.

An index should be useful in order to be effective. Have you ever used an index to look up a topic in a book and not found an index entry because it was referenced by another word? PageMaker will automate the clerical steps in creating an index, but it takes a human to select the proper references for a topic. Unfortunately, there are no computer tools available to completely automate indexing.

Indexing requires planning and time to review and evaluate the chosen references. Perhaps a logical place to start is to evaluate some good and some poor indexes. When creating your own index, expect to need about 5 to 10 index pages per 100 pages of text. For each 5 pages of text, allow about 1 hour for indexing. This will vary depending on the complexity of the book. Using these guidelines, a 100-page book would require 5 to 10 index pages and about 20 hours to complete the indexing process.

PageMaker allows you to create three levels of index entries and has the power to **cross-reference** topics. For this project, you will use one level and the cross-referencing feature. You will index all the subheadings and several other words within the text. Figure 10.6 shows the document and the words to be indexed.

To add an index entry for *Medical*:

1. Click on the page 2 icon (if necessary).
2. Adjust the page view so you can see the area of text around *Medical*.
3. Click on the text tool.
4. Select *Medical* by pressing and dragging the I-beam across the word (see Figure 10.7).
5. Select Index entry... from the Utilities menu (⌘-;).

   The Add index entry dialog box appears, as shown in Figure 10.8. You will use all the defaults.
6. Click on OK.

To add an index entry for *Dental*, using shortcut keys:

1. Select *Dental* (step 4 above).
2. Press ⌘ and ; (semicolon) at the same time.
3. Press (RETURN).

Use Figure 10.6 as a guide for continuing the index entries. Make an index entry for each highlighted word and phrase. To add an index entry for the other headings and the phrase *Work weeks* (in the Scheduling section):

Figure 10.6
Benefit 1 with index entries noted

The Inn at Portage Bay

3
Employee Benefits

Medical

Full time employees are eligible for group medical coverage for themselves and their families. There are several plans from which to choose: Health Maintenance Organizations, Blue Cross, and Rainier Medical plans. Family members include spouse, dependent children up to and including age 18, and dependent college students. Open enrollment periods are established once yearly. During this time, employees may change plans.

Part time employees may self pay for medical benefits at the group rate.

Dental

Full time employees are eligible for group dental coverage for themselves and their families. There are two choices of plans: Blue Cross and Washington Dental Services. Part time employees are not eligible for dental coverage.

Holidays

Holidays are New Year's Day, Martin Luther King's birthday, President's Day, Memorial Day, Independence Day, Labor Day, Veteran's Day, Thanksgiving, and Christmas. Full time employees working these days will be given comp time at the rate of 1-1/2 days for each holiday worked. Part time employees will be paid 1-1/2 times their daily rate for each holiday worked.

Scheduling

Schedules for 24-hour coverage stations will be established for two months at a time. Bidding for schedules will be by seniority. Work weeks include four 10-hour days or five 8-hour days.

Vacation

After six months of employment, full time employees have earned one week of vacation. At the end of one year, full time employees earn a second week of vacation. After one year of employment, vacation is awarded on the employee's anniversary date at the following rate:

Up to 5 years	2 weeks per year
5 - 15 years	3 weeks per year
Over 15 years	4 weeks per year

Part time employees earn vacation after three years continuous part time employment at the full time rate, but in proportion to the number of hours the part time employee works. The average weekly hours for the past year is used to calculate vacation time, rounded to the closest day.

The Inn at Portage Bay

Sick Leave

Employees should notify their supervisor as soon as they know they will be unable to attend work due to illness. An allowance for five sick days per full time employee per year is made and sick leave may not be carried from one year to another. Part time employees are not given sick leave.

Uniforms

All employees whose jobs require uniforms will be given an initial uniform allowance upon employment based on the cost of the uniform and the expected number of shifts the employee will work per week. Smaller uniform allowances will be given on the anniversary date each year.

Employees are responsible for the cleaning and maintenance of their uniforms.

Breaks

Employees are given one fifteen minute break for every four-hour shift. A meal break is given for shifts of eight or more hours. An additional fifteen minute break is given for ten-hour shifts. Meals are the responsibility of the employee. Employees are invited to the Employee Tasting Hour on the first day of each month to sample items from our menu.

Add an additional entry for *Leaves*

Figure 10.7
Selecting the
word *Medical*

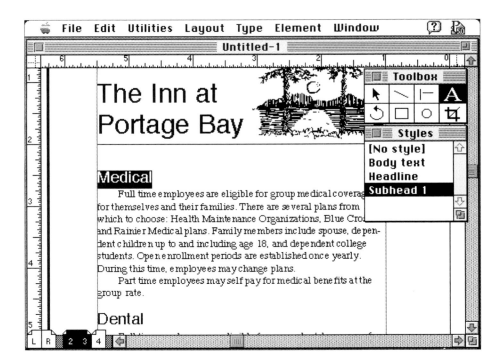

Figure 10.8
Add index entry
dialog box

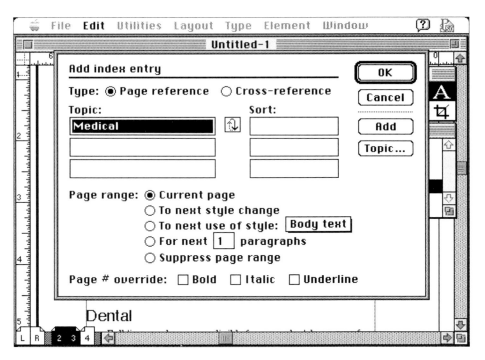

1. Repeat steps 4, 5, and 6 above, adjusting the page view as necessary, or use the shortcut keys.

By this time, you have made an index entry for all of the headings: *Medical, Dental, Holidays, Scheduling, Vacation, Sick Leave, Uniforms,* and *Breaks,* as well as the phrase *Work weeks.* In the next sections you will cross-reference *Illness* to *Sick Leave* and type a different index title for other entries.

Creating a Cross-reference

Cross-referencing allows you to list one topic under multiple titles in the index. In cross-referencing, you list the different words a person might use to refer to a topic and include them in the index with a reference or pointer to the word you use. In our example, the Employee Benefits book calls a section *Sick Leave*. A person might look for this topic under *Illness*, so you will create a cross-reference for *Illness*. You will list *Illness* with a reference to *See Sick Leave*. Because it is the primary reference, *Sick Leave* will have the page number. In a more complex book, there may be several logical ways in which a person will begin an index search. A skilled indexer will include enough terms to help the reader without making the index so large it is unwieldy.

To cross-reference *illness:*

1. Select *illness,* as shown in Figure 10.9.

2. Select Index entry... from the Utilities menu (⌘-;).

3. Replace the *i* in *illness* with a capital *I* (see Figure 10.10).

4. Click on Cross-reference.

5. Click on See, as shown in Figure 10.11.

Compare Figures 10.10 and 10.11. When you select Cross-reference, PageMaker gives you a different set of options than are available with Page reference.

6. Click on X-ref...

Figure 10.9
Selecting *illness*

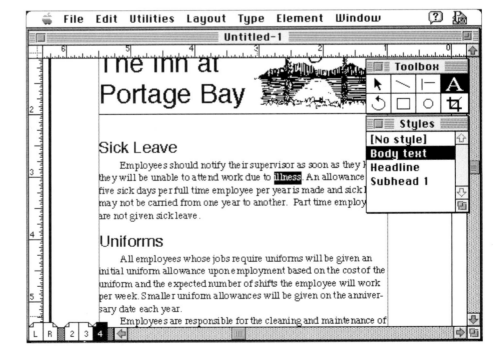

Figure 10.10
Page reference view
of Add index entry
dialog box
(Illness with capital I)

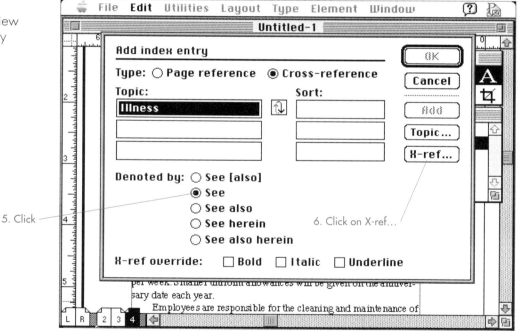

3. Retype with capital *I*

4. Click

Figure 10.11
Cross-reference view
of Add index entry
dialog box

5. Click

6. Click on X-ref...

The Select cross-reference topic dialog box appears, as shown in Figure 10.12.

7. Type *Sick Leave*.

8. Click on OK.

Returns you to the Add index entry dialog box.

9. Click on OK.

Returns you to the Pasteboard.

Figure 10.12
Select cross-reference topic dialog box

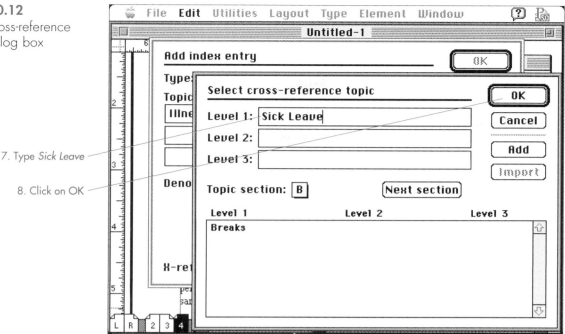

7. Type *Sick Leave*

8. Click on OK

Figure 10.13
Selecting *maintenance of their uniforms*

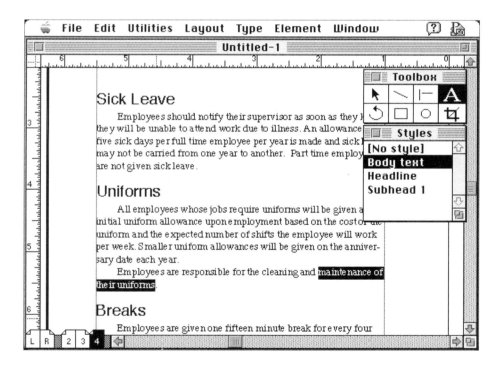

Typing a Different Index Title

You can also type a different index title than the selected text. For example, within the Uniforms section is the phrase *maintenance of their uniforms.* You can select this text and call it *Uniform maintenance* in the index.

1. Select *maintenance of their uniforms,* as shown in Figure 10.13.

2. Select Index entry... from the Utilities menu (⌘-;).

Figure 10.14
Revising an index title

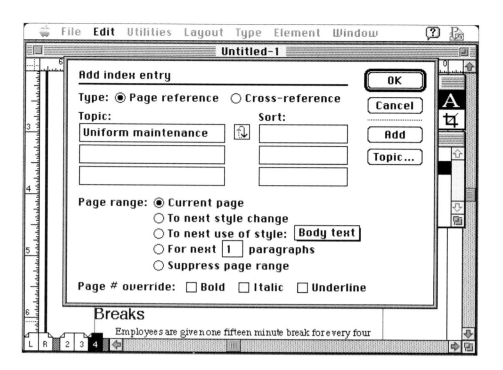

3. Type *Uniform maintenance* for the topic (see Figure 10.14).

4. Click on OK.

Repeat the steps to add an index entry for *comp time* (in the Holidays section on page 2), changing it to *Comp time.*

Looking at the Index

You have identified several index topics for the Benefit 1 publication. There are two ways to review the index at this point. The first is to go into story view; the second is to use the Show index command.

Story View

Within story view you can see which text has been indexed by looking for the index markers (◆) in the text. Index markers may be added using the Copy and Paste commands, moved using Cut, Copy, and Paste, and deleted using the Cut command. In this section you will look at the text you have been working with, but you will not make any changes.

To see the index markers in Story Editor:

1. Click an insertion point anywhere in the publication.

2. Select Edit story from the Edit menu (⌘-E).

3. Use the scroll bars to find indexed text. Figure 10.15 shows one view.

Viewing the publication in story view allows you to see the text from top to bottom and see which topics are cross-referenced. This is useful when changing the index or editing the text.

Figure 10.15
Examining index entries
in story view

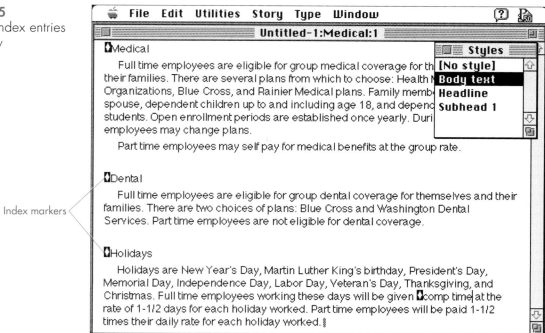

Index markers

Using the Show index Command

The Show index command allows you to review and edit the index prior to creating a final index.

To review the index:

1. Select Show index… from the Utilities menu.

The Show index dialog box appears, as shown in Figure 10.16.

The options in this dialog box allow you to display the next alphabetical section having at least one entry (Next section), add a cross-reference (Add x-ref), change an index entry (Edit), remove index entries from an

Figure 10.16
Show index dialog boxes; the index for each letter may be viewed

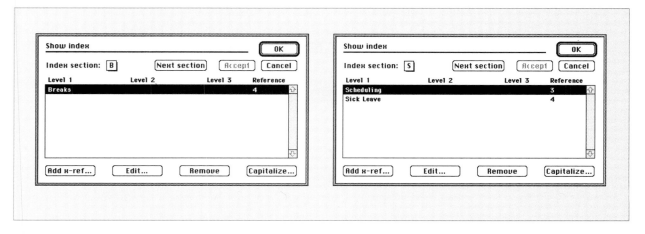

index (Remove), and accept changes while keeping the Show index dialog box open (Accept).

To exit the Show index dialog box, click on Cancel.

Saving the Indexed Publication

You will want to save this publication with all its index entries. In order to keep Benefit 1 in its original form so you can go back and practice again, use the File menu Save as command and save with a different file name.

1. Select Save as... from the File menu.

2. Type *Benefit 1 Indexed.*

You have indexed one publication. At this point you have two versions of the first part of the Employee Benefits book: Benefit 1, which comes on your disk, and Benefit 1 Indexed, an indexed version of the same publication. Your publication window has the indexed version (Benefit 1 Indexed).

The Employee Benefits book has a second publication (Benefit 2), which must also be indexed. You will now open and index it using the steps you learned in the first part of this chapter.

Opening Multiple Publications

A new feature of PageMaker 5.0 is the ability to have **multiple open publications** at the same time. When you select the File menu Open command for a new publication, all other opened publications remain open. In older versions of PageMaker, you could have only one publication open at a time; whenever you opened a new one, PageMaker would close the existing one, saving it or not as determined by you.

When opening Benefit 2, do not close Benefit 1 Indexed. Use the following steps:

1. Open Benefit 2.

2. Select Cascade from the Window menu.

Now you see two title bars, one for each open publication (similar to Figure 10.21). Only one publication is active, as indicated by the highlighted title bar. To change from one publication to another, simply click on the title bar or within the publication. To restore the cascaded configuration, select Cascade from the Window menu.

In the Projects at the end of the chapter, you will experiment with multiple open publications. This is left until then so as not to interfere with the Employee Benefits book.

Using Figure 10.17 and the steps you learned in the first part of this chapter, index Benefit 2 and save it.

Figure 10.17
Benefit 2 with index entries highlighted

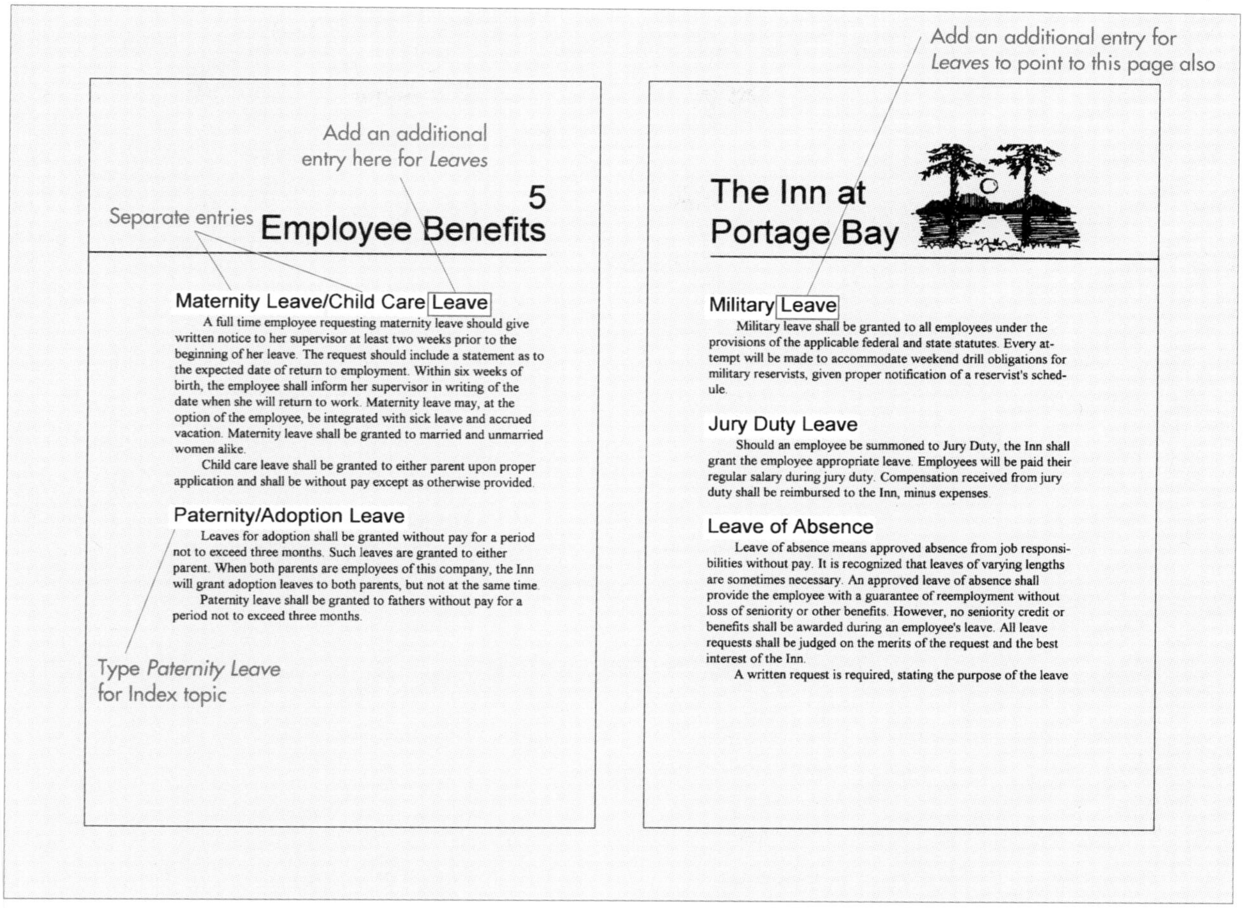

Add an additional entry for *Leaves* to point to this page also

Add an additional entry here for *Leaves*

Separate entries

Employee Benefits
5

Maternity Leave/Child Care Leave

A full time employee requesting maternity leave should give written notice to her supervisor at least two weeks prior to the beginning of her leave. The request should include a statement as to the expected date of return to employment. Within six weeks of birth, the employee shall inform her supervisor in writing of the date when she will return to work. Maternity leave may, at the option of the employee, be integrated with sick leave and accrued vacation. Maternity leave shall be granted to married and unmarried women alike.

Child care leave shall be granted to either parent upon proper application and shall be without pay except as otherwise provided.

Paternity/Adoption Leave

Leaves for adoption shall be granted without pay for a period not to exceed three months. Such leaves are granted to either parent. When both parents are employees of this company, the Inn will grant adoption leaves to both parents, but not at the same time.

Paternity leave shall be granted to fathers without pay for a period not to exceed three months.

Type *Paternity Leave* for Index topic

The Inn at Portage Bay

Military Leave

Military leave shall be granted to all employees under the provisions of the applicable federal and state statutes. Every attempt will be made to accommodate weekend drill obligations for military reservists, given proper notification of a reservist's schedule.

Jury Duty Leave

Should an employee be summoned to Jury Duty, the Inn shall grant the employee appropriate leave. Employees will be paid their regular salary during jury duty. Compensation received from jury duty shall be reimbursed to the Inn, minus expenses.

Leave of Absence

Leave of absence means approved absence from job responsibilities without pay. It is recognized that leaves of varying lengths are sometimes necessary. An approved leave of absence shall provide the employee with a guarantee of reemployment without loss of seniority or other benefits. However, no seniority credit or benefits shall be awarded during an employee's leave. All leave requests shall be judged on the merits of the request and the best interest of the Inn.

A written request is required, stating the purpose of the leave

1. Create index entries for Benefit 2. Use Figure 10.17 as a guide.

2. Save the indexed publication as Benefit 2 Indexed.

You are ready to have PageMaker create the index and table of contents.

Creating Empty Publications for the Index and Table of Contents

PageMaker will create an index and a table of contents for you, but you first have to create empty publications so you have somewhere to put them. To create these two publications, start with the same template used to create the other Employee Benefits publications: Benefit Template. Since this is a short book, the table of contents and index will each be one page long.

1. Open Benefit Template.

Notice that the template has two pages, but the table of contents and index will each need only one. You will remove page 2.

2. Select Remove pages... from the Layout menu.

You want to remove pages 2 through 2.

Figure 10.18
Removing page 2 of
the template to save
as an empty table
of contents

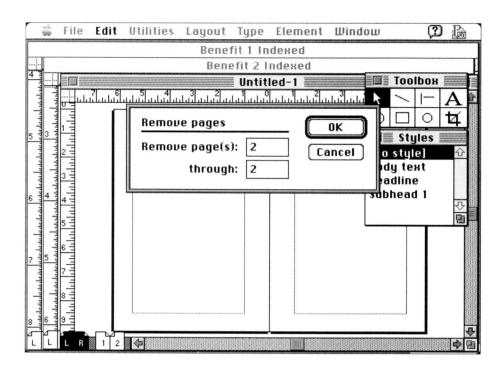

3. Type *2* in the Remove page(s) box.

4. Press TAB once.

5. Type *2* in the through box.

Your screen should match Figure 10.18.

6. Click on OK.

PageMaker will ask if you want to delete the page and all items on it.

7. Click on OK.

Now save the one-page publication twice, once for the table of contents and once for the index, using the Save as command.

8. Select Save as... from the File menu.

9. Type *Benefit TOC*.

Saves one-page table of contents.

10. Click on OK.

The index will fit on one page if there are two columns, so you need to make a two-column page.

1. Click on the page 1 icon (if necessary).

2. From the Layout menu, select Column guides...

3. Type *2* in the Number of columns box.

4. Click on OK.

5. Select Save as... from the File menu.

6. Type *Benefit Index.*

Saves one-page index.

7. Click on OK.

USING PAGEMAKER TO CREATE THE INDEX

PageMaker can do three tasks for a book: create an index, create a table of contents, and print the book. Recall that a book is a set of PageMaker publications defined by a **book list**. You must create a book list for every publication in which you want to do any of these three tasks. This means you must create a book list in the index and create the same book list in the table of contents. You may print from either publication or any other publication that has the book list. But it is not necessary to create the book list more than twice.

Typically, you want the page number of the index listed on the table of contents, so create the index first and the table of contents second.

Creating the Book List

You should currently have the index, Benefit Index, as the top publication window. To create a book list:

1. **Select Book... from the File menu.**

The Book publication list dialog box appears, as shown in Figure 10.19. Note that the current publication is already part of the list. You will click on files listed in the left-hand box to include them in the Book list on the right.

Figure 10.19
Book publication list dialog box

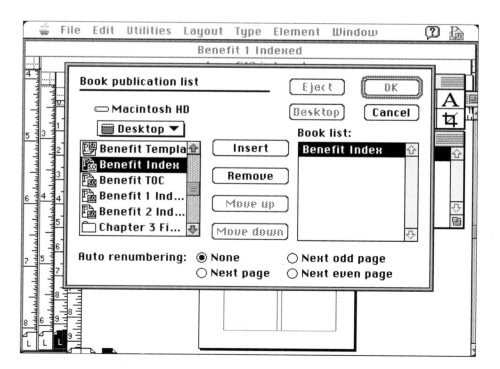

2. Click on Benefit 1 Indexed (if necessary).

3. Click on Insert.

Notice that Benefit 1 Indexed becomes part of the book list.

4. Repeat steps 2 and 3 to add Benefit 2 Indexed and Benefit TOC.

Your list should now have four PageMaker publications, but they are not in the correct order for the book. The correct order is:

Benefit TOC

Benefit 1 Indexed

Benefit 2 Indexed

Benefit Index

To move a publication to the correct location:

1. Click on the publication name in the book list to highlight it.

2. Click on Move up or Move down, as appropriate.

3. Repeat steps 1 and 2 until your book list matches the one in Figure 10.20.

PageMaker can automatically number the pages from 1 through the last page of the book. To do this:

1. Click on the Next page option in the Auto renumbering list (see Figure 10.20).

2. Click on OK.

PageMaker will tell you that Auto renumbering is selected and ask if you want to update the page numbers now.

3. Click on Yes.

Figure 10.20
Book list in correct order

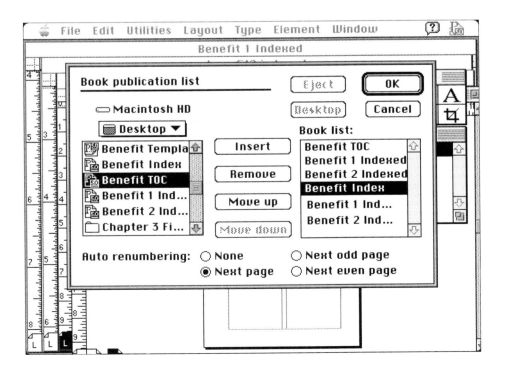

Creating the Index

To create the index:

1. **If necessary, adjust your page view to Fit in window (⌘-W).**

2. **Select Create index... from the Utilities menu.**

3. **Click on OK.**

PageMaker creates the index; a loaded text icon appears so you can place the index story. Three new styles appear in the Style palette—PageMaker's default index styles. You will place the index and change the default styles to conform to those of the Employee Benefits book.

4. **Position the loaded text icon as shown in Figure 10.21.**

5. **Click to place the index.**

The full index is about twice the length of the index from *A* to *L*. Breaking the columns after the *L* entries will make the two columns about the same length, as shown in Figure 10.22.

1. **Press and drag the windowshade to the bottom of the *L* entries. Release.**

2. **Click on the triangle. A loaded text icon appears.**

3. **Adjust the page view to Fit in window (⌘-W).**

4. **Place the loaded text icon at the top of the second column aligned with the *A* entries (refer to Figure 10.22).**

5. **Click.**

To change the style of the word *Index*:

1. **Press ⌘ and click on Index title in the Style palette.**

Figure 10.21
Placing the loaded index text icon

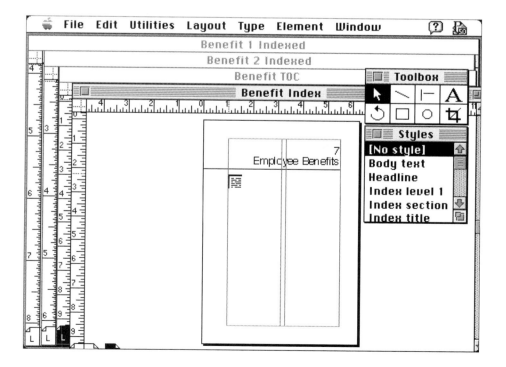

Figure 10.22
The completed
Index page

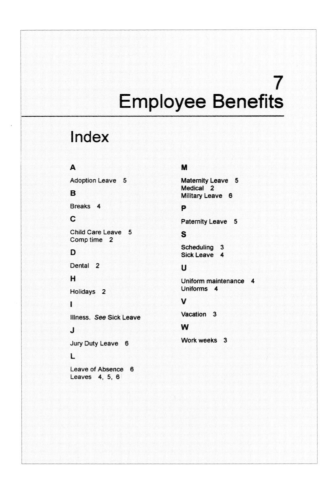

2. **Click on Type...**

   Change to Helvetica, 24 point, Normal.

   Click on OK.

3. **Click on Para...**

   Change alignment to Left.

   Click on OK.

4. **Click on OK.**

To verify the alignment of the two columns:

1. **Pull a ruler guide down from the ruler. Be careful to point to the ruler immediately below the title bar for Benefit Index.**

2. **Adjust the text blocks in the columns as necessary.**

Saving the Index

When you save the index publication, you are also saving the book list. If you want to print at a later date, by opening the index publication you have the option of printing either the index or the entire book.

To save the index:

1. **Select Save... from the File menu (⌘-S).**

The steps to create the **table of contents** are analogous to those used to create the index. First open the table of contents publication, make a book list, create the table of contents, adjust the styles of some of the text, and, finally, save the table of contents.

A good table of contents requires organization and planning. The organization required is similar to outlining, where some topics are identified as major topics and others are subordinate. The planning is related to creating a Style palette. As you define each style, such as Headline, Subhead 1, and Body text, you select whether or not to include that style's text in the table of contents. A good table of contents gives an overview of the publication and helps the reader navigate through the book.

Creating the Book List

You need to create the same book list in the table of contents as you created earlier in the index. You may wonder why you have to repeat this process. PageMaker requires a book list to be created within every publication using a book feature. The table of contents and index are both book features, so both need a book list.

To create the book list in the table of contents:

1. Select Open... from the File menu (⌘-O).

2. Click on Benefit TOC.

3. Click on the page 1 icon (if necessary).

4. Repeat the steps you did previously to create a book list containing the opened publication and:

   Benefit 1 Indexed

   Benefit 2 Indexed

   Benefit Index

   Make sure the four publications are in the correct order.

Creating the Table of Contents

To create the table of contents:

1. Select Create TOC... from the Utilities menu.

   The Create table of contents dialog box appears, as shown in Figure 10.23.

2. Click on OK to accept the standard defaults.

The loaded text icon appears and the Style palette lists the default TOC styles, as shown in Figure 10.24.

3. Place the loaded text icon, as shown in Figure 10.24, and click.

Figure 10.23
Create table of
contents dialog box

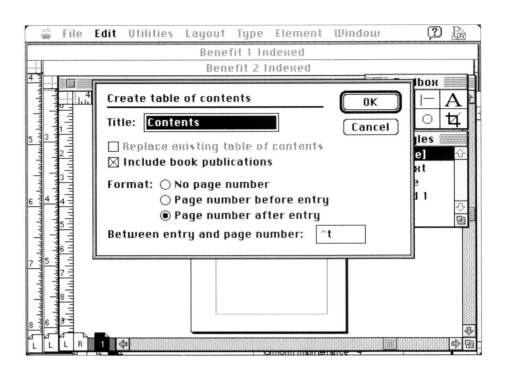

Figure 10.24
Publication window
after creating table
of contents

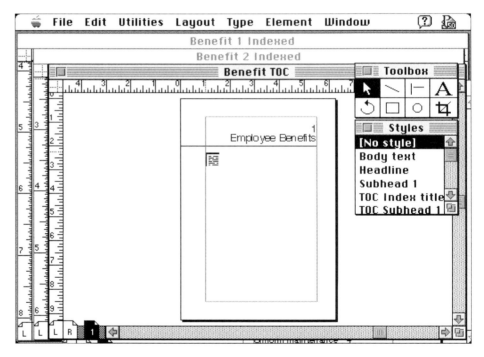

To change TOC title style to Helvetica Normal:

1. Press ⌘ and click on TOC title (in the Style palette) at the same time.

2. Click on Type...

3. Change Type style to Normal (see Figure 10.25).

4. Click on OK.

Returns you to the Edit style dialog box.

Figure 10.25
Type specifications
dialog box for
TOC title

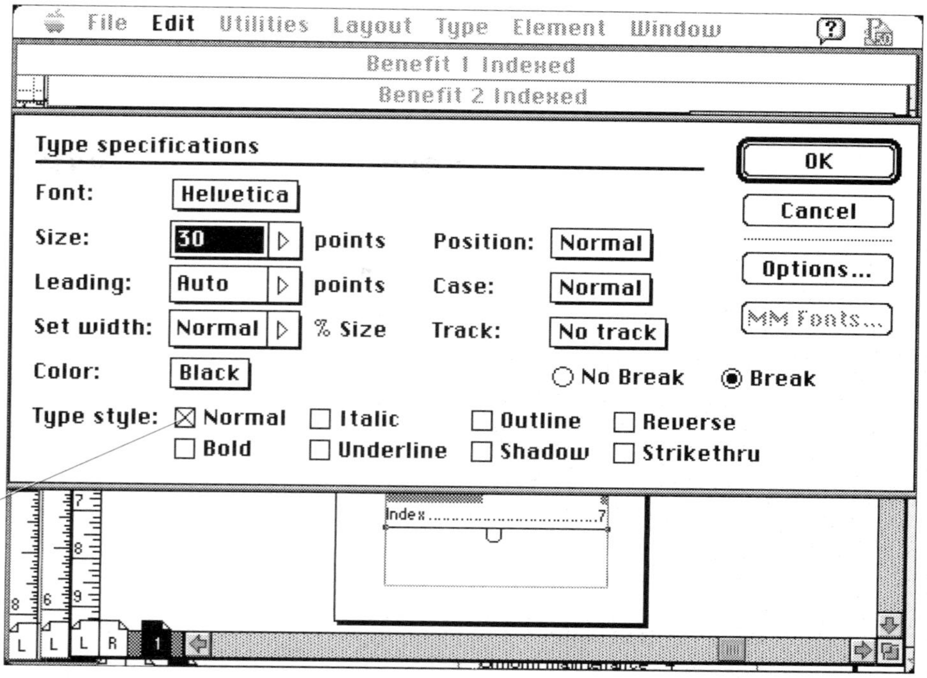

Select Normal

5. Click on OK.

Returns you to the Pasteboard.

The last entry in the table of contents is the word *Index,* and it is in a different style than the other entries. To change it to TOC Subhead 1 style:

1. Select the text tool.

2. Select the *Index* line by pressing and dragging the I-beam over it (see Figure 10.26). Release the mouse button.

3. Click on TOC Subhead 1 in the Style palette.

The completed Contents page is shown in Figure 10.27.

Saving the Table of Contents

To save the table of contents:

1. Select Save... from the File menu (⌘-S).

PRINTING THE BOOK

The last step is to print the book. This can be done from within either the table of contents or index because they both have a book list. You should currently have the table of contents open. To print the Employee Benefits book:

1. Select Print... from the File menu (⌘-P).

The Print document dialog box appears.

Figure 10.26
Changing the style
of *Index*

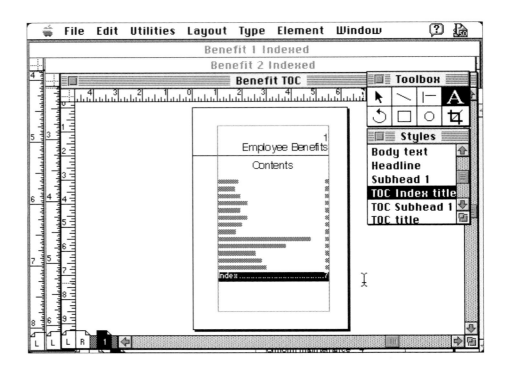

Figure 10.27
The completed
Contents page

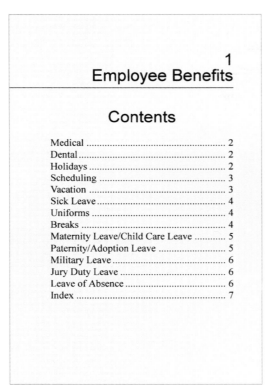

2. Select the Print all publications in book option.

3. Click on the Options button and select Printer's marks.

Your screen should match Figure 10.28.

4. Click on Print.

Close all your publications, saving each one.

Figure 10.28
Print document and
Options dialog boxes

Figure 10.28
Print document and Options dialog boxes

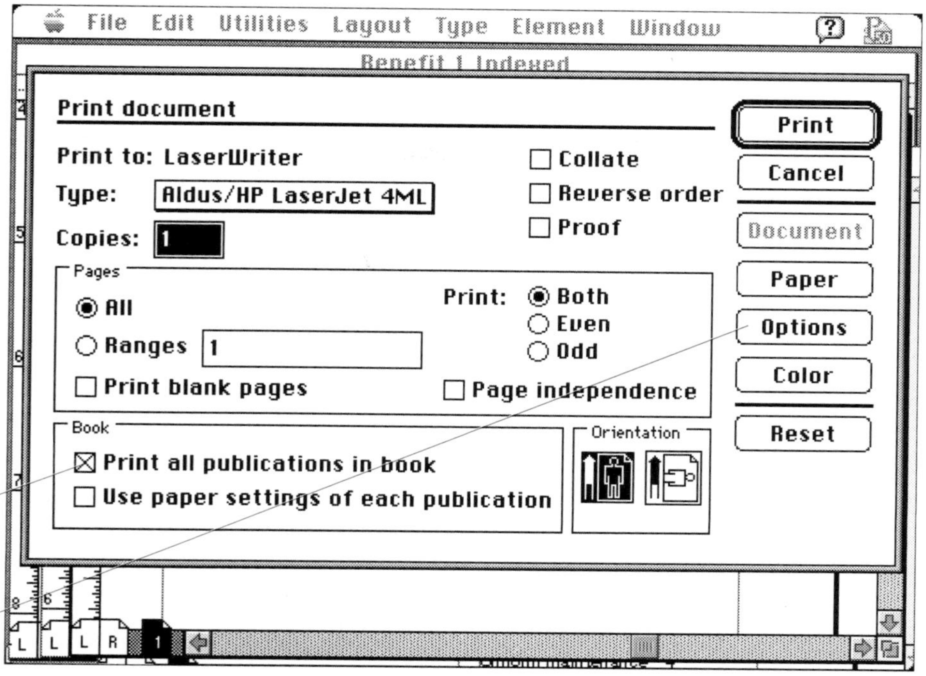

2. Select Print all publications in book

3. Click on Options to select Printer's marks

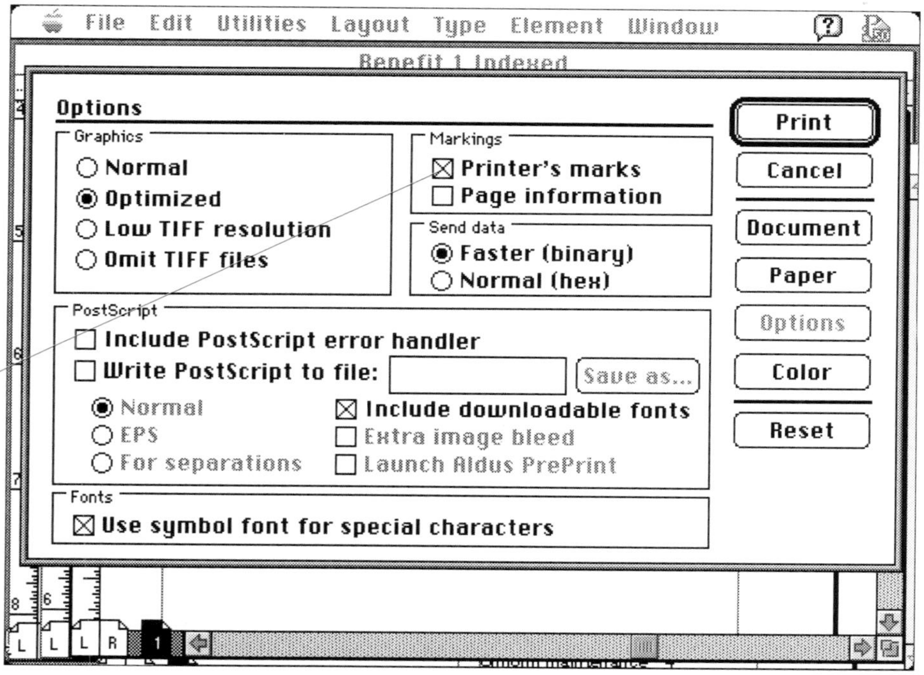

Click on Printer's marks

SUMMARY

Congratulations on publishing your first book! In the process of assembling a long publication, you learned about the importance of planning for the book. The Style palette defines whether a style will have a table of contents entry. Creating an index entry is done with the Index entry command in the Utilities menu. Before creating an index or table of contents, you must create empty publications for each. A book list is a list of several PageMaker publications that will be included in a book. PageMaker automates the process of creating an index and table of contents. Printing is done from a publication containing a book list, typically the table of contents or the index.

KEY TERMS

book	multiple open publications	table of contents
index	book list	
cross-reference		

QUESTIONS

1. Why is it a good idea to plan before creating any documents for a book?

2. List the steps to follow to create a book.

3. How do you create an entry for the table of contents?

4. Describe the process for creating an index entry.

5. The index you created has a page number after *Sick Leave* and a cross-reference after *Illness* (See *Sick Leave*). Why was *Sick Leave* chosen as the primary reference and *Illness* chosen as a cross-reference?

6. In cross-referencing, what is the indexer trying to do?

7. Explain the different things you can learn when you look at index entries in story view and use the Show index command. When would you use the two options?

8. Why do you have to create an empty index and table of contents?

9. Why do you need to create a book list in both the table of contents and index?

10. What are the limitations of PageMaker's indexing function?

11. From where may you print a book?

12. Using Help, answer the following questions.

   (a) How many publications may you have open at once?

   (b) What does the ^t in the Create table of contents dialog box instruct PageMaker to do?

   (c) The maximum length of an index title is _____ characters.

1. Use Benefit Template to create another two- to three-page publication to add to the book. Index the publication. Re-create the book with this additional publication.

2. Create a cover for the Employee Benefits book.

3. This project illustrates the power of multiple open publications. Do the following.

    (a) Open Benefit 1 Indexed and Benefit 2 Indexed.

    (b) Tile (rather than Cascade) the two publication windows.

    (c) Click on the page 4 icon in Benefit 1 Indexed.

    (d) Click on the page 5 icon in Benefit 2 Indexed.

    You are going to copy the Breaks section of page 4 to page 5. You will separate the Breaks section to make it a separate text block, using a technique you learned in Chapter 4.

    (e) Using the pointer tool, click on the text block on page 4.

    (f) Move the windowshade to the end of the Uniforms section.

    (g) Click on the red triangle.

    (h) Place the loaded text icon (containing the Breaks section) after the Uniforms section on page 4.

    (i) Point, hold down, and drag the Breaks text block to page 5, placing it below Paternity/Adoption Leave.

    Create a new index publication, including this altered Benefit 2 Indexed.

    (j) Open Benefit Template and create a book list.

    (k) Remove page 2 of Benefit Template (this will be a one-page index).

    (l) Create the index.

    (m) Print the index.

    (n) Save the index.

    Look at the Breaks section of this index. Compare it to the one you created in the chapter. Notice in the new index that Breaks has two references: pages 4 and 5. Why?

4. Create one book made up of publications the entire class creates. Start by planning the book and creating a class template. Each student should create an indexed publication. Place all the PageMaker publications on one disk and copy the disk to a hard drive. Create a table of contents and index. Print the book.

Quick Reference

CHANGING THE PAGE VIEW

To select:	Press:
Fit in window	⌘-W
25% size	⌘-0
50% size	⌘-5
75% size	⌘-7
Actual size	⌘-1
200% size	⌘-2
400% size	⌘-4

To switch between Actual size and Fit in window, point to the desired area of the page and click the mouse button while holding down OPTION-⌘.

WORKING WITH TEXT

Selecting Text

Text blocks	Use the pointer tool to point to the desired text and click the mouse button.
A letter, word, paragraph, or any part of text	Using the text tool (I-beam): drag the I-beam across the desired text, or
Word	double-click, or

	Paragraph	triple-click, or
	Part of text	click an insertion point at beginning. Move the I-beam to the end, hold down (SHIFT), and click.
	Entire text	Choose Select all from the Edit menu or press ⌘-A.

Selecting Text and Graphics	Multiple items	Use the pointer tool to point to the desired item, hold down (SHIFT), and click. Repeat for each item.
	Stacked item	Use the pointer tool to point to the stack. Hold down ⌘ and click to select the top item. Continue to click until the desired item is selected.
	All items	Choose Select all from the Edit menu or press ⌘-A.

Deselecting Text	Click on a blank area of the Pasteboard or page, or select another item.

Moving or Copying Text	Select the text.
	Choose Cut (to move) or Copy from the Edit menu.
	Choose Paste from the Edit menu.
	Drag the text to the desired location.

Deleting Text	Select the text.
	Choose Clear from the Edit menu or press (DEL).

WORKING WITH GRAPHICS

Selecting Graphics	Single item	Use the pointer tool to click on the graphic.
	Multiple items	Hold down (SHIFT) and click on each item.
	Stacked item	Use the pointer tool to point to the stack. Hold down ⌘ and click to select the top item. Continue to click until the desired item is selected.

Deselecting a Graphic(s)	Click on a blank area of the Pasteboard or page, or select another item.

Moving or Copying Graphic(s)	Select the graphic(s).
	Choose Cut (to move) or Copy from the Edit menu.
	Choose Paste from the Edit menu.
	Drag the graphic to the desired location.

Deleting a Graphic(s)	Select the graphic(s).
	Choose Clear from the Edit menu or press (DEL).

Altering Graphics	Trim imported graphic	Use the cropping tool to point to a handle and drag it.
	Resize a graphic	Use the pointer tool to drag a handle.
	Proportionally resize a graphic	Hold down (SHIFT) and use the pointer tool to drag a handle.
	Draw a circle	Hold down (SHIFT) and draw using the ellipse tool.
	Draw a square	Hold down (SHIFT) and draw using the rectangle tool.

PAGEMAKER ICONS

Toolbox

Tool	Icon	Function
Pointer		Selecting text blocks and graphics
Line	+	Drawing diagonal lines
Constrained-line	+	Drawing perpendicular lines
Text	I	Selecting, entering, and editing text
Rotating	+	Rotating text and graphics
Rectangle	+	Drawing rectangles
Ellipse tool	+	Drawing ovals and circles
Cropping		Trimming graphics

Other

Icon	Name	Used to
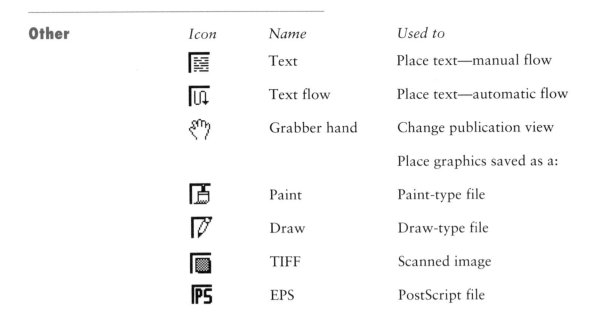 Text	Text	Place text—manual flow
Text flow	Text flow	Place text—automatic flow
Grabber hand	Grabber hand	Change publication view
		Place graphics saved as a:
Paint	Paint	Paint-type file
Draw	Draw	Draw-type file
TIFF	TIFF	Scanned image
EPS	EPS	PostScript file

PAGEMAKER MENUS

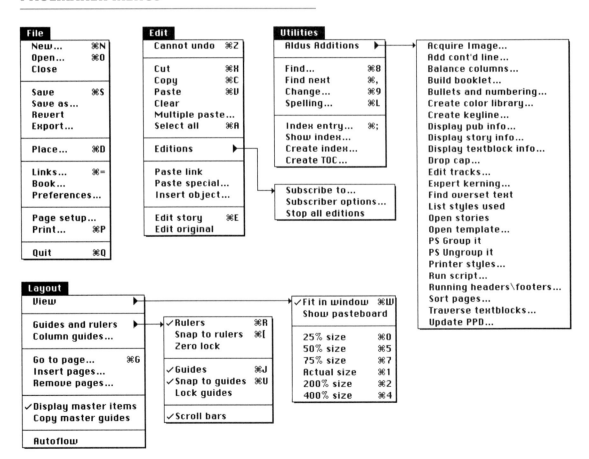

File

New...	⌘N
Open...	⌘O
Close	
Save	⌘S
Save as...	
Revert	
Export...	
Place...	⌘D
Links...	⌘=
Book...	
Preferences...	
Page setup...	
Print...	⌘P
Quit	⌘Q

Edit

Cannot undo	⌘Z
Cut	⌘X
Copy	⌘C
Paste	⌘V
Clear	
Multiple paste...	
Select all	⌘A
Editions ▶	
Paste link	
Paste special...	
Insert object...	
Edit story	⌘E
Edit original	

Editions submenu:
- Subscribe to...
- Subscriber options...
- Stop all editions

Utilities

Aldus Additions ▶	
Find...	⌘8
Find next	⌘,
Change...	⌘9
Spelling...	⌘L
Index entry...	⌘;
Show index...	
Create index...	
Create TOC...	

Aldus Additions submenu:
- Acquire Image...
- Add cont'd line...
- Balance columns...
- Build booklet...
- Bullets and numbering...
- Create color library...
- Create keyline...
- Display pub info...
- Display story info...
- Display textblock info...
- Drop cap...
- Edit tracks...
- Expert kerning...
- Find overset text
- List styles used
- Open stories
- Open template...
- PS Group it
- PS Ungroup it
- Printer styles...
- Run script...
- Running headers\footers...
- Sort pages...
- Traverse textblocks...
- Update PPD...

Layout

View ▶	
Guides and rulers ▶	
Column guides...	
Go to page...	⌘G
Insert pages...	
Remove pages...	
✓Display master items	
Copy master guides	
Autoflow	

Guides and rulers submenu:
✓Rulers	⌘R
Snap to rulers	⌘[
Zero lock	
✓Guides	⌘J
✓Snap to guides	⌘U
Lock guides	
✓Scroll bars	

View submenu:
✓Fit in window	⌘W
Show pasteboard	
25% size	⌘0
50% size	⌘5
75% size	⌘7
Actual size	⌘1
200% size	⌘2
400% size	⌘4

Appears only in layout view

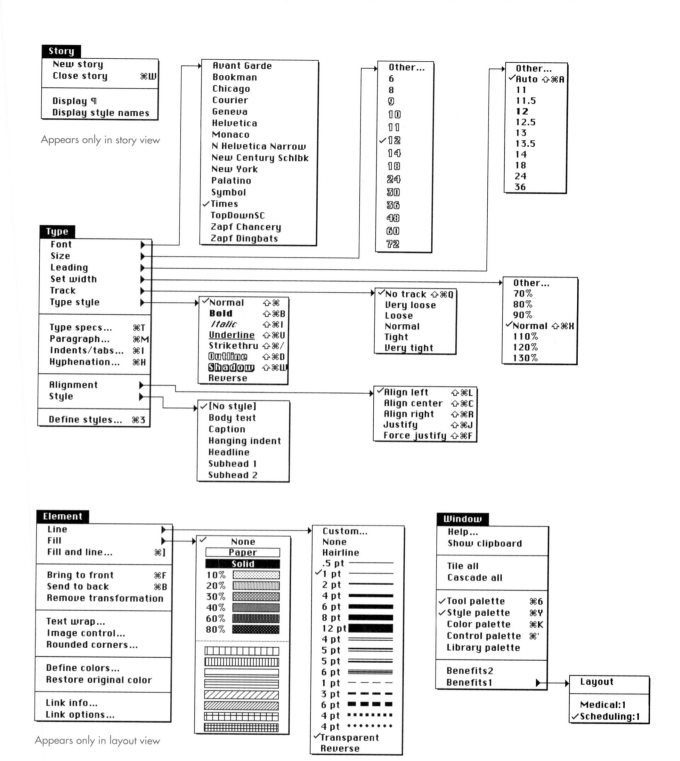

Story

New story
Close story ⌘W

Display ¶
Display style names

Appears only in story view

Avant Garde
Bookman
Chicago
Courier
Geneva
Helvetica
Monaco
N Helvetica Narrow
New Century Schlbk
New York
Palatino
Symbol
✓Times
TopDownSC
Zapf Chancery
Zapf Dingbats

Other...
6
8
9
10
11
✓12
14
18
24
30
36
48
60
72

Other...
✓Auto ⇧⌘A
11
11.5
12
12.5
13
13.5
14
18
24
36

Type

Font ▶
Size ▶
Leading ▶
Set width ▶
Track ▶
Type style ▶

Type specs... ⌘T
Paragraph... ⌘M
Indents/tabs... ⌘I
Hyphenation... ⌘H

Alignment ▶
Style ▶

Define styles... ⌘3

✓Normal ⇧⌘
Bold ⇧⌘B
Italic ⇧⌘I
Underline ⇧⌘U
Strikethru ⇧⌘/
Outline ⇧⌘D
Shadow ⇧⌘W
Reverse

✓No track ⇧⌘Q
Very loose
Loose
Normal
Tight
Very tight

Other...
70%
80%
90%
✓Normal ⇧⌘X
110%
120%
130%

✓Align left ⇧⌘L
Align center ⇧⌘C
Align right ⇧⌘R
Justify ⇧⌘J
Force justify ⇧⌘F

✓[No style]
Body text
Caption
Hanging indent
Headline
Subhead 1
Subhead 2

Element

Line ▶
Fill ▶
Fill and line... ⌘]

Bring to front ⌘F
Send to back ⌘B
Remove transformation

Text wrap...
Image control...
Rounded corners...

Define colors...
Restore original color

Link info...
Link options...

Appears only in layout view

✓ None
  Paper
  Solid
10%
20%
30%
40%
60%
80%

Custom...
None
Hairline
.5 pt
✓1 pt
2 pt
4 pt
6 pt
8 pt
12 pt
4 pt
5 pt
5 pt
6 pt
1 pt
3 pt
6 pt
4 pt
4 pt
✓Transparent
Reverse

Window

Help...
Show clipboard

Tile all
Cascade all

✓Tool palette ⌘6
✓Style palette ⌘Y
Color palette ⌘K
Control palette ⌘'
Library palette

Benefits2
Benefits1 ▶

Layout

Medical:1
✓Scheduling:1

I N D E X